CLASSIC *f*M
A-Z *of* CLASSICAL MUSIC

Professor Stanley Glasser was born in Johannesburg in 1926. After taking a degree in economics he turned to music as a career. Studies in composition in London with Mátyás Seiber and Benjamin Frankel and ethnomusicology studies in Johannesburg with Dr Hugh Tracey were followed by a first-class honours degree in music at King's College, Cambridge, where he also played rugby for King's First XV.

After a spell as a freelance composer, he began his long association with Goldsmiths College, University of London, first as lecturer, then as Head of Music, and finally as the first Professor of Music at the college. During his time there, he built up the music department into one of the largest and most forward-looking in the country.

His compositions reflect his interests in the music of southern Africa in their lively vitality and vibrant rhythms. They include a one-act comic opera, *The Gift*; a Concerto for piano and orchestra; *Lalela Zulu*, commissioned by the King's Singers; and *The Chameleon and the Lizard* for choir and small orchestra, which was commissioned by the London Bach Society with funds provided by the Arts Council of Great Britain.

Since his retirement in 1991 he has become closely associated with Classic fM and he is one of the trustees of the Classic fM Charitable Trust.

CLASSIC *f*M

A-Z *of* CLASSICAL MUSIC

Professor Stanley Glasser

HEADLINE

First published in 1994
by HEADLINE BOOK PUBLISHING

10 9 8 7 6 5 4 3 2 1

ISBN 0 7472 7842 3

Typeset by Phoenix Photosetting, Chatham, Kent
Printed and bound in Great Britain by
Mackays of Chatham PLC, Chatham, Kent

HEADLINE BOOK PUBLISHING
A division of Hodder Headline PLC
338 Euston Road
London NW1 3BH

Contents

To Adam, Sue, Daniel and Simon

Preface

Not so long ago the mayor of a small town held a reception for a famous string quartet who, that evening, had given an exciting concert. His admirably brief speech was not in the least perfunctory. Inspired by the music and its interpreters, his eyes shone, one could even detect a slight tremble in his voice. Clearly the mayor loved music. He concluded his laudatory remarks with, 'Be assured we will invite you back. By then, gentlemen, no doubt you will certainly be able to afford to double the number of players in your group. Good luck!'

Had that good mayor possessed a copy of Classic fM's *A–Z of Classical Music*, idly leafing through its pages of an evening or in between borough council meetings, he would certainly not have made such a *faux-pas*. He would have known that the foursome string group consisting of two violins, viola and cello was a fixed combo going back to about 1750.

The *A–Z of Classical Music* does not pretend to be a scholarly dictionary. Its aim is simple: to give the amateur listener a pile of useful information which offers a wide variety of musical subjects covering several hundred years and relevant to our Western classical tradition.

This reference book contains an enjoyably quirky and varied range of information; it allows you speedily to look up or check on a general matter to do with most of the composers you are likely to come across, the most familiar instruments, one or two musical forms, some musical terms, several critically important operas and other works, a few major conductors and other performers, and a miscellany of odds and ends. Some of the entries are opinionated, others state the bald facts. If some entries seem to be lacking, this is the author's choice; he has had to be selective and can only plead for understanding. It was decided, for instance, to exclude the more obvious voice types. Were he to include every possible entry he could think of, or were he to make any particular entry twice as long, the *A–Z of Classical Music* would have run to two volumes. Your purse might not have liked this.

What should prove of added use are, besides the index, the two lists at the end of the book: one gives the dates of the composers and performers covered, the other offers a selection of recommended CDs. Not all the works mentioned in composer entries feature in this second list; it's up to you to explore further if you like what you hear.

The music of the twentieth century is kept in mind. God, to the best of my knowledge, has not ordained that all works composed after 1900 should receive the thumbs down. Even if we don't much like the ruddy stuff it behoves us at least to become acquainted with it. To listen to, say, a piece by Stockhausen and then stamp up and down, shouting, 'I hate it! I hate it!' may well prove of beneficial psychotherapeutical release.

Melody, to my mind, is the most important communicating element in music. It is the first thing that normally draws us to a piece. I would suggest that Bach's fugues in his *Das wohltemperirte Clavier* (The Well-Tempered Clavier) continue to live, not because of all their foxy technical display, but because the *melos* they contain is so richly attractive. When the role of Rodolfo in Puccini's *La Bohème* is played by a portly, middle-aged tenor, just as soon as he utters the melodic thrust of the composer's music, before our ears and eyes he is magically transformed into the young, handsome, romantic poet, free-living in the Latin Quarter of late nineteenth-century Paris.

Believe it or not, there is *melos* to be found in the music of Bartók, Webern, Messiaen, Lutoslawski, Ligeti or Birtwistle. Admittedly, it is not easy to pick out, but it is there to be discovered after repeated hearings. Of course, it is a new type of *melos* and therefore somewhat strange to our ears. For that matter, have you ever listened to Chinese opera? On a first hearing it will very likely make your melodic hair stand on end.

There are two ways of listening to music. Both are valid. The one is to let the music simply accompany you as a close, invisible friend as you go about your tasks. Nothing wrong with that, I claim. The other is to push all thoughts aside and concentrate on listening *into* the music. Damn it all, you owe it to the composer and performers as well as having paid good money for the experience – playing a CD, listening to the radio, sitting in the concert hall. Listening in this intense way demands some practice – one's attention span is limited. Most professional musicians have a listening attention span of between twenty and forty minutes, so if you can last for, say, ten minutes before your mind begins to wander off, that's pretty good going. Concentrated listening, especially to your favourite works, will bring unexpected additional satisfaction; you will fish out details in the music you hadn't previously heard and you and the music will be drawn even closer to one another. 'Hadn't realised what the left hand was doing in that Chopin nocturne',

'Fancy, the saxophone and flute carrying on like that while the strings and percussion throb away in the *Sabre Dance* of Khachaturian'.

Classical music appears to be growing in popularity. After only two years in existence, for example, the radio station Classic fM has, it is estimated, some five million listeners from John O' Groats to Land's End. Not bad.

I hope you'll find the *A–Z of Classical Music* happily expanding your listening pleasure.

I should like to express my appreciation of Michael Bukht's initiatives and support, and my deep gratitude and warmest thanks to Anna Powell, Lorraine Jerram and Elisabeth Ingles for their encouragement, patience and alert disciplining. One day, as I look up from 'the other place', I will hear them playing gorgeous harp trios with a chorus of angels.

STANLEY GLASSER, London, September 1994

ABEGG – Schumann composed this piano piece in 1830 at the age of nineteen. Still an adolescent, he was enjoying booze-up parties, puffing cigars and dreaming of beautiful girls. The letters a–b–e–g–g spell the surname of a young female acquaintance and form the first five notes of a catchy romantic theme which is then followed by three variations and a finale. He was obviously a fine pianist, for the music is easier to listen to than to play.

ACCELERANDO – an instruction from the composer to the performer to 'step on the gas', to speed up the music. Why use the Italian word? Well, tradition has it that directions for musical expression are usually given in the language of the country from which opera burst upon the musical world in the seventeenth century, to wit, Italy. A well-known example of *accelerando* is Grieg's 'In the Hall of the Mountain King', the fourth and last movement of his *Peer Gynt Suite* No. 1, Op. 46.

ACCORDION – before the arrival of the infamous electric guitar the most popular instrument, together with the harmonica or mouth organ. In the 1930s accordion schools flourished in most towns. (Even Johannesburg, South Africa, boasted three.) In 1937 an international accordion championship was held in London; one participating band hailed from Norwich – all the nine players were women. The accordion is particularly associated with French music-hall and café life; and do you not recollect accordion sounds tootling in the background in a French film or in a screen advertisement for a Gallic product? Very evocative – makes me want to reach out for a glass and a bottle of *Bordeaux rouge.*

AGON – Stravinsky's last ballet, completed in 1957. This musical genius of the twentieth century wrote some twenty-one outstanding works for the stage. The title is an acronym of the Greek letters *alpha/gamma/omega/nu*. The ballet, choreographed by George Balanchine, involves only twelve dancers and has no story. It may be described as mobile sculpture, eye-gripping patterns of movement. There are twenty-six sections in all. *Agon* does not make for easy listening, but be adventurous! Take a deep breath and dive in! Stravinsky himself conducted the first recording with the Los Angeles Festival Orchestra.

ALBÉNIZ, ISAAC – in the history of Spanish classical music, an important composer. A contemporary and big mate of Debussy and Ravel, both of whom were clearly influenced by his piano writing, with its Spanish folk music idiom. In 1868, Albéniz's piano skills at the age of eight were such that, under his father's chaperoning, he made a concert tour of Spain. Like Palestrina in Italy three hundred years earlier, he was robbed by bandits. He toured South America and the USA at the age of thirteen. In 1880 he took piano lessons at Weimar with Liszt. From about 1890 Albéniz gave up his concert career, concentrating on composition; at this time he lived in London for three years. He frequently visited Paris and died in Nice. Albéniz's music often arouses a desire in the listener to roll up the carpet, get out the castanets and dance. Test this claim by listening to his *Suite española* No. 1, Op. 47 for piano, written in 1886.

ALBINONI, TOMASO – a contemporary of Bach and Handel. He came from a well-to-do family, which meant that he did not have to seek professional work. His early compositions were therefore produced as a dilettante, but by the age of thirty he had already written several operas, which were first performed in Mantua. In time he proved to be a prolific composer of Baroque concertos, sonatas, operas and solo cantatas, in which his distinguished melodic gifts are always apparent. Perhaps because of his favourable material circumstances, Albinoni seems to have mixed very little with other musicians, except in the course of performances of his own music. Bach used his keyboard fugues for teaching purposes, and his oboe concertos were the first of their kind by an Italian composer to be published; these concertos lean in character towards operatic aria writing, in contrast to his violin music, which is much more virtuosic. The second movement of his Oboe Concerto in D minor, Op. ix, No. 2 is out of this world. As the solo instrument enters on a long sustained note after the gentle introduction by the strings, the oboe's lyrical qualities are emphasised. You'll probably have goose-pimples each time you listen to this music.

ALPHORN – a.k.a. Alpenhorn – a droll item. One of the longest musical instruments in use: examples range from seven to ten feet in length (two to three metres). In order to be played this dinosaurian sound-source has to be rested on the ground. Swiss countryfolk have been known to call their cattle with a puff or two on the alphorn. And if a sore throat prevents them indulging in the amusing pastime of yodelling to one another across the mountainsides then the alphorn is a handy substitute.

AMERICAN IN PARIS, AN – one of George Gershwin's most ambitious works, composed in 1928. As with his successor, Leonard Bernstein (of *West Side Story* fame), Gershwin had one foot in popular music and one in classical. At present, perhaps more composers could to advantage follow this double path. One remembers the range of music, from jocular to intensely serious, turned out by Byrd, Purcell, Bach, Mozart, Beethoven, Schubert and others. *An American in Paris* serves as a bridge between jazz and the classics. The music is an orchestral tone poem which reflects the impressions an American visitor to that lovely city might have had before the war, and contains blues-type motifs, dance rhythms and nutty effects such as a motor-car horn.

AMADEUS STRING QUARTET – this swinging foursome was founded in 1947 and soon dominated chamber music concert halls on both sides of the Atlantic. In 1970, in recognition of their services to music, the Queen bestowed OBEs on them. To listen to the Amadeus sound is something therapeutic. For example, in the final movement of Haydn's String Quartet in B flat Op. 55, No. 3, the music seems to say, 'Folks! It's Friday! Another working week over! Let's get the hell out of here!'

AN DIE FERNE GELIEBTE – Beethoven's *To the Distant Beloved* for voice and piano is music's first true song-cycle. The difference between a song-cycle and a set of songs is that the former deals with a single sub-ject, whereas the latter involves a variety of topics. Beethoven's titanic and difficult personality caused his love affairs to end unhappily or in frustration. As a consequence it is possible that he created a sort of pin-up in his imagination, a composite phantasy image of his various loves. In any event *An die ferne Geliebte* is an outpouring of painful yearning. In the third, fourth and fifth songs of the group of five he despatches his longing to his love via the movement of cloud, stream and west wind, and with the return of May he envies all the mating creatures of Nature.

ANONYMOUS – composers in the Middle Ages, usually monks, were not that concerned to add their name to the music they created. Uninvolved with collecting royalties, presenting compositions in the concert hall or generally embarking on an ego-trip, they dedicated their works to the glory of God. Scholars, in the study of old unsigned

4

manuscript collections, have labelled them for easy reference Anonymous I, Anonymous II and so on. Worth attention is a motet in a collection originally discovered in a Swiss Benedictine monastery at Engelberg. This three-voiced praise of the Virgin Mary has two texts sung simultaneously – a not uncommon device of the time. Both in Latin, the lead voice sings 'Exquisite bride of Christ' while the other two sing 'Virgin chaste, shining in glory': quite a foxy piece of writing.

APRÈS-MIDI D'UN FAUNE, PRÉLUDE À L' – an orchestral prelude by Debussy which received its first performance in Paris in 1894: unbelievable that such an innovative work was written a hundred years ago. *Afternoon of a Faun* must be considered one of the most original items, in its instrumentation and structure, to be found in the orchestral repertoire. The opening flute solo, about three bars long, provides most of the material on which the entire piece is built. The music captures the quintessential sensuousness of the poet Mallarmé's randy little forest creature, half awake, lost in his languid, erotic thoughts in the heat of the Mediterranean sun. There is exceedingly effective writing for woodwind and the strings seem to convey the very breathing of Mother Earth; no brass except for horns, and the only percussion are two tiny cymbals tinkling no more than ten notes between them. This is a must for those who have not yet come across the work.

ARNE, THOMAS – the leading figure in English theatrical music of the mid-eighteenth century and an important composer of the period. His father was well-off and could afford to send his son to Eton. With his

5

younger brother and sister and with the father acting as impresario, Arne gave a performance of Handel's *Acis and Galatea* at the Haymarket Theatre in 1732. He turned out a steady stream of all types of music of the time; for the stage he wrote opera seria (*Artaxerxes*), opera buffa (*Thomas and Sally*), incidental music (Shakespeare's *As You Like It*, *Twelfth Night*, *Romeo and Juliet* and others), masque (*Comus*) and oratorio (*Judith*), as well as odes, cantatas, songs and instrumental pieces. He wrote the music for *Rule Britannia*, perhaps Britain's second national anthem, and his arrangement of the actual national anthem, *God Save the King/Queen* (an anonymous melody), is still occasionally played today. Burney describes Arne as also being a very fine violinist, an activity he had to give up owing to bad arthritis in his bowing arm. To get some idea of Arne's music have a listen to his cantata *Cymon and Iphigenia* or the Concerto No. 5 in G minor for keyboard and orchestra.

ARNOLD, MALCOLM – one of the finest composers for the screen. He has written over eighty film scores, the best known being his music for *The Bridge on the River Kwai* starring Sir Alec Guinness. In his early career Arnold earned his bread as an orchestral trumpet player. At only twenty-two he wrote a skilful, lighthearted wind quintet (flute, oboe, clarinet, horn, bassoon) for his pals in the orchestra, entitled *Three Sea Shanties*. Each of the three movements is built on a folksong – 'What should we do with the drunken sailor', 'Boney' and 'Johnny come down to Hilo'. Many composers have written wind quintets, but none is as popular among players and audience.

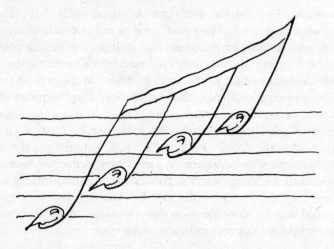

ARPEGGIO – What the hell is an *arpeggio*? No problem. It is simply a clump of notes, not struck at the same time – that's a chord – but spread out in sequence, going either up or down the scale.

ARRANGEMENT – a piece of music adapted from its original version for another medium. Composers have long made arrangements, either of their own works or of works by fellow composers. Bach arranged Vivaldi concertos, Mozart arranged Bach fugues for string quartet, Liszt made virtuosic arrangements of items from Italian and German opera. This activity is not only a form of artistic expression or simply one composer paying homage to another. No, no. The motive is often purely commercial: yes, the arranger is wanting to earn an extra penny or two. If you do not know it, try to listen to Stravinsky's arrangement for piano of his own ballet *Petrushka* – terrific!

ATONALITY – traditionally a composer writes his piece of music with one particular note as the master or 'boss': the key-note. All his pitch ideas stem from this central note. In the sixteenth century, say, this note was easy to discern. As time went on composers became more and more adventurous, and by the arrival of the twentieth century quite a number of them decided that the rule of the 'boss note' was a tyranny and it was overthrown. A radical development such as this has often caused music lovers a bit of an aural headache on first listening to such 'new music'. Do have a listen to, say, Messiaen's *Quatre études de rythme* (Four Studies in Rhythm), composed in 1949, or the first movement of Schoenberg's String Quartet No. 3.

AUBADE – a title that originally described music to be played in the morning, as opposed to *serenade*, music to be played in the evening; in the seventeenth and eighteenth centuries such music was often performed for members of royalty or civic authorities. The *alba* of the troubadours is a distant antecedent; the Spanish use the term *alborada*. Now it is a generic term that may be used for any composition that evokes or has to do with the early part of the day. Attractive examples are Bizet's piano piece *Aubade*, Lalo's *Aubade et allegretto* for strings and wind instruments, Poulenc's *Aubade* for piano and eighteen instruments, Lambert's *Aubade héroïque* for orchestra.

AURIC, GEORGES – a member of a characterful group of six French composers whose music caused a particular stir in the inter-war years. French music for wind has a distinctive attraction. Ever since Berlioz, woodwind instruments have played a significant role in introducing new ideas into French composition. Refer to Auric's Trio for oboe, clarinet and bassoon, written in 1936 – especially the final movement.

BACH, JOHANN SEBASTIAN – belongs to the most renowned family of musicians in the history of European classical music, from which flowed uninterruptedly composers, instrumentalists and singers for two hundred and fifty years from about 1600. Believe it! A phenomenon due to a gene or simply a tradition? Probably a mixture of the two. If you wish, wallow in detail by reference to the *New Grove Dictionary*, Volume 1 of which lists eighty-five Bach music-makers across 102 pages in double columns.

Bach's supreme powers combined unique performing virtuosity with a compositional inventiveness of extremely rare quality, joined with intellectual control; in his time his reputation rested on the former, whereas posterity crowns him with the latter achievement. His output draws together the techniques, styles and general concerns of Baroque music and paves the way for new approaches to be followed in composition which reach another climax in the Classical period of Haydn, Mozart and Beethoven. As a boy Bach was known to have had a very good treble voice, and by the age of fifteen had received a useful general education. At the same time his keyboard facility and practical knowledge of the workings of the organ advanced rapidly – if he had wished it, Bach could have become a first-rate organ builder and repairer. He also possessed a special talent for teaching; by the age of twenty-three he was already attracting organ and composition students. It is estimated that during his lifetime Bach had eighty private pupils.

Bach's professional life was spent in the employ of various courts; sometimes he would move, taking a drop in payment, for the sake of having a better organ at his disposal. A particularly productive period of composition is associated with his stint at Cöthen from 1717 until 1723. There he composed the fifteen two-part and fifteen three-part *Inventions* for keyboard, which, in a way, anticipate the 'symphonic principle', that is, the working and reworking of one particular theme, as well as Book I of the *Forty-Eight Preludes and Fugues* and the sonatas and partitas for solo violin. Bach was married twice, both times happily; his first wife, Maria Barbara, a cousin, bore him at least four children before her early death; his second wife, Anna Magdalena, not only bore him thirteen children but outlived him by ten years, and, very sadly, died in abject poverty. After Cöthen, Bach spent the remainder of his life in Leipzig, where he became Kantor at the Thomaskirche. For some time in his last years Bach suffered from eye trouble, developing cataracts; two operations proved unsuccessful and for almost all of his final two years he was blind.

In England we still too often like to pronounce the name with a dainty 'Bark', whereas it should be uttered with a hefty 'ch' as in 'loch'. The main members of the family were J. S. himself and his three sons W. F., C. P. E. and J. C. What a collection of works these four produced between them; but Daddy Bach is the genius – a word always to be used with caution – with his keyboard, instrumental, orchestral and choral works. For a *magnum opus* refer to the *St Matthew Passion*; for something lighter, the *Italian Concerto* for harpsichord.

In order of age: W. F. haphazardly followed in his father's tradition, and, cursed with a character unable to build a solid professional life, left his family poverty-stricken; C. P. E., the most original of the three sons, produced trail-blazing material through his keyboard works which heralded the musical styles of Haydn and Mozart, and, in contrast to W. F., left his family comfortably off; J. C., known as the London Bach (he spent twenty years in that city, where he died and lies buried in St Pancras Churchyard), demonstrated a graceful style of composition rooted in the world of Italian opera – scholars regard him as having had a singularly lasting influence on Mozart.

BADINAGE – in musical terms 'a bit of a lark'. In early eighteenth-century suites, pieces thus entitled displayed the gavotte two-beats-to-the-bar rhythm, as in Telemann's *Musique de table* or the final movement of Bach's Suite No. 2 in B minor.

BAGATELLE – a lighthearted piece, normally for piano. Note that Beethoven's set of *Bagatelles* Op. 126 are compositionally unusually ambitious. Since its first use by Couperin in 1717 (in his tenth suite for harpsichord), the title *bagatelle* has been used by, for example, Smetana, Saint-Saëns, Sibelius, Bartók and Webern, thus underlining that it has not been confined to a particular period nor a specific style.

BAGPIPE – do not think that this instrument begins and ends in Scotland. Its history goes back to ancient times; some organologists (researchers on musical instruments) believe that one form of the Greek *aulos* may well have been a bagpipe-type instrument migrating from the Middle East. European countries, whether north, south, east or west, record some form of bagpipe. Most of us, however, identify it with the Highland pipe of bonnie Scotland. While its martial use is stirring enough, even more moving is to hear a lament, with its sad melodic contours intensified by improvised ornamentation figures. It is used to marvellous effect in Maxwell Davies's *An Orkney Wedding with Sunrise*.

BAKER, JANET – a singing pin-up of mine, a Yorkshire lass who has conquered the worlds of both opera and solo recital. Her acting talent enhanced her stage presence, while a rare technical virtuosity and the distinctive character of her voice elevated arias in Bach cantatas, Schubert *Lieder*, French *mélodie* and the vocal compositions of many British composers from Elgar onwards. Baker has a list of honours as long as your arm; in 1976 she was created a Dame. Have you heard her in Mahler's poignant *The Song of the Earth* (*Das Lied von der Erde*) or singing a simple Fauré ditty?

BALAKIREV, MILY ALEXEYEVICH – at one time earned his bread as an overseer in the goods department of the Warsaw Railway. In the history of Russian music, consider him the successor to Glinka. His forceful personality rather than creative distinction made him the leader of his four contemporaries – Borodin, Cui, Musorgsky and Rimsky-Korsakov. The critic Stasov termed them 'the mighty handful'; later they became known as the Big Five – quite a suitable name for some contemporary pop group ...

From the mid-1860s, together with Tchaikovsky they established a valuable output of compositions which contributed strongly to the evolution of European classical music and paved the way for Prokofiev, Stravinsky and Shostakovich. No less than eleven concert pianists have recorded Balakirev's oriental fantasy *Islamey* – worth a listen.

BALALAIKA – more Russian info: basically a long-necked, three-stringed lute, for long one of the most popular folk instruments east and west of the Urals. Its strumming tone quality produces listenable solo material but the instrument is best suited as accompaniment to song and dance. As it is available in six different sizes, it is no surprise to learn that balalaika bands have been formed, some of which were sophisticated enough in choice of material and standard of performance to undertake successful international concert tours, mainly between 1920 and 1960.

BALFE, MICHAEL – the creative distinction in English composition which flourished from the time of Dunstable in the fifteenth century faded out after Purcell at the close of the seventeenth; the eighteenth century produced only two real masters – Arne and Boyce. Thereafter, until Elgar who kicked off the great renaissance of English composition in the twentieth century, the only truly successful 'British' composer was the nineteenth-century Balfe, born in Dublin. He was much respected in Italy and France and earned the admiration of Cherubini and Rossini, but more for his baritone voice and his operatic acting. Yet Balfe composed well-received operas, not only in English, but also in French and Italian for Paris and Milan audiences. His great gift was the ability to write immediately appealing, melodious vocal lines. He wrote very little of worth outside his thirty operas; this industrious application duly allowed him to retire for the last six years of his life to a small estate he bought in Hertfordshire. The high point of his output was *The Bohemian Girl*, which ran for one hundred nights at Drury Lane. For those who enjoy musical Victoriana, recordings of this opera are available as well as several of his songs; often lampooned, but really quite charming are his two songs *Come into the garden, Maud* (Tennyson) and *Excelsior* (Longfellow).

BALLADE – a free-form composition, usually for piano; the four that Chopin wrote are the best known. Liszt, Brahms, Franck and Grieg had a go. An example for piano and orchestra is Fauré's *Ballade* Op. 19.

BALLAD OPERA – a rare contribution from England to eighteenth-century musical concerns, in that ballad opera influenced continental music theatre; especially in Germany and Austria, where the genre became known as *Singspiel* (song-play). No need to remind you of the best known of all *Singspiels* – Mozart's *The Magic Flute*. The ballad opera in its early English form consisted of a play with prose dialogue interspersed with songs, some traditional and rearranged, others especially written and full of comedy, with the emphasis on satire. The one most familiar to us is *The Beggar's Opera*. Before he established his reputation as a great novelist (around 1735), Henry Fielding had a hand as author in several ballad operas. Today we also recollect the Brecht/Weill creation of 1928, *The Threepenny Opera* (*Die Dreigroschenoper*), which contains that evergreen hit song *Mac the Knife*.

BARBER, SAMUEL – twentieth-century American composer; a contemporary and great friend of his fellow-American, the composer Menotti, who wrote the libretto for Barber's opera *Vanessa*, first performed at the Metropolitan Opera in New York in 1958. In his early years Barber was also a professional baritone; this may account for his felicitous writing for the voice, proof of which lies in his songs and choral pieces. His musical style is essentially lyrical and diatonic. In 1937 his Symphony No. 1 was performed at the Salzburg Festival, the first American work to be included in this distinguished event. Barber's music is less appreciated in Europe than in his own country, but his *Adagio* for string orchestra, arranged by the composer from the second movement of his String Quartet, is consistently a 'top of the pops' piece in the concert hall and on record. Deservedly so.

BARBER OF SEVILLE, THE (*Il barbiere di Siviglia*) – a superb comic opera by Rossini, first performed nearly 180 years ago in Rome in 1816 at the Teatro Argentina. It was a flop, booed to high heaven, largely because, scholars have unearthed, several unrehearsed and unscripted incidents occurred: the lead tenor, when tuning his guitar, snapped a string; later a cat jumped out of the prompter's box, leapt on to the stage and the cast fell to chasing it hither and thither. Imagine that scene ... The barber hero's name is Figaro; a constant delight is his unique aria *Largo al factotum della città* ('I'm the busiest man in town').

BARCAROLLE – a Venetian gondolier's song, mimicking his boat's gentle motion through the water. Composers have long been attracted to its appeal. You may hear the evidence for this in Chopin's *Barcarolle* Op. 60, Fauré's thirteen *Barcarolles*, Bartók's *Barcarolla* from his *Out of Doors* Suite, Mendelssohn's three *Venezianische Gondellieder* in his *Songs Without Words* collection. All these examples are written for the piano, but barcarolles are also featured in opera – in Weber's *Oberon*, Rossini's *Otello* and, best-known of all, in Offenbach's *The Tales of Hoffmann*. Next time you are gliding along in Venice in a gondola ask the gondolier to render you a song; alternatively make up your own barcarolle while rowing on an English lake.

BARENBOIM, DANIEL – Israeli pianist, conductor and arts director, born in the Argentine. He was left a widower after his wife, Jacqueline Du Pré, a most gifted cellist, died young of multiple sclerosis – a tragedy to tug the sternest heartstrings. Barenboim is already in his fifties, which is hard to believe; it seems only yesterday that he was carving out for himself an international reputation as a dashing young pianist and baton-wielder. But *tempus fugit*, as they say. For me his *tour de force* is the recording of all twenty-seven Mozart piano concertos with him as soloist, conducting the English Chamber Orchestra from the keyboard.

BARITONE – most males around the world naturally sing in this range of the human voice. Situated between the bass and tenor, the baritone singer took a back seat in most medieval and renaissance vocal polyphony. He only came into his own when Mozart created brilliant, baritone roles in his operas *Don Giovanni* (the Don himself) and *The Marriage of Figaro* (Figaro himself). This innovation was quickly followed by his contemporaries and successors, for instance Verdi, Brahms, Wagner, Puccini. The baritone can project a much wider range of characterisation than the tenor or bass, in song as well as opera; proof lies in listening to any recording by the incomparable Dietrich Fischer-Dieskau.

BAROQUE – nowadays a generic term to describe all works written in the hundred-year period from 1650 to 1750. Musical language and style, it must be underlined, never stand still. They evolve from one decade to the next, so there is a clear difference to be heard between the sounds of Bach and those of Purcell, indeed between Bach and his two highly reputed contemporaries Telemann and Vivaldi. Nevertheless there is a Baroque sound, so to speak, which can be distinguished from the preceding Renaissance and the succeeding Classical sounds. You simply pick up the distinctions by constant listening. What a pleasurable task!

BARTÓK, BÉLA – twentieth-century Hungarian composer, an idol of mine. His first name is pronounced 'Bayla' not 'Bella'. Conservative music listeners would describe the three-headed composition monster galumphing around between 1910 and 1950 as having the faces of Bartók, Schoenberg and Stravinsky. Readers, you should know that Bartók put new life into the string quartet, piano writing and the concept of chamber music. He also drew our attention to the riches of folk music – he is revered equally by ethnomusicologists and by classical music pundits. In contrast to most modern composers (British ones an honourable exception) he wrote music for children, amateurs and semi-professionals as well as for the big time. Test my eulogy with his *Out of Doors* suite for piano – an easy entry to Bartók's sound world.

Bartók's music is saturated with peasant culture, mainly that of Eastern Europe. This does not mean arrangements or reworkings of folk music; rather the transmutation of his listening, transcription, analysis and love for this musical language into a personal, highly individualistic style, capable of constant creative exploitation. His six String Quartets are the most distinctive of all twentieth-century efforts in this genre; his writing for the piano introduces a new percussive element to its expressive range. With Stravinsky, he revitalised motor and structural rhythm.

Bartók was courageously anti-Nazi, refusing to play in Germany after 1933 and from 1937 changing his publishers from Universal Edition in Vienna (because of their willingness to follow Nazi tenets) to Boosey & Hawkes in London. He was deeply attached to his mother and did not leave for America until 1940 because of her poor health. The five or six years in the USA until his death were strenuous; he and his wife were at times on the poverty line; the American League of Composers in fact paid his funeral expenses. An act of generosity as well as his pure musical respect for Bartók caused the jazz clarinettist Benny Goodman to commission a chamber work from him. The result was the exciting *Contrasts* for clarinet, violin and piano, first performed and recorded by Goodman, Szigeti (fellow countryman) and Bartók in 1940.

BASSOON – the bass woodwind instrument of the orchestra. Its wide range of tone colour allows composers to write comical effects (Dukas's *The Sorcerer's Apprentice*) or plaintive melody (the opening bars of Stravinsky's *Rite of Spring*).

BAX, ARNOLD – an English composer with strong Celtic ties, emotional and artistic, whose best achievements came in the twenty years from about 1920. His muse was constantly stirred by two concerns: to reconcile the ideal with reality, to reconcile the harshness and magnificence of nature. His tone poem *Tintagel* is an orchestral beauty.

BAYREUTH – pronounced 'by-royt'; this pretty little German town in northern Bavaria was made famous by Wagner, one of the top two nineteenth-century composer geniuses (the other being Beethoven). Wagner chose Bayreuth for the erection of a theatre which he himself would design; he would also supervise its construction, own it, and there hold an annual festival of no other operas but his own. Such has been the case to the present. Today the theatre and festival lie in the hands of the trustees of the Richard Wagner Foundation Bayreuth. First choice as festival director must be made from the members of the Wagner family; the current director is Wolfgang Wagner, a grandson of the great Richard. Talk about Egyptian pyramid or Texas oil magnate dynasties ... 1876 marks the year of the opening of the theatre with a first full performance of his quadrilogy *Der Ring des Nibelungen* (The Ring of the Nibelung).

BBC – British Broadcasting Corporation; a useful whipping boy; doesn't mind being called 'Auntie'; the finest radio and television network in the world. Founded in 1922, when it immediately started broadcasting classical music. Has been in charge of the Proms since 1927; founded the BBC Symphony Orchestra in 1930, the first of many excellent musical institutions under its aegis. The Corporation has commissioned many new works for broadcasting on Radio 3 (formerly the Third Programme), and transmits a fair amount of live opera and other musical events on television. It must be saluted for the huge part it has played in the dissemination of classical music. Call me Colonel Blimp ...

BEAT – the basic pulse in any music to which one can count. Music such as Gregorian chant has no beat – try counting to it. Grouping beats into larger units creates metre, which is merely sound pattern. The most common sound patterns are grouped in two, three or four beats: as examples think of a march, waltz or foxtrot you know.

BEECHAM, THOMAS – English conductor; a maverick man of music who through his character and with his family wealth made a radical advance in the concert and operatic life of British audiences. As a conductor of great skill he introduced works by native composers, above all Delius, as well as giving authoritative performances of more established masters. At the same time he presented operas by Strauss, Wagner and leading nineteenth-century Italian composers. Beecham was knighted in 1916, the year he succeeded to his father's baronetcy. He was a particularly fine interpreter of the symphonies of Sibelius and he recorded prolifically.

BEETHOVEN, LUDWIG VAN – there is nothing, but nothing, to touch this Shakespeare of music. Truly remarkable is the range of human emotion expressed through his orchestral, chamber, solo and vocal works, and the extent of his compositional technique. Don't take my word; just listen, as one example among many, to his Piano Concerto No. 5, nicknamed *The Emperor.*

Beethoven's grandfather and father were both musicians. The father was an only child and married a widow; they had seven children, of whom only Beethoven and his two brothers survived. His general education stopped at elementary school. He was bad at spelling and found it difficult to work out the simplest multiplication sums, yet by the age of eleven his musical gift was already recognised in Bonn, where he was born. At the age of seventeen he earned money by giving piano lessons. When his father turned to drink, Beethoven applied, at nineteen, to be recognised in law as head of the family; here it is already evident that he possessed character and assertiveness.

He visited Vienna and met both Mozart and Haydn, from whom he had lessons. The emperor Joseph II was an influential supporter of the late eighteenth-century intellectual, political and social ideas known as the Enlightenment and Beethoven was much affected by this milieu. Later he returned to Vienna where he settled permanently. Throughout his life he was basically a lonely figure, no matter the number of friends and admirers that gathered around him and no matter how much he was accepted in aristocratic circles. His search for a female companion with whom he could share the deepest intimacy was never realised, despite his many relationships with various women. The reason would seem to be twofold: he idealised such a relationship beyond the bounds of reality; more importantly, the power of his musical creativity was so driving that it uncontrollably overwhelmed all other considerations. Beethoven's hearing steadily deteriorated and in the last nine years of his life he was stone deaf; yet it is in this period that he wrote some of his greatest works, for example, the Symphony No. 9, his last String Quartets (Opp. 127, 130–135), the Piano Sonatas Opp. 109–11, and his *Missa solemnis* in D. The tragic hero is a most potent figure; Beethoven in his life and in his music fits this picture, and this is perhaps why he is the most admired composer in Western music.

BEGGAR'S OPERA, THE – its first run in 1728 at Lincoln's Inn Fields Theatre created a record, with sixty-one performances; in 1920, some

17

two hundred years later, it set another record at the Lyric Theatre Hammersmith, with a run of 1463 performances. To term this stage work an opera is a bit of a joke; actually it is a play with sixty-nine songs – hardly any original – consisting of popular ballads ('Over the hills and far away', 'Greensleeves', Purcell's 'Britons strike home'), country dances, Scottish and French tunes, compiled by John Gay. One of the production's purposes was to deliver a blow against the vogue for Handel and Italian opera – 'Let's have less of this foreign stuff, damn it!'

BELLINI, VINCENZO – how sad that he died young. In Italian operatic development he stands with Donizetti between Rossini and Verdi. Much of his nineteenth-century vocal style was influenced by the folk-song of his native Sicily, proof of which may be heard in his three finest operas, *La sonnambula* (The Somnambulist), *Norma* and *I Puritani* (The Puritans). Bellini tasted success at the age of twenty-six; eight years later he was dead.

Two years earlier, Bellini paid a successful visit to London, where a season of his operas at the King's Theatre and at Drury Lane received much acclaim; the same thing happened a little later in Paris. There he met Chopin and Rossini, whose fatherly advice he much appreciated, and also the German poet Heine. It is in Paris that he first heard a performance of Beethoven's Symphony No. 6, after which he exclaimed, 'this music is as beautiful as Nature'. Bellini had a captivating personality, charming and sympathetic; a contemporary remarked that he was as warm as his melodies. This was, however, only one side of the coin, for he could also be jealous of fellow composers, as he showed in relation to Donizetti who, in contrast, did not hesitate to praise Bellini's operas. Composers are as varied in their make-up as any other group of fellow beings.

BENNETT, RICHARD RODNEY – a leading English composer, now in his late fifties; an outstanding technician and a prime example of our age of eclecticism in music. Want a set of children's piano pieces? Bennett's your man. A concerto for orchestra? Call on R. R. B. Something for choir or strings or wind quintet? Contact Richard. But he is expensive, for he is highly respected and very successful, a true composer, always ready to write for the multifarious musical forces in our society. No doubt you've seen *Murder on the Orient Express*? His music for this film reminds us that he is one of the great cinema composers. Studied with Boulez, no less. His piano repertoire includes jazz playing – boy! can he swing it!

BERCEUSE – those readers whose French is reasonable will know the word means 'lullaby' or 'rocking cradle'. In music the title is appended to quiet, simple pieces, usually for piano, such as Chopin's *Berceuse* Op. 57; but there are also orchestral examples, such as the *Berceuse* in Stravinsky's ballet *The Firebird*.

BERG, ALBAN – Schoenberg was his teacher and friend. Born and bred in Vienna, he belonged to those circles of young folk who rebelled against the hypocritical mores of early twentieth-century Austrian society. His music is more tuneful than his mentor's (see *Serialism*) and easier to grasp. His opera *Wozzeck*, whose hero is an army orderly, is a lament for the little man, and the greatest opera since Debussy's *Pelléas et Mélisande*. Each work in his comparatively small output is a gem, full of melodic substance.

BERIO, LUCIANO – best-known of postwar Italian composers. If you cannot stomach avant-garde music give him a miss. Berio is one of the notorious triumvirate with Boulez and Stockhausen. His works are rich in experimental and daring ideas – the use of electronics, ingenious musical quotation, the exploration of the new sounds possible in the playing of traditional instruments, the breaking down of concert platform formality in performance. Much of his music displays wit and humour. Berio may be considered as a musical reflection of the outburst of invention in science and technology currently upon us. Block one ear if you have to, and with the other listen to his *Circles*, a setting of poems by E. E. Cummings (the avant-garde American poet) for female voice, harp and two percussionists. It's already thirty years old. You may find no need to resort to a reviving double whisky.

BERKELEY, LENNOX – another fine English composer. French ancestry, nature and temperament thankfully prevented him from being swamped by the German-Austrian musical axis – to which not a few composers on our fair island have succumbed. Berkeley espouses rather the world of Fauré, Ravel and Poulenc; in any piece in his nicely varied corpus of music, imaginative ideas, invention, formal balance and tunefulness are always present. Slide into your CD player Berkeley's *Sinfonia concertante* for oboe and orchestra; the composer himself conducts.

BERLIOZ, HECTOR – certainly a larger than life character; consult any biography to learn of his drolleries. He was a quintessential example of nineteenth-century 'romantic' behaviour. BUT – note the capitals – he was a damn' fine composer. *Symphonie fantastique* is an evergreen in the concert hall and there are thirty-nine recordings of his *Roman Carnival* overture (*Le carnaval romain*). Berlioz's knowledge of what an orchestra is capable of doing and his treatise on instrumentation are major contributions to the extension of the nineteenth-century sound palette.

It is well to bear in mind that, as a French composer active in the first half of the nineteenth century, Berlioz was composing in an environment in which literature was the leading art. He had to struggle to have his musical ideas accepted, not only as composer, but also as critic and conductor. Berlioz has received greater recognition in our century than was accorded to him in his lifetime. Oddly enough, considering his mastery of, and treatise on, orchestration, he could play no more than a tin whistle and the guitar. After Berlioz attended a performance by an English company in Paris of *Hamlet*, when he fell in love with the Ophelia, Shakespeare became a lifelong idol for him and he based several compositions on the playwright's works, including the opera *Béatrice et Bénédict*, the symphony *Roméo et Juliette*, the overture *Le roi Lear* and the choral piece *La mort d'Ophélie*.

BERNSTEIN, LEONARD – three reasons why he appears in this musical A–Z: he was one of the most effective popularisers of classical music; he was a distinguished conductor who covered an enormous range of orchestral material; he revitalised the musical with his incomparable score for *West Side Story*. An exemplary composer of the people – an aim of the old Soviet Union not really achieved despite the efforts of Prokofiev, Shostakovich, Kabalevsky and Khachaturian. Get hold of Bernstein's *Chichester Psalms*.

BIRDSONG – who among us has not enjoyed the sound of a bird-call? I myself even find the clucking of hens rather soothing; ducks quack-quacking is not unpleasant; a peacock's squawk, however, can be grating on the ears. Birdsong is really no more than signalling and communication. We romantic humans endow our feathery friends with a non-existent musicality. Musical composition using bird-calls may be traced back to the thirteenth-century round *Sumer is icumen in*, featuring the two-note cuckoo call – most popular of all bird sounds used by composers. In addition, quail, nightingale and lark have been known to make appearances. Here are some examples: Boccherini's String Quintet Op. 11 No. 6, known as the *Aviary*; Beethoven's Symphony No. 6 (the *Pastoral*); Delius's *On Hearing the First Cuckoo in Spring*; Britten's *Spring Symphony*. But the composer on birdsong *par excellence* is Messiaen, whose works are splattered with dozens of bird-calls, used, not simply as decoration, but as essential structural motifs. He made a disciplined in-depth study of birdsong worldwide, and this element plays a major role in forming the character of his music. His *Bird Catalogue (Catalogue* *d'oiseaux*) for piano is a group of thirteen lengthy pieces; each contains a selection of bird-calls to be heard in *La belle France*.

BIRMINGHAM – city situated in the so-called Midlands region of England. As with most conurbations in the UK, the kick-off moment for growth started with the outburst of industrialisation in the eight-eenth century. Birmingham drew attention to itself musically with an annual festival which continued from 1768 to 1912; major musical events in this timespan included first performances of Mendelssohn's *Elijah* and Elgar's *Dream of Gerontius*. The city boasts a rich supply of venues with churches, halls such as the spanking new City Concert Hall, theatres and choral societies. The University of Birmingham con-tains one of the best music departments in the land, while the City of Birmingham Symphony Orchestra, currently under the direction of Simon Rattle, offers an annual season of worthwhile programmes that include a healthy supply of contemporary works. Bless Birmingham for its support of the living composer!

BIRTWISTLE, HARRISON – Britten's successor with regard to stage works, a composer of original and independent outlook. The full-length *Punch and Judy* is unique in its conception and realisation. Equally striking is the shorter *Down by the Greenwood Side*. He has ripened new techniques of composition. In general his music leaves an impression with the listener of starkness, violence, sardonic humour; gentleness and appealing melodic line are only now and again permitted to peek out. Birtwistle has earned a solid international reputation and a knighthood. His latest opera *Gawain* confirms he is as British as a baron of beef.

BIZET, GEORGES – a truly Parisian composer, thoroughly representa-tive of nineteenth-century French opera, yet his Symphony in C, com-posed at the age of seventeen, remains in the current orchestral repertoire. His viewpoint on genius: it is divided into two categories – the type that always has to sweat it out (Beethoven) and the type that expresses itself simply and unselfconsciously (Mozart); Bizet thought he belonged to the latter. Bizet wrote twenty-eight operas. You could be forgiven for not knowing any music from *Les pêcheurs de perles* (The Pearl Fishers) or *La jolie fille de Perth* (The Fair Maid of Perth), but if you are not at least acquainted with his last opera *Carmen*, go forthwith and seek forgiveness from St Cecilia – a broadminded saint.

BLISS, ARTHUR – from 1953 to 1975 Master of the Queen's Music, knighted in 1950. Always a champion of the music of fellow composers.

He produced an impressive output for stage and cinema – incidental music to plays, ballets, opera, film scores. One of his finest pieces, *Music for Strings*, employing the string section of a large orchestra (sixty players), is inexplicably neglected.

BLOCH, ERNEST – Swiss-born, he lived and died in the USA. He consciously aimed to establish himself as a 'Jewish' composer, an aim fulfilled by producing quality works directly influenced by biblical themes, synagogal chant and melodic characteristics common to a wide body of Middle Eastern music. A good impression of his style may be gleaned from *Schelomo* for cello and orchestra and *Concerto Grosso* No. 2.

BLOW, JOHN – with Purcell and Humphrey, Blow led the last group of English composers at the close of the seventeenth century. Thereafter, apart from a handful of exceptions, English composition as a telling force only resurfaced at the beginning of the twentieth century with Elgar. No musicologist has yet offered a convincing explanation for this phenomenon of two centuries of arid composition. Could it be because England in this period exploded into the first industrialised power of modern times, before building an empire so large that on it 'the sun never set'?

Although Blow wrote a charming masque, *Venus and Adonis*, he did not feel the same attraction to the stage as Purcell; instead he produced a large corpus of church music. The motet *Salvator mundi* or *God spake some time in visions*, his coronation anthem for James II, should please your ear.

BOCCHERINI, LUIGI – Italian composer and cello virtuoso, a contemporary of Haydn and Mozart. He is said to have organised, at Lucca in 1765, the first public appearance of a string quartet – hitherto confined to courts and salons. Many of his works were written for his own performance needs. Note the uncertainty of a composer's life: for long Boccherini travelled successfully all over Europe, but at the end of his life, living in Madrid, his material condition rapidly deteriorated; on top of this, within the space of three years he lost his second wife and three daughters. Spare some listening time to his Cello Concerto No. 9 or the two String Quartets Op. 51 of 1795.

BOHEMIA – with Moravia and Slovakia the territory formed the new state of Czechoslovakia in 1918; before that these regions were merely part of the Austrian Habsburg empire. Now, after seventy-five years, the territory is again split, this time in two, with Prague as the Czech and Brno as the Slovak capital. What price tribalism – the curse of mankind (bye-bye Yugoslavia ...). Bohemian composers who belong to the CPL

(Composers' Premier League – my term, not an official organisation) are Smetana, Dvořák, Janaček and Martinů.

BORODIN, ALEXANDER – his life would make a perfect subject for a Hollywood melodrama: illegitimate son of a Russian prince; happily married to a tubercular pianist who joined him 'on the other side' only five months after his own death; ladies regularly attracted to him; admired by Liszt; at the same time as being a composer led the life of a distinguished researcher, teacher and academic in chemistry. Borodin was closely associated with the anti-Teutonic, Russian-music-comes-first movement. His composition list is small but memorable. While busy investigating the behaviour of aldehydes such as valerian and vinegar he turned out the excellent Symphony No. 2 in B minor, the moving String Quartet No. 1 in A and the stirring opera *Prince Igor*, which contains the wild *Polovtsian Dances*. Remarkable fellow, don't you think?

BOULEZ, PIERRE – one of the most influential of postwar composers; also an excellent conductor and a musical theorist of substance. In 1974 he founded in Paris IRCAM (Institut de Recherche et de Coordination Acoustique/Musique), whose purpose, in addition to promoting avant-garde compositions, is to forge a new language for European classical music. He belongs to that élitist sector of contemporary composers who flourished between about 1950 and 1980 and whose time is now perhaps past; such composers did not worry too much over the negative reaction to their music from the ordinary concert-goer. Does this grate on you? Well, have a listen to his exciting Piano Sonata No. 1 – a veritable clattering of jewels of sound – or his exquisite *Pli selon pli* (Fold on Fold) for orchestra.

BOYCE, WILLIAM – the best of the eighteenth-century English composers. He made a comfortable living from composition, turning out fine material for stage (opera, masques, incidental music for plays) and also for orchestra and chamber ensemble forces; his services, anthems, partsongs and odes show a high standard of vocal writing. Boyce's increasing deafness led him to turn to musical research. Between 1760 and 1773 he produced the three volumes of his impressive collection *Cathedral Music*, illustrating the worth of English church music, particularly of the seventeenth century. Go to St Paul's Cathedral if you want to see where Boyce lies buried. And have a listen to any of his eight lively and tuneful symphonies.

BRAHMS, JOHANNES – that he is one of the nineteenth-century greats need hardly be stressed. He had a tough boyhood – had to

23

supplement the family income by playing in the sailors' dives of Hamburg (often while plonking out a dance or drinking song he would at the same time study an orchestral score placed on the stand in front of him – how did he do it?!). A bachelor all his life; there was a period in Vienna when he would veer from strenuous, ascetic creative work – drinking lots of coffee and sleeping little – to sojourns of abandon in the red-light district of the city. Shortly before his death Brahms heard some piano ragtime which he greatly enjoyed. Had he lived a while longer he would have fulfilled his intention of writing some piano pieces in this genre; fascinating ... would he have rivalled Scott Joplin's efforts?

Brahms's father was a street and dance musician who married his housekeeper, seventeen years older than himself; Brahms was their second child. Hungarians fleeing from their failed uprising in 1848 against the Austrians and Russians on their way to America passed through Hamburg; Brahms's contact with them left him with a permanent soft spot for Hungarian music and its musicians, manifested in his orchestral *Three Hungarian Dances* and his collection of four-part *Zigeunerlieder* (Gypsy Songs). Which reminds one that not to be forgotten is his large output of songs; he is certainly among the leading composers of the nineteenth-century German *Lied* – an unmatchable world of song-writing. A comparison between Brahms and Wagner, the two greats after Beethoven and Schubert, underlines that music of the highest quality does not depend on whether a composer is 'conservative' (Brahms) or 'revolutionary' (Wagner), but on what the music has to say and how it is said.

Brahms was the ultimate Late Romantic. Piles of wonderful Brahms to listen to: Symphony No. 4 with one of the finest finales of all symphonies, *Liebeslieder* (Love Songs) for soprano, alto, tenor and bass (SATB) and piano (four hands) – gorgeous melody and a superb display of the variety to be found in waltz rhythm which doesn't simply go 'um-pah-pah'. And there is the finely wrought Clarinet Quintet.

BRANLE – a dance originating in medieval France, performed by a group of couples formed in a circle or a straight line. As has so often happened in dance, the *branle* migrated from the countryside to the court; variations evolved but all had a common triple beat pulse. Rameau's ballets contain *branle*-derived sequences. By 1800 it had faded away, soon to be replaced by the waltz.

BREAM, JULIAN – while still in his teens he had to support a sister and a chronically ill mother. Today he stands as one of the world's great guitarists, and also an outstanding lutenist; his playing is spell-binding. A long list of composers have been inspired to write for him – e.g. Bennett, Arnold (concertos), Britten, Rawsthorne (solos), Berkeley, Henze, Tippett (voice and guitar). Introduce yourself to the world of the lute with Bream playing Dowland's songs and dances.

BRENDEL, ALFRED – one of the most intelligent pianists on the international circuit. His Beethoven and Schubert sonata interpretations will knock you sideways; and, bless him, he keeps one eye on music by contemporary composers. Awarded an honorary doctorate by the University of London.

BRITTEN, BENJAMIN – I regard him as the most renowned of postwar British composers, though some would give this accolade to Tippett. A major opera composer, he revived this genre after Puccini with the very dramatic *Peter Grimes*, considered by many as the best opera since Berg's *Wozzeck*. Britten's piano playing was certainly of concert platform standard; he was also an excellent accompanist and an effective conductor who, with his own works, in an undemonstrative style, communicated to an audience all the subtleties lying in a score. Britten was often nervous of the success of his music; this frequently resulted in intolerance of criticism coming from reviews or from well-meaning and loyal fellow musicians and friends. His word-setting of English, whether in opera, symphony, song or choral piece, is matched only by Purcell's – no mean achievement in a literature-orientated culture. With his friend, colleague and partner, the tenor Peter Pears, he established a unique annual festival (in the month of June) at Aldeburgh – lovely setting, you would not regret attending it. *Serenade* for tenor, horn and strings, Violin Concerto, the chamber opera *The Rape of Lucretia*, *A Ceremony of Carols* for boys' voices and harp – enjoy!

BROADCASTING – you cannot escape the radio or television set; either or both are an integral part of your life. On offer, need I say, are quality programmes for the discriminating and bland ones for those who simply desire sound and/or vision to keep them company. A powerful force worldwide, broadcasting promotes news, information, religion, the arts, education, propaganda, commercial products. There is a growing international dimension – 600 million people have been known to watch a vital football match or some special event in the Olympic Games. Quite soon these sorts of events will draw 1,000 million viewers and listeners. Don't ask about the numbers for a special performance of a Beethoven symphony or a Puccini opera ... although opera and football were successfully combined when Pavarotti sang 'Nessun dorma' from *Turandot* as the 1990 World Cup theme tune. More music, opera and ballet is

25

now broadcast on television than ever before – international piano competitions, Singer of the Year, Young Musician of the Year – and for an event such as the Three Tenors concert in Rome (Pavarotti, Domingo, Carreras) the streets emptied. And now Classic fM has added a new dimension to music on radio.

BRUCH, MAX – a long-lived, modest nineteenth-century German composer. Operas, choral music, songs and instrumental works flowed from his pen, but today old Max is best known for his melodious Violin Concerto in G minor; a second violin concerto did not catch on. Never mind. Many composers would welcome just one hit for posterity.

BRUCKNER, ANTON – nineteenth-century Austrian composer, as a person rather pathetic – parochial, timid, humourless; as a symphonist some consider him as great if not greater than Brahms. Had to find work at seventeen in order to help with the family finances; obtained a teaching job in the Austrian village of Windhaag – duties included farm labouring and muck-speading. Bruckner's chronic lack of self-confidence allowed well-intentioned fellow musicians to press him to make, and themselves to make, ill-considered alterations to his symphonic scores. Decide whether you are pro- or anti-Bruckner by listening, for example, to Symphony No. 7 in E or his *Te Deum*. Personally, I'm sorry to say, I find his music a bore.

BULL, JOHN – a brilliant Elizabethan composer, mainly, of pieces for the virginals. The *Fitzwilliam Virginal Book* has forty of his examples in this genre; he could write complex but musical canons as easily as peas rolling off a log. Bull fled from England to the Netherlands in 1613, never to return. The reason? Well, here's an extract from a letter of 1614 from the English envoy at Brussels, Sir William Turnbull, to James I: he did 'steal out of England ... to escape ... the punishment ... for his incontinence, fornication, adultery and other grievous crimes'. Yet by 1592 both Oxford and Cambridge universities had honoured him, the former with a DMus. O human frailty ... A small selection of Bull's viol consort and virginal music is available on CD.

BURNEY, CHARLES – lived to eighty-eight – pretty good for the eighteenth century. A most important figure in the history of musicological research, he earned a good living as a private teacher well into his seventies. Burney travelled widely; to list some of his friends and acquaintances is sheer name-dropping: Arne, Handel, Padre Martini, Metastasio, Gluck, C. P. E. Bach, Dr Samuel Johnson, Garrick, Haydn.

Interested in astronomy throughout his life, he even published an essay on comets. Never had a university education.

BUSONI, FERRUCCIO – important Italian piano virtuoso, music theorist and composer; a champion of Bach as well as the composers of his time; opposed to the nineteenth-century attitude that classical music must always be lofty – bully for him! Busoni held that of all musical elements melody is the most important and that the finest of all instruments is the voice. As against this somewhat Italianate outlook there is his marathon work for piano, *Fantasia contrappuntistica*.

BUTTERWORTH, GEORGE – snuffed out in 1916 while defending a trench on the Western Front, for which he was posthumously awarded the Military Cross. While an Oxford undergraduate he became attracted to English folksong and dance; he was guided in this respect by Cecil Sharp, the daddy of British ethnomusicology, and by Vaughan Williams. His orchestral rhapsody *A Shropshire Lad* is a sensitive and relaxing piece of music which showed promise for future composition, never to be realised.

BYRD, WILLIAM – indisputably the greatest Elizabethan composer, one of my musical deities. With Palestrina and Victoria he represents the finest achievements in sixteenth-century composition. Familiarise yourself with one or other of his three Masses or any of his motets, say, *Christe qui lux es et Dies*. His enormous output covers sacred and secular choral, consort and keyboard music. Byrd was also a competent businessman, ably managing his financial interests, which mainly involved music publishing and land ownership. He has been described as the Schoenberg of his time in that his artistic mission exercised lasting influence on younger composers such as Bull, Morley, Philips, Tomkins and Weelkes.

CABALETTA – don't ask from where this term originates; none of the experts can explain. It refers particularly to nineteenth-century Italian opera in which, on occasion, the concluding section of an aria (sometimes a duet) has the following form: usually orchestral introduction, voice enters, orchestra on its own again or joined by the chorus, a repetition of the voice section, finally an end bit in quick tempo. Audiences take to cabalettas – 'Come per me soreno' (Bellini's *La sonnambula*), 'Ah, fors'è lui' (Verdi's *La traviata*).

CABARET – here I am not referring to second-rate turns in sleazy dumps but to small venues for evening entertainment which offer intelligent, subtle and sharp-tongued satire in recitation, song and dance. Precedents may be traced back to the close of the seventeenth century. In modern times this art form was launched in 1881 at the Chat Noir in Paris; for the next fifty years it spread around Europe, especially to Berlin, Munich and Vienna. The English developed their own brand of cabaret, known as Intimate Revue; in the early 1950s its main venue was a little Soho club called The Establishment. The peak of Intimate Revue was the *Beyond The Fringe* production in the theatre land of Shaftesbury Avenue, then the BBC television series *That Was The Week*

29

That Was, ending with the double act of Peter Cook and Dudley Moore. Maybe this serious/lighthearted type of entertainment will return one day.

Not a few famous composers involved themselves in writing music for cabaret – Satie, Debussy, Milhaud, Schoenberg. The composers Weill and Eisler brought German cabaret, musically speaking, to its apotheosis. In Berlin the equivalent of the Chat Noir was the Über-brettl, founded in 1901.

CADENCE – one may say this is the musical version of a punctuation mark. The arrangement of a musical passage at the end of a phrase or section would equal a comma or semi-colon; the end of a movement would have a cadence acting as a full stop; quotation, exclamation and ... marks may also have their equivalent cadences. Test your conception of cadences in the next piece of music you listen to.

CADENZA – a composition in which a soloist (instrumental or vocal) is accompanied, usually by an orchestra, may sometimes include a special section called a cadenza. The cadenza is for the soloist alone; its purpose is to show off both his/her technical virtuosity and musicality. In Mozart's time a cadenza would often be left to the soloist to improvise; today it is rare to find a cadenza that is not carefully written out by the composer. Ask yourself why ...

CAGE, JOHN – the twentieth-century composer of experimental music *par excellence*. Born in the USA, widely travelled, acute intelligence, well informed on the arts, architecture and philosophy; also heavily involved in the modern dance movement; his influence, worldwide, reached its zenith in the 1960s. A natural iconoclast, Cage aimed to alter conceptions of music in the composer, performer and listener; his belief was that 'everything we do is music'. Two examples of his music: *4' 33"* – may be performed by any instrument or combination of instruments; the performers sit silently on the concert platform for the given duration (4'33") and the music consists of silence, any rustling from the audience and any extraneous sounds that may filter into the auditorium. *Landscape No. 4* – twelve radios each shared by two performers, volunteers from the audience preferred; one of each pair operates the station selector, the other the volume control; naturally one performance sound will vary from the next depending on what the stations are broadcasting at the time – the cacophony is likely to be the same, however. An English composer much influenced by Cage was Cornelius Cardew. Like Cage's approach to music or not, you now have some idea of what he was about. A surprising amount of his music is on CD. Cage was also an expert on mushrooms.

CALL AND RESPONSE – the exchange between two sets of performers, usually singers and usually a soloist against a group; a common form in African music south of the Sahara, both vocal and instrumental – you can hear its influence in blues and jazz. Often the soloist will create variation and improvisation, whereas the group response material remains fixed. The call and response structure can be discerned in Gabrieli, and even Beethoven piano sonatas.

CALLAS, MARIA – one of the greatest postwar operatic sopranos, she possessed a riveting stage presence which enabled her to play a large variety of roles; her *forte* was Italian opera from Rossini to Puccini. Towards the end of her career her voice, which was uniquely expressive though not always conventionally beautiful, began to fail. Some say this was due to bad early training, others that it was due to vocal abuse; perhaps it was a mixture of both. Enjoy *Maria Callas – Operatic Arias*.

CALVINIST MUSIC – under the influence of the noted French Protestant leader Calvin, church music took on a simpler form. He took refuge in Switzerland, where opposition to Catholic procedures met with sympathy and support. Calvin believed in the power of music to affect human behaviour but he was against the use of instruments at services, concentrating rather on monophonic congregational singing; also, he insisted that all church worship should use the vernacular, not universal Latin. In due course four-part settings of texts were permitted.

CAMBRIDGE – up the Light Blues! Musical activity emanates mainly from the university, which is about one hundred years younger than the one at Oxford. In fact, it got cracking in the third quarter of the thirteenth century as a result of cooperation between dissident Oxford scholars and the monks of Ely. Cambridge was the first university in the world to award music degrees (around 1463); these were honorary or gained through the submission of a composition or 'exercise'. Only as late as the postwar period were fully-fledged undergraduate degrees, at honours level, established. The same applied at Oxford, and the major change came about through the efforts of Dr Hubert Middleton at Cambridge and Professor Jack Westrup at Oxford. The Chair of Music is currently held by the composer Alexander Goehr.

King's College, founded in 1441 by King Henry VI, is renowned for its annual Festival of Nine Lessons and Carols, broadcast on Christmas Eve from its exquisite chapel which D. H. Lawrence described as looking like 'an upturned sow'! The choir of students, not all of them reading music, and schoolboys from the attached King's College Choir School is world-famous, making regular tours abroad and recordings; its present director is Stephen Cleobury.

CAMPION, THOMAS – You *must* listen to his exceedingly beautiful part-song *The cypress curtain of the night is spread*. Campion was a most prolific lute-song composer, as well as poet and physician (he gained his medical degree at the University of Caen in France). He wrote the lyrics for all his songs and his independent poems included some written in Latin.

CANON – it's not that difficult to understand what is a canon. If you are a complete ignoramus in this matter simply think of a round such as *Three Blind Mice*; your voice and those of three companions all sing the same melody but entering consecutively; the result is a musically exciting texture, and at the end of your performance – we won't consider its quality ... your musically fulfilled quartet will have sung a canon *a 4*. Composers have been writing canons from as far back as the fourteenth century. It is a challenge to a composer to write a canon that not only works on paper but is worth listening to. As time marched on the use of canonic technique moved from vocal to instrumental composition. Even today you will find scores that are devoted to or contain canonic passages; Bach is supreme but there are also Mozart, Beethoven, Brahms, Franck, Schoenberg and Stravinsky among the big boys with fine examples.

CANTATA – means no more nor less than a composition for solo voice and/or chorus with instrumental accompaniment; a popular form in the Baroque era. There were sacred and secular cantatas: Bach wrote over two hundred – nearly all sacred. At first the cantata in its layout was pretty similar from one composer to the next, with variations pertaining to Italian, French, German and English traditions; today, however, only my simple definition applies, as witness Bartók's *Cantata profana* or Prokofiev's *Alexander Nevsky* or Stravinsky's *Cantata*.

CANTICLE – a special type of psalm essential to Christian worship. By the fifth century there had been established fourteen canticles to be used in the Service. Today, in the Anglican Church the term applies to the following: Morning Prayer – *Venite, Te Deum, Benedicite, Jubilate*; Evening Prayer – *Magnificat, Cantate Domino, Nunc dimittis, Deus misereatur*. Britten composed five works bearing the title 'canticle'.

CANTILENA – until the start of the fifteenth century the term described single and two-part secular vocal music, emphasising melodic and ornamental line. The nineteenth-century revival of the term was used to qualify a melody that was heavily lyrical for voice or solo instrument.

CANTUS FIRMUS – you may as well know this term – it particularly applies to vocal polyphonic composition of the fifteenth and sixteenth centuries. A composer selects a pre-existing melody, sacred or secular, or even invents a melody himself. This melody, which may be modified or adjusted as convenient, is the spine of the composition; around it are woven normally from two to five parts. Josquin and Palestrina have written Masses using as *cantus firmus* a well-known French folksong of the time, *L'homme armé* (The Armed Man); Josquin's is in four parts, Palestrina's in five.

CANZONA – one of the forerunners of fugue technique. At first it meant an arrangement of polyphonic songs for instruments. By the close of the seventeenth century canzonas became instrumental pieces in their own right, characterised by a sequence of sections in which motifs are passed in imitation from one instrument to another. Purcell's *March and Canzona* for brass, written for the funeral of Queen Mary II, is an immediate illustration.

CAPRICCIO – a term that does not refer to musical form, but, derived from the Latin for 'goat', describes a piece expressing the lighthearted, the whimsical, the fantastic with a bit of bounding about. It can be written for the piano: Mendelssohn (*Andante and Rondo capriccioso* Op. 14), Brahms (Capriccios in D minor and A minor to be found in Op. 116); for orchestra: Tchaikovsky (*Capriccio italien* Op. 45), Walton (*Capriccio burlesco*); as opera: R. Strauss (*Capriccio*); as a piano concerto: Stravinsky (*Caprice*). Nice selection?

CARISSIMI, GIACOMO – seventeenth-century Italian composer known as the first important composer of oratorios; also admired for his cantatas. Appointed *maestro di cappella* (director of the choir) at the Collegio Germanico in Rome, where he remained for the rest of his life, as teacher, musical director and composer. Steadfastly declined offers of more prestigious posts such as succeeding Monteverdi at St Mark's, Venice. Poor at first, in time he became well off through living frugally. His oratorio texts are taken mainly from the Old Testament. He rapidly advanced the evolution of recitative, aria and chorus writing. Carissimi's best-known oratorio is *Jephte*.

CARMEN – Bizet's last opera. Its first performance in 1875 at the Opéra Comique in Paris was a failure; Bizet, already not at all in good health, and now utterly depressed, died within three months. A short while later, in Vienna, *Carmen* took off and has remained one of the most popular operas ever since; it is performed all over the world. If he is looking down from heaven Bizet must certainly enjoy this posthumous success. Carmen is a *femme fatale*, an alluring gypsy girl who is stabbed to death by one of her rejected lovers; the opera is brimful of incident and tuneful music.

CARMINA BURANA – first, a thirteenth-century manuscript containing over two hundred love poems, some quite lewd, in Latin with a few in German, discovered in Bavaria in the nineteenth century. Second, an effective scenic oratorio (it is meant to be staged rather than simply given on the concert platform) popular with choral societies and small opera companies, written by the German composer Carl Orff, who conceived his version for soloists, choruses and orchestra in 1937; he makes use of twenty-four poems extracted from the original collection.

CAROL – so you know what a carol is, do you? You know, for instance, that in medieval times the text of carol songs could be about any subject (but mainly about the Virgin and the Saints at Christmas), that they could even be danced to and the words were in English or Latin; and you know that the festival carol was associated with amorous games (the early sixteenth-century carol by King Henry VIII, *Green growth the holly*, maintains the metaphor of holly/man and ivy/woman). You also know that carols became more rigid and institutionalised in Victorian times; and of course you know that the traditional service for Advent and Christmas comprising nine Lessons and Carols was established at King's College, Cambridge, in 1918; no doubt you yourself can sing lots of carols. Truly, I need not have written anything on the subject.

CARTER, ELLIOTT – hard to believe this American composer is in his eighties, because his music still seems to be so new. One of his techniques is known as 'metric modulation' – don't panic, it simply means the use of different rhythms being played simultaneously. First the basic pulse of one rhythm is emphasised, then another rhythm's basic pulse comes to the forefront, and so on; the resultant texture is at times so thick that the sound becomes meaningless to the ordinary listener. Carter has stated he doesn't mind much if his music goes unappreciated by the majority of classical music-lovers. So there. A marked difference between Carter and his compatriot Cage is that the former dots the 'i' and crosses the 't' of every note he writes; the latter stresses the 'chance' production of sound. Decide on your own reaction to Carter's music with his Violin Concerto or his *Night Fantasies* for piano.

CASTRATO – a male who has been castrated for the purpose of preserving his treble or alto voice. This was essentially an Italian activity which first appeared in the sixteenth century in church choirs. In the seventeenth century, when opera first burst upon the world, women were as yet not permitted to appear on stage, and the castrato fitted in very nicely to take on female characters, with his high voice and the lungs and muscles of a grown man. It is estimated that in the eighteenth century perhaps as many as 4,000 boys were 'treated' – usually between the ages of six and eight. Handel, Mozart, Rossini and Meyerbeer wrote parts for castrati. If you want to hear what a castrato sounds like, there is a CD available entitled *The Last Castrato*, a recital by Alessandro Moreschi (*d*. 1922). The strange quality of the voice is partly due to the original recording, made in 1902–3, but its effect is also mysterious and sepulchral. Puccini was commissioned to write a song for Moreschi as part of an Italian Navy celebration.

CECILIA – we must all love her, for she is the patron saint of music. One story about her goes: around AD 500 a Roman maid of noble birth, Cecilia, dedicated herself to perpetual virginity; however, she was betrothed to an attractive young patrician. She not only persuaded her husband to keep their marital relationship platonic but also converted him and his brother to Christianity. Roman authority did not like this at all and soon the brothers were done away with, as was Cecilia a while later. The bizarre bit is that the first attempt to kill her by suffocation in the steam-bath at her home failed; it was then decided to behead her, yet after several strokes the axe failed to do its job properly and poor Cecilia lingered on for several days. She actually was only taken up as music's patron saint from the fifteenth century. By the time of Purcell, then Handel, Cecilian festivals presenting music and poetry became common. Britten was born on St Cecilia's Day which is 22 November.

CELLO – for long thus called, but originally and traditionally referred to as the violoncello; a lovely-sounding instrument, the bass of the violin family. An important member of the classical string quartet – two violins, viola and cello. You will of course know that the left hand fingers the strings and the right bows them, and that the four strings are tuned in fifths (C-G-d-a); and you will also know that the instrument is played upright and held between the knees. The cello section in the orchestra is placed in front, to the right of the conductor. The present-day version of the cello was fixed by Haydn and Mozart's time; before that different sizes and tunings existed, according to the needs of players and composers in different centres. It is in the twentieth century that the cello truly gained recognition as a fully-fledged solo instrument. The pioneer in this respect was the Spanish Pablo Casals; the great recitalists that followed him include Fournier, Tortelier, Starker and Rostropovich. The cello is capable of producing the most poignant of melodic lines as well as virtuosic passages of dramatic intensity; its additional effects of pizzicato, glissando, double-stopping and harmonics can be extremely effective. There is a long list of cello music, solo and chamber works; one might cite Debussy's Sonata, Ravel's Sonata for violin and cello, and further sonatas by Hindemith, Shostakovich and Britten. Outstanding concertos written for the instrument include those by Elgar, Prokofiev, Martinů and Milhaud; among avant-garde composers, Xenakis and Penderecki have written especially for it.

CHABRIER, ALEXIS-EMMANUEL – a charming and likeable nineteenth-century French composer, appreciated more by fellow musicians than by the public. He wrote operas and songs, but his main creative contribution was to the French piano repertoire, in which he exhibited an adventurous exploration of harmony, rhythm, tone colour and pellucid melodic line; he had a profound influence on Ravel. Lend an ear to Chabrier's *Dix pièces pittoresques*; and of course you know his orchestral rhapsody *España*, with its lively rhythm, tunefulness and imaginative orchestration.

CHACONNE – you need to know this term if for no other reason than for the chaconne movement in Bach's Partita in D minor for violin, Purcell's Chaconne in G minor for strings, the final movement of Brahms's Symphony No. 4 (never mind that it is described as a pas-sacaglia – to all intents and purposes the terms are interchangeable), and the third movement of Britten's String Quartet No. 2. Many forms in classical music have originated from popular dances and songs; the cha-conne seems to have migrated to Spain from Latin America as a dance-song. By the eighteenth century it had been transformed into a piece for instrument or orchestra, having three-beats-to-the-bar, with a firm melody in the bass part and ingenious variation or elaboration in the upper parts. Check my explanation against one or all of the examples cited above.

CHAMBER MUSIC – music written for small forces, to be performed in more intimate surroundings than the grand concert hall or opera house. The character of chamber music is more abstract, demanding strong interplay between the parts, but it need not be at all heavy in spirit – as may be heard in the string quartets of Haydn, Mozart and Beethoven. Many listeners fail to appreciate the riches chamber music has to offer, preferring works for large orchestra or music for the stage. These show a (to my mind) regrettable gap in their listening net, and I would press them to consider Schubert's Quintet in C, Mendelssohn's String Octet in E flat Op. 20, Ravel's *Trois Poèmes de Stéphane Mallarmé*, Bartók's *Music for Strings, Percussion and Celesta*, and Britten's *Serenade* for tenor, horn and strings. I bet a penny to their pound that one, some or all of these works will touch their oofles.

CHANSON – of course *chanson* simply means 'song' in French, but as a technical term it refers to songs set to French texts in the fifteenth and sixteenth centuries. Some were for solo voice, others for three or four parts; the *chanson* had a variety of forms which made it all the more attractive. Dufay's *Vergene bella*, Josquin's *Mille regretz* or Janequin's *Au joly jeu* are appealing examples.

CHERUBINI, LUIGI – an Italian-born composer who spent the majority of his life in France. Born four years after Mozart, he outlived Beethoven, Schubert and Weber. He exercised a marked influence on the development of French opera and made a major contribution to the evolution of French music education. His admirers included Haydn and Beethoven and he was held in high esteem by both traditional French royalty and Napoleon. In the early nineteenth century Cherubini went through a period of mental depression, believing that his composing career had come to an end, and so he turned to the study of botany; in due course, happily, he recovered, but now concentrated on the writing of church music, which brought him new success. His operatic overtures are particularly striking, such as that for *Médée* of which there is a complete recording; his Symphony in D is also worth attention.

CHOPIN, FRÉDÉRIC – the supreme poet of the piano. You are sure to be familiar with some of the pieces from his collections of polonaises, nocturnes, waltzes, mazurkas, *études*, *ballades* and scherzos. He was Polish-born, and his music always exhibits a Slav melodic nuance. His piano technique was second only to Liszt's. So sad about his chronic chest ailment and his troubled affair with the feminist author who called herself Georges Sand and smoked cigarillos. Chopin's major contribution to music's path of change lies in three areas: innovative and lasting harmonic progressions, establishment of the piano as the unmatched instrument of the nineteenth century, the introduction of new subtleties to the treatment of rhythm and tempo. On recital visits to England he was known to have rented a suite of rooms in Little St James's Street, not far from Piccadilly. Perhaps the outstanding interpreter of his music in this century is Artur Rubinstein – select as evidence his complete recording of the *Nocturnes*.

CHORALE – after the breakaway movements of Luther and Calvin from Catholicism, the primary function of music at church services was to ensure the congregation's singing of psalms and hymns. In Germany these became known as chorales. The congregation being made up of amateurs, musically speaking, it was essential that the tunes should be simple, even using melodies already known to them; the texts were to be clear, rhymed and in the vernacular, not in Latin. Then the ruddy composers came along and began to produce all sorts of foxy pieces based on chorale material. There are chorale preludes, fugues, cantatas, concertos, fantasias and variations; Bach made four-part harmonisations of some 360 chorale tunes, admittedly some of these using the same tune several times. Bach has left us some of the finest specimens of the chorale used in the writing of organ pieces – turn your ear to No. 9 of his Orgel-Büchlein *Von Himmel hoch*. Later composers who emulated Bach in this respect were Mendelssohn, Brahms and Reger.

CHORD – see *Harmony*.

CHORUS – a large group of singers, usually amateurs, who sing in unison or in parts. Normally there are four parts – soprano (S), alto (A), tenor (T), bass (B) – each part shared by a number of singers, so now you know what 'such-and-such a work for SATB' means. A chorus may be subdivided into more than four parts or even into two smaller choruses. Usually it is accompanied by an orchestra but it could instead be an organ or a brass ensemble. The term 'choir' refers to a smaller, more skilled group of singers – as may perform at church services or at chamber music venues. There is an extraordinary chorus culture in the UK, of a high standard. Byrd said way back in the sixteenth century, 'since singing is so good a thing, I wish all men [humanity] would learn to sing'. If you can read music just a teeny bit go and join a chorus; there is nothing like singing away for dear life in the company of your fellow citizens.

CIMAROSA, DOMENICO – most popular composer of Italian opera before Rossini. Chucked into jail for sympathising with the republican movement (having written a patriotic hymn in support) after King Ferdinand's soldiers reoccupied Naples; four months in prison and under threat of death sentence; saved as a result of a petition from friends in high places (e.g. Cardinal Ruffo, Lady Hamilton). Cimarosa wrote over sixty operas but one should of course appreciate that none was on the scale of an *Aïda* or *Boris Godunov*. His admirers included Haydn (who through his generous nature seemed to admire everyone), Goethe and Hanslick; his operas were performed from England to Russia. He showed sharp dramatic judgement, a sense of musical light-heartedness, the ability to establish character quickly through recitative, aria, chorus and orchestral accompaniment. You can hear excerpts from his most successful opera *Il matrimonio segreto* (The Secret Marriage), but there's a complete recording of *Il pittor parigino* (The Parisian Painter).

CLARINET – the most popular woodwind instrument. In concert wind bands clarinets take on the role of first and second violins. There are six different sizes of clarinets: the common one is pitched in B flat, which means that the easiest scale (row of notes) to play starts on the note B flat. But don't get a wrong idea here, for the B-flat clarinet is one of the most agile and versatile of all orchestral blowing instruments. Its mouthpiece holds one reed (made of cane), in contrast to the oboe whose mouthpiece holds two reeds. Blow hard on a low note and the sound will jump up twelve notes higher – this is called overblowing. The clarinet's low notes produce either warm or mysterious sounds and comprise the chalumeau register; the middle register is lively and penetrating; its top register, while able to show off quite a dynamic range, especially when the instrument is in the hands of a good player, can burst through quite a blanket of accompanying sounds.

The instrument gradually entered the orchestral and chamber music repertoire from the end of the eighteenth century – no small thanks to Mozart as well as the rise of wind ensemble playing. Then followed important clarinet writing from Weber, Mendelssohn, Berlioz, Wagner, R. Strauss, on to Schoenberg, Bartók, Stravinsky. Clarinet virtuosi feature strongly in the development of clarinet writing and playing – Stadler (Mozart), Baermann (Weber), Benny Goodman (Bartók), Alan Hacker (Birtwistle and Maxwell Davies). Select from Mozart's Quintet K581, Weber's Concerto No. 2 for clarinet, Stravinsky's *Ebony Concerto*, Bernstein's *Prelude, Fugue and Riffs*.

CLASSICAL MUSIC – any society which contains in its musical corpus a division of material that demands presentation by well-trained and informed musicians, to be performed generally or on special occasions, may be described as having classical music in its culture. Some examples outside our self-centred European tradition: Japan, China, India, the Middle East, Africa – quite widespread, huh? The listener of classical music does not need to be knowledgeable, he need only like the stuff. Folk and popular music is much more grassroots-orientated in its aims and objectives. The European classical music tradition stretches from plainsong to the present day and is the most complex and the fastest changing of all classical musics. It is subject to continuously altering aesthetic aims, to the ebb and flow of its society's thoughts and desires, to the pace of technological invention. Today our classical music is 'in the mix'; it exhibits a wide range of compositional intentions, making it harder for the ordinary classical music listener to latch on to. Keep on trying! There are sonic riches to be discovered.

The 'Classical period' is an aesthetic/technical term which applies to music written approximately between 1750 and 1830, after the Baroque and before the Romantic periods. These things are never cut and dried: Beethoven and Schubert, in varying degrees, merge from the Classical into the Romantic period.

CLASSIC fM – a broadcasting phenomenon. In September 1992 a national radio station was introduced that plays nothing but classical music twenty-four hours a day, month in and month out. Would you believe it! By the first half of 1994 its listening figures were lapping five million. Classic fM has to live by its commercials, but this does not seem to have frightened away listeners. It has established the Classic fM Charitable Trust, which each year chooses some charity connected directly or indirectly to music and hands over to it the funds earned in that year by the Trust's activities.

In its second year of existence the station has launched music education programmes to supplement the teaching of music in schools. The inventive triumvirate that currently propels the station's progress is made up of John Spearman, chief executive, Michael Bukht, programme controller, and Robin Ray, head of music repertoire. As it develops, Classic fM intends to increase its support for live performance and the commissioning of works.

CODA – the tail-end of a piece of music, with a concluding function; the piece may be large (an orchestral movement) or small (a song). The coda usually contains material to be found earlier in the piece. Not all pieces have them. Sometimes the coda is overdone, but with Beethoven, even though he wrote nearly 150 bars of coda in the first movement of his Symphony No. 3 (the *Eroica*), all of it is very much part of the musical discussion and is worth listening to.

COLOGNE – a city on the Rhine, with a university. Its church music, at first Catholic-orientated, later included important Protestant material. There is a rich history of secular music performance in Cologne, which became the centre for the Rhineland Carnival; the present format of this carnival goes back to 1823, the year in which opera started there. In addition the city has a history of instrument-making (lutes and keyboard instruments) and music publishing. An electronic music studio under the benign directorship of Herbert Eimert became a centre for electro-acoustic experimentation and composition for young composers, who included Stockhausen.

COLORATURA – the popular meaning of the term refers to a type of soprano opera singer, particularly in the performance of nineteenth-century Italian opera roles, in which she may display her ability to cope with the high, florid passages especially written into her arias to show off technical agility and tone colour. Originally, however, the word is German, 'Koloratur', and is used as a generic term to describe vocal and instrumental ornamentation of all periods.

COMPOSITION – the putting together of clearly organised musical thought. The result may remain in the composer's head, as occurs in cultures other than Western classical music. Improvisation is also a form of composition, usually following certain terms of reference within which the improvisation is disciplined, although the details may vary from one performance to the next; it is a form of rapid composition, as evidenced in transcriptions of music played by jazz composers such as the saxophonist Charlie Parker, which reveals logical invention, imaginative artistic expression and a dramatic drive towards the conclusion of the piece.

By and large, in our own tradition we like to write down what we create. This is because music, like other areas, faces constant technological advance – not necessarily producing better music! but causing notation to become more and more complex; also because there is a demand for a composer's work to be performed in distant venues at which he cannot be present, and also because of the general wish of composers and others to preserve his efforts for posterity, and finally to promote the sales of his scores. Often composers will make sketches for a work in order to help clarify their aims and intentions. The increase in the quality of recording has encouraged us to become passive listeners, via broadcasting, the concert hall and CDs, rather than to make music ourselves; on the other hand, our listening range has greatly increased in sophistication, for there is one helluva large mass of music from which to choose in order to satisfy our inclinations.

CONCERTO – put simply, a composition in which there is interchange between a solo instrument or group of instruments and a larger body of players. By Bach's time there had evolved the *concerto grosso*, a small orchestra divided into a smaller and a larger ensemble (as in his *Brandenburg Concerto* No. 2 – trumpet/recorder/oboe/violin *v.* strings). This sort of concerto is succeeded, for example, by the trail-blazing piano concertos of Mozart, after which follow the grand nineteenth-century concertos (e.g. Brahms's Violin Concerto, Dvořák's Cello Concerto). Then come the twentieth-century adventures such as Bartók's excellent *Concerto for Orchestra* (which should be seen as well as heard), highlighting individual instruments, sections and sub-sections of the large symphony orchestra.

CONDUCTING – the process of directing a body of players and/or singers to ensure that the music performed is well coordinated and adheres as closely as possible to what the composer has written. The notes of the score are dead, though, until brought to life by sounding out, and so it is understandable that what the notes convey may be open to varying interpretations. Some will swear by Toscanini's rather than Von Karajan's interpretation of a Beethoven symphony; one conductor has an histrionic style of conducting (Stokowski) while another is restrained (Boult) – neither need be better nor worse. Conductors abound, but there are few indeed who earn the constant admiration of an orchestra's members, a tough bunch to please. Some conductors are more successful in interpreting choral or operatic works, while others show their best strengths in orchestral music; Solti or Rattle seem to be impressive all-rounders. In addition to requiring a natural aptitude, conducting is a very demanding discipline; it can take years for a conductor to reach his peak. What is not easy to explain is the ability of a conductor to transfix each and every player; it remains a mystery. It is pleasing to note an increase in the number of women conductors.

CONSORT – the small ensemble referred to as a consort in the sixteenth and seventeenth centuries was made up of voices alone or having some instrumental accompaniment at first. Soon 'consort' meant an instrumental group comprising instruments belonging to the same genre, such as viols. A 'mixed' or 'broken' consort obviously refers to an ensemble of instruments of several genres, say, recorder/oboe/viols or violins. This is all you need to know about consorts.

CONTINUO – possesses a complicated history in terms of function, playing style and instrumentation. Its role in music starts from about the beginning of the seventeenth century and peters out about 1790; but note that today there are a goodly number of early music experts who are impressively skilled in continuo playing. Here is the historic sequence, for your needs: (a) church organist has a 'score' of all the parts to be sung by the choir, helps to fill out the sound. (b) Music style changes to emphasise vertical aspects (the harmony) of a piece; a line for a bass part is provided to stabilise the upper parts; this bass part would be for all or some of the following instruments – viola da gamba, cello, organ, harpsichord. So far so good? (c) Then, below each note of the bass part, figures are added to denote which chord should be played and in what position. (d) Continuo parts are provided for instrumental, orchestral and operatic works. You now possess the ABCD of continuo. Today, if you buy a copy of, say, a Telemann trio sonata you will find the continuo part filled in with notes; this is to save you, the non-expert, the headache of having to work out the chords to go with the bass line.

CONTRALTO – the deepest voice of the female singing range, below soprano and mezzo-soprano (half-soprano), and nowadays relatively rare. When we talk of a choral piece being scored for SATB, the A refers to the lower echelon of female singers, who are a mixture of mezzo-sopranos and contraltos. When *contralto* was first used in the seventeenth century it described a male singing falsetto; later it referred to a castrato. The female contralto has character parts in operas, including some by Handel and Rossini and the part of Erda in Wagner's *Ring*. For the concert platform, contralto solos may be found in the music of Brahms (*Alto Rhapsody*), Mahler and Elgar.

COPLAND, AARON – important American composer of our time. At twenty he was already studying in Paris and attending a variety of musical events in Europe. He liked and was influenced by a wide range of works by contemporary composers. However, just as Musorgsky and Stravinsky showed their Russianness in their music, so Copland wanted to underline his American roots, and his first important work in this genre was *Music for the Theatre* (amongst other features it contains jazz-type elements). Copland assisted fellow American composers through personal support, writing about their works, organising festivals. He did much to promote the early understanding of what twentieth-century music was about through publications such as *Our New Music*. If you wish to enjoy pungent rhythms, athletic orchestration and rich melodic line then give ear to *El salón México*, *Billy the Kid* and *Rodeo* (the latter two, orchestral suites from his ballet music). Copland is good for you.

COPYRIGHT – a composer also owns something, you know; it is each piece of music he writes. His ownership is international, although there is less chance of this being recognised in some countries than in others. A composer is likely to give a share of his royalties to his publisher, his recording company or anyone else who may promote his music. From about the end of the nineteenth century copyright law has been steadily built up and refined through a series of international copyright conventions; many countries now have some form of performing right society (PRS) to cover live performances and a mechanical copyright protection society (MCPS) to cover recorded material. Even if a composer writes a work to commission he still retains ownership of the work. In earlier days a publisher would pay a composer outright for his work and hope to recoup his outlay and make a profit on the sale of the sheet music. Still earlier, when the composer was but a member of the staff of a church or court, he would be paid a retainer for his creative efforts and other duties such as the training of a choir and orchestra and supervising the performance of his music. Often his patron would fall behind in payments for a year or more, and the composer would then have nothing but his board and lodging.

Kindly do not assume that with each work he completes a composer is going to start to earn lots of royalties from it; in fact, of the thousands of pieces turned out today, very few indeed earn enough royalties to provide a living and income has to be supplemented by teaching, performing, arts administration or through entirely non-musical tasks. The UK boasts the most efficient and sophisticated copyright processes in the world – something to be proud of. In the past three decades, with the arrival of the photocopy or reprographic machine, there has grown up serious abuse of sheet music. For instance, one copy of a partsong was bought (a true story) but over thirty were distributed to the choir, and when the composer complained he was told the members of the choir had learnt the partsong by heart from the single copy ... most unethical as well as unlawful. Exceptions are often made for music used for educational purposes.

Sometimes a work may 'lie dormant' for ages and then, for one reason or another, suddenly a strong demand for it arises and it will earn substantial royalties; that is one reason why a composer's ownership of his works will continue in most countries for a period of fifty years after his death. The Polish composer Gorecki, who is very much alive, suddenly saw his Symphony No. 3 become popular – were he to choose to have a holiday in England at Southend-on-Sea, meeting the cost would not prove a serious problem. Musical copyright is very complicated and the foregoing is no more than an easy explanation of the subject. But I hope you get the picture, so to speak.

CORELLI, ARCANGELO – mid-Baroque composer. He came from a well-established land-owning family. Music publishing, which was getting under way at the time, greatly assisted in the dissemination of his music. He was generous, good-natured, refined as a person; a pupil, Fornari, became his lifelong great-and-good companion; he never married. Although his was a comparatively small output for his time, Corelli exercised enormous influence on the development of violin playing. As a concert violinist he was in constant demand, and he held a European-wide reputation as a violin teacher: the violin could be said to be Corelli's sole form of creative expression. He brought order and discipline to the functions of the string body. Recommended listening: the twelve *Concerti Grossi* Op. 6 for strings, twelve Trio Sonatas Op. 4 for two violins and continuo.

CORONATION OF POPPEA – see *Incoronazione di Poppea, L'*.

COUNTERPOINT – become friendly with this term. Basically it means no more than the simultaneous utterance of two or more lines of music; it is the linear element to be found in many pieces, large and small. The lines are mainly interdependent rather than independent. Any piece sounding out clearly defined counterpoint should arouse in you a feeling of gut pleasure as much as the elements of rhythm or melody or orchestration. Your ear is mainly used to following the 'top line' of a composition, but with a little added concentration and practice you would greatly enjoy the pleasure of listening 'into' the music.

In Western classical music, the element of counterpoint has a long, evolving history, right up to the present. Composers like to take up the challenge of writing characterful counterpoint. Generally, no large-scale work can really hold together without the exercising of a high level of contrapuntal technique. Swing from Bach's *Two-Part Inventions* for keyboard through Mahler's Symphony No. 4 (with a solo contralto part in the last movement) to Stravinsky's *Mass*.

COUNTERTENOR – in England it was preferred to develop a falsetto voice, and to leave nature alone, rather than to engage in the Italian practice of castrating boys (see *Castrato*). Hence, today England produces the finest countertenors in the world, who are partly responsible for its long and excellent tradition of church choir singing, unmatched anywhere else.

COUPERIN, FRANÇOIS – the most famous of a line of Couperin musicians that continued for some two hundred and fifty years from the end of the sixteenth century. François is an older contemporary of Bach and Handel but hardly followed their Germanic instrumental or Italian operatic inclinations. Although he wrote a substantial number of sacred and secular vocal works and some chamber music, Couperin was essentially a composer of harpsichord pieces. His four volumes of *Pièces de clavecin* comprise some two hundred items and give us a fascinating insight into the urbane French culture of his time; each piece has a title. He was a committed teacher of the harpsichord and his treatise *L'Art de toucher le clavecin* makes relevant reading for serious harpsichord players of today. See how you react, for example, to the contents of his third volume of *Pièces de clavecin – Ordres 13–19*.

CRITICISM – the Shorter Oxford English Dictionary gives one definition of criticism as 'the art of estimating the qualities and character of a literary or artistic work'; not bad – this definition, mark you, goes back to 1674. In music, criticism can at once be helpful or misleading, enlightening or contentious, informative or sheer gobbledy-gook, partisan or detached. Some writers have tried to make a science out of musical commentary by removing personal opinion and merely examining the anatomy of a work, chalking up its factual data; this is analysis rather than criticism.

Today writing on or about music is quite an industry, and it includes critics who range from the inspired to merely what is called puff-reviewing. The contemporary critic has to have a basic viewpoint, has to be widely informed, has to understand his reader's biases, has to be eclectic in his musical tastes, has to possess an attractive literary style, has to risk being disliked by composers and performers, has to risk raising the ire of his readers; he always needs to be studying and listening. That's asking one helluva lot from one individual. Nowadays, with the music market offering such a huge variety of products, a demand has arisen for music critic specialists – on symphonic works, opera, early music, avant-garde compositions and so on; each is an area that demands expertise. Music criticism is an evergreen controversial subject and will never die out. In the end each one of us, once we have heard a piece of music, becomes his or her own music critic.

CRUMB, GEORGE – an American avant-garde composer whom I like very much; why? Because whatever innovations, complexities, abstractions or electro-acoustic devices he may employ, the resultant sound is full of aural interest and beauty. He brings what I call the human touch to the avant-garde camp, not via talk, theory and explanations but through the sounds of his music – proof of the pudding is in the eating … Crumb's favourite poet is the Spaniard Lorca. I wonder what your reaction would be to Crumb's *Songs, Drones and Refrains of Death* (Lorca's words) for baritone, electrified guitar/bass/piano plus harpsichord and percussion, or his piano piece *Little Suite for Christmas AD 1979*?

CUI, CÉSAR – the weakest of the Russian Big Five. Throughout most of his life he wrote operas, one as inadequate as the next; he hardly improved his technique in orchestration; as a music critic he was wildly prejudiced. His father was an army officer in Napoleon's battalions, who remained behind after their momentous retreat from Russia and married a Lithuanian lass. As Borodin was a trained and fully-qualified chemist, so Cui graduated at the Academy of Military Engineering to become a professor and reputed expert on fortifications. Best enjoy Cui through his less ambitious efforts – his songs and piano pieces, say, *Eight Songs* Op. 55 and *Three Waltzes* Op. 31.

DA CAPO – 'capo' is the Italian for 'head' or 'the top'. Usually abbreviated to DC, this is an instruction placed at the end of the second section of a piece of music telling the performer to go back to the beginning of the first section; the performer now plays the first section again, either an exact repeat or with specially written additional bars incorporated in the second playing. 'Segno' means 'sign' in Italian; *dal segno*, DS, is an instruction to the performer to repeat from the 'sign'; so the two terms have pretty similar functions.

DALLAPICCOLA, LUIGI – twentieth-century Italian composer who was the first successful user among his compatriots of serial technique, a compositional technique convincingly established by Schoenberg. His works contain warm, attractive melodic lines. His liberal views caused him serious handicaps during the war period. It is regrettable that there are insufficient examples of his music available on CD, such as his opera *Il prigioniero* (The Prisoner), the choral work *Canti di prigionia* (Songs of Imprisonment), the piano piece *Quaderno musicale di Annalibera* (Musical Foursome for Annalibera) and *Commiato* (which may be translated as 'Final Remarks') for soprano and instrumental ensemble. Available on CD are *Due Pezzi* (Two Pieces) for orchestra and *Due Cori di Michelangelo* (choral pieces).

DANCE – dance and music have always gone hand in hand. The evolution of both is as ancient as man. The first sign of dance may have occurred when some individual's feelings burst out in a flood of elation, accompanied by some sort of musical support. Perhaps both evolved towards a form of community expression, light-hearted or ritualistic (celebrating a wedding or mourning a death). Happily, dance continues to manifest itself as a popular form of social pleasure. The history of our own dance, as an art, may be traced as far back as 1200. The problem we face, however, is that the technique of recording dance steps and general movement accurately through some form of notation was, and still is, comparatively crude compared to musical notation. Thus the history of dance relies on no little detective work, despite the ongoing examination, and continuous discovery, of source material. What is of great assistance in our own time is the availability of the moving camera. Orchestral and instrumental works include numerous pieces rooted in dance music – pavane, gigue, waltz, tango, fox-trot. Large works for dance have been written for stage performance – ballets – from Lully in the seventeenth century to Cage in the twentieth. The earlier French tradition moved eastwards to Russia, which in the late nineteenth and early twentieth centuries produced the equivalent of Olympic gold-medal winners with the ballets of Tchaikovsky (*Swan Lake*), Stravinsky (*The Rite of Spring*) and Prokofiev (*Romeo and Juliet*). Since then the USA seems to have stepped into the forefront with 'modern dance' – the works of Martha Graham, Ruth St Denis and Jerome Robbins, amongst others. Dance activity in England is not far behind with regard to quality of dancers, choreographers, staging and composers. Why not take up some social dancing? You'd enjoy moving to the rhythms of the cha-cha or samba; besides, it'll help you keep fit.

DANSE MACABRE – the title of Saint-Saëns's popular symphonic poem, which, like Liszt's *Totentanz* (Death Dance) for piano and orchestra and Mahler's cantata *Das klagende Lied* (Song of Lament), makes use of the *Dies Irae* plainchant. The 'dance of death' theme was already incorporated in some pieces by the fifteenth century.

DANTE SYMPHONY – a two-movement orchestral work with the titles 'Inferno' and 'Purgatorio' by Liszt, who was inspired by Dante's remarkable poetic achievement *The Divine Comedy*. Then Liszt tagged on a Magnificat for choir which, for some listeners, weakens the effect of the earlier two movements.

DA PONTE, LORENZO – an extremely active Italian librettist who was in great demand. His place in posterity is fixed as the provider of the librettos for three Mozart operas, *The Marriage of Figaro*, *Così fan tutte* and *Don Giovanni*. Da Ponte, a difficult character to deal with and often unreliable, mishandled his affairs to the extent that he decided to emigrate to the USA in the first half of the nineteenth century. There he started a grocery business, of all things, which soon failed, and he ended up as a teacher of Italian language and literature. A rum ending, what?

DARGOMÏZHSKY, ALEXANDER – with Glinka established the ideal of expressing Russianness in classical composition, acting as a model for the succeeding generation of Russian composers; otherwise he was a second-rate composer. He shows melodic gift – consult the songs *I am sad*, *The night zephyr stirs the air* and the opera *Russalka*. No need to go overboard for Mr D.

DARMSTADT – a German town whose modest musical history was advanced after the war with the building of a fine opera house and the establishment in 1951 of an annual conference at which avant-garde music trends are examined and discussed. A bit of a yawn for some of us.

DART, THURSTON – an influential musicologist in postwar England. Thanks to his radical approach, London University, where he held the Chair of Music, eventually boasted the largest number of internally registered music undergraduates, by far, of any university in the UK. To boot Dart was a virtuoso harpsichordist, playing solo or continuo at concerts in the UK, USA and Europe and in numerous recordings. Though he gave a powerful fillip to early music up to the time of Bach through his research, writings, teaching, editing and playing, his vision and erudition enabled him to encourage and assist a variety of musical activity in other areas. He was invited to become president of the British Electronic Music Society, which he accepted with relish. At the entrance to his headquarters at King's College, London, he put up a notice which stated, 'all ye who enter this building leave behind counterpoint' – his reaction to much stuffy music-teaching going on at universities.

DAVIES, PETER MAXWELL – important British composer of the generation born in the 1930s and 40s; his prolific production covers a range of works as wide and as long as a summer's day. In the 1950s at the Royal Manchester College of Music (now the Royal Northern College of Music) he associated with Harrison Birtwistle, Alexander Goehr and the pianist John Ogdon, and this clutch of students earned the title 'Manchester Group'; they championed the European avant-garde, more as a reaction to British musical conservatism of the day than anything else. Maxwell Davies moved to the solitude of Orkney where he helped to promote festivals, some of which featured music he wrote especially for them. His output stretches from the difficult and obtuse to easily approachable music for children. He has steadfastly supported the interests of British composers, and in the recent hullabaloo concerning the continued existence of London's excellent orchestras he threatened to give up his knighthood if certain destructive proposals by the Arts Council of Great Britain were carried out. Cut your musical teeth on Maxwell Davies with his *An Orkney Wedding with Sunrise* for bagpipe and orchestra, *Runes from a Holy Island* for a mixed sextet and *Eight Songs for a Mad King* for male voice and chamber ensemble.

DAVIS, COLIN – British conductor of world class; started musical life studying clarinet at the Royal College of Music and as a bandsman in the Household Cavalry. A remarkably poor pianist, he found difficulty in fulfilling his ambition to become an opera conductor, the first step up the rungs of this ladder being an appointment as a fluent répétiteur. In due course he made it, tenacious fellow that he was, and his repertoire nowadays extends from Mozart to Tippett. Has notched up appointments as principal conductor of the BBC Symphony Orchestra and as music director at Covent Garden (1971–86), seasons with such diverse orchestras as the Berlin Philharmonic and the Boston Symphony, and was the first British conductor to be engaged at the Bayreuth Festival. Davis is knighted, and the more musical knights we have the better!

DEAN, WINTON – a fine example of the best in English writers on music – always lucid, and economical with words; the research is authoritative, and there is a canny grasp of human frailty and of the preoccupations of the society contemporaneous with the subject under study. Dean's reputation rests mainly on his scholarly work on Handel, Bizet and pre-Verdi Italian opera.

DEBUSSY, CLAUDE – if you want to talk about a composer creating his own original sound, this is your man. Ignore any writings claiming that Claude was influenced by such-and-such a composer or by this or that work; much as this may be the case, his sound-world is unique – it really has no antecedent, and any imitations by another composer are second-rate. Yet the originality of his musical thought is such that, from Stravinsky to the present day, he continues to influence composers. It is Debussy, not Schoenberg, who heralds the music of the twentieth century; difficult to believe when recollecting the beauty of his understatement, the immediate rapport his musical lines and contours make with the listener.

Considering Debussy's influence, importance and fame today it is regrettable to have to note that even by the age of forty his royalties amounted to less than £10 a month. His nature seemed to have no desire for a religion, yet he was very superstitious. On a visit to London as a young boy he attended a performance of *H.M.S. Pinafore* and became an admirer of Sullivan; at the time he also met Sir Hubert Parry, director of the Royal College of Music. I share with Debussy his preference for *Tristan und Isolde* above all Wagner's operas. But if one has been nurtured on Verdi, Wagner and Strauss it is not easy to appreciate the achievement and uniqueness of Debussy's opera *Pelléas et Mélisande*, where simplicity and space lie in the music and silence is used as an effective means of expression. Debussy wrote, 'we must agree that the beauty of a work of art will always remain a mystery, in other words we can never be absolutely sure "how it is made". We must at all costs preserve this magic which is peculiar to music and to which, by its nature, music is of all arts the most receptive.'

Both his opera and his sole string quartet upset their respective applecarts; his orchestral pieces reveal new horizons in instrumentation and orchestration; his piano music in terms of poetic expression is surpassed only by Chopin's. Let me cool it – I am sinfully making value judgements. Go and listen to his *Nocturnes* for orchestra or the piano pieces comprising Book I of his *Préludes*.

DE LA HALLE, ADAM – in medieval times poet and composer were often one and the same person. This French *trouvère* was pretty busy in the performing arts in the latter part of the thirteenth century. Musicologists are not sure whether he died in Naples or London. *Tant con je vivrai* is a *rondeau* for three voices, an exquisite example of his words and music writing: 'As long as I live/I will never love another./I will never leave you/As long as I live./Rather I shall serve you./To this task I have dedicated myself, completely, loyally./As long as I live/I will never love another.' If you are in the process of courting, then memorising these words might come in handy.

DELIBES, LÉO – nineteenth-century French composer who wrote almost exclusively for the theatre. Even if you haven't seen the ballets *Coppélia* and *Sylvia* you will surely know some of the music. His most serious work, the opera *Lakmé*, remains in the international operatic repertoire. He gained much of his stage experience as chorus master at the Théâtre Lyrique, where his work involved him in the preparation of operas by Gounod, Berlioz and Bizet. Delibes is a composer of what today would be described as light classics; in this idiom he was highly skilled, fashioning quickly-grasped melodies, adapting various popular dance rhythms to his own needs, providing nicely judged accompaniments. After hearing Delibes you are bound to go away humming or whistling some of the music and even to execute a jaunty step or two.

DELIUS, FREDERICK – here we have a different kettle of fish: an important figure in the early period of the twentieth-century British composition renaissance. A poignant life-story: father a wool merchant in Bradford, for long opposed to his son taking up a musical career; at twenty-two, off to Florida to grow oranges; formed strong emotional ties with Norway and Paris; attractive to and attracted by women; infected with syphilis, of which he was never cured; in Paris met a young student painter who, after six years, swapped her status from mistress to wife; music hardly noticed in England until championed by Sir Thomas Beecham; suffered continuous pain from his illness, which ultimately turned him blind and paralysed; fortunate in obtaining the voluntary service as amanuensis of Eric Fenby, who helped him compose his last works. Delius's music is ridden with melancholy, nostalgia and gentleness. Largely because of his health, moments of energy are few and far between. Considering his condition his output is surprisingly large, and includes music for the stage, orchestra and chamber ensemble, also songs and pieces for choir. You are likely to enjoy his orchestral rhapsody *In a Summer Garden*, and *Two Pieces* for small orchestra (*On Hearing the First Cuckoo in Spring* and *Summer Night on the River*). A high percentage of Delius is recorded; you may yet become a Delius fan.

DELLER, ALFRED – responsible for bringing the English countertenor from out of the church into the concert hall and on to record. He also played a major part in the revival of early music performance in the postwar years, especially lute-song material, with his Deller Consort. Now there is a constant demand for English countertenors in Europe. The part of Oberon in Britten's opera *A Midsummer Night's Dream* was especially written for him; he frequently commissioned composers, bless him, to write pieces for this type of voice.

DIABELLI VARIATIONS – the Viennese publisher Anton Diabelli thought up a foxy idea: he had made up a little waltz tune and, with an eye to earning a thaler or two, invited a number of composers each to write a variation on his modest creative effort. The number of composers grew to fifty-one, including not only Schubert and Liszt – who at the time was but eleven years old – but also Beethoven. Ludwig, never one to do things by halves, went to town and wrote thirty-three variations – his Op. 120. The result was that Diabelli published two volumes of the variations – the first devoted to Beethoven's effort, the others all piled into the second volume. For your curiosity know that on record at the moment there are sixteen interpretations of the Beethoven piece.

DICTIONARIES – nowadays, perhaps more than ever, we ordinary mortals need to understand what is going on around us, in music no less than in other subjects. The prime and most authoritative source worldwide is the English publication *The New Grove Dictionary of Music and Musicians*, sixth edition, editor Dr Stanley Sadie; it comprises twenty huge, heavy, thick volumes. If you wish to delve deeper into any subject contained in the present jolly publication then off you go to consult the 'New Grove'. Dictionaries and encyclopedias containing musical material were already being drawn up from before the eleventh century; these were written in Latin, mainly by scholars for scholars. Before about 1700 musical definitions and explanations treated music as a branch of science. With the steady growth of musical vocabulary, sooner or later there was bound to emerge a dictionary solely devoted to music. The first such, by Walther, was published in 1732. The next milestone occurred in the mid-nineteenth century with publications by the Belgian Fétis and the German Schilling. The first important publication for universal use in English was George Grove's *A Dictionary of Music and Musicians*, completed in 1889. Every few decades another edition with additions and revisions is brought out, 'Grove 6' in 1980; at a guess 'Grove 7' will be born before 2000. In our world of music there has been such a vast expansion and growth of musical knowledge and scholarship that the publication of 'Grove 6' required almost two and a half thousand contributors. At the same time specialist dictionaries have come out on, as examples, opera, early music, instruments, jazz, catalogues of themes. Better stick to this writer's effort if you don't want to become too discombobulated.

DIMINUENDO – quietening down the level of loudness; a synonym is *decrescendo*; in a score their abbreviations are 'dim.' and 'decresc.' The opposite, to get louder, is *crescendo* – which does *not* mean a 'peak' of loudness. Such instructions rarely appeared in scores before the nineteenth century, as performers who knew the musical language and style required were left to follow their own inclinations. From the end of the nineteenth century scores have increasingly been splattered with instructions not only on how to play a phrase but how specific notes should be sounded.

D'INDY, VINCENT – see *Indy, Vincent d'*.

DIRGE – a song or instrumental piece of mourning; the terms *lament* and *threnody* have similar connotations, but pieces so entitled do not usually express that degree of forlornness contained in a dirge. Listen to Britten's setting of the anonymous fifteenth-century *Lyke-Wake Dirge* in his *Serenade* for tenor, horn and strings. Terrific!

DISCOGRAPHY – describes any list of sound recordings for commercial or scholarly purposes. Some listeners suffer from discographic mania, a comparatively harmless condition, in which their prime concern is who recorded what and when, rather than a regard for the quality of the content. But nowadays we do have to take some trouble in deciding which version on CD of, say, Tchaikovsky's Symphony No. 5, Op. 64 we should buy – especially as at present there are some fifty-four recordings of this work to choose from; this is where the viewpoints of writers and commentators on recordings can act as helpful guides. See the list of recommended performances at the end of this book.

DISSONANCE – if you think you don't like dissonance you are wrong; an important reason why you are likely to prefer Beethoven to Dittersdorf, or Chopin to Czerny, is because the former in each case writes music containing more dissonance than is to be found in the music of the latter. Dissonance is the spice of music and we enjoy its resolution to consonance. It is always relative, and what may have been considered dissonant in the thirteenth century becomes mildly consonant in the eighteenth, which in turn breeds its own dissonance palette.

In music theory, discussion on dissonance and consonance for a long time centred around the relationship between musical intervals and largely held good until the naughty twentieth century arrived; since then, many works emphasise unresolved dissonance, composers paying more attention to elements such as rhythm, texture, and new sounds. Of late, however, composers are turning again to the 'd–c' factor, which seems to be fundamental to most of our listening pleasure.

DITTERSDORF, CARL – a contemporary of Haydn and Mozart, a highly successful composer of symphonies and *Singspiel* (a type of opera containing spoken dialogue). As happens to not a few composers he faced straitened financial circumstances at the end of his life, as well as suffering badly from arthritis. He wrote an autobiography, a rare thing for a composer to do at the time, which gives some insight into the musical milieu of his age. Attractive are his Oboe Concerto and his Symphony in E flat.

DIVERTIMENTO – a light-hearted piece written for an instrumental ensemble or for a small orchestra. The close of the eighteenth century produced piles of divertimenti (by which time the title had become stabilised), including examples by Haydn, Boccherini and Mozart. A divertimento was meant to be performed on relaxed occasions, even as background music at a party. Some divertimento-type pieces, just to confuse you, carry instead the title of serenade, cassation, or *Tafelmusik*. Oddly, the divertimento faded out in the nineteenth century – too much romantic loftiness around perhaps – but had a reasonable revival in the twentieth – Bartók's (for strings), Berkeley's (for chamber orchestra), Françaix's (for bassoon and strings) are three choice examples.

DOLMETSCH, ARNOLD – in a long life this scholar and instrument-maker promulgated a new understanding of the nature and performance of early music, especially of instrumental pieces. He began his instrument-making by restoring old instruments but moved on to the construction of harpsichords, clavichords, lutes and viols based on strict authentic principles; the quality of his production soon earned him an international reputation. His book *The Interpretation of Music of the 17th and 18th Centuries* (1915) remains a classic. After settling in Haslemere, Surrey, with the help of friends and enthusiasts he established an annual festival of early music. His son, Carl, has substantially continued and developed the achievements of his father.

DONIZETTI, GAETANO – as a nineteenth-century Italian opera composer he fits in nicely between Bellini and Verdi. In contrast, say, to

Corelli or Delibes, Donizetti was born into wretched poverty. Mayr, a successful composer and *maestro di cappella*, firmly believed in Donizetti's talent and ensured a wide and thorough musical training in his boyhood; Donizetti bore a lifelong gratitude to him. With the capacity to work concentratedly and swiftly, particularly useful when it came to getting opera commissions, Donizetti was soon involved in the operatic life of Italy. He composed some sixty-six operas in the space of about twenty-six years – not bad going, despite the conventions of opera writing laid down at the time. His happy marriage was over after nine short years when his wife died in a cholera epidemic; he never quite recovered from this emotional blow. Donizetti travelled much around Italy and to Paris; at one period he had four operas running there at the same time, which made Bellini and Berlioz quite jealous. Elegance in formal design, a sense of wit and a great melodic gift helped to ensure his success as a composer of comic opera – *L'Elisir d'Amore* (The Elixir of Love) or *Don Pasquale*; also meriting attention are two of his serious operas, *Anna Bolena* and *Lucia di Lammermoor* – no doubt you are acquainted with arias from the last-named.

DOUBLE BASS – the lowest-sounding instrument in the string section of an orchestra. The players stand or sit on high stools while in action. The instrument is not easy to play in tune because of the wide stretch the left-hand fingers need to make to get their normal notes. It is a lovable, friendly instrument, as witness the dozens of concertos and solo pieces written for it, even to the present. The double bass has four strings, more rarely five; the bow is short, almost squat. Good players possess great agility in fingering and bowing. Harmonics on the double bass (obtained by the way the fingers of the left hand touch the strings) produce a haunting, eerie sound. In the orchestra the double bass adds weight to the cello line and emphasises rhythm and pulse. Only from the nineteenth century onwards did it gain significant independence from its lighter comrades, always having played what the cellos play, only an octave lower; today the double bass has an effective orchestral repertoire. The players need to have technical virtuosity and firm intonation, as is required in Schoenberg's *Verklärte Nacht*, R. Strauss's tone poem *Till Eulenspiegel* or Britten's *Young Person's Guide to the Orchestra*.

DOWLAND, JOHN – I vote with those who consider Dowland the greatest Elizabethan lute-song composer. His travels took him to France, Germany and Denmark, where he was highly appreciated – for long he was a favourite at the court of King Christian IV of Denmark. After an extended period of frustration at failing to get a post at the English court he at last succeeded in 1612, when he was appointed one of the King's Lutes – no great shakes, really. Dowland's songs show wide-ranging melodic and harmonic invention, felicitous choice of words (many written by himself) and telling extension of lute-playing technique. His music contains a melancholy characteristic of English song of all periods; but Lully's dictum certainly does not apply to Dowland – 'La musique anglaise est toujours mélancholique, toujours triste et toujours sentimentale'. The three volumes of songbooks he published (the songs were called 'ayres') proved consistently popular in England and abroad; two songs that immediately come to mind are *Come away, come sweet love*, and *Fine knacks for ladies*. There is also his very moving *Lachrimae or Seven Teares* for five viols and lute.

DOWN BY THE GREENWOOD SIDE – Birtwistle's outstanding piece of music theatre, which he describes as a 'dramatic pastoral' for soprano, five actors and chamber ensemble. It is a comparatively short work, like a one-act comic opera, highly entertaining with its whimsy, slapstick, violence, and taunting melodic material. Its subject matter is based on English legend. It certainly can be listened to as well as seen in the theatre, and it is very regrettable that it has not yet been issued on CD.

DREAM OF GERONTIUS, THE – one of Elgar's most impassioned works, and that's saying something. An oratorio for mezzo-soprano, tenor and bass soloists, chorus and orchestra, composed in 1900, one of the high points in his oeuvre. Newman's words ponder over Everyman, on the point of death, facing judgement; worth getting to know.

DRUM – apart from the voice, perhaps man's first musical instrument. Almost any object may be called a drum as long as it emits some degree of resonance after being struck; but once we get beyond this crude description the definition becomes quite sophisticated and has to incorporate the hundreds of different kinds of drums to be found all around the world, which may be beaten, rubbed or even shaken. In some parts of the world the sound is thought to hold magical powers (as with the set of drums in the royal court of the Rain Queen of the Lowedu of the Northern Transvaal). Here we are really concerned with drums in our symphonic orchestra. The largest is the *bass drum*, with a deep sound of inaccurate pitch which may be raised or lowered by screw tension. Then there is the kettledrum or tympanum which comes as a set of from two to five; these *timpani* each have a pitch range of four to five notes, selected nowadays by a foot-pedal attached to the frame. The stretched material which the drumsticks strike is a type of plastic, replacing the old stretched hide. The third of the most common drums in the orchestra is the snare or *side drum*. The frame holds the two stretched plastic membranes with the lower having across its surface the wires, called snares, which give the instrument its characteristic sound. These snares may be released by a metal lever. The top side is struck by a pair of wooden sticks, the ends of which taper into a sort of knuckle which ensures keen definition in the striking. Players have developed a remarkable virtuosity in side-drum playing, with a rich variety of ornaments and effects. If you want to know more about drums and drumming, best seek out a professional player who is likely to keep you engrossed about the world of percussion with description, demonstration and anecdotes.

DUFAY, GUILLAUME – remember the name, for he is the great composer of the fifteenth century; his influence was as wide as that of Bach, Beethoven and Schoenberg in their time. Dufay held numerous posts in France and Italy, but his headquarters were at Cambrai where he lived and died. His music is exciting, though written in a period of relatively little innovation. His masses, motets and secular choral pieces are nearly always in three parts and full of rhythmic vitality, finely wrought polyphony and refreshing melodic contours. Listening to his music stimulates and relaxes the psyche at one and the same time: hark to *Ave regina celorum* or the rondeau *Adieu ces bons vins de Lennoys*.

DUKAS, PAUL – a contemporary of Debussy. He left a short list of works, having, unwisely, destroyed a large number of scores, believing their quality to fall short of his standards. At the Paris Conservatoire he taught orchestration and composition at different periods and he edited some of the music of Beethoven, Rameau, Couperin and D. Scarlatti, so he must have had some musicological expertise. Dukas belonged to the group of French composers who were Wagner-admirers. His friends and colleagues included Saint-Saëns, d'Indy, Debussy and Albéniz. Of his surviving works his *Variations, interlude et final sur un thème de Rameau* for piano and his Symphony in C are important. But the work that is unique in that it continues to be performed and recorded decade after decade is his symphonic scherzo *L'apprenti sorcier* (The Sorcerer's Apprentice), composed in 1897 and based on a ballad of Goethe. This is understandable, since it has rich orchestral colour, harmonic innovation and rhythmic verve. I suppose what helped to maintain its popularity was its appearance in the Walt Disney classic *Fantasia*, with Mickey Mouse drawn as the apprentice; on the other hand, mark you, composers such as Debussy, Schoenberg and Stravinsky held it in high regard.

DUKE BLUEBEARD'S CASTLE – Bartók wrote this one-act opera in 1911; it was rejected as unplayable and had to wait seven years before its quality was recognised. It is possible Bartók may have been influenced by Janáček's masterpiece *Jenůfa*, which had received several performances in Hungary in 1904. Heavy, heavy is the symbolism of the work, but what wonderful music. The two characters, Duke Bluebeard and his new bride Judith, on their wedding night enter a large chamber in his castle. The chamber has seven doors leading off, behind each of which lies a secret, now horrible, now lovely. The Duke tries to persuade Judith not to open the doors but she insists, and a dramatic event occurs with each opening. From the seventh door out step the three murdered wives of the Duke's previous marriages. Judith returns with them through the seventh door and the Duke is left alone – will he find a fifth wife? This is not a 'soap opera', so I can't tell you ... The Hungarians consider *Duke Bluebeard's Castle* as their equivalent of Debussy's *Pelléas et Mélisande*.

DULCIMER – to put it simply, a zither (stretched strings over a resonating body), when struck by beaters and not finger-plucked, becomes a dulcimer. Dulcimers are found all over the world; West European iconography shows them going back to the fifteenth century. The instrument was played by gentility and peasantry alike. East European folk music very often includes dulcimers, either as accompaniment in an ensemble – usually involving clarinet, violin and drum – or as a lead instrument. Large dulcimers may be fixed on to stands and have become concert instruments. Hungarians call both large and small dulcimers *cimbaloms*. If you are in a café or restaurant in Budapest sipping a glass of white Hungarian wine, with a violinist playing romantic melodies in your ear, sooner or later you are also likely to hear the trilling of a cimbalom. Liszt was the first to use it orchestrally, what with his Hungarian background; Kodály, Bartók, Stravinsky and Orff have also made use of the instrument.

DUNSTABLE, JOHN – English composer who flourished in the first half of the fifteenth century; before Dufay the most important composer of his time. Yet there is little detail on his life, employment or movements. In medieval times, at Cambridge, for example, one was considered cultivated if one had studied mathematics, theology and music. Dunstable easily fulfilled this requisite; three extensive treatises on astronomy have been identified as having been written by him. Musicologists think it likely that he was for long in the employ of the Duke of Bedford. There is little doubt that Dunstable had all-round intellectual brilliance. His music shows vocal polyphony entering a period of subtlety and refinement; there is masterly use of isorhythmic technique and purposeful direction for each voice part. In keeping with the convention of the day, his works are nearly always in triple time. Later composers – Binchois, Dufay and Ockeghem – show the influence of Dunstable in their music. Have a go at his motets *Quam pulcra es* and *Speciosa facta es*.

DUPARC, HENRI – here's the oddity: his reputation as a leading composer of nineteenth-century French song (referred to as *mélodie*) rests entirely on thirteen songs he wrote between the ages of twenty and thirty-six. He destroyed a number of early pieces and the remainder is really second-rate. Each of his songs, however, is a jewel, and if you have a feeling for things French his *Chanson triste*, *Extase* and *L'Invitation au voyage* are for you. A sad case, a bit like Delius in that in due course Duparc went blind and became paralysed. His ailment was mainly physical, but he also suffered from a certain psychological problem with special regard to composing. He had two good friends in Chausson and Chabrier. His long post-composition period was filled with the study of a wide range of literature, painting, an interest in non-Western art and in religious contemplation.

DVOŘÁK, ANTONIN – truly put Czechoslovakia on the musical map; a most industrious fellow who churned out orchestral works, concertos, choral pieces and songs, chamber and piano music. All his life he was obsessed with writing opera, but though he completed ten, none was a hit – his rich creative powers lacked the opera feel, unfortunately. His best effort in the genre is *Rusalka* (no connection whatever with Dargomïzhsky's *Russalka*). Like Beethoven he wrote nine symphonies, the most popular being the Symphony No. 9 in E minor, subtitled 'From the New World'. Orchestral players enjoy performing his music because sooner or later in a piece there will be an interesting part for their particular instrument. The easy, melodious sound of his works belies sharp invention and high technical skill – perhaps much like the music of Haydn and Mozart. He drew on his folk music environment continuously. For the first ten years of his adult life Dvořák relied on teaching to earn his bread; by his early forties, however, he achieved international recognition. He travelled widely to conduct or attend performances of his music. There were regular visits to England, where he was always enthusiastically received; Cambridge conferred an honorary PhD; in the 1880s alone his fine *Stabat Mater* received performances in England at London, Birmingham, Worcester, Hereford and Gloucester. Two of his pals were Brahms and Tchaikovsky. He did not much enjoy his professional duties in New York during his stay in the USA in the early 1890s, preferring the company of Czech compatriots and listening to black American music, which he relished. Though never belonging to a political movement, he staunchly supported Czechoslovakian interests; for all his fame Dvořák described himself as 'a simple Czech musician'. Symphonies and other orchestral music, OK, but do give a hearing to some of his chamber music – the Piano Trio No. 3 in F minor, the String Quartet No. 4 in E minor. It is not often appreciated that Dvořák's music plays an important part in the extension of nineteenth-century harmony.

DYAGILEV, SERGEY – a larger-than-life Russian impresario whose activities bridged the late nineteenth and early twentieth centuries. He was one of those *animateurs* who draw forth important works of art. In Dyagilev's case this was chiefly in the realm of ballet, since he had formed the Ballets Russes company. He involved leading dancers, choreographers, painters, stage designers and composers, from the last-named commissioning vital material: ballets from Stravinsky (e.g. *The Firebird*) as well as from Satie (*Parade*), Debussy (*Jeux*), Ravel (*Daphnis et Chloé*), R. Strauss (*Josephslegende*), Falla (*The Three-Cornered Hat*) and Prokofiev (*The Buffoon*).

EDINBURGH – this beautiful city, the capital of Scotland, offers an arts festival, launched in 1947, which is world-renowned; of three weeks' duration, it begins in the third week of August. If you have not yet attended the Festival, do so, if only for a few days – you'll enjoy every minute. There's always a large list of events from which to choose and the Edinburghians, including the B&B landladies, are lovely people. While the emphasis is on music, most of the arts are included. Each year there is rich representation from European and other overseas countries in addition to local and national performers. Of great interest at the Festival is The Fringe, which features offerings from a huge range of individuals and groups, some good, some terrible, involving dance, comedy, theatre, poetry, painting, photography and an assortment of oddities. The only adverse comment on the Festival, now that it has at last a proper opera house (the Festival Theatre, opened June 1994), is that in relation to its importance there is still insufficient commissioning of new works from composers. Perhaps that will now change.

EDISON, THOMAS – for your splendid high-quality CD collection you need to go back to this compulsive American inventor who, in 1870, built the first sound playback machine – how magical that must have seemed to our forebears. A sad curiosity is that Edison had turned deaf at the age of twelve.

EDITING – you may not be aware of it but editing music is a highly important function, particularly when dealing with pre-twentieth-century material. A music editor must be expert in his subject and exercise objective judgement in preparing a work for publication – unlike nineteenth-century editors, for instance, who would often 'improve' the music of Bach, Mozart or Schumann. It is not merely a matter of correcting an erroneous note or two the composer may have written; the editing process is more sophisticated than that. The further one goes back in time the more difficult it is to interpret accurately what the notes in the score mean. This is because a piece of music was often left to the performer to complete, so to speak, since he or she would be familiar with its language, style and convention, and would even be allowed a certain amount of licence in, say, the use of ornamentation, dynamics, improvisation of a cadenza in a concerto, the playing of passages louder or softer, faster or slower, even in the duration of a note. Present-day musicologists are highly trained and often specialise in a particular historical period or in a particular composer; it is from their ranks that editors are most often drawn. Musical notation changes constantly, and often the learning of another musical language is involved. Performers today, when playing early music, require a score in contemporary notation that accurately reflects what the composer of two, three and four hundred years ago actually intended. So spare a thought for, and be thankful to, music editors.

EDUCATION – basically, in modern music education, two types are involved: education of the gifted, those likely to pursue a career in music, and making alert listeners out of ordinary music lovers like you and me. The training which gifted young musicians receive in universities and other specialist institutions is, on balance, not bad, though there's always room for improvement. But that is really outside our scope – let me just say that you will spot the odd reference to particularly outstanding teachers throughout this book.

In Western society, for many hundreds of years, the potential musician would learn from his masters at church or in court, emulating the system of peasant societies, in which the child learns by following the adults' music-making. The end result could be an all-in-one composer, performer, conductor, teacher, administrator – Bach was even considered a reliable organ repairer and hot on keyboard maintenance and tuning.

66

Nowadays we believe that knowing something about music is beneficial to our general development, and the school syllabus satisfies this requirement to some extent, though it is far from ideal. Of late the DES has laid down music education guidelines which incorporate three principles: composing, performing, and listening to music; very acceptable, but success depends on quality music teaching and this is rarer than we might think. We *do* need to know about our musical heritage, we *do* need to know about music beyond our shores, we *do* need to know about music other than so-called classics; how best to mix these into a syllabus that demands the three principles is not at all easy – and it is expensive. Incidentally, what was your music education like?

EISLER, HANNS – a pupil of Schoenberg and occasionally of Webern. Because of his material circumstances their instruction was free. Eisler was so committed to his communist principles (don't forget there is such a thing as secular religion) that the subject-matter of almost his entire corpus of music defends the interests of the so-called working class or attacks so-called capitalist tenets. A lifelong collaboration with Brecht was not interrupted when both had to flee Hitler's régime; after a troubled stay in the USA they returned to the newly created communist state of East Germany. Much experience in writing music for the screen qualified Eisler, in collaboration with Adorno (music theorist and critic), to write a useful book *Composing for the Films* (1947). His apologists claim Eisler's music is not yet fully appreciated. It ranges from the banal to the sophisticated, from simple diatonic melody to subtly-fashioned chamber music; he is the last of the German cabaret-song composers whose tradition goes back to the Überbrettl days of 1900. See what you make of his Septet No. 2 *Zirkus* and the songs *An den kleinen Radioapparat* (To the minor radio official) and *Frühling* (Springtime).

EISTEDDFOD – originally the Welsh word for a 'session' at which, over many centuries, Welsh bards would compete against one another; today it is the name for a competitive festival featuring poetry, music and dance. From Wales this type of festival has sprung up in other lands, particularly those associated with the old British Empire, where it now refers mainly to classical instrumental competitions. The best known of the Welsh eisteddfods is the one held at Llangollen – the International Eisteddfod – which concentrates on folk song and dance and draws teams from every point of the compass.

ELECTRONIC MUSIC – whether you like it or not, electricity in music has come to stay. Pop groups, who have been playing electric guitars for over forty years, will remind you of this; even earlier jazz guitarists – I have in mind Barney Kessel and Wes Montgomery – were using, very musically, contact microphones attached to their instruments and wired to a loudspeaker. Now there are electric pianos, keyboard and wind synthesisers, plus a large selection of other electro-acoustic equipment. Have you come across the vibraphone, a sort of electrified xylophone, which produces some very attractive sounds? It's been around quite some time.

The microchip has made possible an enormous extension to the creation of sound sources. In classical music electro-acoustic composition established itself in the 1930s with works composed by the Frenchman Varèse. The tape recorder has been most useful to composers involved in this field, for it enables them to store a lexicon of sound from which to build up a piece with or without the addition of live instrumental participation. Computers are now increasingly involved, programmed either to store material for the composer's use or even to create their own compositions! If you listen closely to music for film, TV and jingle you are sure to have noticed a good percentage of sound derived from electro-acoustic sources.

Currently many universities and schools run electronic music studios; here, on the more mundane side, a student's performance in song or on the violin can be recorded so that the student, listening to the playback, can observe what is good or bad about it. Postwar composers have written significant works involving electronics: to name but a few, Berio, Birtwistle, Boulez, Penderecki, Pousseur, R. Smalley and Stockhausen – quite an international spread. If you feel some curiosity about all this try Stockhausen's *Mantra*.

ELGAR, EDWARD – it is the music of this composer that marked the beginning of a magnificent renaissance in British composition, continuing to this day. Though aesthetically a late Romantic and influenced by nineteenth-century Austro-German and French masters, he forged a highly individual musical voice. In and around Worcester Elgar's father earned a living as piano-tuner and local organist and also played piano and violin; later he opened a music shop, in which Elgar worked until the age of sixteen. Thereafter, for the remainder of his life, he became a freelance musician, playing the violin, teaching, conducting and composing. While Elgar gained some satisfaction from the comfort and security of middle-class life, at the same time his intense and passionate nature, stifled by the late Victorian and Edwardian code of behaviour, was suppressed – only to be given full vent through his music. This contrast of outer and inner life led to the writing of two types of music, each having Elgar's indelible stamp: on the one hand there were his popular pieces, such as *Salut d'amour* (a piano piece, later orchestrated) and his five *Pomp and Circumstance* marches for orchestra (No. 1 is the most popular, now associated with the Last Night of the Proms concert and containing that sweeping melody with the word-setting Land of Hope and Glory). On the other hand, from a distinguished list, there are his *Serenade* for string orchestra, *Introduction and Allegro* for string quartet and string orchestra, the oratorio *The Dream of Gerontius*, his Violin and Cello Concertos, Symphony No. 1 and *Variations on an Original Theme* (popularly known as *The 'Enigma' Variations*) for orchestra. Elgar was for long happily married. His wife, eight years his senior, died in 1920; as a result, like Donizetti when he lost his wife, Elgar suffered a serious falling off in his creative output.

EPISODE – a useful term to describe a passage or section in a piece of music which acts as a link in its discourse. An episode may or may not include material already presented and may even contain musical ideas which are later taken up in some way or another. Episodes in fugal writing have more narrowly defined functions, closely associated with the fugue *subject* (its 'theme') and with modulation (moving from one key to another). And that's enough on *episode*.

ETHNOMUSICOLOGY – a musical discipline of increasing importance. It is the study of music and society, of music and individuals in their ethnic context. There is little difference, in principle and methodology, in the study of the repertoire and function of Chopi xylophone orchestra music in Mozambique and the study of someone who wishes only to listen to different performances of Beethoven symphonies and little else. Research into the musical ways of different peoples of the world has been going on for the past two hundred years; greater ease of communication and travel and the development of sound and visual recording facilities have caused research and writings in ethnomusicology to snowball in the past five decades. Early ethnomusicologists of this century include von Hornbostel, Bartók and Cecil Sharp. In the UK the principal scholars are normally connected with universities, one of the best-known being the late John Blacking at Belfast. You yourself could prove a worthy subject for ethnomusicological research. Watch out!

EXPOSITION – the opening section of an intensely argued piece of music, when the leading themes and motifs are presented, is termed its *exposition*. The mood of the piece does not necessarily have to be 'serious'. Traditionally the first movement in a sonata, concerto or symphony is written in what is called *sonata form*, which has a tripartite division – exposition, development, recapitulation; but things can

69

already get complicated if one examines the exposition, say, of the first movement of a Mahler symphony. An additional meaning to 'exposition' involves fugue; here the exposition refers to the opening section, in which each part of the fugue will have presented its theme at least once. Now you can turn to your companion at a concert and murmur, 'Splendid exposition in the first movement but the development section was a bit of a let-down, don't you think?'

FALLA, MANUEL DE – a younger contemporary of Albéniz and Granados; the three were instrumental in reviving the Spanish contribution to classical music which had lain dormant since the days of Victoria in the sixteenth century. Debussy and Ravel influenced Falla, but by far the greater influence was the rich variety of Spanish folk music and dance. Some folk musics have greater universal appeal than others; to European ears in this century, that of Spain has exercised wide attraction. There is something atavistic about this material, infused with rhythm, melodic line, dance step, the sound of castanets and guitar, vocal nuance – all combining in a chemistry of sensuous darkness and light, despair and exhilaration. Falla's music reflects all this, but ever in the classical mode. This is his achievement – none of his works is sentimental or merely reworkings of native substances. Note particularly the ballet *El sombrero de tres picos* (The Three-Cornered Hat), the ballet with songs *El Amor Brujo* (Love the Magician), *Noches en los jardines de España* (Nights in the Gardens of Spain), symphonic impressions for piano and orchestra, and the Concerto for harpsichord and five instruments. Dukas and Lorca were good friends. The Spanish civil war gravely upset him and caused his muse to languish; he removed to Argentina, never to return to his homeland.

FANTASIA – in a nutshell, here follows an historical review: musically, a piece in which attention to any conventional form is relaxed in favour of allowing fuller play of the imagination. The title was first used in the fifteenth and sixteenth centuries to describe vocal pieces in which word-setting was not expected to keep to conformist lines. By the seventeenth century the title moved on to pieces for keyboard (virginals and organ) and string consort music, mainly in three and four parts; at this time English masters of the fantasia were Byrd, Bull, Gibbons and Jenkins. Fantasia-writing did not preclude artful contrapuntal interplay. By the time of Bach in the first half of the eighteenth century and Mozart in the second half, the fantasia could therefore be either contrapuntally emphasised (Bach's three-part keyboard sinfonias were originally called fantasias) or moulded in a free-form style, even suspending barlines (as in some of C. P. E. Bach's clavichord fantasias). The nineteenth century spawned fantasias galore for the piano – Schubert's *Wanderer Fantasia*, Schumann's *Fantasia in C major*, Liszt's *Reminiscences from Don Giovanni*. There is comparatively little attention paid to the fantasia in the twentieth century, despite some excellent examples from English composers – Vaughan Williams's *Fantasia on a Theme of Thomas Tallis*, Tippett's *Fantasia on a Theme of Corelli* and Britten's *Phantasy Quartet* for oboe and strings. In postwar composition there are many works not called as such, but which are really no more than fantasias.

FANTASTIC SYMPHONY – Berlioz's *Symphonie fantastique* is one of the unique works in the symphonic genre. In it is introduced the concept of a motif reappearing in each movement – the *idée fixe*. This nineteenth-century Frenchman's work is in five movements instead of the conventional four; it is an apt example of programme music, and the orchestration is masterly. Following Beethoven's nine symphonies few composers really added to the symphonic territory he mapped out; this work makes Berlioz one of those few.

FARNABY, GILES – the Tudor period in England exhibits a rich selection of composers, from Thomas Tallis to Thomas Tomkins. Though Farnaby was not of the front rank, his compositions show how high the normal standard of composition was, as witness his psalm-settings, secular choral pieces and fantasias for keyboard. His early training was more as a joiner than a musician. Full of charm are virginal pieces such as *Giles Farnaby – His Dream*, *Farnaby's Conceit* and *Lacrymae Pavan*.

FAURÉ, GABRIEL – during his professional lifetime as composer, teacher and organist, his influence was wide in France. He enlisted in the army at the time of the Franco-Prussian War and took part in the raising of the siege of Paris. In contrast to not a few of his musical colleagues, Fauré was little influenced by Wagner, although he made a point of seeing most of that master's operas; he evolved an independent style, particularly with regard to melodic and harmonic innovation. With Chabrier, Duparc, d'Indy and Lalo he formed the *Société Nationale de Musique*. An unhappy love affair produced his first quality pieces – a piano quartet, a violin sonata and a *Ballade* for piano which, oddly, the virtuosic Liszt, with whom Fauré was friendly, complained was too difficult to play. The woman he ultimately married seems to have been unable to deal with his creative crises, which may have been the reason why he had several intense liaisons. Until he was about fifty, admiration for his music had been restricted to friends and the salons of the wealthy who enjoyed the avant garde – out of a sort of zoo-syndrome curiosity rather than from informed knowledge; at some of these gatherings Fauré and Proust would meet. Though he was by no means a miniaturist, his best work lies in his songs, as distinguished as those of Duparc, Debussy and Ravel (the song-cycles *La bonne Chanson* and *La Chanson d'Eve*), his chamber music (Violin Sonata No. 1, Piano Quintet No. 2), and his many piano pieces (nocturnes, impromptus, barcarolles). That only his *Requiem* for soprano, baritone, chorus and orchestra is constantly performed belies his thorough knowledge of the musical tradition in French liturgy and his experience in writing for this field. You might do worse than introduce yourself to Fauré's musical voice, if you have not yet met it.

FELDMAN, MORTON – a radical American composer. You will be fascinated by his orchestral *Madam Press died last week at 90*, *For John Cage* (violin and piano), *Why Patterns* (violin or flute, piano and percussion). Influenced in his early days to no little degree by Cage and other avant-garde compatriots. His soundworld stresses softness and delicacy. When they are well performed his pieces can prove quite appealing. An important contributor to the postwar explosion in experimenting with new ways of notating music.

FERNEYHOUGH, BRIAN – one certainly requires a particular listening bias to tolerate the convoluted sounds Ferneyhough creates, whether for solo instrument (*Superscriptio* for piccolo), string quartet (*Quartet for Strings No. 3* – deliberately so titled) or instrumental ensemble (*Funérailles*). An English composer in the avant-garde mould, appreciated in Germany and France more than in his homeland; the music of Stockhausen and Boulez has exercised a major influence on his musical thinking. Will his highly élitist attitude to composition, with its intense intellectual application to musical processes, stand the test of time?

Meaning, will his works migrate beyond the confined attention of specialist listeners? Who can say?

FESTIVAL – you doubtless know that festivals take place all over the world, lasting several days or spread over several months, in which music is often the only or the main feature. Festivals normally occur annually and continue over the years as long as enthusiasm, imaginative programming and, above all, financial support are abundantly available. In the UK alone, each year is likely to offer a handsome crop of at least thirty festivals. Some are biennial (Leeds), some triennial (Birmingham); the best-known annual ones include Aldeburgh (June), Bath (May–June), Brighton (July), Cheltenham (July), Edinburgh (August–September), Glyndebourne (May–August), Llangollen (July). So go out and collect your brochures!

Festivals go back to ancient times when a community would celebrate some ritual or other – the arrival of spring, a religious event. The Olympic Games began as a festival in honour of Zeus and all the athletics were accompanied by music and dance – not much of that in our present-day Olympics, more's the pity, even if, with some stretching, one considers the ice-dancing of the winter Olympics! In the medieval, Renaissance and Baroque eras, festivals would be held at churches and courts to celebrate royal or saints' days. The nineteenth century laid the foundation for that praiseworthy aspect of British culture, the large choral festival – the hardiest is the annual Three Choirs Festival (born in the early eighteenth century), held in rotation at Gloucester, Worcester and Hereford (August–September).

FIDELIO – Beethoven's gift to opera; its subtitle is *Conjugal Love*. Some consider *Fidelio* more successful from the musical point of view than for its effectiveness as a stage work. Interestingly, the opera was first commissioned by Schikaneder, the librettist and producer of Mozart's *The Magic Flute*. By no means unusually in the world of opera, *Fidelio*'s first performance in 1805 was a flop, and success had to wait until 1814 while it underwent several revisions. It boasts no less than four overtures, one of which, entitled *Leonora No. 3*, appears in concert programmes. The plot, set in eighteenth-century Spain, reflects the noble behaviour and faithful love to be found in woman – a sentiment which may be too easily poohpoohed in our own time. In sum, the heroine, Leonore, disguises herself as a young man, Fidelio, in order to enter the service of the villain in whose castle her husband has been imprisoned; after this, that and t'other she rescues him and they live happily ever after.

FILM AND TELEVISION MUSIC – a world of musical riches and an artistic creation of the twentieth century. Take note of the music for any film you may watch – the effect it can have on a scene is magical. Imagine a scene in which a car is driven along a country lane, then stops outside a farmhouse and the driver enters; one piece of music can make you believe he has dropped by for a cup of tea, another that he will surely commit murder. *Tom & Jerry* cartoons would be only half as effective without the music. Even in the age of silent films it was found necessary to supply musical accompaniment.

Music for sound films is now about sixty-five years old and has produced outstanding composers hardly known outside the medium – Max Steiner (over three hundred feature film scores), Dimitri Tiomkin, Elmer Bernstein, John Williams are some of the names associated with Hollywood motion picture production, which at its peak of activity turned out some four hundred films a year. To write film music the composer must possess an eclectic turn of musical creativity, for he has to draw on a wide range of language and style, depending on a film's requirements: historical setting, mood, narrative, characterisation and so on. Indirectly, the film composer has contributed in no small measure to our understanding of twentieth-century classical music, because he writes in its idiom; here the listener is, as it were, subliminally educated.

Classical composers who have written film scores include Milhaud, Shostakovich, Copland, Honegger and Walton. Let it not be forgotten, though, that there is a high percentage of rubbishy film music – bland, perfunctory, clichéd. British film music is of a high standard, in part because classical composers have had the opportunity to write for the medium: Britten, Arnold, Vaughan Williams, Rawsthorne, Richard Rodney Bennett. The same applies to composers for television: Gunning, Horovitz, Carl Davis. The art and craft of film composition has chalked up a history and a sophistication in composition technique such that it has now become a valid subject for research and for study at university and film school. See also *Incidental Music*.

FINZI, GERALD – a minor but valuable contributor to the flowering of twentieth-century English song. Hear proof of this claim in his cantata *Dies natalis* for soprano, tenor and string orchestra, his song-cycle settings of the poetry of Hardy, *A Young Man's Exhortation* and *Before and After Summer*, and his choral pieces *Seven Part-Songs* (Bridges) and *White-Flowering Days* (Blunden), both for SATB. Finzi's idiom is gentle and refined and belongs to a less hectic age. He died, too soon, from leukaemia.

FISCHER-DIESKAU, DIETRICH – a splendid baritone, a Berliner. As a young soldier at the close of the war, aged twenty, he was taken prisoner by the British in Italy. Equally at home on stage or concert platform, he has notched up at least thirty lead roles in opera and a repertoire of more than a thousand songs. His recordings are numerous, from Bach to Henze: Berg's opera *Wozzeck*, the *Lieder* of Schubert, Schumann and Brahms, the *chansons* of Debussy and Ravel. Britten wrote the baritone solo part in his *War Requiem* for Fischer-Dieskau as well as the song-cycle for baritone and piano *Songs and Proverbs of William Blake*, first performed at the 1965 Aldeburgh Festival (Peter Pears is supposed to have selected the text). At the time this latter work, dark and tortuous, must have fitted in with Fischer-Dieskau's feelings, for his first wife had lately died in childbirth. If you wish to set yourself a standard for baritone voice singing, listen to Dietrich!

FITZWILLIAM VIRGINAL BOOK – from the latter half of the sixteenth century until the first three decades of the seventeenth there blossomed in England a mass of significant compositions for keyboard. A line can be traced from here through the expansion of keyboard music right up to the present; it is a fascinating phenomenon. *The Fitzwilliam Virginal Book* is easily the largest collection of virginal music of the time, rich in its parade of dances, sets of variations and adaptations of songs and madrigals. Byrd, Bull, Farnaby, Morley and Tomkins were the most prolific composers. The original manuscript is housed in the Fitzwilliam Museum, Cambridge.

How was this collection compiled? Most of its material might have been lost to us were it not for one Francis Tregian, an immovable Catholic in the time of Elizabeth I and James I who refused to attend Church of England services. As a result he was chucked into the Fleet prison in London in 1609, where he languished until his death ten years later. During his incarceration much of his time was spent in copying out English virginal music. The collection disappeared until Pepusch, a German composer and theorist living in London, died in the mid-1770s, when it was discovered on the disposal of his extensive library. It is thought that perhaps he bought it in Holland. Lord Fitzwilliam acquired the FVB in the 1780s. The edition by Fuller Maitland and Barclay Squire was published in 1894 and dedicated to Queen Victoria. Fascinating?

FLORENCE – one of the most cultivated of European cities, situated in Tuscany. Italians regard Florence as their national cultural centre. From as far back as the thirteenth century it has a distinguished history of achievement in literature, philosophy, architecture and music. If you have not yet done so, and you're 'a vulture for culture', and you have some quidlets to spare, a visit to Florence is not a bad idea. Music was well served by Florence (as you know, 'Firenze' in Italian), with its churches and courts, crafts and commerce: first, the promotion and advance of sacred and secular polyphony; then the birth of opera (by the close of the seventeenth century twelve theatres were running opera – just imagine them to be the equivalent of our local cinemas); on to early oratorio writing and Cristofori constructing the first crude piano. Today the city is a living exhibition of six centuries of fine arts creation, a centre for musicological research and the frequent presentation of new works by Italian and other composers.

FLUTE – normally the top-sounding instrument in the woodwind section of the orchestra. Nowadays it is made of metal and not wood. Held horizontally, it is built in three sections – the embouchure (mouthhole), the middle section with the main keywork attached, the 'foot' section with keywork for the right-hand little finger. It is well to remember that there are many other kinds of flutes throughout the world, some played vertically, and even including a 'nose' flute! If you blow hard (overblow), the sounding note of our orchestral flute will jump up an octave (eight notes). The recorder was usually the 'flute' of the orchestra until the latter half of the eighteenth century. Especially in the Baroque period, in the very popular trio sonatas (two melody parts supported by a harmony-filling part), the flute could substitute for violin or oboe. It was showered with concertos in the eighteenth century by composers from Albinoni to Mozart; twentieth-century composers have paid due attention to it as solo, chamber and orchestral instrument. Here's a selection for you: Bach (Concerto in E minor), Mozart (Concerto for flute and harp in C), Saint-Saëns (*Tarantelle* – flute, clarinet and piano), Debussy (Sonata for flute, viola, harp), Prokofiev (Sonata for flute and piano), Varèse (*Density 21.5* – solo flute), Berio (*Sequenza I* – solo flute). A higher-pitched instrument is the smaller piccolo, lower-pitched the larger alto and bass flutes. The flute is an enormously versatile instrument, capable of rendering very virtuosic swift passages, silvering the violin line in the orchestra, enjoying interplay with its companions in the woodwind section, conjuring up magical, soft, soothing melodies. Long live the flute!

FRANÇAIX, JEAN – not a trail-blazing twentieth-century composer, but his music possesses impressively consistent and firm control over form and instrumentation. French wit, irony, seductive motif, brightness of rhythm, nuance in tonal colours infuse his works, whether for stage or concert platform. A gifted pianist, he frequently participated in performances of his own music. His output includes music for films. Like, say, Mendelssohn or Walton, Françaix established a language and style early in his career which evolved little, yet attractive pieces flowed regularly from his pen; compare the Piano Concertino written aged twenty with his *Hommage à l'ami Papageno* written at seventy-two. A delightful ballet in which cats are the characters, *Les demoiselles de la nuit* (Ladies of the Night), has choreography by Roland Petit. Enjoyable are his *Divertissement* for bassoon and strings and *Petit Quatuor* for saxophones.

FRANCK, CÉSAR – French composer, born in Belgium. Early life dominated by an ambitious father determined to turn his son into a piano prodigy; result? son revolts, leaves the family home; struggles to earn a living eased in his mid-thirties when recognition gained as able writer of music for church services and fine improviser on the organ. In due course he obtained the post of organ professor at the Paris Conservatoire. Franck's music really only got cracking in his early fifties, by which time he had gathered a large coterie of pupils, among them Duparc, d'Indy and Chausson. Liszt thought highly of Franck's organ works. The essence of his musical style and language is rooted in the contrapuntal models of Bach and the harmonic matter of Wagner. He advanced the *cyclic form* (reworking of the same material in different movements of a piece); this compositional technique is already seen in the cyclic Masses of the fifteenth century; there are dribbles of it in

Beethoven and Schubert, while Schumann and Liszt take the technique still further. Two model examples in Franck's corpus are *Grande pièce symphonique* for organ and *Prélude, Chorale et Fugue* for piano. His most popular works today are the *Variations symphoniques* (Symphonic Variations) for piano and orchestra, and the Sonata in A for violin and piano, with its ingenious treatment of canon in the final movement. Franck was not so hot on choral music and song.

FRESCOBALDI, GIROLAMO – Italian composer and organist, active in the first half of the seventeenth century, who knocked his audience sideways with his brilliant performances, much like Chopin and Liszt at the piano and Paganini with his violin later on. Frescobaldi was born in Ferrara, at the time one of the leading musical centres of Italy. He was elected to the Accademia di S. Cecilia, an early musicians' union in Rome, at twenty-one; following a fruitful journey to Brussels he then became organist at St Peter's. Somewhat rough-mannered, he seemed to have been a bit of a ladies' man. His general education was found wanting and a contemporary writer observed, 'all his knowledge is at the end of his fingertips'. Frescobaldi was prolific in the production of keyboard toccatas, canzonas, ricercars and all the dance forms of the time, and at showing off all manner of contrapuntal and ornamentation skills. *Nine Toccatas* would be a pleasant way to become acquainted with his music.

FRICKER, PETER RACINE – of the composers to emerge in England immediately postwar he was a leading light. One of a number of distinguished pupils of Mátyás Seiber, a Hungarian composer and teacher who settled here before the war. Appointed director of Morley College, a noted adult education institute with a marked emphasis on music study, Fricker succeeded two distinguished predecessors – Tippett and Holst. Administrative demands increasingly interrupted his composition, and when the opportunity arose to spend a year at the University of California at Santa Barbara, in 1964, he sped there, where he settled; by 1970 the Chair of Music was conferred on him. His works, large and small, are brimful of contrapuntal ingenuity. More frequently than not they are sombre in mood, serious in intent. This may account for the absence of any recording to date of his music. It is much to be regretted that, for example, his *Wind Quintet, Litany* for double string orchestra or *A Wish for a Party* for male choir are not yet on CD.

FUGUE – some say fugue is a technique, others that it is a form; what it is for sure is one of the most demanding of all contrapuntal disciplines devised in European classical music. A fugue piece is written in two or more parts whether for keyboard, voices or instruments. Each part has to make constant use of the theme, known as the *subject*. At all times the composer is compelled to think linearly. To write a fugue as an exercise is not that difficult, but to make it into an exciting piece of music sometimes eludes the most gifted. Some composers couldn't care a toss about fugue, others consider the writing of a characterful fugue a challenge – Ravel is an example of the former, Beethoven of the latter. Fugal writing evolved in the second half of the seventeenth century from several other contrapuntal forms.

Bach is the supreme master of fugue. In his time it had become embedded in the music culture, and many an inferior contemporary could bash out a fugue before tea; in contrast, today fugue is some distance away, like say Mars, from current musical language and style. So contemporary composers may well have to sweat it out in order to produce a convincing fugue, and some do decide to have a go. The fact that many composers have written pieces which they call fugues and many have simply introduced in a piece substantial sections which are deliberately fugal has caused the indecision as to whether fugue is a form or only a technique; let us perhaps say it is both. Fugue in mood can be happy, sad, dance-like, contemplative – it does not have to be 'serious'. To the ordinary listener, without understanding in detail the processes going on, fugue can prove utterly exhilarating, exciting, as its subject and the subsidiary material are manipulated between the parts. Do not be timid about fugue! Here is a handsome list of fugue or fugal writing to set you off: Bach (*Forty-Eight Preludes and Fugues* for keyboard, and *Brandenburg Concerto* No. 4, last movement), Handel (choral fugues in the oratorios *Messiah*, *Saul*), Mozart (finale of the 'Jupiter' Symphony, No. 41, K551), Beethoven (Piano Sonata Op. 111, first movement), Brahms (conclusion of *Variations on a Theme of Handel*, piano), Verdi (the final scene of his opera *Falstaff*), Bartók (*Music for strings, percussion and celesta*, first movement), Shostakovich (*Twenty-Four Preludes and Fugues*, piano).

FUX, JOHANN JOSEPH – Baroque Austrian composer and theorist. He has the odd distinction of having served three Habsburg emperors – Leopold I, Joseph I and Charles VI. A sufferer from gout, in order to attend the first performance of his opera *Costanza e Fortezza* in Prague he had to travel all the way from Vienna in a litter. Fux was a popular composer in his time, with operas, oratorios and other sacred vocal music to his name. Little, however, has survived and musicologists can only ponder on his output of several hundred works, assisted by documents and a thematic catalogue drawn up by Koechel, the music bibliographer best known for making a chronological list of Mozart's works. Fux's name is important in the world of music, hardly for his compositions, which one suspects are likely to have been boring, but for his textbook on counterpoint, *Gradus ad Parnassum*, which influenced the teaching of the subject right up to the close of the nineteenth century.

GABRIELI, GIOVANNI – Italian composer who was taught by his uncle, Andrea. Both played vital roles in establishing Italy as the leading musical country in the latter part of the sixteenth century; both were born and died in Venice. On his uncle's death Giovanni succeeded him as principal composer at St Mark's, and many young composers came to study with him; of the foreign contingent the German Heinrich Schütz was the most important. He concentrated on sacred vocal and instrumental music; because of his position he was able to hire the best singers and instrumentalists in and beyond Venice. He used a technique known as *cori spezzati* – the breaking up of a choir or instrumental ensemble into two blocks, high and low, extended in his hands by voices accompanied by instruments; the upper choir would be supported by flutes and strings, the lower by bassoons and trombones. At times he would write for as many as four choirs and at special performances at St Mark's the choirs would be placed at different points in the church. Thus our Giovanni was the first successful creator of live stereo- and quadrophonic sound! He wrote much music for brass, mostly with the title 'canzona' or 'sonata'; the number of parts would range from four to fifteen. Gabrieli was one of the first composers to write in expression marks into his scores such as loud or soft. Some brass pieces worth your attention are *Canzon in echo* for ten parts and *Sonata XVII* for fifteen parts.

GALOP – in the middle of the nineteenth century it was the habit to end a grand ball with a *galop*, a fast, two-beats-to-the-bar, invigorating and jolly dance, which, it was hoped, would send everyone home in high spirits; the format would involve couples as part of a quadrille group. A witty galop appears in Offenbach's *Orphée aux enfers* (Orpheus in the Underworld). The following also wrote galops: Schubert (*Galop and Eight Ecossaises*), Liszt (*Grand galop chromatique*) – both for piano, Bizet (in his little suite for orchestra *Jeux d'enfants* – Children's Games), and even Prokofiev (as many as three galops in his ballet *Cinderella*) and Shostakovich (in *The Gadfly Suite* for orchestra).

GASPARD DE LA NUIT – a set of three piano pieces by Ravel which show off his distinctive keyboard style. The work is inspired by a set of poems of Aloysius Bertrand. 'Gaspard' is a name for the devil. The pieces are headed *Ondine* (a water nymph), *Le gibet* (the gallows) and *Scarbo* (a goblin).

GAVOTTE – this jolly dance originated in Brittany, that part of France, as you know, which has Celtic ties; it is still danced there and indeed in other parts of France. The accompaniment is usually the small French bagpipe called a musette, or a violin, plus a drum. From the sixteenth to the eighteenth centuries the dance was just as popular at court as with the peasantry; there are even gavotte songs. Its rhythm is two-beats-to-the-bar and built up in four-bar units. The basic dance step routine is hop-step-step-jump. Try this out with one of the following – the gavottes in the first two of Bach's Six English Suites for harpsichord, in Schoenberg's Suite for piano Op. 25 or in Prokofiev's *Classical Symphony*, third movement. Rameau inserted gavottes in his ballets and one may be found in Mozart's opera *Idomeneo*.

GAY, JOHN – an English poet and playwright much involved with music. One may say that he is the inventor of the ballad opera, in revolt against the plot and character source of opera at the time, which were commonly drawn from Greek mythology. The most enduring example is *The Beggar's Opera*, which he produced in 1728; in further revolt, this ballad opera contains popular songs of the day, not arias. The successors to *The Beggar's Opera* were, regrettably, lacking in invention and the audience gave the thumbs down to *Polly* and *Achilles*. Gay also wrote one of Handel's best librettos, that of *Acis and Galatea*. Brecht and Weill created a very successful modern version of his hit with *Die Dreigroschenoper* (*The Threepenny Opera*).

GEBRAUCHSMUSIK – a term used to describe music composed in the 1920s which aimed at deliberate simplicity, direct appeal to the ear, and could even be played as background music at social functions; much as would apply to the numerous divertimenti of the eighteenth century. German composers like Hindemith and Weill led the way in this type of composition; you will enjoy Hindemith's *Kammermusik No. 1* for twelve instruments; his *Gebrauchsmusik* short opera *Hin und Zurück* (There and Back) is not yet recorded – more's the pity. At one time the term was used to apply to film music, music for radio plays, music for amateurs, home and school. But this is now passé.

GENEVA – one of Switzerland's most beautiful cities; Liszt gave a piano course there in 1835 in support of the newly established music conservatoire (come to think of it, Liszt was a remarkably generous fellow throughout his life). The nearby Abbey of Solesmes had a marked influence on early church music practice; with the Reformation movement Calvin replaced the Mass with congregational psalm-singing, church organs were demolished or sold, music for relaxation and amusement was banned. By the eighteenth century secular music reappeared and in the nineteenth and twentieth centuries the Abbey undertook important research in the study of Gregorian chant. Dalcroze worked in Geneva in the early years of this century – he was the inventor of eurhythmics (bodily movement to the accompaniment of music and precursor of present-day aerobics). Today Geneva is a centre for international instrumental competitions. Ansermet founded there the fine Orchestre de la

Suisse Romande, promoting the music of Debussy, Ravel and Stravinsky.

GERHARD, ROBERTO – a Spanish composer who settled in England in the 1930s as a result of his grave opposition to Franco's forces in the Spanish Civil War. He was a pupil first of Granados and then of Schoenberg. His style is a mixture of his Catalonian heritage and the tenets of Schoenberg. He settled in Cambridge after the war and in due course received an honorary DMus. from the University. His fine opera *The Duenna* is not yet recorded, nor his *Violin Concerto* nor his Symphony No. 3, *Collages*, which was inspired by watching clouds on an aeroplane journey. But you can get a feel of his rhythmic vitality and his imaginative orchestral colouring from his *Albada* and *Alegrías* (a concert suite from his ballet of the same name). There is also a *Fantasia* for guitar.

GERSHWIN, GEORGE – died, during an operation to remove a brain tumour, before he was forty; one of the most renowned American composers. His fame, rightly, rests with his output of numerous popular songs, most of which have memorable melodies and lyrics of quality (*I got rhythm*, *Embraceable you*, *But not for me*, for instance), and his folk opera *Porgy and Bess*, which even achieved a season at Glyndebourne, and which was the climax to a large number of musicals. His brother Ira wrote the lyrics for many of his songs. Gershwin wanted to study with Ravel who, gracefully declining, said, 'With the money you earn from *your* music I should be studying with you.' The main influence on Gershwin was undoubtedly jazz and the blues; this may already be observed in his *Rhapsody in Blue* for piano and orchestra, composed at the age of twenty-five. Sometimes one regrets that not more American composers have made use of that country's most important musical contribution to the twentieth century, namely, jazz. Efforts by Gershwin in this direction are *An American in Paris*, *Cuban Overture*, *Piano Concerto in F*; though here the works are sometimes limited in the development of material, this defect is balanced out by Gershwin's extraordinary gift for melody. He was a first-rate improviser at the piano; he notated eighteen of the improvisations on his songs in *George Gershwin's Song-Book* and there are also his *Preludes* for piano.

GESUALDO, CARLO – a highly neurotic and off-beat sixteenth-century Italian composer, both Prince of Venosa and Count of Conza, a veritable nobleman. Soon after he married Maria d'Avalos he caught her 'in flagrant intensity in fragrant sin' and promptly murdered her; he was then twenty-five. All that happened, it seems, was that Gesualdo retired to his estate until the scandal subsided, and there began to concentrate on composition; until then it was but a secret pastime – apparently nobles were not expected to compose. In due course he visited Naples and then Ferrara, which at the time was a brilliant musical centre. He married again but this too proved to be a failure. He belonged to the avant-garde circles of Ferrara and Naples. Gesualdo lost both his sons, one from each marriage; from 1595 he became more and more morose and kept to his estate, immersed in composition and suffering long bouts of depression. His six books of five-part madrigals and his two books of sacred songs are evidence that his music is striking and full of subtle nuances. Listen to his five-part motet *Ave, dulcissima Maria* and his five-part madrigal *O sweet my treasure*. An interesting sideline is Stravinsky's orchestration of a Gesualdo madrigal which he calls *Monumentum pro Gesualdo*.

GIBBONS, ORLANDO – a most important English composer of the early seventeenth century. He was a chorister in the chapel of King's College, Cambridge, later joining the College as a student. He was accepted in the Chapel Royal under James I in 1603; Cambridge awarded him a Mus.B. in 1606 and Oxford a DMus. in 1622. By profession he was a keyboard player, which is apparent in his organ and virginal pieces; these show great individuality, as does his church music. Gibbons also made a very valuable contribution to the music of the Anglican service – the *Second Service*, having a solo voice with independent organ accompaniment as well as the full choir doubled by the organ; this formal arrangement is considered a particularly English innovation. His anthems (the English motet) *O clap your hands* for eight parts and *This is the record of John* for alto, five viols and five-part choir are outstanding. Musicologists consider Gibbons as the pioneer of violin music in England and pioneer of the trio sonata in Europe. He died of apoplexy which, today, I think, we would describe as a stroke.

GIGUE – a dance believed to have originated in England, where descriptions of the 'jig' may be found in fifteenth-century records; its usual rhythm is two-beats-to-the-bar in triplets. The gigue was one of the most popular of Baroque instrumental dances and was a standard movement of the suite, usually the final one. The French lutenist Gautier, who for three decades was a court lutenist in England, introduced the dance to France; it then migrated to Germany and Italy. Pachelbel and Froberger wrote gigues for organ and there are gigues in each of Bach's French Suites for harpsichord. Gigues appear in English masques and other stage events in the seventeenth century, and in the works of Lully in Paris. More modern examples are Schumann (*Four*

Piano Pieces, Op. 32), Debussy (*Images* for orchestra), Stravinsky (*Duo Concertante* for violin and piano), Françaix (*Sonatine* for piano).

GINASTERA, ALBERTO – Argentina's and indeed one of South America's leading composers, who settled in Geneva. A large part of Ginastera's life was spent in helping to develop Argentina's musical growth by teaching, organising concerts and the example of his own compositions. In due course recognition came from the USA and this led to a stream of commissions; Ginastera's music is now performed worldwide. In 1968 he received an honorary DMus. from Yale University. Of his four operas, two – *Bomarzo* and *Beatrix Cenci* – were at one time banned in Buenos Aires for their overt sexuality and violence. Latin freshness and vitality may be heard in his *Tres Danzas argentinas* for piano, *Pampeana No. 2* for cello and piano, and in his ballet suite *Estancia*.

GLASS, PHILIP – twentieth-century American composer who studied at Chicago University, at the Juilliard School and with Nadia Boulanger in Paris. There he met the Indian musician Ravi Shankar, who exercised a marked influence on Glass's approach to composition; essentially this meant the relegation of harmonic concerns in favour of emphasis on rhythmic procedures. Glass's music falls under the umbrella of *minimalism*, a musical movement and aesthetic which reacted strongly against the intellectually directed world of composers such as Stockhausen, Boulez, Xenakis and Maderna. The simpler, more approachable sounds that emerged from the minimalists, while full of subtle treatment of instrumentation, motif and form, attracted a new public to contemporary music. Glass undoubtedly has a following as a popular classical composer. See how you take to him with *Company* for strings, *Dances* Nos. 1–5 for chamber ensemble or his piano piece *Mad Rush*.

GLAZUNOV, ALEXANDER – a much respected Russian composer of the generation following Tchaikovsky and Borodin. His main teacher, with whom he retained a lifelong friendship, was Rimsky-Korsakov. Glazunov's career received valuable promotion from Mitrofan Belyayev, a wealthy patron of the arts. In some twenty-five years as director of the St Petersburg Conservatoire he revised the curriculum, raised the standard of staff and students, and defended the autonomy of the institution. He always sought to help needy students, one of whom was Shostakovich. He also opened an opera studio and launched a students' symphony orchestra. On his visits to England Glazunov studied teaching methods at the Royal Academy of Music and Royal College of

Music. The peak of his musical creativity manifests itself in the ten years to 1907. During World War I and the revolutionary period immediately after Glazunov suffered much deprivation. In 1928 he left for Paris, where he lived until his death. In 1972 his remains were transferred to St Petersburg (then Leningrad) and interred in an honoured grave. I think you would enjoy his Symphony No. 7 in F, Op. 77, and his two concertos, one for violin and one for saxophone; the latter is not as odd as may first appear, for the instrument grew in popularity from the end of the nineteenth century and regularly appeared in concert performances by military bands.

GLEE – a simple, light-hearted English song, harmonised in three or four parts and performed informally; in the seventeenth century the texts of glees centred around the subject of eating and drinking and, as one might expect at the time, the singers were male. But by the early nineteenth century the material of the texts had greatly broadened and glee singers included the fairer sex. Glee clubs sprang up all over the place. Today the singing of glees is usually confined to after-dinner activity on special occasions at universities and colleges. A bit of gleeful information.

GLINKA, MIKHAIL – it was freely admitted by Tchaikovsky and the Big Five (Balakirev, Borodin, Cui, Musorgsky and Rimsky-Korsakov) that Glinka launched the nineteenth-century Russian nationalist school. His general studies in St Petersburg produced satisfactory results, more out of his natural intelligence than hard work. Thereafter he spent his days hanging around salons enjoying the life of a dilettante and, his family being well-off, indulging his passion for travel. But note that during all this time he would be composing, though hardly anything of importance. His first triumph, at the age of thirty-two, came with his opera *A Life for the Tsar*; the plot deals with a Russian peasant who, at the cost of his life, leads astray a band of Poles seeking to kill a seventeenth-century Tsar. In this work there is ample evidence of Glinka's sharp ear for and love of Russian melody, rhythm and speech inflexion. His second opera, *Ruslan and Lyudmila*, while containing many worthy and even exciting moments, has not achieved the same success. The disappointing reception at its first performance left Glinka, not surprisingly, very dejected. He left for Paris in 1844; the most important event of his stay was the striking up of a friendship with Berlioz and his thorough study of the Frenchman's scores. Then he left for Spain, where he lived for a couple of years, enjoying its life and music; of his Spanish-influenced music the best example is his *Spanish Overture No. 1*. The sum of Glinka's achievement in the history of Russian music is threefold:

harmonic progressions not common to Western traditions, reference to Russian legend and literature, treatment of Russian melodic material. He died in Berlin and, like Glazunov eighty years later, his body was taken back to St Petersburg.

GLISSANDO – a musical effect that can be either witty or serious. It refers to the sliding of a musical note up or down; this sliding may be short, from a note to its immediate neighbour, or it may be as much as two and a half octaves, as with the famous clarinet glissando which opens Gershwin's *Rhapsody in Blue*. Sometimes unwanted glissandos occur, as when a singer, thinking to intensify the feeling of the music, swoops up or down, thereby marring the intention of the melodic line; the same can happen with a violinist or cellist.

GLUCK, CHRISTOPH – a German composer and an important pioneer in eighteenth-century opera. Gluck's early years were little enough distinguished and his education, both musical and general, was haphazard. He arrived in Prague at the age of fourteen and, with his enterprising bent, soon acquired a post as church organist. Later he went to Milan, where his composition technique was markedly advanced by the teaching of Sammartini. His hidden operatic talent emerged at the age of twenty-seven, when an opera of his was performed in that city – no great shakes but full of promise. Both his music and personality appealed to the Viennese aristocracy and from 1756 (the year Mozart was born) he made a comfortable living; he adapted French *opéra comique* to Viennese tastes, and at this time he took on the young Dittersdorf as an amanuensis. Musically Gluck jumped to the fore with his late operas, the so-called 'reform' works such as *Orfeo ed Euridice* (Italian version performed in Vienna in 1762), its French version *Orphée et Eurydice* (performed in Paris in 1774), *Alceste* and *Iphigénie en Tauride*. With such works Gluck lifted operatic writing on to a new plane. He replaced the stiff formal procedures to be found in the librettos (Metastasio's were the most popular) of the 'old school', recitatives and arias, in which action and emotion are highly stylised, by emphasising the musical and dramatic drive of plot and character. As with Handel and Mozart he could achieve the most poignant effect through simple melody. In his hands the orchestra played a far greater role in the unfolding of the drama. His purely instrumental and orchestral pieces are of minor importance – don't bother about them.

GOEHR, ALEXANDER – a postwar English composer who, in his student days at the Royal Manchester School of Music (now the Royal Northern School of Music), was a member of an influential quartet with the composers Maxwell Davies and Birtwistle and the pianist John Ogdon. Goehr is the current holder of the Chair of Music at Cambridge. On completing his studies he earned his living first as copyist and translator, then as BBC programme producer of orchestral concerts. His father, the conductor Walter Goehr, a former pupil of Schoenberg, exercised an early musical influence on him; perhaps from him Goehr inherited his high principles and powerful musical intellect. His composing technique is full of complex devices, the control of which is masterly – the Piano Trio Op. 20, the String Quartet No. 2, Op. 23. Some believe his works tend to be too austere or over-involved and would like to see more examples on the lines of *Naboth's Vineyard*, a short piece of music-theatre in which his stern tendencies are more relaxed and the music becomes more approachable to the ordinary listener. Goehr's recordings include *Lyric Pieces* for wind quintet, trumpet, trombone and double bass and *Sinfonia* Op. 42 for orchestra.

GOLDBERG VARIATIONS – an extended piece by Bach for harpsichord, originally with the title *Aria with Thirty Different Variations*. One is not quite sure how it got its popular title. Perhaps Bach wrote it for his brilliant harpsichord pupil Johann Goldberg, but there is no absolute proof of this. Of greater interest is the work itself, which is ingeniously planned in sets of three variations, each set consisting of two variations in free style followed by a variation in canon; the final variation is a *quodlibet* – several melodies appearing at the same time in counterpoint. Very foxy! The theme is repeated simply at the end, just as it was presented at the beginning. If you don't know this work it is certainly worth a listen.

GOLLIWOG'S CAKE WALK – one of the most popular of Debussy's piano pieces; it is the sixth and last piece of his suite *Children's Corner*, written for the amusement of his daughter, nicknamed Chou-chou. Since it is not too difficult to play, pianists of all abilities like to have a go. The left hand has an oompah bass related to American ragtime, while the right hand unfolds a jolly, humorous tune; in contrast, the middle section is somewhat wistful. Surely some of the readers who are pianists have plonked out this piece with telling panache at some time or other.

GORECKI, HENRYK – a Polish composer of worth who has lately gained much fame through live performances and broadcasts of his Symphony No. 3 (Symphony of Lamentation Songs). Gorecki studied with Messiaen in Paris and has won numerous international awards. The character of his music is a mixture of almost static sounds which can be transformed into violent explosions, as in *Genesis II* for fifteen instruments; his instrumentation and orchestration are quite original, not so much for exploiting new sound sources from any instrument as for the way he combines them. His inspiration lies mainly in Polish peasant culture, Polish liturgical music and sixteenth-century Italian polyphony. Not a bad mixture. You might well be moved by his *Symphony No. 3* and *Old Polish Music* for brass and strings. Very more-ish.

GOTTSCHALK, LOUIS – a remarkable character in the world of classical music, a nineteenth-century American pianist who churned out dozens of piano pieces, some very original, some banal. Gottschalk's parents were sympathetic to his musical talents and sent him off to Paris at the age of thirteen. Chopin, hearing him give a recital at sixteen, was fulsome in his praise. In Europe Gottschalk gave recitals in which he included his own compositions and these went down a bomb – *Bamboula – danza des nègres* and *Le Bananier – chanson nègre* are two examples. He returned to the USA for his first tour there, where he played at more venues than he had planned since, on the death of his father, he had to earn extra funds to support six younger brothers and sisters. To suit the comparatively unsophisticated audiences in some American towns at that time, his titles and compositions often turned bland or banal – *The Maiden's Blush, Battle Cry of Freedom, Fairy Land*. After touring the Americas to an almost unbelievable extent he finally settled in Brazil. A bizarre finale: while playing a piece of his with the title *Morte!!* he fainted at the piano and died a while later. There is something pathetic about his life; he was a sort of sideshow character with lots of natural pianism at his fingertips and an abundance of goodwill and affection, all flowing along uncontrollably. Gottschalk is certainly important to the early history of American music. Only since the 1930s has research begun on his output. He has written some attractive pieces for piano four-hands such as *Marche de Nuit* or *Ses yeux: polka de concert*; recordings of his piano music are surprisingly numerous.

GOUNOD, CHARLES – an important French composer in the third quarter of the nineteenth century. He spent four years in Rome on winning the Prix de Rome at the Paris Conservatoire; as opposed to Berlioz, he enjoyed life there and the music, hearing Palestrina sung in the Sistine Chapel, being introduced by Mendelssohn's sister Fanny to the music of Bach, Beethoven and her brother. Gounod turned to opera, writing five for the Théâtre-Lyrique which are still respected today. Gounod took French opera beyond Meyerbeer, whose style dominated the scene for thirty years. In *Faust*, for example, the usual cardboard figures are replaced by more flesh-and-blood characters, even in the smaller roles. *Faust*, incidentally, was Queen Victoria's favourite opera. Gounod's creative activity was interrupted by the Franco-Prussian War of 1870–71; he and his family decided to take refuge in London, living in Blackheath for three years (a blue plaque is attached to the house in Morden Road commemorating his stay). While in London Gounod churned out ballads and sentimental songs of the kind so popular with the English in mid-Victorian times. He also started an affair with a highly neurotic and tempestuous lady called Mrs Georgina Weldon which did him little good. Such is human frailty. Musicologists note that, on his return to Paris, the quality of his music deteriorated. Gounod turned back to his first love, church music, and in the last twenty-two years of his life wrote twelve Masses. He influenced a large number of composers including Massenet, Tchaikovsky and Fauré. Both Mendelssohn and Gounod, like Puccini and Richard Strauss a generation later, were able to express the ideals and dreams of the contemporary middle classes. Besides the operas *Faust* and *Roméo et Juliette*, worth noting is his *Petite Symphonie* for ten wind instruments and his *Messe solennelle de Sainte Cécile*.

GRAINGER, PERCY – in a word, born in Melbourne, studied in Germany, settled in London in 1901, then became a naturalised American in 1918 after a four-year stay in New York. Grainger was composer, pianist and folksong collector all in one. He gave piano recitals in England and toured extensively. In 1905 he joined the English Folk Song Society and introduced the wax cylinder phonograph to the process of collecting and transcribing British folksongs, of which in four years he collected some five hundred examples. He struck up valuable friendships with Grieg and Delius. Grainger was a bandsman in the US Army for two years – 1917–19; in 1921 he settled permanently in White Plains, NY. To his great grief his mother committed suicide in 1922.

In composition Grainger rejected the tradition of Brahms and Wagner. He might be regarded as an early avant-garde composer: his music is filled with experiments and unconventional ideas and processes. Nevertheless, his compositions include simpler, more approachable material as well, here influenced by his folksong knowledge, as in *Colonial Song* for military band, *Country Gardens* and *Handel in the Strand*, both arranged for orchestra. It is sad to have to say that he died an isolated, disillusioned man. Research on Grainger is still young and we will learn more about him as time goes on.

GRAMOPHONE – in these days of the CD, to which no doubt will be added in due course still finer artefacts for recorded music, let us spare a thought for the jolly old gramophone. The mechanical process of recording reigned for fifty years to about 1925. In England the leading manufacturer went under the title of the English Gramophone and Typewriter Company. Flourishing recording companies grew up in the USA, France, Italy and Germany. Caruso's recording from Leoncavallo's opera *Pagliacci* of 'Vesti la giubba' (which might be rendered as 'put on now the clown's costume') was the first record to sell over a million copies. Very early on recordings were made by some most distinguished names such as Brahms, Grieg, Sarasate, Kreisler and Patti. With the introduction of the electrical recording system the frequency and dynamic range of sound could be transferred more accurately on to disc. Thus the advent of the 78 rpm (revolutions per minute) disc, with a playing time of under five minutes. A large Beethoven symphony would then require five discs, ten sides. The long-playing disc, the LP, arrived at the end of the 1940s and by the mid-Sixties had become the normal disc to buy for every kind of music. It was a relief to be able to replace the easily breakable 78 by the hardier LP – though it was prone to warping – and through the use of microgroove technique it offered between twenty and twenty-five minutes' worth of music per side.

For us ordinary listeners the most important fact about the gramophone is that it has given musical pleasure to millions of people. With regard to classical music, not only has the gramophone increased familiarity with the works of well-known composers but it has also enabled us to meet and become attached to music which has deserved a wider public but has perforce been neglected – the music of Berlioz, Mahler and Sibelius are some instances, not to talk of the large Early Music repertoire. The gramophone has paved the way for more critical listening and for raising the standard of performance, be it soloist, string quartet, orchestra or opera company. Gradually archives of recordings are building up, allowing us to compare the performance of a Mozart symphony by a contemporary conductor with a predecessor forty years ago. Today there is an ever-growing commerce in the buying and selling of old recordings, as with books and paintings. You yourself may be the owner of some rather valuable 78s or LPs!

GRANADOS, ENRIQUE – a Spanish composer and pianist who died at sea. The story is that after the success of his opera *Goyescas* at the New York Metropolitan Opera in 1916 Granados was invited by President Wilson to give a recital at the White House. This caused him to miss a boat that would have taken him directly back to Spain, and instead he had to sail home via England. Crossing the English Channel his boat was torpedoed by a German submarine. Granados was picked up by a lifeboat but seeing his wife struggling in the sea he dived into the water to save her, and both were drowned. A ghastly tale and a sad musical loss.

Granados's main output consists of piano music and songs. A younger colleague of Albéniz, he was part of the Spanish musical revival. He was a great admirer of the music of Schumann, Liszt and Grieg. The opera *Goyescas* grew out of an earlier piano suite of the same name consisting of six pieces; via rhythm, harmony and keyboard colouring they give a dramatic account of a painting by Goya, his favourite painter. In addition to his twelve *Danzas españolas* and seven *Valses poéticas* there exists on CD a handsome selection of his piano music. A fine example of his song writing is the collection *Quince Tonadillas al estilo antiguo* (Fifteen songs in the antique style).

GRAPHIC NOTATION – much of the world's music is not notated; but in the complicated Western system of notation the attitude is essentially that a composer's notes are fixed for all time and the performer simply reproduces what appears on the written or printed page. But our notation is constantly changing, and in about 1950 avant-garde composers began to express their musical intentions on paper in exceedingly radical ways. This was due partly to the influence of sounds being produced in the electronic music studio which traditional notation, quite obviously, was unable to record. Also there was a strong reaction to the stranglehold exerted by, say, a score of Webern's on a player who had to account for the over-written symbolic instructions occurring almost from bar to bar. Stockhausen, Cage, Feldman and Penderecki were among those who made up new symbols and even new ways of laying out a score. It is this category of musical symbol that is known as graphic notation.

No overall communality of graphic notation has yet been arrived at. Each composer of such a score will often make up his own set of symbols and may even alter the symbols from one piece to the next. The composer will instruct in his writing, explain his new symbols, entrust to the performer a freedom of playing where the latter bears the onus of realising the deliberately limited guidance coming from the composer; the intentions of both composer and player will, of course, be discussed at rehearsal. In some graphic scores the number of pages of explanation and instruction may equal the number of pages of actual music. After some forty years now graphic notation seems to have got stuck and may be on the way out; but it may well be succeeded by greater use of computer programming. Go to a good music library and look at a score of Penderecki's *Threnody* or Cage's *Concerto* for piano and orchestra.

GREGORIAN CHANT – in medieval times Gregorian chant was one of the five principal repertoires of Latin liturgical chant (the others being Old Roman, Gallic, Mozarabic and Ambrosian). It may be considered the starting point of European classical composition. St Gregory the Great, Pope from 590 to 604, has given his name to this chant, but his relationship to it is unknown. The Book of Psalms is the principal source of its texts; its manuscripts go back to at least the eleventh century. Let it be understood these chants are numerous. Although they are unaccompanied single-line melodies they are in every way compositions; their suppleness of line is magnificent and they stand out for their shape and singable quality. The music normally lies within an octave range. Rhythm is certainly present but there is no pulse; chant in fact is musical speech, and rhythm is used to mark the stressed and unstressed syllables of the text. A variety of forms can be found. The sublime melodic-rhythmic flow of Gregorian chant may be noted in the particular example which I recommend you listen to: the *Ite, missa est*.

GRIEG, EDVARD – the most important composer Norway has yet produced. He flourished in the latter part of the nineteenth century and played a leading part in the surge of musical nationalism that appeared then throughout Europe. He first studied in Leipzig. In Denmark he met the Danish composer Niels Gade, a close friend of Schumann and Mendelssohn; he also met Hans Christian Andersen, some of whose poetry he later set to music. Grieg gained an enthusiastic supporter for his music in Liszt; in Rome in 1869 he handed Liszt his Piano Concerto and after playing it through at sight Liszt gave his thumbs-up. In Rome Grieg also met Ibsen for the first time; the incidental music to Ibsen's play *Peer Gynt* was completed in 1875. All the time he was active as concert pianist and conductor.

Grieg's listening to and study of Norwegian folk music shows a steady upward curve, and he much enjoyed swapping information on composition and folk music with his American friend Percy Grainger. From his pen there flowed one hundred and forty songs; he claimed his sole inspiration for these was the interpreter, his wife, Nina; their union was a lifelong, happy one. He did not excel at writing orchestral music but the Piano Concerto, the *Peer Gynt Suite* and the *Holberg Suite* for strings remain evergreen favourites. These and his songs and piano pieces secure his reputation as a composer whose music is much enjoyed by audiences and listeners. The ten books of *Lyric Pieces* for piano contain many gems; he possessed a great gift for melody. Grieg's compositions made a significant contribution to the extension of nineteenth-century harmony.

GRIFFITHS, PAUL – one of England's leading postwar writers on music, with special reference to contemporary composition and performance. Griffiths's style displays the English tradition: thoroughly informed, dispassionate, clear and concise. He began writing music criticism at the age of twenty-four and for ten years (1982 to 1992) served as a critic on *The Times*; currently he is the London-based critic for *The New Yorker*. Griffiths is the author of several books as well as an opera librettist. *The New Grove Dictionary of Music and Musicians*, 6th edition, contains a number of authoritative and extensive articles on contemporary music by him.

GROVE, GEORGE – editor of the first edition of *Grove's Dictionary of Music and Musicians*, which was completed in four volumes in 1889. He himself contributed many of the articles, the most important of which were on Beethoven, Schubert and Mendelssohn. You'll be surprised to learn that by training Grove was an engineer; at the age of twenty-one he was sent out by his firm to Jamaica to supervise the building of a lighthouse, and later for the same purpose to Bermuda. His father was a flourishing fishmonger and venison dealer in Charing Cross. He began to undertake biblical research while acting as secretary to the Society of Arts. Steadily he educated himself in music, attending concerts and buying scores; for some forty seasons he contributed analytical notes to the programmes of the Saturday Concerts at Crystal Palace. In due course his research reputation was as high in music as it was in biblical studies and he even produced a geography primer for the publisher Macmillan. He developed close friendships with Sullivan and Clara Schumann, met Brahms in Vienna, and entertained Wagner in London – he was known to have complained that the Love Scene in Act 2 of *Tristan und Isolde* was too realistic! O happy Victorian! Grove played a leading role in establishing the Royal College of Music in 1883 and then finding the funds, from a wealthy Leeds engineer, Samuel Fox, to pay for a new building; he became the RCM's first director, a post he held for eleven years. He received a knighthood in 1882. All in all a truly remarkable person.

GROVES, CHARLES – a very fine English conductor, knighted in 1973. During his tenure at Bournemouth and Liverpool he not only raised the standard of performance of the orchestras but also educated concert-goers in a wide selection of works. He took the Royal Philharmonic Orchestra on a visit to the USA, the Royal Liverpool Orchestra to Warsaw, was a frequent guest conductor in Germany and conducted seasons in Australia and South Africa. Groves was much at home with twentieth-century music and always had time to see and offer advice to young composers, conductors and students. His recordings include works by Haydn, Mozart, Schubert, Mahler, Elgar and Delius.

GUIDO D'AREZZO – a Benedictine monk active in the first half of the eleventh century. His fame as a music theorist is still with us; in medieval times the influence of his writings was paramount. Guido propagated a system of notation laid out in lines and spaces, the principle of which remains in current practice. He also established a method of sight-singing, the crux of which was naming six pitches *ut, re, mi, fa, sol, la*. He settled in Arezzo for the last eight years of his life. Guido's treatise *Micrologus* discusses chant and polyphonic music, and may be considered as the earliest comprehensive account of musical practice. He also earned a high reputation as a teacher of church singers.

GUITAR – a plucked instrument having six strings whose pitches, in ascending order, are E A d g b e′; simply run a finger across these strings and already there is a delightful sound. The guitar's resonant wooden body, shaped like a woman's torso, has a flat back and its fingerboard has frets to guide pitch changes; it is played by plucking or strumming the strings. At the end of the fingerboard are pegs which regulate the tuning; its range is about three and a half octaves. The guitar has been popular since the end of the seventeenth century. Today it is fully established as a concert instrument, with a large and growing repertoire

that includes pieces written for it in the eighteenth century. The Spaniard Fernando Sor was the leading player and composer of guitar music in the late eighteenth and early nineteenth centuries.

The pleasure of the guitar is that while it can sound ravishing in the hands of a professional player it also allows the amateur to attract the listener's ear. Mark you, it is certainly an instrument that requires practice. Segovia was the first great twentieth-century guitarist and the first to encourage composers in general to write for the instrument. In 1920 Falla wrote the guitar piece *Homenaje pour le tombeau de Claude Debussy*; the first guitar concerto was written in 1939 by Castelnuovo-Tedesco – Concerto No. 1 in D for guitar and orchestra. Boulez included it in his *Le Marteau sans maître*, as did Maxwell Davies in the ensemble which accompanies his opera *The Lighthouse*. In England there is a steady output of writing for it, partly because of its three guitarists of international stature: Julian Bream, John Williams and Timothy Walker, as well as many other fine players. Composers who have written substantial pieces for guitar include Berkeley (*Sonatine, Theme and Variations* for solo guitar), Arnold (Guitar Concerto) and Rodrigo (*Concierto de Aranjuez*). The instrument is also very suitable for the accompaniment of song – Britten (*Songs from the Chinese*) and Walton (*Anon in Love*). Segovia's influence spread to South America, where guitar compositions of major worth have come from Villa-Lobos (Brazil) and Ponce (Mexico).

It may be worth reminding ourselves that in Africa south of the Sahara the guitar has long been the leading instrument of townsfolk who have developed new playing techniques. The electric guitar, rampant in pop music, and where use of fingers and fingernails is usually out of the question, a plastic plectrum being a more practical replacement, has still to be taken up by classical composers. The only common element between the electric and acoustic guitars are the six strings, tuned to the same pitches, and the fingerboard; the body of the electric guitar can be almost any shape because its function as a resonator is not required.

GURNEY, IVOR – a minor composer whose importance lies in his worthy contribution to the twentieth-century English song revival. Gloucester-born, Gurney was both composer and poet. Two of his fellow students were Ivor Novello and Herbert Howells. His studies at the Royal College of Music were interrupted by the First World War; serving in France, he was badly wounded, gassed and shell-shocked. In due course he resumed study at the RCM where he was taught by Vaughan Williams. Thereafter he returned to Gloucester. His inability to earn a living from either composition or poetry caused serious depression, added to which he had never properly recovered from his physical and mental war injuries. Finally Gurney had to be admitted to a mental hospital in about 1922 and, sadly, he never recovered his health. His legacy is his songs and a volume of poetry edited by Edmund Blunden in 1954. Choice examples of his songs are *Down by the Salley Gardens*, *Sleep*, and *An Epitaph*.

GUY, BARRY – a virtuoso double-bass player and avant-garde composer. While still an apprentice draughtsman and having to help with the family finances, he took evening part-time composition lessons with Stanley Glasser at Goldsmiths College; at the same time he studied with Graham Collier, jazz composer, double-bass player and writer. He then went to the Guildhall School of Music and Drama, where his teachers were Buxton Orr and Patric Standford. As a double-bass player, apart from solo performance he is equally at home in a conventional orchestra, avant-garde chamber ensemble or jazz band. Guy's compositions are varying blends of traditional writing, jazz, avant-garde techniques and electronics. His works have been performed in France, Italy and Germany as well as in England – works such as *Incontri* for cello and orchestra and *Play* for chamber ensemble.

HABANERA – an alluring dance which originated in Cuba and is supposed to have been named after its capital, Havana (Habana). Stately in movement and rhythm, it spread to other South American countries. The habanera has provided the rhythmic ground for a variety of Latin American dance music. In Argentina, where the *tango* originated, the habanera emerged as its slow version, in contrast to the wilder, more notorious, faster version. By the mid-nineteenth century it was being played and danced to in Spain, and its popularity soon spread to France and other European countries. *La paloma* is perhaps the best-known habanera worldwide, yet hardly anyone can name the composer – Sebastian Iradier, who wrote it in 1861. Bizet drew on Iradier's habaneras for his opera *Carmen* and Chabrier, Debussy, Ravel, Albéniz and Falla all made use of the rhythm. If you're over forty then dancing to the strains of a habanera immediately makes you look ten years younger.

HACKER, ALAN – an English clarinet virtuoso; he studied at the Royal Academy of Music, to return later as a teacher. He was a founder member of the avant-garde Pierrot Players, who after a year or two turned into the Fires of London; in both guises their programmes were mainly devoted to works by young English composers. Hacker is able to execute chords, glissandi and a rare selection of other effects not easily achieved by fellow clarinet players. At the same time he is an authority on the early history of the clarinet and its repertoire. He has given first performances of many pieces by, among others, Boulez, Goehr, Maxwell Davies and Birtwistle.

HAFFNER, SIGISMUND – a burgomaster of Salzburg whose significance to us is his tie-up with Mozart. The *Serenade* in D major, K250, was written for a Haffner family wedding in 1776 and in 1782 the 'Haffner' Symphony No. 35 in D major, K385, was composed in celebration of Sigismund's elevation to the equivalent of a knighthood. So if you decide to commission a composer to write a work for you there's a chance that one day your name may appear in a music dictionary.

HAITINK, BERNARD – a Dutch conductor who has visited our shores many times. In 1961, aged thirty-two, he became the Amsterdam Concertgebouw Orchestra's youngest principal conductor ever. For twelve years, from 1967, he held the post of principal conductor and artistic adviser of the London Philharmonic Orchestra. With one or other of these two orchestras he toured the USA, Russia and the Far East. Haitink's reputation is also high as an opera conductor – Mozart, Stravinsky, Janáček – at venues which include Covent Garden and Glyndebourne. Pleasingly, he is a committed champion of works by contemporary composers. His CDs include all the symphonies of Bruckner and Mahler and the tone poems of Liszt.

HALÉVY, FROMENTAL – French composer, teacher and writer, active in the first half of the nineteenth century. His music teacher, Cherubini, had a marked influence on his musical development. Winning the Prix de Rome, he left for Italy in 1820. On his return to Paris in 1822 Halévy turned to opera-writing, which at that time was the only way for a French composer to make progress. As a teacher at the Paris Conservatoire he included Gounod, Saint-Saëns and Bizet among his pupils. His brother Léon wrote several librettos for him. The majority of his forty operas and ballets were well received and placed him with Meyerbeer as the leading lights in French grand opera of the time; Scribe was his most frequent librettist. Halévy's most important opera is *La juive* ('The Jewish Girl'), much admired by Wagner. The structural writing in Halévy's compositions is generally weak, often mechanical and repetitive, but this is balanced against some very imaginative orchestration, especially in regard to woodwind and brass; this feature impressed even the intolerant Berlioz. Bizet married Halévy's daughter, Geneviève.

HALLE, ADAM DE LA – see *De La Halle, Adam*.

HANDBELL – a bell, varying in size according to pitch, with a clapper inside and a handle of wood or a leather loop. It is either tapped with a hammer, usually when used in the orchestra, or swung, when used in team bell-ringing. Organologists trace the existence of handbells as far back as 1600 BC in China and some centuries later they are also found in Japan, India, Egypt and Africa. Early Christians, in their steady trek from Mediterranean Africa into Western Europe, are recorded as having carried handbells. Everywhere, the bell seems to have religious significance – both joyous and mournful. Handbell choirs or teams, ringing the changes, were firmly established in English village life by the mid-nineteenth century. A set of handbells can range from as few as four up to sixty in number; each ringer with his two, three or four bells has to ensure successful realisation of his part in the music, so disciplined attention and cooperation is vital. A rich variety of music has been turned out for the medium – original compositions, arrangements, solos, and combined with voices. There is little or no handbell-ringing in the rest of Europe; it seems to be a particular English phenomenon, which still flourishes. The Handbell Ringers of Great Britain was formed as late as 1967, with a membership of over 100 teams. Handbell-ringing did cross the Atlantic, and in the USA the American Guild of English Handbell Ringers was formed in 1954, boasting 1,000 teams. The Whitechapel Bell Foundry has been in existence since the sixteenth century and is still going strong. While its main product is the making and repair of church bells, the firm's flourishing export trade includes the manufacture and sale of handbell sets. Nice to know that here is yet another musical activity earning foreign currency for the UK.

HANDEL, GEORGE FRIDERIC – German-born naturalised English composer. In greatness the only composer that can compare with him in the age of the Baroque is Bach; they were exact contemporaries, though Bach predeceased him by nine years. Born in Halle, Handel studied law at the university there as well as getting in some thorough training in harmony, counterpoint and composition, and learning to play the harpsichord and violin; he moved to Hamburg to continue his studies. Handel scored his first success with an opera composed in 1705, *Almira*; another forty-two were to follow in due course. In itself his opera output is not impressive, but considering the huge pile of other material he turned out in his lifetime, it's good going.

From Hamburg, Handel went to Italy, first to Florence and then to Rome. At this time, apart from France, the rest of Europe was musically parochial compared to Italy, with its advanced activity in opera, oratorio, cantata and instrumental music. A not unusual event of the time was to hold keyboard contests. Handel undertook one with Domenico Scarlatti, son of Alessandro; honours were even but Handel was considered the superior on the organ; pleasantly, friendship and mutual admiration were the result. In Rome Handel produced dozens of cantatas; he arrived there comparatively untrained and gifted, and left trained and sophisticated, possessing a confident command of melody formation and writing for the voice. Handel was now twenty-five. A 'temporary' stay in England was prolonged until from about 1712 London became his home for the rest of his life. For the first three years he was a guest in Lord Burlington's town house, where he enjoyed a routine of composing during the day and attending to theatre duties in the evening. His first London operatic success, *Rinaldo*, received fifty-three performances; Queen Anne gave him a pension of £200 in order to keep him in England. Later he wrote three orchestral suites, in F, D and G major, commonly entitled *Water Music*; some or all of these suites were played to accompany the barge trip of George I from Whitehall to Chelsea up the Thames. In 1719 he was appointed as resident composer at the manor home, Cannons in Edgware, of the Duke of Chandos; here he turned out the eleven *Chandos Anthems* and *Acis and Galatea*, an entertainment modelled on the English court masque tradition.

A movement was started to establish Italian opera on a long-term basis under the title Royal Academy of Music (no relation to the later creation of the famous conservatoire), with Handel as the music director and the King's Theatre as the venue. The success was such that for eight years from about 1720 to 1728 London became the operatic centre of Europe. At this time Handel's operas included *Radamisto*, *Ottone*, *Rodelinda* and *Alessandro*. This was show business, and how. Handel came to create a level of oratorio unmatched in Europe and unique to English musical culture. While his operas have largely faded out, despite brave attempts in the twentieth century to revive them, his oratorios, *Messiah* of course, but also, say, *Saul*, *Israel in Egypt* and *Semele*, continue to be performed generation after generation as well as having been popular in his own time. *Esther* was the first oratorio heard in London; its success was such that plans were made to transfer it to the King's Theatre, but the Bishop of London had forbidden sacred subjects to appear in an opera house. Deftly, Handel arranged that the performance should be presented without action and with a little décor only, in the manner, perhaps, of a Coronation Service. This was permitted and the work was enthusiastically received by the audience. During the rehearsal of *Music for the Royal Fireworks* (with the absence of the fireworks!) in Green Park, 12,000 people attended and traffic was held up for three hours.

Handel was known for his dry sense of humour; also for his generosity, not only to charity but to fellow musicians. He was a founder member of a charity set up in 1738, now known as the Royal Society of Musicians of Great Britain, to help elderly and ill musicians, and he assisted in establishing a hospital for foundlings by holding concerts as well as making direct gifts. He is buried in Westminster Abbey.

HANSLICK, EDUARD – influential German music critic, born in Prague. After graduating as a doctor of law, he was soon attracted to music, its nature, aesthetics and function; he wrote articles and books on the subject, and gave lectures on music appreciation. His friendship with Brahms caused him to become a staunch supporter against the Wagnerites, earning Wagner's enmity (and a send-up as Beckmesser in *Die Meistersinger*). Hanslick attained a full professorship at Vienna in music history and aesthetics in 1870; six years later, at the age of fifty-one, he married a young singer, Sophie Wolmouth, which proved a happy union. He is undoubtedly the first critic to turn to musicological considerations: in-depth study of scores, analysis, examining a composer's background, pondering the genesis of a piece of music – studying Shakespeare's play before seeing Verdi's *Otello*; yet he firmly believed in the practical side of music, taking piano lessons for most of his life. He held that the element of melody was the essence of music and that a composer's creativity would fall with any decline in health.

HARMONICA – a lovable little instrument available to amateur and professional alike. Its ancestor is the Chinese *sheng*, with which Europe became acquainted at the end of the eighteenth century. By the 1850s the most successful European manufacturer was Matthias Hohner of Trossingen, still going strong today; by 1879 his factory had produced 700,000 harmonicas, 60 per cent of them exported to the USA. Hohner's brought out a chromatic harmonica in the 1920s which quickly gained a wide reputation through its use by the virtuoso Larry Adler. The instrument is played horizontally cupped in the hands. Notes are obtained by blowing and sucking; a lever attached at one end shifts the mouthboard, allowing every note in the chromatic scale to be sounded; the sound is produced by causing reeds in the casement to vibrate. In case you have an urge to rush out and buy a harmonica, bear in mind that beyond a certain level it is not an easy instrument to play. It attained postwar respect from composers of classical music: pieces by Milhaud and Seiber, *Romance* for harmonica and strings (Vaughan Williams), *Rumanian Fantasy* for harmonica and orchestra (Chagrin), concertos by Arnold and Benjamin; many more composers have included it in their compositions.

HARMONICS – question: what makes, say, a flute sound different from an oboe or clarinet, though all three are playing the same note? Answer: the differing strengths of the pure sounds that go to make up that note in each of the three instruments. A note you hear sung or played is not unsullied. Only pure sounds are virgin, and these are called harmonics (or overtones). The nearest thing to a pure sound you are likely to hear outside an acoustic laboratory will come from a tuning-fork; the pips sounding on the hour on BBC radio are very near a pure harmonic. When we say that X's voice or Y's violin-playing has 'a lovely, pure tone' we are being poetic, not scientific. This is all you need to know about harmonics. More than this and things get very complicated.

HARMONIUM – in about 1840 the Frenchman Alexandre Debain, improving upon earlier prototypes, developed a keyboard instrument, with compression bellows operated by the feet, which he called a harmonium. The instrument is capable of playing louder or softer because when the air current flows over the free-vibrating reeds or metal tongues, the pitch of the note is not changed, only its strength. Until the late 1920s the harmonium was popular as a domestic instrument, very useful for church services and apt as sound accompaniment to silent films; it has often proved an acceptable substitute for the organ and for a time was even taught in music colleges. Composers have made use of the harmonium for special effects and tone-colours, such as

Hindemith in his short comic opera *Hin und Zurück* (There and Back); Schoenberg adapted two Strauss waltzes for piano, harmonium and string quartet.

HAROLD IN ITALY (*Harold en Italie*) – Berlioz wrote this work for Paganini, who was just as much at home on the viola as on the violin. Paganini had lately acquired a viola made by Stradivarius, the most famous of the seventeenth-century Italian makers, and wanted to show it off. Berlioz's effort, however, was rejected, since the viola part he had written was hardly a test of the maestro's scintillating virtuosity; and so Paganini never performed it. *Harold in Italy* is a programme symphony in four movements, composed in 1834, based on excerpts from Byron's poem *Childe Harold*. Berlioz includes reflections of his own sojourn in Italy, and the viola solo part represents himself as well as Byron's character. This work was his second symphony, appearing four years after his first – the striking *Symphonie fantastique*.

HARP – truly a heavenly instrument; its sounds can conjure up magic, mystery, romance. The most adept at capturing the soul of the harp in classical music are the French composers; one need only cite the two Impromptus respectively by Fauré and Roussel for solo harp, Saint-Saëns's *Morceau de concert* for harp and orchestra, Debussy's *Danse sacrée et danse profane* for harp and strings and Sonata for flute, viola and harp, Ravel's *Introduction et allégro*. It was via the opera house that the harp first entered the orchestra, to be used more for special effects than anything else – Gluck's *Orfeo* (1762), Meyerbeer's *Robert le diable* (1831), Donizetti's *Lucia di Lammermoor* (1835). But it was Berlioz who brought it into the symphony orchestra by writing substantial parts for it in his *Symphonie fantastique* and *Harold en Italie*. In the last quarter of the nineteenth century the harp's position in the orchestra was raised even more – Richard Strauss's tone poem *Don Juan* (1888) and Sibelius's *Swan of Tuonela* (1893) are a couple of examples. Substantial cadenzas for the harp even appeared – Rimsky-Korsakov's *Capriccio espagnol* (1888), Tchaikovsky's three ballets *Swan Lake*, *Sleeping Beauty*, *Nutcracker* (1876–92). In the twentieth century Berio and Boulez were two of the composers who devised new sound effects possible on the instrument.

The harp of today has seven pedals. Each can be notched up twice, thus the name double-action harp; one notch up, the pitch of the string rises a semitone; a second notch up, a further semitone. All manner of interesting chords can be obtained with this pedalling business. The section nearest the player contains a richly reverberating soundbox. The length of the strings decreases, with the pitch rising, as the strings run towards the player, who finger-plucks them on either side; the low strings plucked slowly can create a threatening, sombre sound. One of the best-known characteristics of the harp is the glissando, in which a finger is run across the strings away from or towards the player. An Egyptian tomb dated about 2500 BC contains a relief depicting a harpist and singer performing. Various versions of the harp are found in many areas in Africa south of the Sahara, as well as in South America and Asia.

HARPSICHORD – like the piano, the harpsichord is a stringed keyboard; the main difference is that the strings are hammered in the piano, whereas they are plucked in the harpsichord. Essentially the harpsichord is an instrument of the Baroque, when it was used in thousands of pieces as a solo instrument, part of a chamber ensemble or an orchestra. In opera it became indispensable, especially in recitative accompaniment; in due course, as keyboard writing began to move towards the piano, for quite some time the harpsichord remained alive and well in the opera house. However, by 1800 even this role had disappeared. Harpsichords were constructed with the finest materials and decorated with subtlety and refinement. Many believe that the apotheosis of harpsichord writing was attained by Bach. You are likely to agree if you listen to some or all of his two-volume *Forty-Eight Preludes and Fugues* (Vol. I, 1722; Vol. II, 1742), brimful of melodious and rhythmic music, now light, now serious, now simple, now intricate, now pure dance music, now contemplative. Almost the entire output of Domenico Scarlatti consisted of delightful sonatas for harpsichord, equally varied in style but with a Spanish accent. Interest in the instrument has been revived in the twentieth century, first, because it is part of what one may call the early music movement; secondly, composers enjoy its sharp, clean sound. It is used in ensembles and orchestras, and not a few solo pieces have been written for it. A most excellent work is Frank Martin's *Petite Symphonie Concertante* for harp, harpsichord, piano and strings; Falla wrote a Concerto for harpsichord with flute, oboe, clarinet, violin and cello. There are even songs with harpsichord accompaniment.

HARRIS, ROY – a composer who made a worthy contribution to the development of the more traditional side of American classical music. Harris only started to compose in his mid-twenties; with Copland's support he obtained funds to spend two years studying in Paris under Copland's old teacher, Nadia Boulanger, who attracted a steady stream of young American composers over several decades. On his return to the USA Harris taught at various universities and organised several music festivals; he mixed with folksingers and researchers such as Burl Ives, Alan Lomax and Woody Guthrie, who had a marked influence on his style. From 1961 Harris was composer-in-residence at the University of California at Los Angeles. His music often contains a sweep and breadth evocative of the luxurious spaciousness of western America. Appealing is his Symphony No. 3 and, on a smaller scale, the *Lyric Study* for flute and piano.

HARVEY, JONATHAN – English composer with a deeply spiritual bias. A graduate of Cambridge, he now teaches at Sussex University. Harvey's first influences, Bartók and Tippett, were succeeded by Schoenberg and Messiaen and then, to some extent, by Stockhausen and Maxwell Davies; but he has forged his own style. He has a firm command of electro-acoustics, and manipulates this element with confidence to suit his creative requirements. His music is intensely worked out, sometimes too much so, bringing to bear on his ideas complex solutions which appeal to the élitist rather than to the ordinary listener. But in *Bhakti* for chamber ensemble, in the Cello Concerto, and even in *Ritual Melodies* for quadrophonic tape, there are many attractive sounds.

HAYDN, JOSEPH – I suppose everyone knows that, with Mozart and Beethoven, Haydn forms the great triumvirate of the Classical period. Haydn was the first-born, so to speak; in his early youth he could still hear the music of the high Baroque and in his ripe years he had intimations of the coming of the Romantic age. Of the Big Three Haydn is the most characteristically Classical; in his hands the triumph of symphony, string quartet and piano sonata was assured. Formal poise, thematic manipulation, firm control over instrument and orchestra are to be found in his music again and again.

After a tough start in Vienna, Haydn worked his way up the ladder, gaining recognition for his early symphonies and string quartets. Then he married, a lifelong but unsuccessful union; he had really preferred his wife's sister but settled for second-best, more to please the daughters' kindly father. By 1761 Haydn's standing was such that Prince Paul Esterházy, the head of one of the wealthiest and noblest families of the Habsburg ruling class, desperately wanted to engage him for his court. This opportunity was certainly a large material and musical step up for Haydn; in fact he remained in the Esterházy employment continuously until 1790 – quite an innings. His duties required him to compose music according to the prince's needs, and his life was bound by fairly strict limits. Prince Paul died in 1765 and was succeeded by his brother, Prince Nikolaus, who turned out to be a very effective patron. Eisenstadt, the initial centre of operations, was succeeded by a new palace built in Hungary, where the family owned a large estate with a hunting lodge. The parade of music-making at the new venue, Eszterháza, over twenty-five years is truly remarkable: concerts were provided twice a week, a small opera house was built in which most of Haydn's operas were performed, there were constant visits from important personages – the French ambassador, the Empress Maria Theresa, Archduke Ferdinand and the Imperial Court and so on and so forth. Haydn had to supply a continuous flow of every kind of composition for all this, and had little time to move outside the charmed circle. Yet such was his great creative talent that his music was his advertisement, receiving performances here, there and everywhere, and by the 1770s his reputation was securely international.

Mozart had such a high regard for Haydn's music that he dedicated to him six of his finest string quartets. Haydn did not get on so well with Beethoven, a man of very different temperament, who was his pupil for a while. In 1790, when Prince Nikolaus died, Haydn was at last free to pay the first of his two visits to London. In 1790 he spent several months there, fêted by one and all including the royal family. He was greatly stimulated by the London atmosphere and was staggered during the Handel Commemoration to hear the oratorios *Messiah* and *Israel in Egypt*; these works definitely influenced his later oratorio writing (*The Creation, The Seasons*) and Masses. A work of particular emotional depth is *Seven Last Words of our Saviour on the Cross*, commissioned for Cádiz Cathedral for the three-hour Good Friday Service. After his second London visit, in 1795, by which time he had produced the twelve excellent 'London' symphonies and received an honorary DMus. from Oxford, Haydn settled in Vienna; until 1803 he paid regular visits to the Esterházy estate. In the year of his death the French army conquered Vienna, but Napoleon placed a guard of honour in front of his house.

A selection of his works to consider: the *Surprise* Symphony, No. 94 in G; the oratorio *The Creation*; the Piano Trio No. 28 in E; Six String Quartets, Op. 76, No. 2 in D minor; the Piano Sonata No. 18 in E flat.

HEIFETZ, JASCHA – one of the twentieth century's greatest violinists. In his childhood his family was so poor that his father, his first teacher, was known to break up a piece of furniture for the fire so that his son's fingers would be warm enough to practise his exercises and pieces. Heifetz at the age of six was able to perform the Mendelssohn Violin Concerto; at the age of eleven, in Berlin, he performed Tchaikovsky's. He finally left Russia – he was born in Vilna (Lithuania), in 1917 – to undertake a concert tour in the USA; needless to say it was a triumph, and in 1925 he became an American citizen.

Heifetz on the concert platform could give the impression of a cold-hearted performer. This was created by his expressionless face, with almost no movement of his body; even responding to explosive applause, he was unsmiling. But if one simply listened to his playing one heard a tone of remarkable warmth and fiery emotion; his bowing and fingering were perfection itself and he was unmatched for his virtuosity, which appeared effortless. The finest of the works he commissioned is Walton's Violin Concerto. In his chamber music performances, with Feuermann, Primrose, Piatigorsky and Rubinstein, he had the ability to blend his violin tone perfectly with the whole. You need to hear a recording of Heifetz's performance of Bach's *Chaconne* to be zonked forever as a Heifetz fan.

HENZE, HANS WERNER – important postwar German composer whose unusually prolific output may be described as pan-European, for he is quadrilingual and the titles of his pieces may be in German, French, Italian, English or even Spanish. Mozart is his favourite composer in a range of musical models which give his works an eclecticism but without loss of individuality in musical language or style. In contrast to a composer such as Birtwistle, who is notoriously uncommunicative, Henze is articulate on his works in both talks and articles. He left Germany in 1953 to settle in Italy, eventually at Castel Gandolfo. In 1963 he visited the USA, where Bernstein conducted the first performance of his Symphony No. 5. For ten years (from 1966) he was a raving Marxist, perhaps as a reaction to the Nazi régime and inspired by the ideal of a universal brotherhood.

Henze's relationship with England is strong: his opera *We Come to the River* was performed at Covent Garden, his *Kammermusik* for tenor, guitar or harp and eight instruments is dedicated to Britten, his opera *Elegy for Young Lovers* had a season at Glyndebourne and Frederick Ashton commissioned for Covent Garden a ballet, *Ondine*, in which Margot Fonteyn danced the lead, with Henze as conductor. Auden and Kallman provided the librettos for two operas, the aforementioned *Elegy for Young Lovers* and *The Bassarids*. You might lend an ear to his song-cycle *Voices*, *Ragtime and Habaneras* for brass band and the Double Concerto for oboe, harp and strings – the last-named commissioned by the Swiss conductor Paul Sacher.

HÉROLD, FERDINAND – French composer of *opéra comique*; his output in this genre was unbelievably popular throughout the nineteenth century. Hérold was another Prix de Rome winner, but his stay in Rome lasted less than a year, for he was already suffering from tuberculosis, and he moved further south to Naples. There he taught the two daughters of the King of Naples and had his first opera performed – *The Young Henry V*. Back in Paris he was soon churning out operas for performance at the Opéra and the Opéra-Comique. Here are some statistics to illustrate his popularity: *Marie* received a hundred performances within a year, four hundred in ten years; *Zampa, ou La fiancée de marbre* (The Hard-Hearted Fiancée) five hundred by 1877, and *Pré aux Clercs* a thousand by the end of the nineteenth century; the last two were his greatest triumphs. Poor Hérold was too ill to attend the first performance of *Pré aux Clercs* and did not live to witness its success. *Zampa* impressed Wagner, which is saying something; yet, apart from the ballet *La fille mal gardée* (The Wayward Daughter), the only music of Hérold's that survives today is *Zampa*'s overture; that's how it can go with music. The climax of *Zampa* is a sort of feminist reverse of the Don Giovanni story; here the pirate Zampa dies in the arms of a marble statue, an image of a young girl he deceived and deserted, after placing a wedding ring in jest on the statue's finger.

HINDEMITH, PAUL – a most important German composer between the two World Wars; he was a concert violinist and violist as well – in 1929 he was the soloist at the première of Walton's Viola Concerto – and could also play many other instruments. At twenty he became leader of the Frankfurt opera orchestra and later married the music director's daughter. Hindemith's teaching career started in 1927 in Berlin at the Hochschule für Musik. From 1934 the Nazis began attacking him: his music was boycotted, he was accused of perpetrating decadent atonal works, of associating with Jews and of parodying a military march used at Nazi rallies; after the first performance of his symphony, *Mathis der Maler*, its conductor, Furtwängler, was dismissed from the Berlin Oper.

Hindemith left Germany in 1938 and soon became professor of theory at Yale University. He died somewhat embittered, since his music, which had become decidedly bland in character after about 1935, began to be neglected following the rise of a new avant garde from about 1950. In the decade from 1920, by contrast, his works are full of adventure and free of selfconscious theorising. The irony is that he always wished for ordinary people to play and to listen to his music with easy enjoyment; to this end he turned out sonatas for almost the whole range of instruments of the orchestra. His ideal was to create a new form of Baroque contrapuntal harmony; the acme of this aim may be heard in the piano work *Ludus Tonalis*, a series of fugues interspersed with interludes. *Mathis der Maler* (Mathias the Painter), the earlier symphony, was turned into an opera of the same name; it deals with the time of the Peasants' Revolt in Germany and is about the painter Mathias Grünewald, who gives up his art to commit himself to political action, becomes disillusioned and returns to his painting. To get some idea of Hindemith's range of writing the following works are suggested – the symphony *Mathis der Maler*; *Concert Music* for brass and strings; *Die junge Magd* (The Young Maiden), song-cycle for contralto, flute, clarinet and string quartet.

HISTOIRE DU SOLDAT, L' (The Soldier's Tale) – a music-theatre work with narrative by Stravinsky, written in 1918. The story deals with a soldier returning from the wars, whose most precious possession is a violin. He meets the devil, who persuades the soldier to part with his instrument in exchange for a magic book that can predict the rise and fall of share prices. The soldier becomes wealthy and marries a princess, but yearns for his violin; by a ruse he retrieves it and is cursed by the devil, who warns him never to look back; the silly ass of a soldier forgets this threat, looks back and perishes. Stravinsky's music is permeated with attractive melody and rhythm and includes dance numbers – Ragtime, Waltz, Tango, to which the princess swings and sways. What works so well is the instrumental ensemble, made up of clarinet, bassoon, cornet, trombone, violin, double bass and percussion; Stravinsky's treatment of these instruments in various combinations is nothing short of brilliant, with the final cadenza on percussion alone perhaps symbolising the rattle of the soldier's bones.

HODDINOTT, ALUN – Welsh composer and teacher. He studied for a time privately with Arthur Benjamin in London; he was appointed to the Chair in Music at the University of Cardiff in 1967. Hoddinott founded and ran, as artistic director, the Cardiff Festival of Contemporary Music; with this event and other involvements he did much to promote contemporary music in South Wales. The early pieces in a large output show the influences of Rawsthorne and Bartók.

113

Doubles, a concertante for oboe, harpsichord and strings, and *A Contemplation upon Flowers*, for soprano and orchestra, are two attractive examples of his musical language and style.

HOGWOOD, CHRISTOPHER – he has played a significant role in the postwar Early Music revival in England. As an undergraduate at Cambridge his subjects were classics and music; at the time he was much influenced by Raymond Leppard and Thurston Dart, major authorities in seventeenth- and eighteenth-century music. Hogwood is a distinguished harpsichordist. Many listeners have been drawn to his specialist period by his informed, concise and well-presented talks on BBC radio. In the early 1970s he founded the Academy of Ancient Music, which he directs and which specialises in accurate interpretations of Baroque and early Classical music. In 1967, with David Munrow, he was a co-founder of the Early Music Consort. He has a long and varied list of recordings to his name.

HOLLIGER, HEINZ – an outstanding oboist, born in Switzerland; also a minor composer. For a time he had composition lessons with Boulez in Basle. His concert tours have included programmes with his wife, Ursula, a harpist, and his Holliger Ensemble. His rare command of his instrument has enabled him to produce many effects such as harmonics, double trills, glissandos and even chords; on some occasions he has stuck a microphone up his oboe to create unheard-of sounds. While many distinguished composers have written works for him – Berio, Henze, Krenek, Martin, Penderecki and Stockhausen – Holliger remains interested in, and committed to, the performance of oboe music of all periods. His recordings cover a rich selection of music for or involving his instrument.

HOLST, GUSTAV – in the generation after Elgar, he and Vaughan Williams are the leading English composers. Holst was a particularly influential teacher among school pupils and amateurs, an area of musical instruction to which he strongly committed himself. His lasting friendship with Vaughan Williams began when they were students together at the Royal College of Music. Later, it was from Vaughan Williams and Cecil Sharp that he built up a sound knowledge of English folksong. He also developed an abiding interest in Hindu philosophy, expressed in his one-act opera *Savitri*.

In 1905 he became musical director at St Paul's Girls' School at Hammersmith, a post he retained to the end of his life. Two years later he was put in charge of music at Morley College, an adult education institute which has maintained its distinction to this day. There he prepared and presented Purcell's *The Fairy Queen*, its first airing since 1697. His heavy teaching routine allowed Holst only to compose at weekends. In 1916 he completed his most exciting and popular work, *The Planets* for large orchestra. His commitment to amateur music-making produced the fine oratorio-type *Hymn of Jesus* for chorus, female semichorus and orchestra, first performed at the Queen's Hall in 1920, three years after it was written.

His daughter, Imogen Holst, has thoroughly recorded his life and music; writer, conductor and administrator, she had a long spell at Aldeburgh as one of its artistic directors, working closely with Britten and Pears. Holst was unconventional about religion, kindly to amateur musicians, hard on professionals. You will enjoy his *Morris Dance Tunes* for orchestra, *Seven Part Songs* for female chorus and strings and the *St Paul's Suite* for strings. *The Planets* of course you already know.

HOMOPHONY – a term to describe music in which one part concentrates on the melodic material, while the other parts simply act as accompaniment. This is in contrast to polyphony, in which all the parts, with varying degrees of importance, share the melodic material. Understandably, music of a popular nature is usually homophonic, for the aim and ambition here is to let the ear quickly grasp the melody or tune, with or without words.

HONEGGER, ARTHUR – a Swiss composer who was born and died in France. His name was associated with Les Six, a group of composers whose aim was to take an iconoclastic view of late Romantic music and its aesthetics. Honegger is best appreciated for his choral dramas – *Le roi David* (King David), *Jeanne d'Arc au bûcher* (Joan of Arc at the Stake), *Nicholas de Flue* – and his extensive list of chamber and instrumental music. The first of three symphonic movements, *Pacific 231*, describing a steam engine's journey from departure to arrival, and later set to film, is perhaps his most notorious work; the other two, *Rugby* and *Mouvement symphonique No. 3*, are not so well known. An exceedingly charming piece for chamber orchestra is his *Pastorale d'été* (Summer Pastoral), as are his *Concertino* for piano and orchestra and *Concerto da camera* for flute, cor anglais and strings. His five symphonies, though suffering from a degree of pedestrianism, contain many stimulating and orchestrally effective moments. Honegger also turned out a large number of scores for radio and film.

HORN – did you know that if this brass instrument, all nicely curled up, with its widely flared bell were to be stretched out it would measure as much as nineteen feet! In a large orchestra, which would carry four horns, two frequent effects always go down well: first, playing in unison in the upper part of their range – very stirring; secondly, playing slow, four-part harmony – very stately. A solo horn playing a melody with the orchestra in accompaniment can be magical. In contrast to the trumpet, with its cup-shaped mouthpiece, the horn's is conical. It is far from easy to play well and even the best of players can sometimes crack a note. Sound is produced by lip vibration against the mouthpiece, the lips acting as vibrating reeds. Surprisingly, the horn is more agile than you might think. Its four valves channel the vibrating air column through different lengths of pipe, thus allowing for the production of any note in the chromatic scale. The model pitched in F is the one most commonly employed in orchestras; it has a range of nearly four octaves. Some of the effects that can additionally be produced are muting, obtained by either placing the right hand up the bell or inserting a specially shaped mute made of metal or cardboard; and pointing the bell up in the air (*campana in aria* – bell in air), playing loudly to produce a very brassy, lusty sound – this also looks good. Reiteration of notes, by tonguing, is easy, trills less so, while glissandos are harder to play. Among composers who are now part of the establishment, as it were, some superb horn passages have been written: Beethoven (Piano Concerto No. 5), Mahler (*Das Lied von der Erde* – Song of the Earth), Debussy (*La Mer* – The Sea), Stravinsky (*Le Sacre du printemps* – The Rite of Spring), Bartók (*Concerto for Orchestra*).

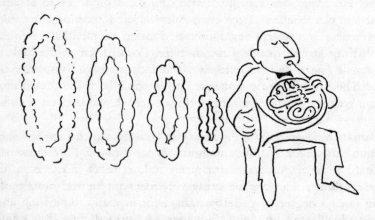

HOROWITZ, VLADIMIR – American pianist, born in the Ukraine, one of the most brilliant of twentieth-century keyboard virtuosos. In 1933 he married Toscanini's daughter Wanda. At eighteen he gave a series of concerts in Kharkov, for which he was paid in food and clothing. He landed up in the USA in the late 1920s, settling there in 1940. Of a highly strung disposition, he was sometimes forced to take time out from recital-giving and recording; a particularly long break occurred from 1953 to 1965. Horowitz's interpretation of any piece he elects to play is entirely his own, in the belief that the performer's rendering is an addition to what the composer may have written. Just listen to his performance of any Beethoven piano sonata, some Schumann or Prokofiev or the Liszt arrangement of Saint-Saëns's *Danse macabre* – here the keyboard starts to sizzle.

HOWELLS, HERBERT – English composer and teacher whose close friends and colleagues included Walter de la Mare, Vaughan Williams and Boris Ord, music director of King's College Chapel, Cambridge. A good deal of chamber and organ music flowed from his pen and he made a valuable contribution to the development of twentieth-century English song, yet his reputation rests chiefly on his sacred choral works – anthems, canticles, services, motets, masses. *Hymnus Paradisi*, a requiem, for soloists, chorus and orchestra, is considered his finest work; it was composed three years after the loss of his nine-year-old son from spinal meningitis. Howells's distinction is his true grasp of the refinements of chapel choir music – *Chichester Service* for SATB and organ, the *Missa Aelis Christi* for SATB *a cappella*, the anthem *Like as the hart*, a *Nunc dimittis* for double choir, his sacred partsong *Long, long ago*.

HUDDERSFIELD CHORAL SOCIETY – founded in 1836, the widest-known of the Yorkshire choral societies; it has given concerts in Europe and the USA and made many recordings including Handel's *Messiah*, Elgar's *Dream of Gerontius* and Walton's *Belshazzar's Feast*. It is a fine example of the best in the continuing English amateur choral society tradition. Back in the 1930s it had a remarkable membership of 400; today it has settled down to about 230 – still not bad! Sir Malcolm Sargent was its music director for over thirty years.

HUMORESKE (*humoresque*) – a term originating in Germany which described short literary presentations to do with our 'humours' or moods. Schumann was the first to use it as a musical title in his piano piece Op. 20; it then became quite a frequent title in the nineteenth century for short pieces of a relaxed character – Dvořák, Humperdinck, Tchaikovsky, Grieg have all written humoreskes. I cannot imagine that today composers like Berio, Boulez or Stockhausen would wish to write one ...

HUMPERDINCK, ENGELBERT – minor German composer straddling the nineteenth and twentieth centuries. He struck gold with the delightful opera *Hänsel und Gretel*, first performed in 1893 at Weimar with Richard Strauss conducting; in that same year it was produced in over fifty theatres. For a time Humperdinck acted as amanuensis to Wagner, assisting him in the promotion of *Parsifal*, his main task being to copy out the score. In 1885 he got a cushy job as private musician to A. Krupp, the wealthy German industrialist. Later he became a reader and adviser to the publishing firm of Schott. Another work of his which attained success was the incidental music to *Königskinder* (The King's Children – also called The Goosegirl), which grew into an opera, first performed in New York in 1910. Oddly, both these operas germinated from groups of songs. Humperdinck also composed impressive incidental music for Shakespeare plays produced by Max Reinhardt in Berlin.

HURDY-GURDY – a mechanically bowed instrument, introduced to Europe from the Middle East via Spain and well known during the Middle Ages. At this time one of its functions was to act as a resource in the teaching of music at monastic schools, to help perform sacred polyphony and to assist singers with their intonation (singing in tune). In the secular realm it became popular as an instrument accompanying *chansons*, sometimes doubling the vocal line, sometimes adding preludes and interludes. By the eighteenth century in France the aristocracy took the instrument to its bosom for use at fêtes, at which everyone was dressed as a shepherd or shepherdess in the vogue for rustic fantasy. Concurrently, wandering minstrels, beggars and blind musicians were playing the damned thing in the streets. You may be surprised to learn that both Haydn and Mozart included parts for the hurdy-gurdy in some of their lighter music, while an arrangement existed of Vivaldi's *Four Seasons* for hurdy-gurdy, flute, violin and *basso continuo*. Usually the instrument was shaped like a viol; it had a keyboard with tangents that pressed on the strings when pushed down. Drone strings are a feature of the instrument; the earlier version had two drones and one melody string; later versions had four drones and two melody strings. The mechanical bowing is achieved by a resin-covered wooden wheel which is made to rotate by a crank. Hurdy-gurdys are to be seen and heard in folksong and dance groups in certain parts of France and Spain.

HYMN – originally a narrative poem in ancient Greek culture, evolving to a single-line Latin chant in praise of God and by the fifteenth century becoming a polyphonic setting at Vespers of major feast days – there are at least twenty-three hymns for these occasions. Since the Reformation, metrical hymns have played an important part in Protestant worship, now sung by the congregation and not confined to the church choir. In England the Wesley brothers, John and Charles, in the eighteenth century ushered in a new era; words and tune were aimed at arousing the religious emotions of the worshippers. By the nineteenth century there was a great flowering of English hymnody and special hymns were assigned to different liturgical functions in the church service and calendar. Many hymn publications came out, culminating in 1861 with *Hymns Ancient and Modern*. By 1912 sixty million copies had been sold. Fair takes your breath away. The Victorian hymn remains our favourite; there is little doubt that churchgoers still enjoy hymn singing. As yet, twentieth-century classical music has not been able to find a means, with but a few exceptions, of adding new material to enrich the established repertoire.

IBERT, JACQUES – French composer who won the Paris Conservatoire Prix de Rome in 1919. For the stage he wrote twenty-nine works including seven ballets, more than eight film and radio scores and several very effective pieces for outdoor entertainments. Like Ravel's *Bolero*, Ibert's *Little White Donkey* (from *Dix Histoires* for piano) achieved immense popularity; while welcoming the royalties earned, both composers cursed these pieces, for it was a long time before the public stopped drawing a curtain over their far more important works. Ibert's style is elegant, vigorous, expressive, yet full of French restraint. He composed his Trio for violin, cello and harp for his daughter, a professional harpist. His piano pieces are a joy to listen to and among his orchestral works his symphonic poem *Escales* (three impressions of the ports of Palermo, Tunis and Valencia) is full of easy melody and rhythm. Of contemporary musical language and style, Ibert maintained, 'all systems are valid, provided that one derives music from them'. Of mild interest is the detail that he wrote a cadenza for Mozart's Bassoon Concerto in B flat K191.

ICONOGRAPHY OF MUSIC – this term describes the study of music through works of art. Musical iconography as a research discipline only

121

got going at the beginning of this century; after nine decades it has proved to be of great help in musicological research. The musical iconographer's task is not simply to identify the performers and the instruments, or to describe the conditions of performance as illustrated in a painting, photograph, sculpture or print. All the subject matter in, for example, a seventeenth-century painting referring to music has to be carefully analysed and weighed up, in order to arrive at an understanding of what the painting may reveal about the history of the instruments, the performance practice then current, the cultural and intellectual attitudes of the time. An engraving exists based on an account by Charles Burney of the chorus and orchestra for the Handel Commemoration Ceremonies of 1784. It provides useful evidence for the following: the number of players assigned to each part in the orchestra, the different instruments in the continuo group, the size and seating arrangements of the choir, the size and specification of organ and harpsichord. The musical iconographer's task is not confined to earlier music alone; the study of photographs of the nineteenth and twentieth centuries, and film, can reveal important information about stage settings, concert halls, opera costume, and facets of instrumental performance. Similarly, images of composers, their families, teachers, friends and places where they would hang out – all can be helpful in establishing the milieu in which composers worked. Next time you visit an art gallery pay special attention to any painting that includes a musical reference; become your own musical iconographer!

IDOMENEO, KING OF CRETE (*Idomeneo, Re di Creta*) – a three-act opera by Mozart, first produced in Munich in 1781. He had been composing operas since the age of twelve (1768 – *La finta semplice*, The Simple Pretence), but *Idomeneo* is his first operatic masterpiece. The plot, in a word, deals with Idomeneo who is sailing home from the Trojan Wars when a storm strikes the ship; he makes a deal with Neptune that in return for his safe landing he will sacrifice the first person he meets on shore. This turns out to be his son, Idamante, who, it so happens, has gone potty over the captive Trojan princess Ilia. To make matters more complicated she is already betrothed. After much hoo-ha the sea god releases Idomeneo from his vow and his son marries the princess.

IMPROMPTU – a fairly short piece, nearly always for piano, varying in style but composed with an attractive air of improvisation. Schubert wrote eight appealing examples, of which No. 4 in A flat major of the D899 set is perhaps the most delightful.

IMPROVISATION – a short definition of improvisation is: the making and performing of music that is not written down. A reliable knowledge of the language and style of the music in which an improvisation is performed is, of course, necessary, otherwise the improvised passage or piece will sound chaotic or directionless. One may say that good improvisation is instant composition. While it is a minor aspect of classical music, it is already to be found in early medieval times, when a singer would make up a second part against a notated Latin chant. We have here the beginning of counterpoint. The Baroque era produced improvisation when performers were allowed various ways of decorating a melody with ornamental figures or filling out the skeleton bass line of the continuo part. Later, in the Classical period, concertos would leave the cadenza sections to the improvisatory skill of the soloist. There is little doubt that many piano pieces in the nineteenth century started off as improvisations, especially those which were transcriptions of songs or excerpts from operas. In the twentieth century, since the war, improvisation has been encouraged by avant-garde composers; the results thus far have not found much favour with listeners, because they have no terms of reference with which to follow the differing improvisatory processes. Before the advent of recording, comment on the history of improvisation is to some extent conjecture. Take note that, in non-Western cultures, improvisation is a normal element in music-making.

INCIDENTAL MUSIC – the term refers to music supporting a stage, film, radio or television production. Its function lies in the same category as scenery, costume and lighting. Before opera was truly born, at the end of the sixteenth century, early religious dramas were effectively enhanced by musical insertions. Since then, and still today, incidental music is rarely absent from the theatre, cinema or broadcasting. Composers often turn their incidental music into a suite for further performance – a way of earning extra shekels. Shakespeare and Greek drama have drawn forth much fine incidental music – Mendelssohn's to *A Midsummer Night's Dream* (which contains a comic funeral march to the Pyramus and Thisbe sub-plot, scored for clarinet, bassoon and timpani); Sibelius's to *The Tempest*; Vaughan Williams's to Aristophanes's *The Wasps*; Grieg's to Ibsen's *Peer Gynt*. Of course, poor examples of this genre of composition are often glaringly obvious. A score that is right for its purpose will subtly highlight the key moments of the action, whereas a bad one will be intrusive – even if interesting in its own right. Thus in the latter case an audience will always be conscious of the music, whereas in the former the effect can often be subliminal – one would only notice the music by its absence. Shakespeare's *Hamlet* has incidental music for the theatre by Shostakovich and for the screen by Walton in Laurence Olivier's production. Geoffrey Burgon's music for *Brideshead Revisited* and Barrington Pheloung's for the *Inspector Morse* series are two fine examples for television.

INCORONAZIONE DI POPPEA, L' (The Coronation of Poppea) – the first opera to deal with an historical subject, for it is set in Rome in the time of Nero (a part written, inappropriately enough, for a castrato). This three-act opera is Monteverdi's last, produced in Venice in 1642. It contains most of the basic ingredients necessary to a popular dramatic plot – conflict, betrayal, variety of emotion, nuances of love-making, triumph of lady getting her own way – all expressed through a rich parade of music: recitative, arioso, aria and choral number, accompanied by a large orchestra.

INDY, VINCENT D' – a French composer who came from a rich aristocratic family. He served with distinction in the Franco-Prussian War of 1870–71. His outlook on music was always rather conservative. His teacher was Franck and he belonged to the French Wagnerites – his opera *Fervaal* was dubbed the 'French *Parsifal*'. He helped to establish the Schola Cantorum, which for a time rivalled the Paris Conservatoire; pupils who passed through his hands included Roussel, Satie and Varèse. His composition and teaching methods were based on strict traditional lines, and d'Indy considered the musical world of Debussy and Ravel as decadent; later he could barely tolerate the works of Schoenberg, Stravinsky or Prokofiev, or even Les Six. His ethos was that of the late nineteenth-century aesthetic – Art for Art's Sake. It should be stressed, however, that d'Indy was remarkably informed and possessed a highly cultivated mind. *La légende de Saint Christophe* (1915), an opera of some quality, caused a bit of a shindig with its mild anti-semitism and forceful expression of all his artistic and political prejudices. If d'Indy grabs you, some idea of his music will be gleaned from his orchestral triptych *Jour d'été à la montagne*, Op. 61, and his String Quartet No. 2 in E, Op. 65.

INTERMEZZO – this term was used first to describe short entertainments involving music placed between acts of Renaissance comedies. Later it was applied to lighthearted scenes interspersed for relaxation in the course of eighteenth-century opera seria. In the nineteenth century the least intense movement in a chamber-music work might be given the title of intermezzo, as in the third movement of Mendelssohn's Piano Quartet No. 2. The Dorabella variation in Elgar's '*Enigma*' *Variations* is very much an intermezzo. Bartók heads the fourth of five movements in his *Concerto for Orchestra* 'intermezzo'. For us the most familiar intermezzos are the three for piano in Brahms's Op. 117; note that he wrote fourteen other piano intermezzos scattered through Opp. 76, 116, 118 and 119.

IRELAND, JOHN – an English composer who was orphaned in his boyhood, the effect of which may have caused him to lean towards the mystical, the transient and an idealistic dreamworld. Ireland flourished in the first half of this century. While he was a composition teacher at the Royal College of Music, Arnell, Britten, Bush, Moeran and Searle passed through his hands – quite an impressive bunch. Ireland much admired the music of Debussy, Ravel and Stravinsky, which did not prevent the expression of his strong streak of English lyricism. He was made a Fellow of both the Royal College of Music and the Royal Academy of Music, and Durham University gave him an honorary DMus. His *Concertino pastorale* for string orchestra has much charm, as do some of his songs, and many of his piano pieces such as *Amberley Wild Brooks*, *For Remembrance* and *Island Spell*.

ISORHYTHM – in simple terms, isorhythm describes a melody whose rhythmic pattern is repeated continuously, as in the nursery rhyme *Twinkle, twinkle little star*. As a technique in composition it is most commonly found in fourteenth- and fifteenth-century motets. Here things get more complicated: an individual line of music may have both a melodic and a rhythmic pattern, but each is of a different length, so that the patterns fall out of synch. When this process is applied to more than one line, as in a three-part motet, then we have a complexity of sound which the ear does not find easy to separate into details, but the composite effect is most attractive. Machaut, Dunstable and Dufay all wrote distinguished isorhythmic motets.

ITALIAN SYMPHONY – a name given to Mendelssohn's Symphony No. 4 in A, Op. 90. He started to compose it during his eight-month sojourn in Italy in 1830–31, completing it a year later; it is broadly inspired by the vitality he found in the Italian folk and folk music he met, and is the most popular of his symphonies.

IVES, CHARLES – one might say Ives is the father of twentieth-century American classical music. Though he was familiar with a number of important European composers, especially Bach, his background and upbringing and his independence of musical thought produced a flow of highly individual compositions. His father, the youngest bandmaster in the Union Army during the Civil War, is considered responsible not only for Ives's early musical training, but also for his experimental and uninhibited approach to composing. In his school days Ives proved to be an able sportsman; at Yale University, according to the athletics coach, he could have been a first-class sprinter, but instead concentrated on his musical studies. Throughout his life he wrote, on the one hand, music which could be easily appreciated by his ordinary fellow citizens, and on the other, works that were complicated, sometimes convoluted, involving intricate counterpoint, polytonality and cross-rhythm.

Ives earned a very successful living as an insurance salesman; while he was developing his business the only time at his disposal for composing was at weekends. Yet his output is large and varied, and is evidence of massive mental and physical energy as well as quickness of musical thought. In 1918 he suffered a severe heart attack, after which he never recovered his full health. His double life as composer and insurance salesman had taken its toll, and from 1926 his musical creativity fell away rapidly: he had burnt himself out. If you do not know any of Ives's music have a listen to his orchestral pieces *Central Park in the Dark*, *Three Places in New England* or *The Unanswered Question*. Then there is his piece for clarinet, bugle, violin, bells and piano duet *All the way there and back*.

JACOB, GORDON – English composer known for his attractive, practical, workaday compositions and for his succinct, highly informed book *Orchestral Technique*, one of several he wrote while a teacher of theory and composition at the Royal College of Music. Jacob himself studied at the RCM under Stanford and Howells. A teacher from 1926 to 1966, he numbered among the students who passed through his hands Malcolm Arnold, Imogen Holst (daughter of Gustav), Antony Hopkins, Elizabeth Maconchy and Bernard Stevens. For a time he took evening classes at Morley and Birkbeck Colleges. Clarity, conciseness and imaginative treatment of his material may be heard in Jacob's Concerto for harmonica and orchestra, or the Suite for bassoon and orchestra.

JANÁČEK, LEOŠ – a Czech composer, today ranked with Smetana and Dvořák. He was a slow developer, poor for most of his life, earning a pittance from a variety of teaching posts. As a composer he only really matured at fifty; outside Moravia he was unrecognised before he turned sixty, and the first time it could be said he was comfortably off was at the age of seventy. Throughout his life there was not a time when he was not involved in some way with opera – writing, revising, planning – and unaccompanied choral pieces. His creative drive was essentially instinctive, although his knowledge of the music of the masters was sound; he possessed a deep understanding of Moravian folk music.

He was a close friend of Dvořák, with whom he took an inspiring walking tour of Bohemia. By 1921 his circumstances at last were such that he could return to his native village, Hukvaldy, to buy a cottage. With the help of Rosa Newmarch, who championed his music, he visited England for a week in 1922 to enjoy a concert of his chamber music at the Wigmore Hall. Janáček's wife, whom he married when she was sixteen, could offer little support to his musical life; in due course he began an unconsummated relationship with Kamila Stösslová, thirty-eight years younger than himself and the wife of a Bohemian antique dealer, who inspired, or was the subject of, much of his operatic, vocal and instrumental music.

Together with Schoenberg and Hindemith he was elected in 1927 to the Prussian Academy of Arts. A remarkable upsurge of creativity occured in the final twelve years of his life, when he produced the finest of his eight operas – including *The Makropoulos Affair* and *From the House of the Dead* – as well as the *Glagolitic Mass* for SATB, organ, chorus and orchestra, and *Nursery Rhymes* – eighteen pieces and an introduction for choir and instrumental ensemble. To become acquainted with his music you could do no better than to listen to his song-cycle *Diary of One who Disappeared* and *Mládí* (Youth) for flute, oboe, clarinet, bassoon and bass clarinet.

JERUSALEM – today this Middle Eastern city is divided in two parts: the new city, capital of Israel, and the old city which is under Israeli administration. Biblical scholars have ascertained that in about 1000 BC King

David established Jerusalem as a music centre, laying down detailed musical functions: a group of Levites should devote themselves entirely to music-making; the musical forces were to be based on the symbolic number of twelve; drums, rattles and other noisy instruments were barred; plucked strings and a small choir would accompany the psalms, which were to form the basis of Christian and Jewish sacred song through the ages.

In due course Greek, Roman and Muslim conquests destroyed the development of Hebrew religious music. Jerusalem grew into a tripartite Jewish, Muslim and Christian religious centre, and there is little doubt that Hebrew melody and text influenced both Byzantine and Ambrosian chant. The first European-type orchestra heard in Jerusalem was the Turkish Army Band, which played at Muslim festivals and at official functions. Postwar premières of works by leading composers include Milhaud's *David*, Stravinsky's *Abraham and Isaac* and Dallapiccola's *Exhortatio*. A. Z. Idelssohn is considered the pioneer of Jewish music research. The Hebrew University of Jerusalem contains the Jewish Music Research Centre and its music department, very active in undergraduate and postgraduate studies, has a busy electronic music studio.

JOACHIM, JOSEPH – one of the leading nineteenth-century violin virtuosi. At twelve he received much help and guidance from Mendelssohn. At fourteen he paid his first visit to England; later he gave concert tours there on an annual basis. At Cambridge he conducted the first performance in England of Brahms's Symphony No. 1, and in Berlin at the age of twenty-one his performance of Beethoven's Violin Concerto established the work in the violinist's repertoire. His close friendship with Brahms was helpful to the composer's development, especially in the writing of his Violin Concerto Op. 77. At the end of his life, when recording was in its infancy, Joachim recorded several pieces which are now of important archival interest.

JOLIVET, ANDRÉ – French composer who, in his boyhood, displayed equal talents for painting, literature and drama. Schoenberg's music had a marked influence on Jolivet; equally, the iconoclastic compositional inclinations of Varèse attracted him so much that he spent three years learning Varèse's approach to composition. With Messiaen, Baudrier and Lesur he formed the group *Jeune France*, whose aim was to establish an outlook on composition independent of Austro-German or neo-classical musical aesthetics. In Jolivet's oeuvre may be found the ever-growing European desire to incorporate elements of non-European musics. This may be heard in his Concerto for trumpet and orchestra, his Concerto for ondes martenot (a type of electronic guitar) and orchestra and *Mans* – six pieces for piano. More relaxed, lighter pieces which you will definitely enjoy are the divertimento *Cabrioles* for flute and piano and *Petite Suite* for flute, viola and harp.

JOPLIN, SCOTT – dubbed the King of Ragtime, this black American composer and pianist began to write down his own compositions after a concert visit to Chicago. Joplin's first publication was *Maple Leaf Rag* in 1899. The structure of his piano pieces became more extensive, and in due course he also wrote two operas based on ragtime, *A Guest of Honor* (the score of which was lost) and *Treemonisha* (1911 – first performed only in 1972). It is in the 1970s that Joplin's music was revived, thanks to the musicologist Joshua Rifkin; the choreographer Jerome Robbins produced a delightful ballet, *Elite Syncopations*, based on Joplin rags (and named after one of them); the score of the film *The Sting* also made use of his rags. There is a recording of *Treemonisha* and many of the rags are available on CD – charming, melodious and inventive piano music to which you could shuffle around as well as listen.

JOSQUIN – really Josquin Desprez, the greatest of the Renaissance composers before the mid-sixteenth century; first active in northern France. He paid two visits to Italy, but by 1505 he had returned to France where he remained until his death. The extent of his reputation may be judged by the singular attention given to his music by the publisher Petrucci, who issued three books of his Masses alone; normally each book would be a compilation of music by several composers. Josquin's works were regarded as models of composition by composers and writers on music alike, and he was Luther's favourite composer. After his death, unscrupulous publishers were prone to placing his name above others' music in order to increase sales. There is still much research awaiting musicologists, but there is little doubt of the importance of Josquin's position, both in his own right and as a link from the music of his predecessors Dufay and Ockeghem to that of his successors Palestrina, Lassus and Tallis. Your listening pleasure will be increased by spending a while with, say, Josquin's six-part motet *Benedicta es, celorum regina* or his three-part chanson *Que vous madame*.

JOUBERT, JOHN – English composer of South African descent; Reader in Music at Birmingham University. A number of talented composition students have come under his guidance, of whom the most distinguished is John Casken. Joubert's output is large and varied, not only in medium but in range of complexity. He adjusts his material according to whether the commission is for amateur forces – Symphony

No. 1 for the Hull Philharmonic Society – or professionals – Symphony No. 2 for the Royal Philharmonic Society, a demanding work for any crack team. This approach to composition is determined by Joubert's belief that the composer has a responsibility to society as well as to art. Proof of the pudding is in the tasting: listen to his *Pro Pace Motets* for SATB *a cappella* and his *Chamber Music for Brass Quintet*, Op. 104.

JUPITER SYMPHONY – the popular name of Mozart's Symphony in C major K551, which he wrote in 1788. Mozart's son said that the title was given to the symphony by the London impresario Salomon; it may have been inspired by the first movement, the opening of which is certainly regal and dignified. The coda of the final movement combines its five thematic ideas in a dramatic climax of contrapuntal ingenuity. This symphony is the last of the forty-one Mozart composed in his all too short life.

KABALEVSKY, DMITRY – a Russian composer who seems always to have toed the Communist Party line; in 1940 he became a Party member and after the decree of 1948 he dutifully pursued its tenets. If not very trail-blazing, his career as a Soviet composer was consistently successful. Despite all the political subservience Kabalevsky has turned out much attractive music. In the Soviet Union he was best known for his vocal works – songs, operas and cantatas; but abroad his reputation was built up on his orchestral, concerto and piano music. Worth hearing are his *Twenty-Four Preludes* for piano, the suite for small orchestra *The Comedians* and his Violin Concerto in C Major, Op. 48.

KAGEL, MAURICIO – Argentine composer who settled in Germany; equally active in film and drama; his avant-garde works frequently incorporate these additional interests. Some consider works such as his music/film *Ludwig van* or his nine-section stage piece *Szenische Komposition* (Scenic Composition) somewhat outrageous. Kagel's creative joy lies in the production of material that seeks to establish new ways of considering music, of breaking down traditional concepts and assumptions. He is a sound experimenter and musical iconoclast, much influenced by Cage and Stockhausen. Kagel is the musical equivalent of the literary and philosophical movement known as deconstructionalism. You may wish to enjoy some modest masochism with his *Musi* for plucked strings or *Rrrrrr: five jazz pieces* for clarinet, saxophone, violin and piano.

KARAJAN, HERBERT VON – one of the twentieth century's more colourful conductors; an Austrian who clocked up a remarkable list of achievements following his first success at the age of twenty-one, when he conducted *The Marriage of Figaro* at Ulm. After a temporary blip because of his Nazi associations his career took off and in due course he became principal conductor of the Berlin Philharmonic – his main orchestra – and director of the Vienna Staatsoper; he was also involved with the Salzburg Festival. He made numerous recordings not only of the traditional repertoire but also of twentieth-century works, and conducted seasons with the Philharmonia, La Scala and many of the other crack orchestras of the world. He had a keen interest in musical aesthetics and therapy, offset by an image as a bit of a playboy, which was enhanced when he qualified to fly his own plane, and proved to be a skilled yachtsman. Nice.

KATERINA ISMAYLOVA – see *Lady Macbeth of the Mtsensk District*.

KELLER, HANS – an influential British music critic, born in Austria. Although he never produced a major book on music, his many articles supplied much food for thought among professional musicians as well as opening up new vistas of musical appreciation for the ordinary listener and concert-goer. In 1959 he joined the BBC Music Division, where he held a substantial number of posts over a period of some twenty-five years. Keller was an authority on Schoenberg, on Gershwin and on Britten (who dedicated his String Quartet No. 3 to him), and possessed a penetrating knowledge of the music of Haydn and Mozart.

KEY – what does this little word mean when applied to music? Mozart's Piano Sonata No. 12 K332 is in the key of F major, Chopin's Waltz Op. 34 No. 2 is in A minor – so what? Well, it does matter in the music written between, say, 1650 and 1900. All music is expressed through a group of notes called a *scale* or *mode* which, in their basic form, are laid out in ascending order; the number of notes in a scale may vary from three to more than twelve, when casting one's eye over the musics of the world. In European classical music in the period mentioned, there are two scales in use, the diatonic eight-note scale, of which there are two 'flavours', the major and the minor; and the chromatic scale of twelve notes. The starting note is called the *tonic*; the relationships between the notes of the scale, whatever the pitch of the tonic, remain the same. So, if the tonic is A, the relationship of note B to A is the same as note D is to note C when C is the tonic. No doubt this is all as clear as mud. Don't panic. Just remember that this system is termed 'functional harmony', and composers would choose different keys either for practical purposes – the range of the soprano voice, for example, or the fact that a natural horn (without valves) would be pitched in the key of F – or because they associated particular feelings or moods with certain keys. Generally, but not always, major keys are associated with brightness and lighter emotion, whereas minor keys tend to bring out the dark or sad aspects of thought and feeling. This difference certainly applies to the Mozart and Chopin examples quoted above. (See also *Signature*.) In any event, don't trouble yourself too much over which keys your favourite works are pitched in; let not your listening pleasure be marred by such petty technical talk.

KEYBOARD – in the evolution of European classical music, keyboard instruments have played an immensely important role in the development of musical language: the organ in the Middle Ages, the virginal in the Renaissance, the harpsichord and organ in the Baroque era, the piano in the Classical and Romantic periods as well as in the first half of the twentieth century, and now the electronic piano and synthesiser. The earliest extant written-out music for keyboard is dated 1320. Its notation would not be understood by you or me; the experts have to translate its meaning for us. Composers have often thought out new ideas and effects while seated at the keyboard; its music has at times influenced vocal and instrumental compositional material. It plays little or no role in non-European musics.

What exactly *is* a keyboard? It is a row of those shiny white and black things a performer presses down with his fingers; they are called levers, technically, and range from those of the lofty cathedral organ to those on the piano accordion of the people. The levers set into motion vibrations which sound a range of pitches, more of them for the harpsichord than for the clavichord, more for the organ than for the piano. The synclavier, a Rolls Royce version of the synthesiser, can create a myriad of pitches; thus far classical composers have hardly begun to explore or exploit the potential of such electronic instruments. Currently keyboards are of three basic types: stringed, in which the levers pluck the string (harpsichord, clavichord) or strike it (piano); pipes, in which the levers cause bellows to make the air vibrate in the pipes (organ); electronic pulses, which generate acoustic frequencies (electric piano, synthesiser). Yes, the keyboard will be with us for a long time yet.

KHACHATURIAN, ARAM – a twentieth-century Soviet composer of Armenian descent. His music represents the more attractive side of the socialist realism aesthetic. Khachaturian's material is simply presented, full of attractive melody and rich orchestral or instrumental colour; he was at his best when writing for the stage or screen. At the Moscow Conservatory he studied with Myaskovsky, who also taught Prokofiev; in 1948, with the latter and Shostakovich, he suffered the Stalinist attack on 'new' music. You will greatly enjoy his two ballet suites, *Spartacus* and *Gayaneh* (which contains the popular Sabre Dance), the Piano Concerto and his Trio for clarinet, violin and piano.

KING'S SINGERS – British vocal ensemble consisting of two counter-tenors, tenor, two baritones and bass. The group was formed in 1968 and is still going strong; its original members were Nigel Perrin, Alastair Hume, Alastair Thompson, Anthony Holt, Simon Carrington and Brian Kay, all except Holt choral scholars at King's College, Cambridge. The unique sound, known for its balance, nuance, dynamic range and virtuosity, that the King's Singers have created is unmatched; not a few imitators have attempted and failed to follow suit. Their style is an imaginative adaptation of two markedly different traditions: the Renaissance consort repertoire and the American close-harmony 'barber-shop' quartet, which later developed into such famous groups as the Mills Brothers, the Ink Spots, the Four Freshmen and the Hi-Los. To their credit, the King's Singers regularly commission works from composers, for example, Bennett, Berio, Glasser, Ligeti, Patterson and Penderecki. Their distinctive arrangements of a rich variety of material come from crack arrangers such as Gordon Langford and Daryl Runswick, and not a few from within the ensemble itself.

KLANGFARBENMELODIE – What the hell is this? I'll try to tell you. As you may know, the German language allows for the process of combining what in English would be several short words into one long word. *Klangfarbenmelodie* is an apt example; the term simply means sound-colour melody and was coined by Schoenberg as long ago as 1911. He maintained, and proved (in the third piece, entitled 'Colours', of his *Five Orchestral Pieces* Op. 16) that a succession of notes given differing utterances – each played by a different instrument, or appearing at octave transpositions – could produce a structural device in composition. Webern, his pupil and crony, developed this device extensively. Of course, *Klangfarbenmelodie* technique should not be taken literally as applying only to single notes, but rather in terms of motifs and divisions of a melodic line. You may like to know that the Tswana of Botswana and the Pedi of the northern Transvaal have long practised *Klangfarbenmelodie*, as found in the flute ensembles of their folk music.

KLEINE NACHTMUSIK, EINE (A Little Night Music) – the title Mozart gave to his *Serenade* in G major K525 for strings, written in 1787; it is in four movements (originally in five, but the second movement, a minuet, is now lost). You are certain to know this popular piece – a pleasure to relax with after work or after having listened to one of the operas from Wagner's *Ring* or a 'heavy' Bruckner symphony.

KLEMPERER, OTTO – one of the most noted conductors of the twentieth century, the first half in particular. Until 1933 he was extremely active in Berlin in presenting works by contemporary composers – he gave first performances of compositions by Stravinsky, Schoenberg, Hindemith, Janáček and Weill. He then emigrated to the USA, but returned to Europe after the war and in 1955 was appointed principal conductor of the Philharmonia Orchestra of London. His operation for a brain tumour in 1939 greatly sapped his energy and health and for a time he was unable to accept conducting engagements. Yet at the age of seventy he achieved new heights in his career, with numerous recordings and much demanding concert activity. What Klemperer is most admired for are his interpretations of the symphonies of Beethoven, Brahms and Mahler. Interestingly, he took composition lessons from Schoenberg in Los Angeles at the age of fifty.

KNABEN WUNDERHORN, DES (The Youth's Magic Horn) – a collection of German folksongs and texts published in 1808. It is of interest to us because Mahler made extensive use of the texts and melodies: there are three different ones in each of his Symphonies Nos. 2, 3 and 4. More importantly, he produced three lots of settings – nine songs with piano, ten songs with piano or orchestra and two songs with piano or orchestra; thus he drew on a total of twenty-four items in all from the collection.

KODÁLY, ZOLTÁN – Hungarian composer, ethnomusicologist and music educator. He and Bartók were lifelong friends and together undertook continuous research into Hungarian folk music, which greatly influenced their composition. A majority of Kodály's music is written for voice; he believed that 'our age of mechanisation leads along a road ending with man himself as a machine; only the spirit of singing can save us from this fate'. The struggle to establish recognition of the value of music education, an appreciation of the country's rich heritage of folk music and respect and encouragement for its composers was a long, hard slog, with success achieved only after the war. He proved that the practice and understanding of music in schools raised the standard of general academic achievement in the pupil, and these policies, known as the 'Kodály method', have spread to many parts of the world. Other than folk music the major influence on Kodály's composition was Debussy. This is not to say in any way that his works are pale imitations of the music of the French composer, as proved in any of the following: the orchestral pieces *Concerto for Orchestra*, *Háry János Suite*, *Dances from Galánta*; the choral works *Psalmus Hungaricus* for tenor, chorus and orchestra, *Missa Brevis* for chorus and organ.

KOECHLIN, CHARLES – a comparatively minor French composer, more of a musicologist. His teachers were Massenet and later Fauré, whom he idolised. Later, one of his most distinguished pupils was Poulenc. His more successful works are in the field of chamber and instrumental music – Sonata for viola and piano, *Nocturne chromatique* for piano, as examples – rather than orchestral, which incline towards longwindedness.

KOUSSEVITZKY, SERGE – American conductor of Russian birth; he began his professional life as a double-bass player. He married, in 1905, the daughter of a wealthy tea merchant, which gave him much independence. In addition to his material fortune it should be underlined that he was a conductor of great talent. After the Russian Revolution of 1917 he left the USSR; by 1924 he was in the USA, to become principal conductor of the Boston Symphony Orchestra, a post he held for twenty-five years. During this period he commissioned Stravinsky's *Symphony of Psalms*, Ravel's Piano Concerto, Hindemith's *Konzertmusik*, works from Prokofiev, Roussel and a long list of American composers including Gershwin, Copland and Barber. He established the summer school and concerts at Tanglewood, and the Berkshire Music Center. In 1941, after the death of his wife Nathalie, he established the Koussevitzky Music Foundation in her memory. One of the early composers to benefit from its funding was Britten with *Peter Grimes*, the Foundation's first opera commission.

KREISLER, FRITZ – legendary violinist of the later nineteenth and early twentieth centuries; the youngest child ever to gain admission to the Vienna Conservatoire, aged seven. From the age of twelve he had no further instruction and, it seems, hardly ever practised. Yet there is no later master who fails to admire his tone, rhythmic control and effortless perfection; perhaps the younger Heifetz was his nearest rival. Kreisler was also a bit of a composer. His most successful and popular items were what one might call 'encore' pieces, which he claimed were written by various minor eighteenth-century composers, until in 1935 he confessed that he himself had composed them; this sorely grated on many established critics, who had been taken in by Kreisler's ruse.

KRENEK, ERNST – American composer of Austrian birth. His prolific output reveals numerous sources of influence – late Romanticism, serial technique, neo-classicism, jazz, electronic music. Krenek has suggested that this diversity reflects his complex personality. His first wife was a daughter of Mahler, his second an actress, his third a composer. His musical eclecticism, which was never really fully integrated in his compositional style as it was in Stravinsky, is an early example of a characteristic that may be discerned in many twentieth-century composers. *Jonny spielt auf* (Johnny Strikes Up), an opera in two parts and eleven scenes, is Krenek's most popular and successful work. The range of his style may be gauged from his Symphony Op. 34 for wind and percussion, *Lamentatio Jeremiae prophetae* Op. 93 for *a cappella* chorus and *Echoes from Austria* Op. 166 for piano.

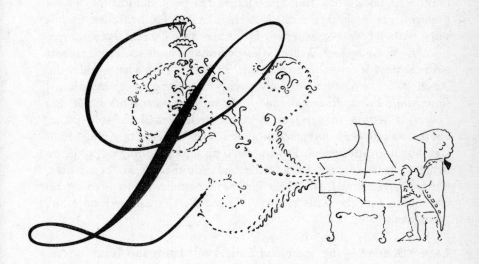

LADY MACBETH OF THE MTSENSK DISTRICT – also known as *Katerina Izmaylova*, the name of the heroine. Outstanding opera in four acts (1932) by the young Shostakovich. This brilliant work, with its gory and satirical plot, full of powerful, lyrical line and orchestration, was banned by the Soviet authorities after a hundred and eighty performances (as well as many more abroad). Considered vulgar and coarse, it was not 'allowed back' in the Soviet Union until 1962. The sum of the plot is: wife seduced by employee on the family estate during husband's absence; father-in-law who himself has designs on the wife discovers the situation, is fatally poisoned by her; husband returns and is killed by employee; couple sent to Siberia; there employee becomes enamoured of a fellow female convict; wife drowns herself and rival. No 'happy ever after' here!

LALO, EDOUARD – nineteenth-century French composer, who achieved success only in his fifties; before that he made his way as a string player and teacher. The revival of interest in chamber music in Paris in the 1850s is largely due to Lalo's activity in this area. His best-known work, *Symphonie espagnole* Op. 21 for violin and orchestra, was first performed by Sarasate in 1874. His several attempts at writing opera ended in failure. Of Lalo's other music, also appealing are his Cello Concerto and his orchestral suite *Namouna*.

LAMBERT, CONSTANT – English composer, conductor and writer on music – his book *Music Ho!*, first published in 1934, did much to air the problems contemporary music was then facing. He had close friendships with fellow composers – Heseltine, Van Dieren, Rawsthorne, Berners, Lutyens, and Walton who dedicated *Façade* to him. Lambert held the post of music director from 1931 to 1947 of what is today the Royal Ballet; when he was only twenty-one Dyagilev commissioned from him a ballet, *Romeo and Juliet*. His most popular work is *The Rio Grande*, a setting of a poem by Sacheverell Sitwell for solo piano, chorus, strings, brass and percussion; in it may be heard the influence of jazz which greatly appealed to Lambert, his understanding of this genre being more instinctive than intellectual. Another of his best works, sensitive and refined, is *Aubade héroïque* for orchestra, inspired by his experience with the ballet company during the German invasion of the Netherlands.

LAMENTATIONS – the combined Offices of Matins and Lauds on the Thursday, Friday and Saturday of Holy Week are called *Tenebrae* ('darkness'); the extinction of fifteen candles, one after each psalm, leaves the final text to be said or sung in utter darkness, *in tenebris*; a very spiritual and dramatic effect can be created. In the first Nocturn of Matins on the above-mentioned days are sung portions of the Lamentations of Jeremiah, the third of the seventeen Prophetical Books of the Old Testament. From the fifteenth century to the present day there have been numerous settings of excerpts of these very beautiful, mournful verses, from Dufay and Josquin to Stravinsky and Krenek.

LA MER (The Sea) – three symphonic sketches, as Debussy described these pieces, completed in 1905. In whatever medium he might select, Debussy had the ability to transfer into sound the tactile quality of elements in nature – mist, moonlight, rain, the sun's heat – and this is magically expressed in highly original orchestration and imaginative treatment of motifs in the three movements of *La Mer*: 'The sea at daybreak', 'The play of the waves', 'The dialogue between the wind and the sea'.

LÄNDLER – an Austrian folk dance in slow time, three-beats-to-a-bar. It is an outdoor dance; the routine contains hopping and stamping, often involves clapping, and can include throwing the female over the male dancer's shoulder – not always an easy thing to do ... The word derives from the old Austrian name for the country's upper region. *Ländler* melodies show the influence of Alpine folksong, with their frequent arpeggio figures and the occasional appearance of yodelling. Several sets of Schubert's dances for piano are *Ländler* and the Austrian symphonists Haydn, Mozart, Bruckner and Mahler would sometimes have their minuet or scherzo movements in *Ländler* style; Weber, Beethoven and Brahms also used its rhythm. In the process of refinement, by the third decade of the nineteenth century the *Ländler* turned into the waltz.

LANDOWSKA, WANDA – a Polish keyboard player who was markedly responsible for the revival of harpsichord playing and research in the twentieth century. In 1900 she moved to Paris, where she began her research into seventeenth- and eighteenth-century keyboard practice. She gave her first public recital in 1903 and in 1909 Pleyel built her a large new two-manual harpsichord, according to her specifications. In Basle in 1919 she played harpsichord continuo in a performance of the Bach *St Matthew Passion* – the first time this was done this century. From 1925 to 1940 she ran a school for Early Music study near Paris, which she had to leave as the Germans approached the city; she had to abandon a library of some 10,000 volumes as well as her collection of instruments. At the age of seventy she recorded all of Bach's *Forty-Eight Preludes and Fugues*.

LARK QUARTET – an excellent example of Haydn's string-quartet writing, composed in 1790; it received its nickname from the high passage played by the first violin in the opening statement of the first movement.

LASSUS, ORLANDO DE – sixteenth-century Franco-Flemish composer; he and Palestrina became the most admired composers of their time. Apparently, as a boy Lassus had an outstanding treble voice and was soon singing in various churches and courts in Italy. Shortly after returning to the north, he accepted a post at the court of Duke Albrecht V of Bavaria in Munich, where he remained until his death. In addition to providing music for the ducal chapel, his duties included choir training, the supervision of manuscript copying, writing works for special sacred and secular events and directing performances. Apart from journeys to France and Italy, occasioned by the needs of the court, Lassus settled into a comfortable and stable routine at Munich. The correspondence between himself and Wilhelm V, successor to Albrecht V, shows him to be on companionable terms with his patron; letters were exchanged in a mixture of Latin, Italian, French and German.

Enormously prolific and versatile, Lassus turned out Masses, motets, passions and other liturgical music; madrigals, chansons and German *Lieder*, music exercises for his students. Like Palestrina, he was conservative, though fully aware of the latest goings-on in musical composition elsewhere. Two typical motets are the four-part *Exaltabo te Domine* and the six-part *Agibus tibi gratias*.

LAWES – an important name in English music of the first half of the seventeenth century. The two brothers, Henry, the elder, and William, the younger, link the last of the Tudor composers with Purcell. Henry concentrated on songs, of which he wrote over four hundred. He was appointed to the Chapel Royal, was a friend of Milton's and host to society, who attended musical parties at his home. He complained regularly about the over-abundance of foreign music in England. William was the more prolific and versatile and is considered the most important composer of dramatic music before Purcell. To this must be added a wide range of instrumental music, especially his consort suites of fantasias and dances; his 'Harpe' consorts are perhaps the earliest examples of chamber music to include a harp. William wrote the music for many court masques and entertainments. He was friendly with Charles I before he became king; later he fought with Charles against the Puritans and was killed in battle. If you desire to hear some music by the Lawes brothers try Henry's songs, such as *Amintor's welladay*, *Man's life is but vain*, *Sitting by the streams*, and William's consort music, for instance *Pavan of Alfonso*, *Consort Sett a 6* in D minor.

LEEDS – an important musical city in the UK. The first recorded public concert, held in the Assembly Room, was in 1726. The steady development of fine choral singing led, as in other northern towns, to the establishment of various societies to promote oratorios and madrigals. Some time after Paganini's visit in 1832 annual concert seasons took root. One special occasion was the opening of the town hall in 1858. Another was its lighting by electricity in 1880, celebrated by a concert with Sterndale Bennett conducting; on this occasion the triennial Leeds Music Festival was launched (from 1970 becoming biennial), at which Sullivan frequently conducted. The Festival's international reputation grew with the commissioning of works from composers including Dvořák, Massenet, Sullivan and Stanford; Elgar's *Caractacus* and Walton's *Belshazzar's Feast* both had their premières at the LMF. Leeds is now the home of Opera North and the triennial Leeds International Piano Competition, started in 1963. The university's Chair of Music is presently held by Julian Rushton, an authority on Berlioz.

Nearby is Harewood House, venue for many musical performances and seat of the Earl of Harewood, opera supremo extraordinaire.

LEHÁR, FRANZ – Austrian light opera composer and conductor of Hungarian origin. His first international hit was *Die lustige Witwe* (The Merry Widow) in 1905; at one stroke this restored the fading fortunes of operetta and confirmed Lehár as the leading twentieth-century composer of the genre, in the same league as the likes of Offenbach and Johann Strauss II a bit earlier. No mean achievement is the fact that his last work, *Giuditta*, was written for the Vienna Staatsoper, produced in 1934; a hundred and twenty radio companies relayed the first performance. The tenor Richard Tauber played an important part in promoting Lehár's later operettas and in their filming, with which the composer was much involved. During World War II Lehár was in the odd position of having a Jewish wife while *The Merry Widow* was one of Hitler's favourite bits of music. Today Lehár's villa at Bad Ischl is a museum devoted to his life and works. He wrote thirty-eight operettas, some containing the rhythms of pre-war social dancing such as the foxtrot, tango or shimmy. Lehár and Puccini were close friends. Some of his other operettas are *Vienna Wives, The Land of Smiles, The Count of Luxemburg*.

LEIPZIG – one of Europe's leading musical cities. What is interesting is that it has never been used as a residence for nobility or high church officials, and thus musical taste developed according to its middle-class inclinations. This is not to say that growth was confined to secular music; St Thomas's Church was for long the centre of the city's musical life. Before things were interrupted by the Thirty Years War (1618–48), composers such as Praetorius, Scheidt and Schütz had dedicated works to Leipzig's city council. Bach became Kantor and music director in 1723, but was soon disillusioned by having to deal constantly with the shortsightedness of the council members; yet his output of music there, especially of cantatas, was quite remarkable. A new Gewandhaus ('Cloth Hall') was built in 1781 and soon regular performances of works by Haydn and Mozart and later, Beethoven, were given in it. The great developer of the Gewandhaus's reputation, and hence of Leipzig's, was Mendelssohn, truly meriting a pat on the back: he conducted its orchestra for twelve years until his death; broadened its repertoire, raised the players' salaries and standard of performance (perhaps the one naturally followed the other!); gave the first revival performance of Bach's *St Matthew Passion* in 1841 and presented many premières. Three conductors, Arthur Nikisch, Furtwängler and Bruno Walter, maintained the city's adventurous reputation until Nazism choked things off – in 1936 the music of Mendelssohn was banned and his statue outside the Gewandhaus was destroyed. Aerial bombardment wiped out the now famous hall in 1943, although the orchestra is still going strong. To date Leipzig has not been able to recapture its former musical glory.

LEITMOTIF – a term which describes a clear-cut musical idea that undergoes transformation, mainly in the operas of Wagner, starting with his *Der fliegende Holländer* (The Flying Dutchman), and reaching its most complex operation in his *Ring* cycle. The demarcation between *Leitmotif* and instrumental or orchestral theme is that in the former the material is tied to what goes on on the stage, whether it be description, mood, character, conflict; whereas in the latter case the material undergoes change in purely abstract musical argument. Wagner could never have developed the *Leitmotif* concept without the models of Haydn's, Mozart's, Beethoven's and Schubert's orchestral, chamber and instrumental output – this despite Wagner's predecessor, Weber, having used the technique comparatively crudely in his operas *Der Freischütz* (The Free-Shooter) (1821) and *Euryanthe* (1823). Berlioz's *idée fixe* and Liszt's thematic metamorphosis may be considered allied techniques. A Wagnerian *Leitmotif* can have a range of alterations which are remarkable for their imagination and invention, and which often go undetected by the untutored ear.

LEONCAVALLO, RUGGIERO – Italian composer and librettist. To us he is known for one work – the opera *Pagliacci*; rather rum, but how many composers would not mind being famous for just one of their compositions and all the shekels that go with it? Leoncavallo gained a degree in literature from Bologna University; in the early part of his musical career he had to earn his bread as a café pianist. The idea of *Pagliacci* stems from his recollection of a case tried by his father, a magistrate, in which a middle-aged actor murdered his unfaithful young wife. The opera, in two acts, is often coupled with Mascagni's *Cavalleria rusticana* (*Cav* and *Pag*), and was given its first performance in Milan under Toscanini in 1892. Leoncavallo was one of the early composers to become seriously involved with gramophone recording; he wrote the words and music for the popular song *Mattinata*, which Caruso recorded in 1904, and in 1907 he conducted a recording of *Pagliacci*, the first complete opera recorded in Italy. Poor Leoncavallo wrote eleven other operas, none of which took off.

LIBRARIES – for the ordinary classical music lover most civic libraries can be pretty useful, and often they are not exploited as much as they deserve. If one is gradually building up a collection of CDs it may be that one is not sure whether a particular work will appeal, and so a final decision can be made after borrowing the item from the library. Then again, one may enjoy a pre-hearing of a work that is going to be performed at a live concert, on the radio or TV, or at the opera house. There is also the opportunity to browse through dictionaries, to take out books on particular subjects and, if one reads music, to borrow a score which, when it is followed with the music, can add a dimension to one's listening enjoyment. For the music scholar of today, libraries, of course, are an essential resource. The more expert and specialist the scholar the more necessary are those libraries which hold archival material. Libraries containing some form of musical information can be traced back to the eleventh century and earlier. Anyway, if you do not do so already, you could do yourself a favour by making more use of your local library – musically speaking.

LIBRETTO – the name (little book) given to a text especially written for a musical stage work. The text can be expressed in prose or in poetry; it can be highly stylised or in free form. It is likely to contain material for solo setting, for dialogue, for chorus, as well as material for action and description. A composer may choose material already existing and adapt it to his ends; or he may shape it in co-operation with the librettist. At one extreme, Wagner wrote his own librettos; at the other, Metastasio peddled his libretti to all and sundry, sometimes reselling the same one to half a dozen different composers, at the time (the eighteenth century) quite a normal thing to do. Some composers have had long and successful collaborations with librettists – Da Ponte and Mozart, Boito and Verdi, Scribe and Meyerbeer are examples.

LIED – the word is simply the German for 'song'; as a term in composition, however, the two most important areas it covers are, first, the German polyphonic *Lied* of the fifteenth and sixteenth centuries; secondly, the Austro-German nineteenth-century piece for voice and piano. The polyphonic *Lied* describes part-writing in Germany mainly in the fifteenth century, and could apply to purely instrumental pieces as well as vocal; in the sixteenth century the increasing influences of the French *chanson* and the Italian madrigal caused it to wither slowly away. The nineteenth-century *Lied* became a much more characterful and powerful element in music. It was Vienna-based, and a continuous tradition may be traced from before Schubert at the close of the eighteenth century to Schumann, Brahms, Wolf and Mahler, ending with Webern in the twentieth century. The quality of the texts ranges from the high poetry of Goethe and Heine to the verses of mere poetasters; weak material is often transformed into an exquisite musical jewel. This small-form genre covers an exceedingly wide range of human emotion, with, as one might expect, an accent on the subject of love. I don't know why, but many *Lied* fans are unattracted to opera and vice versa.

LIGETI, GYÖRGY – a Hungarian composer now resident in Germany. In his early years he undertook some research into East European folk music and he still reflects the distant influence of Bartók. His avant-garde inclinations caused Ligeti some difficulties with the communist régime, and after the 1956 uprising he left for Vienna. Today he is internationally recognised as one of the greatest of postwar composers. Ligeti possesses a remarkable composition technique; each work from his pen offers a new listening experience and, what is more, in contrast to his fellow avant-gardists he shows a sense of humour in his music. With Birtwistle he has taken opera writing a step beyond Britten's achievements. When his opera *Le grand Macabre* is revived again in London, try not to miss it. (By the way, in pronouncing his name put the accent on the first syllable.) He wrote settings of nursery rhymes on commission from the King's Singers. You might cut your teeth on Ligeti with the *Bagatelles* for wind quintet and *Hungarian Rock* for harpsichord.

LISTENING – it is only natural that an ordinary listener's first response is to the melodic line in a piece of music; the element of melos, melodic tissue, seems to be a fundamental requirement by the ear. Melody is not synonymous with simple, sentimental slush – Stravinsky's *The Rite of Spring* owes at least half its success to its melodic content and Bach's *Forty-Eight Preludes and Fugues* still attracts the ear, not because of all the foxy technique employed but because of the melos permeating each item. It is unfortunate that composers of importance in the period 1950 to 1980, approximately, practised a musical aesthetic in which the element of melody took a back seat.

The good news is that many younger composers are beginning to pay attention again to this aspect of music. Yet a lover of classical music has a responsibility to the composer to 'listen into the music', to hear what is going on under the melodic line – the interplay of parts, the orchestration, the composer's shaping of the music. This all requires more concentrated attention on the part of the listener. Repeated hearing of a work pays dividends; it is like digging into the ground to find gold. What is the woodwind doing in a Mahler symphony while the violins sing the melodic line? What is the left hand doing in a Chopin nocturne while the right hand arabesques all over the keyboard? By the way, if you were to ask me to define a good melody, I couldn't. Time alone proves the quality of a melody.

148

LISZT, FRANZ – Hungarian pianist and composer; a remarkable character and musician, certainly the finest of all nineteenth-century pianists
and perhaps the greatest pianist of all time. As a composer he could
write pop music – for example, his piano pieces *Quatre valses oubliées*
(Four Forgotten Waltzes), his piano transcription of themes from
Donizetti's opera *Lucia di Lammermoor* – or highly involved compositions such as his Sonata in B minor, one of the great piano works of the
nineteenth century. Liszt must have had an enormous supply of mental
and physical energy, to service his many recitals, always adding to his
repertoire; to produce literally hundreds of compositions; to teach; and
to have time for his busy socialising. He was outstandingly generous
with his time, money and influence, banging the drum for worthy
causes, assisting other composers, contributing funds to institutions. His
pianistic stardom brought him into contact with all the leading musicians, artists and writers of the time as well as a colourful parade of
European nobility. He had numerous mistresses, drawn from a rich variety of social levels, and it is said he was making love four days before he
died at the age of seventy-five. Liszt epitomised the romantic heroism of
the nineteenth century. In many ways his musical thinking was in
advance of Wagner's (his son-in-law in due course). His creative originality extended the potential of pianism – try his Piano Concerto
No. 2 – produced the symphonic poem, evolved the technique of the
transformation of themes, and expanded the world of harmony in terms
of tonality, chord progression and chromaticism. In sum, old Franz was
one helluva guy.

LIVERPOOL – as this northern city grew in importance as a trading port and its population turned more cosmopolitan, the demand swelled for the arts and entertainment, and its first music festival was given in 1766. The first concert hall, built twenty years later and seating 1400, cost £4526 6s 4d. The Liverpool Philharmonic Society was active by 1844, and was able to borrow musicians from nearby Manchester's Hallé Orchestra if it wanted to have a big musical do. The Philharmonic Hall opened in 1849; destroyed by fire in 1933, it was rebuilt in 1939. The prefix 'Royal' was granted to the Liverpool Philharmonic Orchestra in 1957. Of the many conductors who have directed it, the most important, from 1880, are Max Bruch, Charles Hallé, Henry Wood, Thomas Beecham, Malcolm Sargent, Hugo Rignold and Charles Grove. When Sargent became its resident conductor in 1942 the many recording contracts he secured raised the orchestra's reputation to its zenith. The Chair of Music at the university is held by Professor Michael Talbot, an authority on Albinoni and other eighteenth-century Italian composers.

LOCKE, MATTHEW – an important seventeenth-century English composer preceding Purcell, who was much influenced by his dramatic music and his chamber works. He was a somewhat vituperative character who, like Henry Lawes, constantly railed against the excess of foreign music and musicians. (Today he would unhesitatingly be voting with Parliament's Euro-sceptics!) He and his great friend Christopher Gibbons composed *Cupid and Death*, the only seventeenth-century English masque whose complete score is extant. Besides much incidental music, Locke's body of work includes some fine examples of pieces for strings – dance suites in the main, scored mostly for two violins or viols and continuo – and a volume of twenty-two pieces for harpsichord, *Melothesia*, which includes the first recorded instructions in English on the rules of realising a figured bass. On CD are *Musick for His Majesty's Cornetts and Sackbutts* and *Consort 'ffor seaverell ffriends'* made up of twelve suites of dance music for violins.

LUCIA DI LAMMERMOOR – Donizetti's opera in three acts, taken from Sir Walter Scott's novel *The Bride of Lammermoor*, first performed in Naples in 1835. It is one of Donizetti's best stage works and remains in the repertoire of most opera houses; the role of the soprano heroine is testing vocally and dramatically for any diva. A nice, juicy plot: Lucia is in love with her family's enemy, Edgardo; during his absence her brother forces her to marry another; at the wedding ceremony Edgardo unexpectedly returns and curses her for betraying him; Lucia goes berserk and stabs her bridegroom (famous Mad Scene); Edgardo kills

150

himself. We then all go home having satisfied our atavistic urges and our dramatico-musical desires.

LULLY, JEAN-BAPTISTE – Italian composer born in Florence, who became France's leading seventeenth-century composer; he was also a violinist and dancer. Lully's distinctive contribution is to the stage and his creation of the genre known as *tragédie en musique*. He was brought to France at fourteen to serve in a noble household, and while there he had the opportunity to hear a large selection of contemporary French music at balls, concerts and other social events. It is at these that Lully displayed his dancing abilities, which so impressed the fourteen-year-old king, Louis XIV, that he nabbed him for his own court. In 1653 king and composer danced in a ballet together, the first of many occasions. By 1662 Lully was Master of Music of the Royal Family. He proved to be a first-rate businessman, making various deals to the advantage of his musical interests; he set up a monopolistic Académie Royale de Musique and tried to suppress all opposition. As his wealth increased, so his character became less likeable. The manner of his death is somewhat bizarre: while conducting a church performance of his *Te Deum* Lully accidentally hit a toe with his stick; an abscess developed and gangrene spread rapidly, which left him beyond hope of recovery.

For all Lully's machinations and personal shortcomings, his immense contribution to French music should not be forgotten. There are three stages in the development of his theatre works: first, the *ballet de cour*, a courtly amateur entertainment made up of dances and choruses; each ballet had a team of one composer for the vocal music, one for the instrumental, a poet, a choreographer, a 'machinist' (sets, décor), a master of revels, and was produced by the royal or courtly patron. Secondly, the *comédie-ballet*, not as 'serious' as the *ballet de cour* with its mythological or allegorical subjects, concentrated on the comic, the satirical and on wit. Thirdly, the *tragédie lyrique* or *tragédie en musique*, which is essentially French *opera seria*; preceded by an overture, its five acts have continuous music and the plots are drawn from Greek mythology or from Italian and Spanish medieval romances. On CD are the overtures to the operas *Proserpine* and *Cadmus et Hermione* and there is a complete recording of *Alceste*. Personally I find Lully's music much less interesting than Purcell's, but you may think the opposite.

LUTE – a plucked string instrument that flourished in Europe from medieval times until the eighteenth century. With the revival of Early Music in the twentieth century there are today some very fine lutenists, and often it is played by professional guitarists such as Julian Bream. There are many types all over the world. The European lute has a vaulted body constructed of separate wooden ribs bent and glued together. The soundboard is flat with carved soundholes; attached is the neck with fingerboard, at the end of which is the pegbox, usually at a right angle to the neck and with tuning-pegs; the strings are laid in pairs called courses and the normal lute has five courses. Many paintings depict lutes, their players and accompanying singers. Masses of music was written for the lute as solo instrument, as song accompaniment, or as part of an ensemble. In England it could be considered to attain its apotheosis in the lute-pieces and lute songs of the Tudor composer John Dowland.

LUTOSLAWSKI, WITOLD – Polish composer, pianist and conductor. He emerged as a composer of international status only in the early 1960s, aged fifty. Since then his works have been regularly played in the chief concert halls of Europe and America; he often conducted live performances and recordings of his orchestral music. For a time the English composer John Casken studied with him in Warsaw. During the war, when Poland was under Nazi occupation, Lutoslawski earned a living as a café pianist. His musical language and style were at first influenced by Bartók. Listening to works by Cage coincided with a change of direction; this resulted in passages in later compositions which may be termed controlled improvisation – there are moments when each part is permitted to play and repeat a given phrase at its own tempo, to be stopped on the direction of the conductor. Lutoslawski reminds us of the rich output of music from East Europe in the twentieth century which should act as a necessary balance against the Austro-German tradition, from Stravinsky and Bartók, Shostakovich, Prokofiev and

Martinů, to Lutoslawski and Ligeti, to Pärt and Gorecki. Two very fine orchestral pieces by Lutoslawski are *Chain 3* and *Mi-parti*.

LUTYENS, ELISABETH – twentieth-century English composer and daughter of the architect Sir Edwin Lutyens. The influence of the Second Viennese School (Schoenberg, Webern and Berg) on her music caused her to suffer neglect until the mid-1960s, when the English music establishment became less outraged by non-tonal works. Her composition is always finely fashioned and terse, and ranges from opera to incidental music for film and radio; perhaps her most effective writing lies in her chamber music. From Dame Ethel Smyth on, England has steadily produced a growing number of female composers of marked talent – composition by women may already be found in the nunneries of the sixteenth century – and Lutyens could be considered the most senior of postwar female composers. Particularly attractive examples of her style are *Driving Out the Death* for oboe quartet and her group of choral pieces *Verses of Love*.

MACDOWELL, EDWARD – the best-known American composer before the twentieth century. He spent twelve years, 1876–88, studying and teaching in France and Germany, his most influential composition teacher being Raff, director of the Conservatoire at Frankfurt; at the same time he was active as a pianist. Liszt recognised MacDowell's talents and gave him much encouragement. On his return to the USA he settled in New York where, in 1896, he became the first Professor of Music at Columbia University. By this time his stature as composer, pianist and teacher was nationally recognised. Four years before his early death the first onset of mental illness appeared; from then on fate allowed him only periods of rationality. MacDowell's works are cast in a late Romantic vein, with evidence of much influence from European masters, especially Grieg. He did not possess the individuality and character of Charles Ives, which is not to say MacDowell's music is unappealing, as may be heard in his Piano Concerto No. 2 in D Minor Op. 23 or in his piano pieces *Woodland Sketches*, Op. 51.

MACHAUT, GUILLAUME DE – the most important composer of the fourteenth century; as was not uncommon in the period, he was also a poet. His achievement and reputation ensured that all his life he had

155

employment with the highest ranking members of the church and nobility. At first Machaut's composition concentrated on the Mass and motet; later, however, he moved into writing secular polyphonic song. Machaut's large output is representative of the Ars Nova style of the period, which stressed the use of duple time as opposed to the previous restriction of triple time. This is evidenced in his secular – virelais, ballades, rondeaux – as well as sacred pieces; isorhythm, too, is used frequently. Most of his output is for three parts, although he also wrote monodic songs. Machaut's music is characterised by imaginative and skilled polyphonic rhythmic ingenuity and catchy melodic line. Hear this for yourself in his ballade *Plourés dame*, his isorhythmic motet *Dame, je sui cilz* or the rondeau *Dix et sept cinc*. By the way, it is at this time that texts in at least two different languages (normally French and Latin), set in one piece, make an increasing appearance.

MACKERRAS, CHARLES – distinguished Australian conductor who was knighted in 1979. In his early days he was a fine oboist. He has made two very successful arrangements for ballet of music by Sullivan – *Pineapple Poll* and *The Lady and The Fool*. Mackerras's conducting career displays an enviable versatility, particularly in opera, from Gluck and Handel to Janáček and Shostakovich. For a number of years from 1977 he was chief guest conductor of the BBC Symphony Orchestra. At the same time Mackerras has shown consistent support for a large number of contemporary composers.

MACONCHY, ELIZABETH – English composer who has played an important part in the flowering of British composition in the twentieth century. Her younger daughter, Nicola LeFanu, is a prominent composer in her own right. Her *Piano Concertino* (1930) received its first performance while she was studying in Prague; since then Maconchy's output has ranged from opera to pieces for amateurs. In 1977 she was made a CBE. Her musical world may be heard at its clearest in her chamber music, especially her string quartets of which she has produced thirteen; here there is revealed a full and easy command of the medium, terse musical thought and a wide emotional range. Recommended is her String Quartet No. 6, a fine example of her music.

MADAME BUTTERFLY (*Madama Butterfly*) – a two-act opera by Puccini that rivals his *La Bohème* in popularity, first performed at La Scala, Milan, in 1904. The combination of a heart-tugging plot, highly memorable vocal melody and imaginative orchestration is a winner. What is it all about? An American Navy officer marries a Japanese geisha girl who, for love, forsakes her religion; the cad deserts her, leaving her with child; in due course he returns with his American wife to reclaim the offspring; thrown into dark despair, the girl kills herself.

MADERNA, BRUNO – the first avant-garde composer to emerge in postwar Italy. Among his pupils were Berio and Nono who, together with their master, initiated radical approaches to composition in the decades between 1950 and 1980. Maderna regularly lectured at Darmstadt, the mecca of avant-garde composers, and finally settled there. His works reveal a constant state of experimentation involving atonal techniques, free play on material by the performers, electro-acoustics and even physical perambulation by conductor and instrumentalists. Maderna was in no way concerned to please the traditional concert-goer; rather, his musical and intellectual gifts, which were undoubted, were directed at an élitist coterie. Time alone will test the efficacy of this genre of music in the concert hall; if it fails it will merely provide research material for musical theorists and musicologists. You can see what you think of Maderna's music from his *Aura* for orchestra.

MADRIGAL – a term which describes settings of secular verse to music. The madrigal has two periods: the fourteenth-century version is almost entirely for two parts, only sometimes for three; it is possible that in either instance the low part may have been written for an accompanying instrument. The madrigal of this period originated and flourished in northern Italy. A complete gap comes before its second flowering, from, approximately, 1520 to 1640, when it became the most popular form of secular composition throughout Europe, with the Italian composers leading, from Festa to Monteverdi; a poet whose verses were frequently set is the fourteenth-century Italian, Petrarch. The number of parts ranged from three upwards, but the most common were four- or five-part settings, sometimes with instrumental participation; the subject matter usually expressed the many nuances of love. Marenzio is perhaps the giant among the Italians. England produced some outstanding madrigal composers, amongst whom were Weelkes, Wilbye, Gibbons and Tomkins. It may be that you have had the pleasure yourself of singing madrigals and agree it is a particularly enjoyable bit of music-making.

MAHLER, GUSTAV – the most important Austrian composer at the close of the nineteenth century. His professional life, right from its beginning in minor posts to his international recognition and triumphs, was ceaselessly filled with stress, except for summer periods spent in the Austrian countryside; even then he was hardly relaxed, because he would be making up for lost time in his commitment to composition. Mahler basically earned a living from conducting opera. His approach was to become completely involved with a production; he would refuse to accept traditional procedures for well-established operas, reworking and rethinking the material according to his own very independent outlook. This brought him regularly into conflict with management, company and audience – on top of which his temperament was far from easy to accommodate. Yet he achieved new standards of opera performance, which were at first grudgingly and later enthusiastically recognised.

The question is, why did he not reduce his opera workload (once he conducted nineteen different operas in one month) to make more room for his creative writing? It does not seem to have been financial need alone. There must have been a deep-seated psychological motive behind such a situation, and the odd thing is that Mahler never wrote an opera himself (his effort at nineteen, the score of which is lost, can be dismissed). His record of composition rests chiefly in a narrow field of ten symphonies (the last of which was not completed) and a number of song-cycles or song-sets, usually with orchestral accompaniment, of which *Das Lied von der Erde* (The Song of the Earth) is justly the most famous. But this corpus of music creates a huge and special world of sound, magnificent in its conception, organisation and range of emotional expression. As a symphonist he has a leading position in the great Austro-German tradition; his extension of symphonic thinking includes the use of song, chorus, the breaking up of the large orchestra into chamber ensemble groups, the extension of the number of movements, the use of motifs common to two or more movements; and the music overflows with melody. You would do well, if you are not yet acquainted with them, to listen to his Symphony No. 4 and the above-mentioned *The Song of the Earth* for tenor, contralto and orchestra, a setting of seven Chinese poems translated into German.

MALIPIERO, GIAN FRANCESCO – Italian composer and musicologist, active mainly in the first half of the twentieth century. His achievement as a researcher is marked by his transcription of early Italian music, the editing (1926 to 1942) of Monteverdi's complete works and the editing of some works in the complete edition of Vivaldi's music; since he was largely self-trained as a musicologist, however, his research work has shortcomings, which have been corrected by later experts. Malipiero's compositions are likeable, if not particularly distinctive, as evidenced in the *Grottesco* for small orchestra or String Quartet No. 3 *Cantari alla Madrigalesca*.

MANCHESTER – in 1744 Manchester was still a small country town when public concerts first started; by 1777 a concert hall holding an audience of 1000 had been built and twelve concerts each winter season were presented. The German Charles Hallé established a permanent orchestra in 1858 and conducted the Hallé Concerts for the next thirty-seven years in the Free Trade Hall; their reputation attracted Hans Richter, who retained his post as conductor for twelve years from 1899. Hallé took the orchestra regularly to Liverpool, Bradford and Edinburgh; made sure a proportion of cheap seats was always available; educated the public's musical taste; and presented contemporary music of the time. Between Richter and John Barbirolli's twenty-seven-year stint with the Hallé Orchestra from 1943, important conductors included Hamilton Harty, Beecham, Sargent. The Free Trade Hall, destroyed in an air raid in 1942, was reconstructed in 1951, now with an audience capacity of 2500. To its credit the Hallé Orchestra has never ceased to promote contemporary music right up to the present. The Manchester College of Music, started by Hallé, now flourishes as the Royal Northern College of Music under the praiseworthy direction of Sir John Manduell, and the university has a strong music department, the Chair of Music currently held by Professor Ian Kemp, the noted authority on Tippett. Musicians who spent their student days in Manchester include the composers Rawsthorne, Birtwistle, Maxwell Davies, Goehr and McCabe, the pianist John Ogdon, the bassoonist Archie Camden and the singer Richard Lewis.

MANDOLIN – a small, plucked string instrument of the lute family; mainly used in Italian folk music, especially in the Naples area and the south, and in eighteenth-century opera. Its resonator is a deeply vaulted, pear-shaped body to which is attached a short neck with fretted fingerboard. The back of the body is made up of strips of wood glued together; the front has a large soundhole and is usually decorated with mother-of-pearl or exotic wood. The eight strings are arranged in double courses and tuned in fifths in the same pitches as the violin. The mandolin sound is strong and sonorous. Playing technique involves plucking with a plectrum rather than with the fingers as in the classical guitar, and a characteristic sound is the use of tremolando. In the twentieth century several composers have written mandolin pieces, but in the main it has been used to increase orchestral colour – Mahler in his Symphonies Nos. 7 and 8, Schoenberg in *Variations for Orchestra* Op. 31 and *Serenade* Op. 24, Stravinsky in his ballet *Agon*. Vivaldi wrote a concerto for mandolin.

MARCH – any music used for the purpose of keeping a body of people marching in step, whether a group of soldiers or a processional movement. March music should contain strong beats and simple, clear rhythmic patterns. Marches grew out of drumbeat signals employed by European armies with accompanying trumpet calls, as far back as the sixteenth century; by the eighteenth century military bands were adapting popular tunes and items from oratorio and opera, for marching purposes; instrumental colour was influenced by Janissary music – music of the élite corps of the Turkish army. In the nineteenth century classical composers were writing marches for opera or purely as orchestral and instrumental music – Schubert, Schumann, Berlioz, Wagner, Chopin, Mahler, for instance – and in the twentieth century too – Bartók, Stravinsky, Honegger. Two great specialists in march-writing are Sousa (*The Liberty Bell*) and Alford (*Colonel Bogey*). Marches have different tempos for different purposes and may be used for weddings, funerals, or sporting functions. Children and adults alike enjoy moving to snappy marches, though some, even soldiers, by their clumsy gait suggest they possess two left feet.

MARENZIO, LUCA – sixteenth-century Italian composer and singer, one of the greatest madrigal composers of the Renaissance; two examples in support of this claim: the five-part setting of Petrarch's *Crudele acerba inesorabil' morte* and the twelve-part *Qui di carne si sfama*. For most of his life he was employed by influential Italian cardinals; as an illustration of the freedom available to a musician of the time, Cardinal Luigi d'Este once proposed to give Marenzio as a gift to the King of France!

160

And, as often happened to his coevals not only in Italy but in France and England, Marenzio might have to wait months before receiving the agreed remuneration for his services, meanwhile being expected to live on his music manuscripts and fresh air. Though Marenzio was published widely, the only time he left Italy was to serve for a period at the Polish court; it is thought that the northern climate ruined his health, for he died shortly after his return to Rome.

MARTIN, FRANK – twentieth-century Swiss composer; his ancestors were French Huguenots who fled to Geneva in the eighteenth century, and his father was a Calvinist minister. After World War I he lived for a time in Zurich, Paris and Rome. On his return to Geneva he became associated with Emile Jaques-Dalcroze and his method of rhythmic musical education; he was also busy as a pianist and harpsichordist. Martin's music began to receive wider recognition from the early 1920s. At first, in addition to Bach, he was influenced by the early Romantics; later he was taken up with the music of Debussy and Ravel, and then with Indian and Bulgarian rhythms and with folk music in general. His best-known work, its fame thoroughly merited, is his two-movement *Petite symphonie concertante*, commissioned by the conductor Paul Sacher and written for double string orchestra with solo harp, harpsichord and piano.

MARTINI, PADRE GIOVANNI – eighteenth-century Italian writer on music, teacher and composer. His music does not, one may say, have the kick of a 'Martini cocktail', being produced in a pretty conservative mould; nevertheless his output was profuse: sacred and secular, symphony and sonata. At the age of fifteen he decided he wanted to be a monk and was sent to a Franciscan monastery, becoming ordained as a priest at twenty-five. Apart from odd visits to several other Italian cities, Martini spent his life in Bologna where he was born. His erudition was mixed with a fund of generosity, and his huge correspondence reveals substantial contact with popes and European rulers as well as with musicians – performers, historians and composers. It is estimated that more than a hundred pupils passed through his hands, among them J. C. Bach and Mozart.

MARTINŮ, BOHUSLAV – twentieth-century Czech composer. Although he showed early promise as a talented violinist, the urge to compose took complete hold of his ambitions by the age of twenty. After a spell as violinist in the Czech Philharmonic Orchestra he left for Paris in 1923, where he lived in acute poverty for the next seventeen years. In 1931 he married a dressmaker, Charlotte Quennehen, who took on much additional work in order to enable Martinů to keep composing. During the occupation of Paris by the Germans he was blacklisted by the Nazis and fled to the south of France, during which time he slept many nights on station platforms; finally he and his wife managed to leave Lisbon for America in 1941. Martinů never really settled down in the USA, even though he was appointed to the chair of composition at Princeton University. He returned to Europe, living first in Nice, then in Rome and finally in Switzerland. He never went back to Czechoslovakia. Throughout his life the flow of music from his pen was ceaseless: we still do not possess the full measure of his output. His musical language and style are vigorous and independent. Happily, there are many recordings of his works, including the Piano Concerto No. 3 and the *Nonet* for wind quintet, string trio and double bass.

MASCAGNI, PIETRO – Italian composer, known for his one short opera, *Cavalleria rusticana* (Rustic Chivalry), which he wrote at the age of twenty-five and which was first produced in Rome in 1890. Try as he might, none of his sixteen other operas had even modest success. Like Leoncavallo, he is a one-opera man; yet there are individual arias from these operas and several songs which merit greater exposure – Pavarotti has recorded his canzona *Serenata*. Regrettably, during the war he threw in his lot with the Fascist régime, one imagines more out of creative desperation than political sentiment. Shortly after hostilities ended Mascagni died of despair and disillusionment in a seedy hotel room in Rome.

MASQUE – a form of entertainment that developed in England during the sixteenth and seventeenth centuries. Its origin is to be found in the festivals, pageants and revels of the Renaissance in Italy and France. The masque would be created, mounted and played at courts, from the monarch's downwards. It was a theatrical presentation with an allegorical or mythical theme, in which the participants were usually the lords and ladies themselves, dressed in theatrical costume; they would be involved in parade, declamation, song and dance and be accompanied by a band of musicians. From Henry VIII's introduction of the first masque in 1512 it proved popular, until after the Reformation when it passed into theatre houses which the public would attend – for the price of a ticket, of course. The leading masque creators for most of the first half of the seventeenth century were the poet laureate, Ben Jonson, and the architect Inigo Jones. James Shirley's *The Triumph of Peace* (1634), the most elaborate of all masques, cost Charles I a mere £21,000; the financial equivalent today, one supposes, must be over £2 million. A masque is an elaborate affair; beginning, middle and end would involve sets of dances – almans, branles, pavans, galliards, corantos, voltas; in between would be declamations, dialogue and theatrical effects supported by scene changes and instrumental pieces. The duration of a masque could be as long as four or five hours. Undoubtedly the masque is a precursor of opera and theatre.

MASS – in musical terms the ritual of the Eucharist is of crucial importance in the Middle Ages and early Renaissance for the development of monophonic and polyphonic styles. In the fifteenth century the polyphonic Mass Ordinary became one of the seminal forms of European classical music. Two important secondary versions are the Requiem Mass (Mass for the Dead) and the Missa Brevis (Short Mass). The basic movements of the Mass Ordinary are Kyrie, Gloria, Credo, Sanctus, Benedictus and Agnus Dei. Music of great beauty is to be found in Masses written by Machaut, Dunstable, Josquin, Palestrina (who made over ninety settings), Victoria, Byrd, Carissimi, Bach, Haydn, Mozart, Beethoven, Bruckner, Vaughan Williams, Stravinsky. And this is a much abbreviated list. The Masses of the composers quoted above all reflect the musical language, style and aesthetic of their period – in case you may have the impression that music for this purpose has a retrogressive bias. Try Palestrina's six-part *Missa Assumpta est Maria* and Stravinsky's *Mass* for mixed chorus and double wind quintet.

MASSENET, JULES – nineteenth-century French composer. He won the Prix de Rome at the Paris Conservatoire and during the three statutory years in Rome he had an opportunity to become acquainted with Liszt. On his return to Paris he earned his first pennies from playing percussion in the Opéra, playing the piano in cafés and teaching. His first opera to be performed at the Opéra-Comique in 1867 was *La grand' tante*, and from then on he produced a steady stream of successes. Massenet became the most prolific opera composer of his generation in France. Of the thirty-six he wrote, perhaps *Thaïs*, *Werther* and *Manon* are the finest. Many of his operas, as may also be found in Richard Strauss and Puccini, explore the psychology of female sexuality. Massenet was no trail-blazer and was ever out to please his public, but, with Strauss and Puccini, he expressed through the opera house some fundamental aspects of western European middle-class preoccupations and aspirations.

MATHIAS, WILLIAM – twentieth-century Welsh composer, pianist and teacher. He studied composition with Lennox Berkeley at the Royal Academy of Music and in 1969 was appointed professor of music at Bangor. Mathias is one of the most technically able and fluent composers Wales has ever produced. His early works show the influence of Berkeley, Bartók and Vaughan Williams, while later works are reminiscent of Walton, Tippett and Stravinsky. His mature writing, which concentrates on symphony, concerto and chamber music, reveals an independent voice rich in orchestration and melodic line, to be heard in his Symphony No. 2 *Summer Night*, Op. 90, and the suite for brass band *Vivat Regina*, Op. 75.

MAW, NICHOLAS – twentieth-century English composer who studied with Lennox Berkeley and Paul Steinitz at the Royal Academy and later in Paris with Nadia Boulanger. A turning point in his creative output was the BBC Proms commission of 1962, *Scenes and Arias*, which explores an individual mixture of serial technique and tonality. Confidence and clear direction are apparent in his appealing *Life Studies*, eight movements for fifteen solo strings, and the orchestral piece *Odyssey*.

MAXWELL DAVIES, PETER – see *Davies, Peter Maxwell*.

MAZURKA – a Polish country dance originating in an area near Warsaw where the folk were called Mazurs; there are variations, but all are in triple time with either the second or third beats accented. The dance is performed by groups of four, eight or twelve couples. In early mazurkas the accompaniment was provided by a bagpipe known as the *duda*. Chopin wrote some fifty mazurkas, extending the original characteristics into piano art pieces; this genre in his output contains some of his most daring harmonic progressions. Glinka, Borodin and Tchaikovsky wrote mazurkas. For range of mood possible, compare Chopin's Mazurkas in B flat, Op. 7 No. 1 (joyful) and A minor, Op. 68 No. 4 (sad).

MEISTERSINGER VON NÜRNBERG, DIE (The Mastersingers of Nuremberg) – the only one of Wagner's operas to be cheerful and lighthearted, first performed at Munich in 1868. The plot: a young nobleman is ambitious to enter the Mastersingers' singing contest in order to win the hand of a beautiful maiden, whose father has promised her to the winner; the nobleman is ignorant of the rules of the contest, but with the help of a wise and good-hearted cobbler he triumphs over the nitpickers; his prize song receives the acclaim of judges and populace and the maiden is more than happy to become his bride. The overture is a *tour de force* of technical construction showing pliability in the orchestration and summarising the leading motifs that will appear in the course of the opera; at one moment in the score Wagner has five of the motifs sounding together in ingenious counterpoint.

MELISMA – this term comes from the Greek for 'song' and applies to any group of five or more notes sung to a single syllable. Melisma is found in musics all over the world and can extend to twenty or thirty notes. It is not suited to some vocal styles, such as the German *Lied*, where it rarely appears; Handel, on the other hand, could never have constructed his wonderful oratorio vocal fugues without the use of melisma. Some writers believe that melismatic utterance goes back to prehistoric man, who may have expressed one intense emotion or another in this manner; there can be, indeed, something profoundly moving when a voice sings a melody on one syllable, such as is found in Gregorian chant. An extreme example is Pérotin's *Viderunt Omnes*, where the 'Vi-' syllable goes on for what seems like minutes.

MELLERS, WILFRID – English composer and musicologist. In 1964 he was appointed to the Chair of Music at York University in order to launch a music department which has become one of the half-dozen most distinguished in Britain. But, more importantly, in his seventeen years there he revolutionised undergraduate music studies, and his tenets were followed in varying degrees by all other university music departments, including Oxford and Cambridge. Simply put, he abolished the compartmentalising of musical subjects and instead made the student carry out personal investigation, under tutorial guidance, into a chosen subject involving all aspects of the nature of music. At the same time he pursued his composition, the language and style of which may be seen to best advantage in, for example, his 1969 Proms commission *Yeibichai* for soprano, scat singer, choir, jazz trio, orchestra and tapes or *Threnody* for eleven instruments. Since the 1930s Mellers has published numerous articles and books, the subjects of which range from Couperin to Vaughan Williams to the Beatles to *Beethoven and the Voice of God*.

MÉLODIE – from the eighteenth-century French *romance* and the German *Lied* emerged a nineteenth-century genre of French song described as *mélodie*; it is a setting of a text usually with piano accompaniment, sometimes with chamber ensemble or orchestra. Berlioz is the first important composer to write this type of song, his most telling example being the set of six songs for mezzo-soprano or tenor and orchestra, *Les nuits d'été* (Summer Nights), 1841. After Berlioz, Gounod established models later followed by Massenet, Delibes, Bizet, Saint-Saëns, Lalo, to mention but a few. By far the most effective writer of *mélodies* was Duparc, whose reputation rests on no more than thirteen songs; these characterful vocal pieces reveal very positive piano accompaniment and enhanced harmonic invention. *Mélodie*-writing continued well after the *Lied* with Debussy, Ravel, Satie, Les Six, Françaix, even as late as Messiaen.

MELODY – worth a remark or two, since of all the elements that may comprise a piece of music melody and rhythm are the most fundamental. Melody could be defined as a succession of notes which, to the ear, seem to belong to each other and which have a logical progression differentiating them from mere, unformed noise. It is not quite synonymous with tune, as tune is implicitly simpler and more restricted in its linear ambition. Melody is to be found in all musics of the world and its character is determined by the culture in which it is created. There is a particular five-note (pentatonic) scale common to Zulu, Hungarian and Chinese music which has produced hundreds of melodies; yet the melodic family characteristic of each cultural group is demonstrably very different from the other two. Quite fascinating. Whether a melody is good or bad is entirely a subjective judgement.

MENDELSSOHN, FELIX – one of the finest composers of the first half of the nineteenth century, born in Hamburg. Though he wrote attractive music of great quality, his musical language and style hardly developed beyond its level at about the age of eighteen. His earliest surviving manuscript is a piano piece entitled *Recitativo* which he composed at the age of eleven; the musical calligraphy is that of a mature adult. Mendelssohn came from a cultured Jewish family that had converted to Christianity. In his adolescence he was fortunate enough to strike up a friendship in Weimar with Goethe, who taught him about art and German literature; in turn Mendelssohn increased Goethe's understanding of Haydn and Mozart but failed to convert him to an appreciation of the music of Beethoven.

From 1825 the Mendelssohn home in Berlin became the most active cultural salon in that city. Mendelssohn's heroes were Bach, Mozart and Haydn, whose works influenced his own composition despite his natural leanings towards Romanticism. In 1829 he mounted and conducted the first performance of Bach's *St Matthew Passion* since the composer's death; the effect of this was to revive an abiding interest in Bach's music. At eighteen he wrote his most popular piece, the overture to Shakespeare's *A Midsummer Night's Dream*. In 1829 he made his first journey to Britain and on a trip to Scotland paid a visit to Sir Walter Scott.

Mendelssohn was extremely active as a conductor, and his musical direction at the Gewandhaus in Leipzig was one of the high points in his career. On his later London visits he had regular audience with Queen Victoria, to whom he dedicated the *Scottish Symphony* (Symphony No. 3, 1842); in all he visited Britain ten times. Two out of many works worth getting to know are his oratorio *Elijah* and his Violin Concerto.

MENOTTI, GIAN CARLO – twentieth-century American composer of Italian birth. Menotti is essentially a composer of opera, having written twenty-two, of which *The Consul* is considered his masterpiece: it has been translated into twelve languages and performed in over twenty countries. *Amahl and the Night Visitors*, commissioned by the NBC, is the first opera written especially for television. Menotti has written the librettos of most of his operas. *The Medium*, a tragedy in two acts for five singers, dance-mime and chamber ensemble (1948), ran for 211 performances on Broadway – not bad for a twentieth-century opera. Apart from the dramatic or comic attributes to be found in his stage works, Menotti's musical language and style are comparatively traditional and therefore more readily approachable. In 1958, Menotti launched the annual summer Festival of Two Worlds at Spoleto, Italy, which has become quite a prestigious event.

MENUHIN, YEHUDI – a world-class violinist, humanist and musical ambassador, born in New York and settled in England since 1959. He made a sensational début in Paris at the age of eleven; a few months later in New York he achieved international celebrity status with his performance of the Beethoven Violin Concerto. At the age of sixteen, in 1932, he recorded Elgar's Violin Concerto with the composer, then aged seventy-five, conducting. Menuhin has always taken a great interest in other musics, collaborating in performances of Indian music with Ravi Shankar and recording jazz duets with Stéphane Grappelli. During World War II he gave more than five hundred concerts for Allied troops. He became a conductor of international status and started a boarding school for musically gifted children.

Menuhin has commissioned or given first performances of numerous works by contemporary composers. Bartók wrote for him the Violin Sonata, the greatest piece for solo violin since Bach. Among his many awards is a knighthood. In every way Menuhin is a rare, noble member of the human race.

MESSIAEN, OLIVIER – twentieth-century French composer of great originality and a virtuoso organist. His father was a scholar of English who translated the complete works of Shakespeare; his mother was a poetess of some distinction. At the age of twenty-two he became the principal organist at La Trinité in Paris, a position he held for more than forty years. With Jolivet, Lesur and Baudrier he founded a mutual self-help group in 1936 called *La Jeune France*; its development was interrupted by the outbreak of war. Messiaen was taken prisoner in 1940 and while captive in a Silesian camp he composed his *Quatuor pour la fin du temps* (Quartet for the End of Time) for clarinet, piano, violin and cello, performed in 1941 before 5,000 prisoners. Apart from Schoenberg he has exercised the greatest influence on postwar composers. The essential characteristics of his musical style are: non-European devices, especially as regards rhythm and scale; the Catholic liturgy; reiteration of short, clear motifs; the transliteration of birdsong. Messiaen's knowledge of bird-calls worldwide was at the level of a professional ornithologist's. If one is able to acclimatise one's ear, so to speak, there is listening pleasure to be gained from works such as *Oiseaux exotiques* (Exotic birds) for piano, eleven wind instruments, tuned and untuned percussion; and *Des canyons aux étoiles* (From the canyons to the stars) for piano, horn and orchestra.

MEYERBEER, GIACOMO – German composer who became the leading figure in French opera from about the second half of the nineteenth century. Although he began to compose stage works pretty early on, his reputation was mainly as a piano virtuoso. He established himself as an opera composer during a nine-year stay in Italy. With the first performance in Paris of *Robert le diable* (Robert the Devil) in 1831, he achieved eminence in one fell swoop as Europe's leading opera composer. Thereafter he wrote sixteen more operas, of which *Les Huguenots*, *Le prophète* and *L'africaine* were most successful; he died during the final rehearsals of the last-named. Because of his desire to supervise productions of his stage works all over Europe he never fully settled in Paris, the centre of his triumphs, but preferred to hire hotel suites or private lodgings rather than buy a house. With each opera Meyerbeer would have specific singers in mind; if one dropped out for any reason, he would rewrite that singer's part to suit the replacement. Wagner was an early admirer of Meyerbeer, through whose help the productions of *Rienzi* and *The Flying Dutchman* were advanced. Meyerbeer knew how to use his skills and imagination, his singers, librettists and staging, to win unheard-of popularity with audiences – much like Andrew Lloyd Webber today.

MEZZO-SOPRANO – this describes a female voice pitched between the higher soprano and the lower contralto; its registration balances in colour that of the two other female timbres. The mezzo-soprano is more athletic in fast passages than the contralto but less so than the soprano. Mezzo-soprano roles in opera include Azucena in Verdi's *Il Trovatore*, Flora Bervoix in his *La Traviata*, Mignon in Ambroise Thomas's opera of that name, Frasquita and Mercédès in Bizet's *Carmen*, Octavian in Strauss's *Der Rosenkavalier* and Clytemnestra in his *Elektra*, Larina in Tchaikovsky's *Eugene Onegin*, Fricka in Wagner's *Die Walküre* and Delilah in Saint-Saëns's *Samson et Dalila*. Some meaty roles such as Carmen herself or Rosina in Rossini's *The Barber of Seville* can be taken by either a mezzo or a soprano, more usually the former. The voice type lends itself to 'trouser' roles like Prince Orlofsky in Johann Strauss's *Die Fledermaus*. Often secondary soprano roles are really meant for the mezzo-soprano voice. Writing for it is not as rare as you may at first think.

MILHAUD, DARIUS – prolific and versatile twentieth-century French composer. Already before World War I he had developed the habit of regular travel, which did not stop when he was confined to a wheel-chair with rheumatoid arthritis. More than any other composer he developed and refined the technique of polytonality (writing a piece using more than one key simultaneously); he was also much influenced by jazz and folk music, and was a member of Les Six in the 1920s. This was due to the common ground shared with the other five composers (Poulenc, Auric, Honegger, Durey and Tailleferre) in their reaction to nineteenth-century Romanticism and its aesthetic rather than to common compositional methods. His final work reached Op. 441, his output covering all aspects of composition from opera and symphony to music for the amateur and the classroom; in Milhaud's case, as opposed to the creative fecundity of Bach, Mozart or Schubert, there is much material that is slight and given to note-spinning despite impressive technical competence. But such works as his ballet music *L'homme et son désir* (Man and his Desire) and *La création du monde* (The Creation of the World) or his Violin Concerto No. 2 are full of finely fashioned melodic and rhythmic material, with imaginative orchestration.

MINUET – originally an elegant dance originating in France in the mid-seventeenth century; three-beats-to-the-bar, it became extremely popular until about 1800. The minuet's dance steps were quick and small, and produced cross-rhythm movements to the beats of the music; the form was binary (in two sections) and the music would begin on the first, strong beat. Its character changed when it became purely instrumental in the first half of the eighteenth century; Mozart and Haydn later developed still more sophisticated versions for their sonatas and symphonies, adding a second minuet, called a *trio*, immediately after the first. Louis XIV, who was himself a raving minuet dancer, would not have approved. The minuet with trio was the only Baroque dance form that did not become obsolete in the Classical period. Becoming faster and showing more fervour, it mutated into the scherzo, a title used most prominently by Beethoven; one may measure how far it had travelled by comparing the two minuets in Bach's Suite No. 1 for cello with the second-movement scherzo in Beethoven's Symphony No. 9.

MODULATION – any music of the eighteenth and nineteenth centuries that you listen to contains modulation, so you'd better know what it means; you are likely to come across the term when reading programme notes at concerts. It's quite simple for you as a listener, if not for the student or composer. Any piece from those two centuries is written in a key – a set of pitches chosen by the composer which he uses in order of importance; were the entire piece to remain in one key it is likely you would get a feeling of flatness in the music. The composer changes key or modulates by moving his set of pitches up or down; this adds interest to the music, believe me, and is as necessary as other elements such as melody, rhythm, counterpoint and orchestration. In Bach's time modulation was a comparatively simple process, effective however; by the time we get to Wagner and Skryabin it has become so subtle and sophisticated it is almost anarchic. Thereafter modulation either returns to a crude simplicity or is thrown to the winds. See also *Key*.

MOERAN, ERNEST JOHN (E. J.) – a twentieth-century English composer of Anglo-Irish descent, a contemporary of Vaughan Williams, Delius, Bax and Holst. It is said that Moeran had a bush-tracker's knowledge of the pubs of Soho and could lead a company of fellow-musicians with unerring accuracy to any named watering-hole in the area in the densest fog. The earliest influences on his style and language came from the music of Delius and Ireland, while his melodic line emerged from his intimate knowledge of the folk music of East Anglia, where he grew up. Moeran's best works are among his chamber music and compositions for small orchestra – the *Fantasy-Quartet* for oboe, violin, viola and cello and the orchestral piece *Lonely Waters*, both of which contain music of attractive sensitivity and nuance.

MONTEVERDI, CLAUDIO – Italian composer, his reputation already established by 1600 at the age of thirty-three. What confirms him as the greatest composer of his time, and a musical force essential to a consideration of the development of European classical music, is his output of madrigals, of which he wrote some two hundred and fifty, and the dramatic and musical worth of his operas. Monteverdi was born in Cremona and spent his professional life in the Italian cities of Mantua and Venice. He accompanied the Mantuan Duke Vincenzo I on two trips outside Italy, the first to Austria and Hungary in connection with the campaign against the Turks, the second to Flanders, where the Duke went for a cure at Spa. He was appointed *maestro di cappella* of St Mark's, Venice, in 1612. A droll incident: on his return journey to Cremona from Venice, after his interview for the above post, he was robbed by highwaymen. Like Bach in the eighteenth century and Stravinsky in the twentieth, Monteverdi had the knack of melding the traditional with the contemporary. This may be clearly noted in the corpus of his madrigals, which combine established procedures with new forms, and show increased harmonic dissonance and an extension of emotional expression, created by him and known as the *stile concitato*. In the genre of opera, then in its infancy, through works such as *L'Orfeo*, *Il ritorno d'Ulisse* (The Return of Ulysses) and *L'incoronazione di Poppea* (The Coronation of Poppea) he laid the foundations for operatic development in the latter half of the seventeenth century. In both instances, madrigal and opera, he reflected the rich range of human psychology and feeling, hitherto a rare element in musical composition. On CD are to be found the above listed operas and his eight books of madrigals. A source of much listening pleasure awaits you.

MORLEY, THOMAS – English composer, editor and theorist. His *A Plaine and Easie Introduction to Practicall Musicke* (1597) is one of the most important musical treatises in the English language; very readable, it gives us a reliable insight into English musical thought and composition of the time. Morley was canny enough to secure a good income through publishing rights. His final publication, *The Triumphes of Oriana*, was a collection of madrigals from nearly two dozen fellow composers written in honour of Queen Elizabeth I, and included two of his own efforts. He was largely responsible for introducing the Italian influence to this area of English music. Although he wrote sacred music-services, anthems, psalms and motets, as well as solo songs and instrumental works, his best pieces are his madrigals, especially the lighter variety known as canzonets, in settings ranging from two to six parts: try his five-part madrigals *Now is the month of Maying* and *My bonny lass she smileth*. There is nothing to prevent you from relishing the pleasure of singing a two-part Morley canzonet. Simply invite a friend or member of the family to join you, and if neither can read music find someone who can plonk out each part on the piano and learn the brief piece by ear; a performance at any party will guarantee you sustained applause.

MOSES UND ARON (Moses and Aaron) – an opera in three acts by Schoenberg, who wrote his own libretto; only the first two acts were finished, but they are dramatically and musically complete in themselves. The musical forces are huge, involving a large choral cast and orchestra. The setting is Egypt and Mount Sinai in Biblical times. God, speaking from the burning bush, assigns Moses the role of prophet, but Moses lacks the eloquence to state God's words and his brother Aaron is made the mouthpiece (Moses is a speaking part, Aaron a lyric tenor). The main message is that God requires no sacrifice from the people but only devotion; the demoralised Israelites greet this message with derision, which Aaron quells by performing three miracles; after praying on the mountain Moses returns to find the people worshipping the golden calf, which he destroys, but the people then follow a second image, the pillar of fire, and Moses is left in despair.

MOTET – for five hundred years, from the mid-thirteenth to the mid-eighteenth century, the motet was one of the leading forms of polyphonic music, mainly for unaccompanied voices; as time went on instrumental participation increased. It reached its apotheosis in the works of Josquin and his successors. It was not until the fifteenth century that the leading voice gradually moved from the lowest to the highest part of the polyphony; later, increasing attention was given to tonal painting of the text. By 1650 the motet was on the decline and we find that even Bach's huge output contains only six motets. In the nineteenth century a dribble of motets came from Gounod, Saint-Saëns, Franck, Bruckner. From its Franco-Netherlandish base it spread to Italy, Spain, Germany and England in the early sixteenth century. Its peak period offers some of the most beautiful vocal polyphonic works of all time. Here is a selection: *Planxit autem David* (Josquin), *Assumpta est Maria* (Palestrina), *O magnum misterium* (Byrd), *Ave Maria, gratia plena* (Victoria), *Quo nate Dei* (Schütz).

MOTHER GOOSE SUITE (*Ma mère l'oye*) – a composition by Ravel in two versions, of which the second is better known; it is a suite depicting fairytale characters. It was first written for piano four-hands, then Ravel orchestrated it (adding movements and interludes) as a children's ballet. The music is full of delicacy and charm, overflowing with melody, and the instrumentation and orchestration underline Ravel's remarkable talent in this area of composition.

MOZART, LEOPOLD – composer, violinist, theorist and father of the one and only Wolfgang Amadeus. By 1763 he had gained the position of deputy Kapellmeister at the Salzburg court. In 1747 he married, but of his seven children only two survived to adulthood – Wolfgang and his sister Maria Anna. In 1756 Leopold published the most important of his writings on music, *Versuch einer gründlichen Violinschule* (The Foundation of Violin Practice), which brought him fame in European musical circles. But in 1760 he gave up his violin teaching and composition in order to devote himself, outside his court duties, to the education of his two children. The genius of his son changed Leopold's life; he felt the phenomenon to be a holy mystery and considered it his divinely ordained task to foster it. He undertook numerous artistic and educational journeys, often at great financial risk, accompanied either by the entire family or by his son alone. It may be said that Leopold gave up his own life to his son's advancement; his high intelligence, musical insight and administrative efficiency were all marshalled to the interests of the boy. The latter part of his life turned to sadness, as their intimate relationship deteriorated. Wolfgang never seemed to obtain secure posts appropriate to his gifts and his association with Constanze Weber was a worry. Leopold died, dejected, four years before Wolfgang's own death. And so he did not witness the horrid financial straits Wolfgang had to face in his last days.

MOZART, WOLFGANG AMADEUS – more so than Haydn, his senior by twenty-four years, and Beethoven, his junior by fifteen years, Mozart excelled in every musical medium current in his time; scholars claim him to be the most universal composer in the history of Western classical music. Child prodigies are not that rare, but there is none that stands comparison with Mozart: he learnt pieces from his sister's piano book at four, composed at the age of five, with his father and sister was giving public concerts aged six, started to play the violin without being taught at seven, and first published pieces when he was eight. The period between 1763 and 1766, with Mozart continuously composing, was spent in concert-giving, starting from and returning to Salzburg, taking in numerous venues in Germany, France and the Netherlands and including a fifteen-month stay in London. During this time he suffered two serious spells of illness – possibly these taxing journeys were a contributory factor. By the age of ten Mozart had become a seasoned professional performer. Under his father's tutelage he learnt arithmetic, Latin, Italian and some French and English; otherwise he had no formal schooling. Further travels took place and by 1772 he had visited Italy three times.

From the age of twenty-one Mozart commenced making professional journeys without his father; his chit-chat, light-hearted letters home, some proposed madcap schemes and his misuse of money greatly perturbed his father, whose replies were filled with advice, pleadings for caution and warnings against misspent time. His relationships with his mother and his sister, nicknamed 'Nannerl', continued to be reasonably smooth. Mozart had been having quite a long relationship with Constanze Weber, much to the displeasure of his father, and he finally married her in 1782 at the age of twenty-six. His professional life was constantly hectic and pressurised, full of ups and downs, despite his fame, and now there was the added weight of domesticity, largely because Constanze's lack of sophistication contributed little to his musical interests rather than because of shortcomings in her character. Of their six children only two survived. Regrettably, from now on the Mozarts suffered a steady financial decline until his much too early death at the age of thirty-five. His burial in a mass grave was customary at the time for the ordinary folk of Vienna, but Mozart was not 'ordinary folk'.

The psychology and wide emotional range of Mozart may be traced in his twenty-seven piano concertos, for example No. 17 in G, K453, and No. 27 in B flat, K595. His inventiveness can be simply tested by examining the expositions of his mature piano sonatas' first movements, each one different from the next though following the established format. His symphonies range in emotional content from the joyous to the deeply painful. His operas, chiefly *Don Giovanni*, *Così fan tutte* (All Women so Do), *Die Entführung aus dem Serail* (The Abduction from the Harem), *Le nozze di Figaro* (The Marriage of Figaro) and *Die Zauberflöte* (The Magic Flute) have been longer in the repertoire than those of any opera composer. The music referred to here is but a small section of his output; from the age of twenty-one, when ill-health steadily dogged him, Mozart turned out some twenty-seven compositions each year. In terms of his life and character Mozart remains a phenomenon beyond rational explanation.

MUSGRAVE, THEA – twentieth-century Scottish composer, another in the steady stream of highly talented women composers which Britain seems to be producing, pro rata, more than any other country. Is it perhaps that women in general are more equal here than elsewhere? Musgrave's attractive, relaxed social persona belies the force and thrust of her music; every piece she produces is finely fashioned and purposeful. Her creative achievement is proved in that Musgrave now has her hands full writing only to commission, not a few of which have come from the BBC. Her output stretches from full-length opera to music for children, thus contributing to the tradition of serious writing for amateur forces begun by Vaughan Williams and still continuing, a tradition which leading composers of many other countries, unhealthily for music, have chosen to ignore. You may hear the Musgrave sound in her orchestral work *Song of the Enchanter* or, in contrast, *Rorate coeli* for chorus.

MUSIC DEALING – here is a nice little account of a subject that hitherto may never have entered your head, namely, the publication and sale of sheet music and musical scores. The publishing of music kicked off at the beginning of the sixteenth century. Only music of the day was published, right up to about 1830; at that date you could not pop into a music shop and order a vocal score of Handel's *Messiah* or a Mozart piano sonata, but you could certainly buy a copy of a Schubert song or a Chopin waltz. But reprints of popular pieces or new ones by established composers were issued almost as soon as music publishing began. The publishing/printing house also served as distributor and music shop. In order to increase turnover the publisher sought export orders, and, just as today, these were obtained at international book fairs, which were already flourishing in the sixteenth century, the best being at Lyons, Frankfurt and Leipzig. The publisher-dealer's shop of the seventeenth century now also offered items from other publishing houses; two notable trade ties were Frankfurt/Leipzig and London/Amsterdam. Antiquarian music dealing burgeoned only in the nineteenth century, with the rise in the study of the 'science of music'. The development and refinement of musical scholarship and research from the close of the nineteenth century right up to the present has produced some very profitable music publisher/dealer/antiquarian concerns. The welcome growth of university music departments, the expansion of the musical holdings of libraries and the increase in the number of listeners that can read music have together created a market the size of which must fill the Italian Petrucci, the first great printer/publisher, with the utmost envy as he looks down on his twentieth-century offspring.

MUSICOLOGY – not an easy term to define. Certainly it has to do with musical scholarship; that is to say, it does not include in its remit the active functions of composing and performing; rather it studies, assesses and comments on composition and performance – of all periods, including our own. This is a complicated enough task in itself; but as research digs deeper and wider, so more factors enter the musicologist's orbit. He has to consider the life and character of a composer – if this is his subject; the aesthetics in force at the time; performance venues; the history of the musical forms employed; the social and political events of the time; the connection with the other arts such as dance, drama, film and, in our time, recording and television; as well as the influence from non-European musics. The good musicologist not only has to exercise the sharpest part of his intellect but offer a large slice of imagination; he requires the patience of a sleuth and an obsession with detail. The musicologist's world is so vast now that there is no longer a place for the eighteenth-century all-rounder. Specialism is perforce required – in nineteenth-century Italian opera, for instance, one expert may concentrate on Donizetti, while another covers the gamut of the subject; the two are interlocking and both are necessary. Musicology deserves three cheers from the ordinary listener, since indirectly its discoveries have percolated down to composers and performers; to programme notes and record-sleeve write-ups; and have caused recordings to be made of pieces we would otherwise not have had the pleasure of hearing.

MUSIC THERAPY – I have yet to come across a person who does not like *some* kind of music or other. Our response can be purely physical – we tap the foot, march, nod the head or sway the body – or deeply emotional, even spiritual; here, even if a flow of thought ensues, a physical reaction also takes place – the pulse quickens or slows down. A theory has been put forward that, heaven forbid, Beethoven is greater than Shakespeare, because he communicates more deeply than the word, beyond the word, as it were. Be that as it may, there is something inexplicably profound about music; this has been recognised in the Old Testament, and in most cultures since. And at the same time this recognition has accorded it healing powers. It is certain that music can have a therapeutic role. Currently, however, there does not seem to be any sure theory on how it works with regard to either physical or mental ill-health; but there is ample evidence of its beneficial effects. Children seem to respond more than adults, manic depressives more than schizophrenics and women more than men.

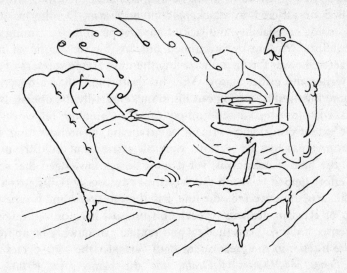

Of all the elements of music, rhythm is seen as the vital therapeutic factor: it has the power to focus energy, to bring structure into the perception of temporal order. Music can stimulate the withdrawn patient into a more alert response, both cognitive and social, to his environment. In emotional illness it can make the patient more accessible, and for physical disability it can be used to organise the acquiring of muscular skill and control. Making music helps patients to gain the confidence required to deal with speech disabilities; in both individual and group therapy, healing and recuperation is advanced through the use of singing, dancing, clapping and percussion games. Music therapy has played an important part in helping with disorders such as brain damage, autism, cerebral palsy, muscular dystrophy and spasticity. In sum, however, it is far from reaching its potential, because the funds for research and training are lacking, and it is still generally considered of minor importance in mental and physical health care.

MUSORGSKY, MODEST – nineteenth-century Russian composer whose greatest achievement lies in his operas and songs. At the end of a highly unstable life he left a pile of unfinished compositions; yet his music shows him to be the most individual of his contemporaries, who include Tchaikovsky and Musorgsky's fellow members of The Five (Balakirev, Borodin, Cui and Rimsky-Korsakov). The emancipation of the serfs put the Musorgsky family in financial difficulties and he had to spend two years helping his brother run the family estate; with little material improvement achieved, he was forced to enter the civil service.

He had already started to drink heavily, and after the loss of his mother in 1865 he suffered an attack of *delirium tremens*. Despite his difficult personality, unreliability and lack of application in the sustaining of creative effort, Musorgsky hiccupped out, as it were, music of marked character; he was fortunate in having the unswerving support of a leading writer and critic, Stasov. After his death more than a dozen hands became involved in sorting out his music, especially the operas. Because he failed to use recognised compositional techniques, his work was to some extent distorted: rewriting, re-arranging, re-orchestrating, adding or cutting passages or sections were all carried out industriously and with the best of intentions; yet it must be acknowledged that some of this effort helped to bring the worth of Musorgsky's music to a wider public. His attractive melodic line, based on folksong and on the inflections of Russian peasants' speech, his unusual harmonic thought, and his sense of drama both musical and textual can quickly be appreciated by the listener in the great opera *Boris Godunov*, the song-cycles *Sunless* and *Songs and Dances of Death*, and the piano suite *Pictures at an Exhibition* (which Ravel later arranged for orchestra). A powerful orchestral work is *Night on the Bare Mountain*, customarily performed in the version by Rimsky-Korsakov.

NAPLES (*Napoli*) – in the hundred years between 1650 and 1750 Naples produced a distinctive brand of Baroque opera which remains its most noted contribution to music. When Alessandro Scarlatti moved from Rome to Naples he was taken with its local comic opera, made up of vernacular texts and local characters, humour and situations. His stage gifts and superior compositional technique elevated this genre in the works he wrote between about 1690 and 1710, so that Neapolitan opera achieved a reputation and exercised an influence in the rest of Italy and elsewhere. Further developments came with the use of Metastasio's early librettos, which laid the foundation for the strict format of opera seria, the chief operatic diet for almost the remainder of the eighteenth century. Pergolesi, Piccinni and Paisiello were the later propagators of Neapolitan opera.

An influence on aria-writing was the Neapolitan solo song with instrumental accompaniment. To this day Italian popular song retains in its character elements of its southern original – sentimentality and languor, spiced by biting, comic twists. Another important contribution from Naples was the development of intermezzo insertions between the three acts of opera seria; these were musical comedies performed during the two intervals to provide relief from the serious goings-on of the main item of the evening. It may be of passing interest to note that Naples was founded as far back as the sixth century BC by Greek settlers; by 326 BC, after it had been conquered by the Romans, it became a holiday resort with two theatres – one open-air and the other covered. It is known that one of the great Middle Ages trouvères, Adam de la Halle, spent several years in Naples, which indicates that it already had a flourishing artistic life.

NATIONAL ANTHEMS – don't pooh-pooh these; every country under the sky has one. It seems to be a socio-psychological necessity; as soon as some land throws out its foreign ruler of one sort or another one of the first things it does is to produce a national anthem. In 1980 it was estimated that there were in existence about 180. There is great variation in musical quality and complexity to be found; some have texts, sometimes with more than one verse, others are little more than fanfare flourishes with no texts; there is also a genre which is international or 'supra-national', such as the *Internationale*, used as a left-wing revolutionary song, or the black South African *Nkosi Sikelel' i Afrika* (Lord, bless Africa), which has existed for many years as a pan-African anthem. In style an anthem can be hymnal, march-like or even operatic; it may be specially written or have roots in folk music. The oldest of all is Great Britain's *God Save the King/Queen*, going back to 1745. National anthems are performed on celebratory occasions – for a head of state, at a gala charity opera performance, or at sports meetings; at the Olympic Games, thus far, the winner of a particular event has his/her country's national anthem played after receiving the gold medal.

NEUMATIC NOTATION – attempts to record music by means of graphic signs may be traced back more than 1500 years and are not confined to Western Europe alone: evidence of the use of musical signs was found in Japan, China and India. In all cases the signs were applied to religious music. Those for Latin liturgy are called neumes, and were written above the texts. If a neume applies to one note it is called a 'simple'; applied to two or more notes, it is a 'compound'. In the age of the neume things were rather complicated, since neume systems varied from one region to another, almost on an ethnic basis – in Western Europe, Central Europe, Poland, Russia, Italy, Spain, Byzantium they were all slightly different. It is from neumes that our present system of notation gradually evolved.

NEWMAN, ERNEST – the leading British music critic in the first half of the twentieth century, who achieved international recognition. He received no formal musical education and for fourteen years earned his living as a bank clerk; during this period he not only studied musical scores and writings on music but also discovered his linguistic talent, eventually gaining a thorough knowledge of nine languages. By 1899, his thirty-first year, Newman had chalked up two books – *Gluck and the Opera* and *A Study of Wagner*. He became a music critic for the *Guardian* in 1905, moved to the *Birmingham Daily Post*, then to the *Observer* and finally in 1920 to the *Sunday Times*, where he remained until his retirement in 1958 at the age of ninety. He spent nearly twenty years working on his major achievement, his four-volume *Life of Richard Wagner*. Newman gave weekly broadcasts for the BBC and, being interested in sport, especially boxing, as a sideline he wrote articles on this subject for the *Evening Standard*.

NICOLAI, OTTO – a German composer and conductor whose contemporaries were Schumann, Mendelssohn and Chopin. He was responsible for establishing the well-known Philharmonic Concerts in Vienna, and was among the last in the tradition of German composers undertaking study in Italy. For much of his life Nicolai earned his living from teaching and as a pianist and singer; even when his reputation grew as a conductor of orchestras and choirs he never achieved the material comforts he deserved. In his short-lived existence he wrote five operas, of which his last, *Die lustigen Weiber von Windsor* (The Merry Wives of Windsor), proved a major success, but only after his death. This opera, based on the *Falstaff* theme, proved to be the finest of all early German Romantic comic operas. Its overture is still frequently performed in concert halls throughout the world.

NIELSEN, CARL – Danish composer who made an important contribution to symphonic writing in the first half of the twentieth century, producing six symphonies of great weight. In contrast, he also turned out collections of songs in a deliberately popular idiom. Nielsen played a leading role in the development of Danish musical life. It took some time before the worth of his music was recognised outside the Scandinavian countries. His style incorporates an individual brand of harmonic and contrapuntal techniques, while his treatment of thematic and motivic ideas is distantly akin to Wagner's use of the *Leitmotif* principle. Felicitous examples of Nielsen's music may be heard in his Flute Concerto, Clarinet Concerto, Wind Quintet and the two volumes of *Danish Songs*.

NOCTURNE – a piece given this title evokes the quiet, meditative aspect of night. Chopin's piano Nocturnes are the best known of the genre, but it is the minor Irish composer John Field to whom Chopin is indebted for the creation of this atmospheric music. It was Field, indeed, who first used this French version of the Italian 'Notturno', often found in eighteenth-century pieces, and who, through the use of the sustaining pedal of the newer piano, and by employing a certain kind of keyboard ornamentation, introduced a particular stream of nineteenth-century compositions of a lighter form. Other composers who produced music in this vein include Fauré, Tchaikovsky and Grieg. Debussy's *Trois nocturnes* ('Nuages', 'Fêtes', 'Sirènes') for orchestra create a high point of impressionist aesthetic, while Bartók's suite for piano *Out of Doors* contains the movement *Musiques nocturnes* (The Night's Music), which offers a remarkable evocation of the activity and sound of nature at night. Of Field's eighteen piano nocturnes, Nos. 1, 5 and 12 will give you a fair idea of his idiom, while Chopin's Op. 72 No. 1 and Op. 9 No. 2 will illustrate the advance made on Field's pioneering. In either case the music will not put you to sleep; nocturnes are not lullabies.

NONO, LUIGI – twentieth-century Italian avant-garde composer. His musical studies, including composition with Malipiero, came fore and aft of a law degree at Padua University. In 1955 he married Schoenberg's daughter Nuria. It is difficult to reconcile Nono's involvement with composition that essentially has a highly sophisticated intellectual basis, and includes the use of complex electro-acoustic techniques, with his sincere commitment to leftist politics: his music certainly excludes any possible appreciation from the man-in-the-street. You may judge for yourself with *La fabbrica illuminata* (The Illuminated

Factory/Building) and *Variazioni canoniche* (Canonic Variations) for chamber orchestra.

NORMA – Bellini's opera in two acts. He considered *Norma* his best opera, and Wagner was full of praise for it, extolling its rich flow of melody. Behind the plot may be seen Bellini's support for Italy's attempts to overthrow Austrian rule. Norma, a Druid priestess, who has vowed chastity, has two sons out of wedlock by the Roman pro-consul; she discovers that he is having an affair with a novice priestess; she fails to persuade him to give up the affair, and then confesses that she has betrayed her country and religion; she is condemned to be burned at the stake; moved by her courage, the pro-consul decides to share Norma's fate.

NOTATION – a visual representation of musical sound, for instructing performers or simply as a permanent record of music heard or imagined. Musical notation usually manifests itself in a society which has developed a script for language. The need to differentiate between various pitches and durations necessitates the placing of notes in a range of vertical and horizontal positions. In this way a series of horizontal lines to fix the placings has evolved, called a stave; in Western notation this consists of five lines along which the notes are strung. Each part in a piece of music requires its own stave; for example, a keyboard piece will have two, one for each hand, while a piece for large orchestra may have as many as thirty-four or more. The term *score* is used to describe the lay-out of a piece containing four or more staves running simultaneously. Vertical lines are drawn across the stave which divide the music into 'bars' or 'measures'; these bar lines help to clarify the beat units, the timing, in which the music is conceived.

NOVELLO, VINCENT – a mid-nineteenth-century musical jack-of-all-trades, being composer, organist, choirmaster, conductor, editor and publisher. His father, an Italian pastry-cook, settled in London and married an English girl. Novello helped to expand the activities of choral societies by publishing vocal scores of oratorios and similar works for choir. He promoted the music of Bach, Haydn and Mozart. When he learnt that Mozart's sister was suffering from poverty and ill-health in Austria he raised a subscription and journeyed with his wife to Salzburg to present the funds to her; at the same time he had the opportunity to gather valuable biographical information on the composer. Novello was frequently requested to design and test new organs, and his home was a welcome venue for such notables as the writer Charles Lamb, the poets

Shelley and Keats, and Mendelssohn. His eldest son, Alfred, continued the publishing work of his father, ultimately establishing the great publishing house of Novello & Co. and in 1844 founding the *Musical Times*, which is still in existence today.

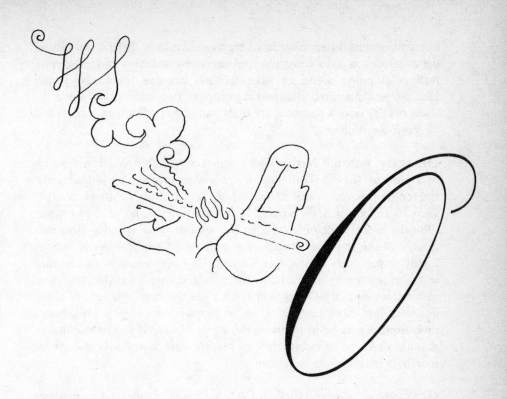

OBBLIGATO – a term to describe an accompanying part in a piece of music, second in importance only to the part that carries the leading melody. A clear and moving example is the violin solo in the Benedictus of Beethoven's Mass in D. The term was actively used in the Baroque period to apply to an instrumental solo which accompanied an aria supported by a basso continuo. At this time, too, keyboard accompaniment usually had no more than a bass line with figured harmony; the filling in was left to the player (a similar practice is found today in jazz, where the pianist accompanies the solo singer or instrumentalist). When the keyboard part was fully written out by the composer the instruction given was 'obbligato' – the player was obliged to play what the composer had written.

OBOE – one of the most attractive of woodwind instruments; examples of oboe-type instruments are to be found in many parts of the world. The pipe has a conical bore and the mouthpiece has two reeds; the bell is flared, but its larger sister, the *cor anglais* (English horn), has a bulbous bell. However it came to Europe, the oboe today is descended from the Renaissance shawm; its present form was developed in Amsterdam in the seventeenth century. A plethora of music has been written for it as a solo instrument, in addition to its regular place in orchestral and chamber works. It is capable of uttering the most beautiful of melodies as well as skipping along in light staccato passages. Presently, Heinz Holliger is considered its leading virtuoso. Two contrasting pieces to show off the oboe's potential are the Concertos by Richard Strauss and by Vaughan Williams.

OBRECHT, JACOB – Netherlands composer who flourished in the second half of the fifteenth century, a contemporary of Josquin; like Britten he was born on St Cecilia's Day, 22 November. Apart from two visits to Ferrara in Italy where, during the second, he died of plague, Obrecht spent most of his life in the area of what is today Belgium, mainly in the towns of Bruges, Antwerp and Cambrai. While he was highly respected as a composer he seems to have been poor at carrying out administrative, financial and choir supervising duties. He was close to his contemporary Ockeghem in terms of the northern style of composition, but more traditional, in an output full of vocal polyphonic invention, as may be heard in his motets or Masses. If you're at all interested in this type of music listen to his five-part motet *Salve crux* or his four-part Mass *Ave regina celorum*.

OCARINA – the word is Italian for 'little goose'; a pleasant instrument made of terracotta for amateurs to tootle on; it is carrot-shaped. Because the column of air inside when made to vibrate behaves as a simple resonator, any sounding note is a pure tone, free from overtones. Though its European origin is Italian and dates back to the nineteenth century, the ocarina is also native to South and Central America, especially Colombia, Peru, Costa Rica and Guatemala. If you can't play an instrument but would love to make music in the bath or while sipping a relaxing drink after a long day, go out and buy yourself an ocarina.

OCKEGHEM, JOHANNES – a Netherlands composer who with Josquin, Dufay and Obrecht forms the great quartet of European composers of the latter half of the fifteenth century. In contrast to his countryman Obrecht, Ockeghem was occupied continuously in France, with only sporadic visits to the north. Records of the French court show that he was engaged as a singer at the age of twenty-three; from then on he remained in royal service, steadily rising in position until by the age of forty-four he was musical top-dog. As was common at the time he also held a variety of additional posts concurrently. His motets and Masses display not only beauty of polyphonic line but an intricate, sophisticated compositional technique quite distinctive for the period. His four-part

Mass *Pro defunctis* is an example; he also wrote highly attractive chansons – the three-part *Tant fuz gentement* is typical.

OCTAVE – the sound distance between any two notes is called an interval; the simplest of all intervals is the octave. Crudely, if you sing a note in the middle register of your voice and then try to sing the same-sounding note but higher or lower, sounding respectively 'thinner' and 'thicker', you will be singing, more or less, the interval of an octave. If your original note is sung at, say, 440 vibrations per second, the upper octave note will vibrate at 880 and the lower at 220 per second. The octave, in fact, is the interval by which a scale, of any kind, is identified. It is the easiest interval for the ear to recognise. If you yourself can't do this, don't get dejected and say you're tone deaf; no one is tone deaf – your ear simply requires a little bit of 'training'.

ODE – in the Greek and Roman civilisations an ode was a poem meant to be sung in honour of a special person or occasion, and in the fifteenth and sixteenth centuries there was a vogue for setting these ancient poems to music. In the seventeenth and eighteenth centuries composers began to write odes of a cantata-like nature. English ode-writing in this vein had a particularly long life, having one of three purposes – to praise a monarch, as an act of thanksgiving or as a tribute to St Cecilia, the patron saint of music. Odes were often included in court masques; in the later seventeenth century, among English composers who wrote birthday or welcome odes were Locke, Blow and Purcell. An ode would contain verses for solo or duet with continuo support and verses for chorus with instrumental ritornellos. Purcell wrote the most characterful examples, filled with technical ingenuity and rich melodic lines, in a variety of tempos, as evidenced in his *Ode to St Cecilia's Day* of 1692. Handel's similarly entitled *Ode* of 1739 and the one celebrating Queen Anne's birthday in 1713 are both strongly Purcellian. By 1820 ode-writing was petering out; the only two later works that bear special mention are Beethoven's Symphony No. 9, in which the last movement is a setting of Schiller's *An die Freude* – Beethoven, not Schiller, called it an ode (Ode to Joy); and Schoenberg's setting for reciter and instruments of Byron's *Ode to Napoleon*.

OFFENBACH, JACQUES – French composer of German origin. His father, a bookbinder, music teacher and cantor at a synagogue in Cologne, took him in his early teens for further musical study in Paris. There Offenbach soon entered the world of Parisian music and theatre, with one comic opera succeeding another. Nevertheless, he was at the same time active as a concert cellist, and appeared on concert platforms with Anton Rubinstein, Liszt, Joachim and Mendelssohn. Often he would be his own impresario; in addition to encouraging works from Delibes and Guiraud, he put on operas by Mozart and Rossini. His first great success came in 1858 with *Orphée aux enfers* (Orpheus in the Underworld). Having always to work under severe pressure, Offenbach would often rely on the help of arrangers as well as reworking previous material – not uncommon among opera composers going right back to Handel. After further marked successes, such as *La belle Hélène* and *Barbe-bleu* (Bluebeard), Offenbach was able to afford a handsome house in Paris and a villa in Normandy but, always a poor businessman, in 1874 he was forced into bankruptcy. He gradually built himself up again, though never reached his previous material position, and did not live to see the triumph of his best work, *Les contes d'Hoffmann* (The Tales of Hoffmann), the only one that can really be described as an opera. Offenbach's ingenious, witty plots and his jolly and tuneful music helped to establish the form of operetta, a genre developed further by Johann Strauss, Sullivan and Lehár which was in turn transformed into the twentieth-century musical.

OISTRAKH, DAVID – Russian violinist of international standing; the Soviet authorities seemed to allow him to travel as he pleased. In 1927, at the age of eighteen, he was asked by Glazunov to be the soloist in the first performance of the composer's Violin Concerto at Kiev. He performed the Bach Double Concerto with Menuhin in Moscow in 1945. Oistrakh paid particular attention to promoting twentieth-century concertos – by Elgar, Sibelius, Walton, Prokofiev, Khachaturian and Shostakovich. He taught his son, Igor, who is also a gifted violinist. When opportunity allowed, he and Prokofiev would play intensely competitive chess.

OPERA – it is well known that Dr Johnson described opera as an 'exotic and irrational entertainment'. However true this description may be, opera is an art form second only in popularity to the cinema and perhaps its offspring, the musical. While music is the chief element in opera, its effect and success rely also on its combination with a number of other arts – literature, poetry, painting, design, lighting. The success of a particular opera has often depended on the singer, or the impresario, or the staging and costumes, rather than on the composer. There was a time when an aria, for example, would be entirely rewritten by the composer if the intended singer changed, for whatever reason. Opera style varies according to a country's cultural and theatrical traditions. In Italy the emphasis was on vocal melodic line, in France on situation, in Germany on philosophical concepts, in England on the importance of text – which is not to say that cross-fertilisation has not been continuously at work.

In current repertoire the most popular opera composer remains Puccini, closely followed by Mozart, and behind these two Verdi and Wagner. Opera is expensive to mount; this, and a change in musical taste from the beginning of the twentieth century, combined to cause a decline in both output and demand, but a few works have been triumphant exceptions to this state of affairs: *Pelléas et Mélisande* (Debussy), *Der Rosenkavalier* (Richard Strauss), *Wozzeck* (Berg), *Peter Grimes* (Britten), *Punch and Judy* (Birtwistle). In the past two decades, however, the writing and production of opera has increased, which is encouraging. The superficial appeal of opera may be spectacle, but its quintessence is the quality of the music written for the singing voice, which touches in us something words cannot reach. It is this aspect of the medium that causes us to suspend a desire for realism on the stage; the more 'artificial' the opera, the more likely is it to be a successful work of art.

The output of opera writing in the eighteenth and nineteenth centuries is quite amazing; hundreds were written – good, bad and indifferent, like the production of films today; in fact going to the opera was equivalent to cinema attendance in our own time. My personal choice for a parade of operas down the centuries would be *L'incoronazione di Poppea* (Monteverdi), *Dido and Aeneas* (Purcell), *Orphée et Eurydice* (Gluck), *Don Giovanni* (Mozart), *Rigoletto* (Verdi), *Tristan und Isolde* (Wagner), *La Bohème* (Puccini), *Wozzeck* (Berg), *The Rape of Lucretia* (Britten), *Le grand Macabre* (Ligeti), *Gawain* (Birtwistle). If you can work your way through these eleven you will fully understand what opera is about.

OPUS – the Latin for 'work'. In music the habit of attaching 'opus' to a composition commenced early in the seventeenth century, and became the norm in the eighteenth and nineteenth. Thus Opus 20, abbreviated to Op. 20, would mean the work was the twentieth the composer had written. Sometimes a group of pieces would fall under one opus, such as Haydn's string quartets Op. 50, of which there were six, thus numbered Op. 50 No. 1 to Op. 50 No. 6. At this time it would often be the publisher and not the composer who would number the work. Because of this, many instances occur in which the numbering does not follow the sequence of composition; of Haydn's divertimentos for string quartet Op. 17, No. 1 was written after No. 2, and No. 3 after No. 6. But do not let these chronological hiccups confuse you; whatever the ruddy opus number, simply enjoy the music. Usually it was not the practice to number songs and operas, or minor pieces. Sometimes the numbering was listed under a cataloguer's name. So it was with Mozart, whose large output was first properly put in chronological order by Koechel; the last piano concerto, 1791, is numbered K595.

ORATORIO – essentially an oratorio is a sub-division of opera; it is a dramatico-musical work of substance, meant only for concert-platform performance and thus devoid of scenery, costume and lighting. Its format follows that of opera, normally having an overture, solo and duet arias, instrumental interludes, and chorus numbers. As with opera, the oratorio originated in the seventeenth century. The texts usually deal with religious subjects. The largest output occurred in the seventeenth and eighteenth centuries, but the genre continues to be used to the present day. In the twentieth century secular texts have been introduced – Tippett's *A Child of Our Time* and Stravinsky's *Oedipus Rex* (though this is partly an opera). A very attractive example of eighteenth-century oratorio writing is Handel's *Saul*, which also illustrates the increased role of chorus numbers. Because of Handel's influence and the considerable choral society tradition, oratorio was most consistently composed and performed in England over the last two hundred years, with commissions not confined to British composers alone – Mendelssohn's *Elijah*, Haydn's *Creation* and Spohr's *Calvary* are but three examples. Twentieth-century English oratorio writing which displays the dramatic, narrative and contemplative characteristics typical of the best in this genre are *The Dream of Gerontius* (Elgar), *Belshazzar's Feast* (Walton) and the *War Requiem* (Britten).

ORCHESTRA – one of the magnificent achievements of Western music culture is the orchestra. In 1607, at the performance of Monteverdi's opera *L'Orfeo* the orchestra numbered thirty-nine players; for his *Der Ring des Nibelungen* nearly three hundred years later Wagner wrote for an orchestra of ninety-eight, while the instrumental forces demanded for Richard Strauss's opera *Elektra* (1908) and Schoenberg's *Gurrelieder*, a cantata for solo voices, choruses and orchestra, are nearly three times Monteverdi's requirements. A good part of the pleasure in attending an orchestra performance in the concert hall lies in watching as well as listening to what is going on. At one time it was feared that recordings, broadcasts and even electro-acoustic creations would sound the death-knell of live orchestral playing; this, thankfully, has not proved the case. Music also has a social function; however large our CD library, we need to hear music in the company of fellow beings as well.

While a group consisting solely of brass or woodwind or a mixture of the two should properly be called a band, the term 'orchestra' should be reserved for a group of players in which the main body consists of bowed string instruments plus any number of woodwind, brass and percussion. Since Wagner's time the orchestra has hardly grown in size, but there are two features which characterise twentieth-century orchestral performance. The one is the increase in the number and variety of percussion instruments; the other is the number of fine works that have been specially written for smaller forces – termed a chamber orchestra – Tippett's *Concerto for Double String Orchestra*, Stravinsky's *Pulcinella* Suite, Messiaen's *Couleurs de la cité céleste* (The Colours of the Heavenly City), spring to mind. As can be imagined, orchestras are expensive to run – as princely courts in earlier times knew only too well – and cannot survive on ticket money alone; they require subsidising and support from foundations, civic bodies, arts councils and business sponsorship in order to meet public demand and continue in existence.

ORCHESTRATION – a term which describes the technical skill and art of handling orchestral forces to express the musical ideas of the composer. Many composers first write their music in what is called 'short score', on three to five staves, before fully orchestrating it in the final 'full score', and it is here that things can go wrong. Poor orchestration can blur musical intentions, whereas ingenious treatment of the instruments can make poor material sound attractive. While, in the first half of the seventeenth century, orchestral parts were open to a choice of instruments, depending on what and who was to hand, the growing medium of opera demanded a firmer and more specific use of them. By the time of Handel and Bach, orchestration reached its first level of sophistication; an effect much enjoyed then was colour contrast – between a smaller and a larger group, or between strings and woodwind. By the following, Classical, period conventions were established, yet there could be a marked difference in the quality of orchestration, depending on the aural imagination of the composer: witness the difference between a symphony by Dittersdorf and one by Mozart. From Beethoven to Tchaikovsky, both marvellous orchestrators, the nineteenth century proved to be one in which tone colour through instrumentation was one of the most important characteristics. Brahms and Wagner illustrate two types of fine orchestrators – the former obtained beautiful and exciting effects with little innovation, whereas the latter brought into the orchestra new instruments and new devices; the same contrast can be seen later between Stravinsky and Shostakovich. Music of the twentieth century offers a rich variety of bold, exciting orchestration, e.g. Bartók's *Concerto for Orchestra*, Stravinsky's *The Rite of Spring*. Debussy (*La Mer*) and Ravel (*Daphnis et Chloé*) are indisputable masters of orchestration; it is strange to realise that most of Ravel's orchestral works were first composed as piano pieces.

ORFF, CARL – twentieth-century German composer and music educationist. At the age of twenty-nine, having already had much experience as a music-teacher, he co-founded in Munich a school for gymnastics, music and dance with the purpose of exploring new relationships between music and movement. From here on he began to build and develop his method, *Orff-Schulwerk* (Orff-School Work), which has had for many decades a worldwide influence in primary school teaching, being adopted in Britain after the war. Orff's basic belief was that no child is unmusical, that through proper teaching and suitable resources any child can develop some perception of rhythm, pitch and musical form, and can enjoy taking part in group creative improvisation. In 1961 the Orff Institute was established to provide full-time and holiday courses for teachers from all over the world, to promote research into children's musical development and the use of the Orff method in music therapy. As a composer he wrote mainly for the theatre. His hit number, which is regularly performed all over the world, is his 'cantata profana' *Carmina Burana*, the Latin and old German texts of which are taken from a medieval monastic collection of poetry, and which contain comments and reflections on love and sex.

ORGAN – some people cannot stand this instrument, others believe there has never been nor will there ever be a musical instrument to equal it. At the age of twenty-one Mozart wrote to his father that the organ 'in my eyes and ears is the king of instruments'. It has been pointed out that before the Industrial Revolution the organ, together with the clock, was the most complex of all mechanical instruments yet developed. The organological study of the organ is vast, and organ-

192

builders of the past have reputations to equal the great violin-makers of seventeenth-century Italy. Although today there are very effective electric organs, no organ buff would spend a moment comparing them to the great instruments in European churches and cathedrals.

The organ is a wind instrument consisting of one or more rows of pipes, which are made to sound when air is pumped under pressure from a wind-raising device and enters the pipes by means of valves operated by a keyboard, with or without an additional foot keyboard. In medieval times organ pipes were imported to Europe from England, where they could be produced more cheaply because of the tin mines in Cornwall. The wind-producing mechanism was at first worked by manual bellows operated by an assistant; this was superseded in time by mechanical action and later by electrical control. Most composers you can think of have written for the organ, either as a solo instrument or in accompaniment. In purely musical terms Bach is held to be its greatest composer and exponent. Towards the close of the nineteenth century and in the early twentieth new repertoire of worth was not forthcoming. But then Messiaen came along with a fresh attitude to composing for the organ, giving it a new lease of life. It is of interest to compare, say, Bach's Fantasia and Fugue in G minor, BWV 542 with Messiaen's *La Nativité du Seigneur* (The Birth of the Lord).

ORGANOLOGY – the term does not mean the study of organs; it is derived from the Greek *organon* meaning 'tool' or 'instrument'. Organology is the study of instruments; it is worth remembering that it does not deal with the music they make, but rather with their classification which, basically, may be divided into three: where and for what purpose an instrument is used, how it is played, and its physical features.

ORGANUM – a type of medieval polyphony or vocal counterpoint which may be traced back to before the tenth century. From the twelfth century its chief feature was to have one part sung in long, sustained notes, usually an existing melody, called the tenor. Above it one or more parts would improvise countermelody, at first note-against-note, then ornamentation of the tenor melody, later using independent material. The texts are always taken from Latin liturgy.

OVERTURE – there are two sorts of overtures, the type that introduces a stage work and the type written for concert performance; two respective examples are Mozart's overture to his Singspiel *The Magic Flute* and Brahms's *Academic Festival Overture*. It is usually of moderate length; it may be no more than a piece of musical floss, as found in many nineteenth-century French comic operas, or it may have serious musical

193

ambition, as Elgar's *Cockaigne Overture*. Opera overtures of lighter vein were often written with no other purpose than to give an audience time to settle down before curtain-rise.

OXFORD – this university town is first mentioned in 912. Although some instruction had been going on previously, the origin of the university commenced with the enforced migration of foreign students from Paris around 1170, and it became a corporate institution at the end of the twelfth century. Mainly to provide living accommodation and keep control of the students, colleges began to be founded in the thirteenth century. Music was taught alongside arithmetic, geometry and astronomy in the medieval period. BMus. and DMus. degrees date from the early sixteenth century; the post of *choragus* – superintendent of music – became a professorship in about 1848. The present incumbent of the Heather Chair of Music is Brian Trowell, a noted musicologist and an authority on opera. Several libraries have major musical holdings; of these the most important are the Bodleian Library and Christ Church. The Faculty of Music houses the Bate Collection of wind instruments. Of particular interest is the Sheldonian Theatre, designed by Wren, in which musical performances have regularly taken place since it opened in 1669. The Oxford Choral Society, the oldest in the city, was founded in 1819. The English Bach Festival started in 1963 and since 1970 has been held jointly in Oxford and London; its programmes include works by Bach's contemporaries and music by twentieth-century composers.

PACHELBEL, JOHANN – a leading German composer and organist of the later seventeenth century, producing an important output of Protestant church music. He was born and died in Nuremberg. Though he lost his first wife and their first-born in a plague, his second wife bore him five sons and two daughters; four of the sons became well-known musicians in their own right and one of them, Carl Theodor, emigrated to the British American colonies in about 1730. Pachelbel was the most influential German composer after Schütz and before Bach. He established a large repertoire of liturgical organ music – chorales and Magnificat fugues – as well as secular music for the instrument – toccatas, ricercares, fantasias and chaconnes. His music for harpsichord includes suites and variations, and his vocal music consists mainly of sacred concertos, some of which were accompanied by brass and timpani in addition to strings and continuo. For listening: Canon and Gigue in D for strings.

PADEREWSKI, IGNACY – pronounced 'pa-der-ev-ski', not 'pa-der-oo-ski'; internationally famous Polish piano virtuoso flourishing in the second half of the nineteenth century and first half of the twentieth. His fame and earnings allowed him to set up a foundation for young composers in the USA in 1896, and competitions for composition and for drama in Poland in 1898. After Polish independence at the close of World War I, Paderewski became Prime Minister and Minister for Foreign Affairs from 1919 to 1922 – the first pianist to attain such high political office, and the most musically gifted head of government in history! He died in the USA during World War II, while once again working in the cause of his invaded country. He supervised a new edition of Chopin's works, not published until after the war. In 1936 he appeared in the British film *Moonlight Sonata*. Paderewski was himself no mean composer; try his *Polish Fantasy* for piano and orchestra.

PAGANINI, NICCOLÒ – nineteenth-century Italian violinist, perhaps the greatest ever virtuoso of the instrument; when Liszt first heard him playing it caused the pianist-composer to rethink his own approach to keyboard-playing. Paganini added to music the element of virtuosity as a valid aspect of artistic expression. His programmes were always to consist largely, and often exclusively, of pieces composed by himself, calculated to show off his special attributes. Paganini left Italy to give concerts elsewhere only at the age of forty-six, by which time his playing was mature and effortless, able to meet the most remarkable technical challenges. In 1831 he gave 103 concerts in England, Scotland and Ireland. Paganini was also a brilliant performer on the mandolin and viola (see *Harold in Italy*). His playing and ability to hold an audience spellbound at court, in salon or in concert hall gave rise to numerous anecdotes, not a few being quite untrue – far-fetched ones on the lines of his having sold his soul to the devil and such-like nonsense. Worth listening to are his twenty-four *Caprices* for solo violin and his Violin Concerto No. 2.

PAGLIACCI – the Italian word for 'clowns' and the title of Leoncavallo's most popular opera, cast as a prologue and two acts. A short work, it is usually presented as part of a double bill with Mascagni's *Cavalleria Rusticana*. The plot is not complicated: the leader of a troupe of strolling players discovers that his wife has a lover and murders her in the course of the play they enact before the audience. The opera is an apt example of Italian *verismo* style.

PAISIELLO, GIOVANNI – eighteenth-century Italian composer. At the age of twenty-six he settled in Naples, where he established himself as an acclaimed composer of comic opera. His reputation reached the ears of the Empress Catherine II of Russia, who offered him a lucrative appointment at the court in St Petersburg; he remained there for more than six years. Returning to Naples he joined the court of King Ferdinand IV, and was put in charge of all secular music. Lorenzi, the best Neapolitan librettist of the time, provided Paisiello with well-shaped plots and lots of comic humour and the resultant music, lively and melodious, made for sure-fire hits. He wrote over eighty operas in addition to other works; compare Paisiello's *The Barber of Seville* with Rossini's version.

PALAEOGRAPHY – the study of the history of writing. In music this discipline is applied to the study of notation, with particular reference to establishing the period and date of the material, localising the script or printing, examining the paper on which the music appears, and noting changes in conventions. Often this study will help to ascertain whether a piece of music is indeed such-and-such an author's or no more than a fake. Just as palaeography has been extended to consider location and model of music printing presses, in time it may conceivably involve the study of computers and computer graphics with reference to musical notation.

PALESTRINA, GIOVANNI PIERLUIGI DA – sixteenth-century Italian composer, regarded by many as one of the greatest representatives of the entire age of vocal polyphony; certainly, with Byrd and Lassus, one of the finest composers of the latter half of the century. He spent most of his professional life in one church post or another in Rome. While Palestrina wrote many madrigals, conservative in style but nevertheless much admired, such as *Vestiva i colli*, his main creative effort was constantly engaged in realising the function and aesthetic aims of Catholic church music in the age of the Counter-Reformation. He wrote 104 Masses, 375 motets, 68 offertories, some 65 hymns, 35 settings of the Magnificat and four or five settings of Lamentations – this on top of his many other tasks. A bit of a workaholic – as composers often are.

From popes and cardinals down, his genius received full recognition. There were many types of Masses and motets of the time in terms of structure and treatment of material; Palestrina covers them all. He preferred to write for five parts but, especially in his motets, the scoring ranges from four to as many as twelve parts. It is rare for a composer of that time to be regularly considered from one generation to the next, right up until the present; this is largely due, as with Bach, to the fact that Palestrina's music was used as a model in the development of disciplined, contrapuntal writing for budding composers and music students in general. But don't let this academic cloud put you off. To become a Palestrina fan listen to his six-part *Missa Papae Marcelli* (Mass for Pope Marcellus) and his eight-part motet *Hodie Christus natus est*.

PANUFNIK, ANDRZEJ – twentieth-century Polish composer, conductor and pianist, naturalised British. He learnt the rudiments of music from

197

his mother, who was English. During the war he wrote patriotic songs under a pseudonym and as a pianist gave illegal concerts, often in cafés, and sometimes in partnership with his countryman Lutoslawski. His pre-1944 compositions were burnt in the Warsaw uprising. After the war he was active as a conductor in Poland, Berlin and London; in the 1950s he visited the Soviet Union, led a Polish delegation to China and, with Honegger, was vice-president of the UNESCO International Music Council in Paris. Panufnik moved to London and later had a two-year spell as director of the Birmingham Symphony Orchestra. His musical creativity reached full maturity in the 1960s; his works exhibit a strong command of form, within which is expressed an intensity best described as romantic. He believed in Pope's dictum: 'Order is Heav'n's first law'. Two examples of Panufnik's style are the Symphony No. 9 and the orchestral piece *Autumn Music*.

PARRY, HUBERT – English composer, scholar and teacher, one of the main figures in the nineteenth century who began to revitalise English composition and musical study, presaging Elgar, Vaughan Williams and others. He assisted Grove with the first edition of the now famous musical dictionary, and succeeded him as director of the Royal College of Music in 1894. Of his books, *The Art of Music* (1893) and his critical biography of Bach are of historical interest. Parry wrote a large number of works for English choral festivals, many songs and a rich variety of other pieces. His anthems accurately reflect English musical taste of the time; the anthem *I was glad* was specially composed for the crowning of Edward VII in 1902 and has been sung at every subsequent coronation; it remains in the cathedral repertoire. A work of dignity and charm is his *Lady Radnor's Suite* for string orchestra. In sum, he was a jolly good musical chap.

PARSIFAL – Wagner's last opera, completed in 1882 and produced that year at his festival theatre in Bayreuth. Wagner termed the work a 'sacred drama'; in contrast to his earlier operas, *Parsifal* teems with musical, religious and ethical symbolism. The three-act structure is deliberately simple and static. The plot: the king of the Knights of the Grail has long suffered from a spear-wound inflicted by Klingsor, the Grail's enemy, and can only be healed by a 'holy fool'. Parsifal, who fits this description all too well, rolls up, resists the temptations of the flower maidens in Klingsor's magic garden and captures the spear, thus healing the king's wound. Slow spectacle, great music.

PÄRT, ARVO – twentieth-century Estonian composer. Early influences on his composition were Prokofiev and Shostakovich; he then passed through a period in which the manipulation of technical devices, especially those centring on serialism, dominated his music, as in his Symphony No. 1. Now he has arrived at a highly individual language and style, proving very popular in the concert hall, that produces subtle, sophisticated material which is yet appealing to the ordinary listener. Pärt has a strong devotional religious bias in him which is expressed in his music, for example, *De Profundis* for four-part voices, organ and percussion. Other works of interest are *Cantus in memory of Benjamin Britten* for string orchestra and bell, and *If Bach had been a beekeeper* for harpsichord, electric bass, orchestra and tape.

PARTITA – a synonym for 'suite' which first took root in Italian instrumental music in the second half of the seventeenth century. Earlier the term was used to describe a variation or a set of variations on a traditional melody, and it is interesting to note that Bach used this meaning of the term in his chorale partitas. By about 1720, however, the suite form of partita had become fully established; the best known are Bach's three for solo violin, six for keyboard and two for lute. In the early Classical period partitas consisted of a mixture of dance and non-dance movements. Since then the term has been used occasionally; a felicitous twentieth-century example is Walton's very effective three-movement *Partita* for orchestra.

PARTSONG – a composition intended for choral singing, usually secular in character; it is normally a single entity. As choral singing developed swiftly in England at the end of the eighteenth century, a demand arose among amateur singing groups for short choral pieces as well as the more extended works. From the second half of the nineteenth century composers have produced a steady stream of partsongs for mixed, male or female choirs, from Vaughan Williams's *Silence and Music* to Maxwell Davies's *Lullaby for Lucy*. The partsong genre is not bound by any particular language or style and is essentially 'democratic', in the sense that any good amateur choir should be able to give a convincing rendering of what the composer has written. Which is not to say that more demanding partsongs are not composed, usually with a crack group in mind such as the BBC Singers.

PASSACAGLIA – this term today is interpreted as a composition having a set melody in the bass, a ground bass, over which variations are written. Examples of passacaglia, given all sorts of subtle and sophisticated treatments, in twentieth-century music are to be found in Schoenberg's *Pierrot Lunaire*, Berg's opera *Wozzeck* (Act 2 Scene iv), Hindemith's Sonata for cello and piano, Copland's *Passacaglia* for piano, Walton's

Symphony No. 2. The Mark 1 model is the passacaglia writing of Bach, but before him 'passacaglia' applied to a standard form of ritornello on the guitar to accompany certain types of French, Italian and Spanish songs; the basic unit consisted of four bars in three-beats-to-the-bar rhythm. The passacaglia is not dissimilar to the chaconne, but note that in the Baroque period the former favoured a minor key whereas the latter fancied major keys. Why the twentieth century seems to have taken up passacaglia writing is that, as in the Baroque period, there is an emphasis on the organisation of melodic line. During the Classical and Romantic periods, by contrast, emphasis was laid on the way parts function together, so there was little or no interest paid to passacaglia; a noteworthy exception is the final movement of Brahms's Symphony No. 4.

PASSAMEZZO – an Italian dance having two-beats-to-the-bar, popular for about a hundred years between 1550 and 1650; the music was usually organised on a framework of eight basic chords, revolving for the length of the piece, orientated towards either a major or a minor key. At first this dance was played on the lute or the guitar; later, however, it appeared in keyboard and orchestral suites. By the later eighteenth century composers were no longer interested in the passamezzo, paying attention rather to the minuet.

PASSEPIED – a French court dance and instrumental form usually in three-beats-to-the-bar; it ran fairly contemporaneously with the passamezzo. The passepied appeared in many French operas and ballets – Lully, Rameau – and was extensively used in keyboard and orchestral suites – Couperin, Quantz, Telemann, Bach.

PASSION – the story of the Crucifixion recorded in the Gospels of Matthew, Mark, Luke and John. Polyphonic settings of the texts have been made since the fifteenth century. After 1600 Passion composition was concentrated in German-speaking regions, couched in a form that was halfway between a biblical reading and an oratorio. In the eighteenth century several approaches to setting Passion texts had evolved, the most common using the text of a particular Gospel; thus Bach's unique *St Matthew Passion* of 1729; his earlier *St John Passion* (1723) is less frequently performed nowadays – it does not have the drama and grandeur of the later one. He is supposed to have written another three, but the music has disappeared – most probably used for bookbinding or for wrapping. From the later eighteenth century the writing of Passion music has become a rarity; one of the latest examples, and impressive, is Penderecki's *St Luke Passion* of 1965.

PASTORALE – in music, a work that evokes or represents the country-side, especially with shepherds. Pastoral poetry of the Renaissance provided texts for numerous madrigals, and by the end of the sixteenth century a tradition had grown up of presenting pastoral plays with music which made an important contribution to the development of opera, in both Italy and France. In the seventeenth and eighteenth centuries pastoral themes were used in numerous cantatas; musical effects such as drone basses, double reed instruments and flutes were employed. It would be nice if composers nowadays would write pastoral-type works to be performed in the parks and open spaces of our towns and cities; updated in subject matter, these could prove enjoyably relaxing on summer evenings.

PASTORAL SYMPHONY – this is not a nickname for Beethoven's Symphony No. 6 in F major, Op. 68, for it was actually published in 1809 with the title *Sinfonie pastorale* and approved by him. The symphony is unusual in that it has five movements; Beethoven's inscriptions for each movement are: 'Awakening of cheerful feelings on arrival in the countryside'; 'By the brook'; 'Merry-making of the country folk'; 'Storm'; 'Song of the shepherds'. This work received a terrific boost in popularity from its inclusion in Walt Disney's famous full-length cartoon film *Fantasia*.

PATTERSON, PAUL – twentieth-century English composer who possesses a marked versatility of musical language and style; always present, though, is his own individual stamp. He studied with Richard Stoker and Richard Rodney Bennett and has extensive knowledge of the music of Penderecki and Ligeti. Patterson also uses electro-acoustic techniques to convincing musical ends. Currently he is professor of composition and twentieth-century music at the Royal Academy of Music. In good British fashion he has treated composition for education and for amateurs with the seriousness these areas deserve. Two samples of his music that will interest you are his *Mass of the Sea* for solo voices, chorus and orchestra and, in contrast, *Comedy* for five winds.

PAYNE, ANTHONY – twentieth-century English composer and writer; his wife, the soprano Jane Manning, is a distinguished interpreter of contemporary music, having given first performances by, and commissioned works from, a rich variety of composers. Payne's works, large or small, are finely fashioned and full of ingenuity – his *The World's Winter* for soprano and chamber ensemble and *A 1940s Childhood* for flute and guitar or harp are apt examples. His writings, which are wide-ranging, show consistent scholarship and clarity, whether they are concert reviews, journal articles, or special studies on such composers as Schoenberg, Bax and Delius.

PEARS, PETER – English tenor who achieved international fame both on the concert platform and in the opera house. Pears is best known for interpreting the music of Britten, with whom he shared a lifelong companionship. Britten first performances include the *Michelangelo Sonnets* and *Serenade* for tenor, horn and strings (1942), the lead role in *Peter Grimes*, the opera that marked the reopening of the Sadler's Wells Theatre in 1945, the Male Chorus in *The Rape of Lucretia* (1946), Quint in *The Turn of the Screw* (1954) and Aschenbach in *Death in Venice* (1973). Pears was one of the founders of the English Opera Group and the Aldeburgh Festival. He was recognised as a leading interpreter of the Schubert and Schumann song-cycles; as the Evangelist in Bach's Passions and in Elgar's *Dream of Gerontius* he displayed an intense and subtle vocal expression, and he gave consistent support to contemporary song. He was knighted in 1977.

PEETERS, FLOR – twentieth-century Belgian organist, teacher and composer. Before Olivier Messiaen it was Peeters who revived the flagging organ repertoire, with a steady stream of compositions which were skilfully structured and which extended the potential of the instrument. Proof lies in his organ pieces *Concert Piece* Op. 52a and *Variations on an Original Theme* Op. 58. During the war Peeters refused to play for the Germans and as a consequence his passport was confiscated. Pupils came from all over the world to study with him and he also undertook numerous organ-playing and teaching tours of the USA. In 1971 King Baudouin elevated Peeters to the peerage with the personal title of baron, only the third musician since 1830 to receive this honour.

PELLÉAS ET MÉLISANDE – Maeterlinck's play attracted three composers: Fauré made a Suite from the incidental music he wrote for it; Schoenberg wrote a symphonic poem inspired by it; and Debussy composed an opera which is the most ambitious and distinguished of the three works. Debussy set Maeterlinck's play almost as it stood, cutting only four unimportant scenes. The opera consists of a succession of short, concentrated scenes which illustrate Rousseau's definition of existence – 'nothing but a succession of moments perceived through the senses'; the setting is the fictional kingdom of Allemonde in legendary times and the characters are set in a landscape of illusion. It is a highly original work, to which Maeterlinck at first objected.

202

PENDERECKI, KRZYSZTOF – twentieth-century Polish composer who, with his fellow countrymen Lutoslawski, Gorecki and Szymanowski, has exercised a marked influence on contemporary composition and who, with the Russian Prokofiev and Shostakovich and the Hungarian Ligeti, has offered a healthy counterbalance to the world of Boulez, Stockhausen and Berio. A most remarkable piece, illustrating his vivid aural imagination and understanding of writing for strings, is the *Threnody for the Victims of Hiroshima* for fifty-two strings. After a lengthy list of works of avant-garde character, Penderecki has lately turned to a more approachable style of writing as evidenced in his Symphony No. 2, which is by no means devoid of the Penderecki personality but involves traditional symphonic principles and some regard for tonality. Treat the string piece as a must for listening.

PEPUSCH, JOHANN – long-lived German composer and theorist. From the age of fourteen he was employed at the Prussian court until, towards the close of the seventeenth century, he decided to leave Germany after witnessing the execution without trial of a Prussian officer accused of insubordination; he wanted to put himself 'under the protection of a government founded on better principles'. He settled in London, where he remained for the rest of his life. After gaining his DMus. at Oxford he became musical director for the Duke of Chandos and was later involved in the production of the two ballad operas, the evergreen *The Beggar's Opera* and *Polly*. Pepusch wrote mainly verse anthems and secular cantatas. From about 1732 he seems to have given up composing to concentrate on teaching and antiquarian book interests; it is in his vast collection of books and scores that the Fitzwilliam Virginal Book was discovered. Of historical interest is his theoretical work, *A Treatise on Harmony*. The composition *Kammer-Sinfonie* in D minor for strings is a good example of his conservative but not uninteresting style.

PERCUSSION INSTRUMENTS – in the present century there has been a great mushrooming in the number and variety of percussion instruments used in classical music – not only in the orchestra but also in chamber music. In the majority of cases these instruments are sounded by being struck, but the group also embraces instruments that are scraped, shaken and even plucked; they may be pitched or unpitched and in each case may be membranophones (the sound is produced by vibration of a membrane – pitched: kettle drum or tympanum; unpitched: bass drum) or idiophones (sound produced by the vibration of its own material – pitched: xylophone; unpitched: castanets). Gordon Jacob in his book on orchestration refers to percussion instruments as belonging to 'the kitchen department'; however, composers are capable of producing a great variety of sheer musical beauty in the use of percussion – from the spare employment of tympani in Haydn and Mozart symphonies to Stravinsky's *Rite of Spring* or Bartók's marvellous Sonata for two pianos and two percussion players. The Mexican composer Carlos Chavez has written a *Toccata* for six percussion. The extraordinary virtuoso percussionist Evelyn Glennie, profoundly deaf, has commissioned or had composed for her a whole range of exciting pieces. Since World War II especially, many non-Western percussion instruments have been introduced, such as the West African gong or bell.

PERFORMANCE PRACTICE – this involves the study of the relationship between the written notes and the actual sounds, and also the way music is performed in different historical periods. One may say that musical notation is a set of instructions from the composer to the performer on how he wishes his music to sound. Whether Bach would be pleased or not, any one of his preludes and fugues for harpsichord sounds very different when rendered on the piano; the same goes for a Haydn symphony as performed in his time, compared to a performance in the Royal Festival Hall by a leading London symphony orchestra; and should a brass work of Gabrieli be played anywhere but in a church? With the ever-increasing refinement in musicological research the problem of authenticity in performance of music of the past has become a vexed one. And with regard to new demands on the performer by contemporary composers, a whole world of fresh performance practices has arisen. Again, select any five conductors directing a performance of, say, Tchaikovsky's Symphony No. 5, and you will hear differences in tempo, dynamics and attention to compositional detail. There will always be differences of opinion and preferences. Yet, as one and one equals two, the composer cannot do without the performer and vice versa. The performer sounds out what the composer had in mind. It has been known for a composer either to pour a thousand curses on the performer or else smother him with delighted kisses.

PERGOLESI, GIOVANNI – an Italian composer who played a leading part in the development of eighteenth-century comic opera. And he lived only to the age of twenty-six; he seems to have been sickly from his childhood, may have had a limp and may have suffered from tubercular disease. Until the age of twenty-one he still had student status, and was employed at various courts and chapels, composing furiously. Pergolesi's first stage work was an opera seria, *Salustia*, but shortly after there followed his first comic opera, *Lo frate 'nnamorato* (The friar in love), which established his reputation in this field. His best-known stage work, still performed today, is his intermezzo in two parts, *La Serva Padrona* (The Maid as Mistress), in which a chambermaid tricks her master into marrying her. The work was inserted between the acts of his opera seria *Il prigioniero superbo* (The Haughty Prisoner) and contains the quintessence of Neapolitan comic opera, full of vitality and attractive melody. In addition to his opera writing Pergolesi composed a goodly supply of sacred works, of which the *Stabat Mater* for two solo voices and strings stands out, as well as chamber cantatas and arias.

PERIODICALS – the intellectual life of any particular age is clearly reflected in its periodicals or journals, and even magazines. Music has for long had its own periodicals. At the close of the seventeenth century musical periodicals merely published collections of songs; a hundred years later they were generally divided into two sections – one dealing with the practice of music, the other with its theory. In the nineteenth century the periodical had become a vehicle for discussion among musical connoisseurs, with newspapers devoting a section to more general discussion of the arts including music. Today there exists a vast range of musical periodicals – in Great Britain alone the following is a very short selection: *Early Music, Classical Music, Musical Times, Opera, Journal of the Plainsong and Medieval Society, Psychology of Music, The British Music Yearbook, Music Business Weekly, Royal School of Church Music Journal, Royal Musical Association Yearbook, The Gramophone Classical Record Catalogue, British Jazz Society Journal, Music and Theatre Digest.* Enough?

PERLMAN, ITZHAK – Israeli violinist with an international reputation. At the age of four he lost the use of his legs as a result of poliomyelitis; by the age of ten he had given numerous public concerts in Israel and made his professional début in the USA at the Carnegie Hall in 1963. In 1970 Perlman initiated his own master class at the USA Meadowbrooks Festival. His playing is distinguished by its rich tone and easy virtuosic technique. In addition to his authoritative grasp of the eighteenth- and nineteenth-century repertoire Perlman is known for his sympathetic attention to concerto, chamber and solo violin music of the twentieth century.

PÉROTIN – French composer who flourished in the second half of the twelfth century in Paris; he may have been associated with the cathedral of Notre Dame. Pérotin composed in the early medieval forms of organum, conductus and discant; these are simply various aspects of early vocal counterpoint. He made a major contribution to the early development of the motet. His music for two, three and four parts is of great beauty and you should make a point of listening to some examples, such as *Alleluia, Nativitas* and *Sederunt principes V. Adiuva*.

PETER AND THE WOLF – a work of particular charm which Prokofiev composed in 1936 for narrator and small orchestra, and which is continuingly popular with both children and adults. Each of the characters of the story is associated with a specific instrument and tune; their combination from time to time underlines Prokofiev's compositional ingenuity.

PETER GRIMES – an opera by Benjamin Britten first performed in 1945, which immediately brought international recognition for the composer. After Puccini, and except for Berg's *Wozzeck*, the world of opera writing had been badly ailing; the advent of *Peter Grimes* showed that this aspect of music theatre could still be a force. Its text, by Montagu Slater (derived from George Crabbe's poem *The Borough*), updated twentieth-century libretto writing at one stroke; the music showed how successful vocal and orchestral writing could be in contemporary terms. The spine of the plot deals with a fisherman, a loner, accused by his village folk of murdering his apprentice boy; he finally commits suicide. The music, with great dramatic conviction, portrays the fisherman's tortured soul, his community and the moods of the sea. The opera has a prologue and three acts.

PETRASSI, GOFFREDO – twentieth-century composer. He and Dallapiccola are the most important Italian composers of their generation. At the Conservatorio di Santa Cecilia and the Accademia di Santa Cecilia he proved to be a highly successful teacher of composition; British composers who studied with him include Kenneth Leighton, Peter Maxwell Davies, Gordon Crosse and Cornelius Cardew. Petrassi's musical language is heterogeneous but his style is distinctive; the sum of his progress is expressed through the eight Concertos for orchestra composed between 1931 and 1972. Regrettably, to date little of his music is recorded. A piece for guitar, *Nunc*, expresses his idiom in a nutshell.

PETRUCCI, OTTAVIANO – Italian music printer active in the late fifteenth and first half of the sixteenth century. He was the first to print polyphonic music from movable type. In 1498 he was granted a licence by the Doge of Venice which gave him exclusive printing rights for twenty years. In 1501 he issued his *Harmonice musices odhecaton A* (one hundred songs in harmonic music, 'A' being the first of a proposed series), which actually contained ninety-six pieces, mainly three- and four-part French chansons plus a few pieces from Flanders, Italy, Germany and Spain. The B and C volumes were published by 1504. Other of his publications included lute tablature, Masses and motets. The effect of Petrucci's achievement was to initiate the widespread dissemination of polyphonic music.

PFITZNER, HANS – German composer and conductor. Although he lived to the mid-twentieth century his most important works were written before 1920. He detested the Nazi régime, during which he worked quietly as an accompanist and local conductor. His house with all his possessions was completely destroyed during a bombing raid on Munich, after which Reger's widow gave him a piano. Of his varied output the work by which he is best known is his opera *Palestrina*, completed in 1917, which Pfitzner describes as a 'musical legend'; the preludes to each of the three acts are sometimes performed in the concert hall. The plot deals with the artist's conflict with society, as expressed in Palestrina's clash with the Council of Trent in the sixteenth century over what is required of church music; this sentiment has something in common with Wagner's *Die Meistersinger* and Hindemith's *Mathis der Maler*.

PHYSICS OF MUSIC – we should bear in mind that, as we listen to our favourite piece by Bach, Beethoven, Brahms or Bartók, a mass of sound activity is going on to do with the science of vibration theory. This aspect of music-making doesn't really concern you but at least you should be aware of it. Musical sounds are complex things, even when only a solo violin or clarinet is played. Any musical instrument, including the voice, offers a combination of vibrations to produce its particular character, and of course when a group of instruments is playing together as an ensemble or an orchestra, matters become even more intricate; frequency of vibration, tonal colour, size and shape of the playing area are involved. Also involved is the behaviour of the ear – of our organs the one about which, still, least is known. Consideration also has to be given to whether an instrument is bowed, struck, blown or plucked. What has long been established is that sound travels in wave forms of marked complexity. With the age of electricity the physics of music has advanced into fresh areas of study, such as recording and its transmission via broadcast, LPs, tapes, CDs and laser reproduction. To all this you need only remark 'Really?' and carry on with your joyful listening.

PIANO – I would say that, as the lion is the king of beasts, so the piano is the king of instruments; from Mozart to the present by far the largest amount of solo music composed has been for the piano. Its peak was perhaps reached in the nineteenth century, despite some quite wonderful examples of piano-writing appearing in our own century. Cristofori, keeper of instruments at the Medici court in Florence, had already constructed in the 1720s several examples of the piano which in action and quality of sound were not far short of models of the early nineteenth century. His main achievement was to develop a hammer action which could strike the string and fall back quickly into its inert position. Improvements were steadily made as regards soundboard, strings, wooden frame and pedals. The leading builders of pianos were the

208

Germans; names still famous today are Bechstein, Blüthner, Bösendorfer (Austrian) and Steinway. English, French and American firms have also contributed to the piano's evolution, while the Russian Petrov and the Japanese Yamaha models, particularly the latter, have effectively entered the postwar market. For a quick parade of solo piano music, say, six pieces, my personal choice is: Beethoven's Sonata No. 23 in F minor (the *Appassionata*), Chopin's *Scherzo* in C sharp minor No. 3, Brahms's three *Intermezzos* Op. 117, Liszt's *Hungarian Rhapsody* No. 2 in C sharp minor, Debussy's *Prélude* No. 10 (*La cathédrale engloutie*), Bartók's *Allegro barbaro*.

PICCINNI, NICCOLÒ – Italian comic opera composer flourishing in both Italy and France in the second half of the eighteenth century. He was not a trail-blazer like his contemporary Gluck. His career took off in Naples, and before his departure for Paris his opera were also very successful in Rome. Piccinni's most famous opera, *La Cecchina* (also known as *The Good Girl*), deals with an orphan girl who loves and is loved by her master; this arouses jealousy among her fellow servants and opposition from the master's family; it is revealed, however, that the girl, La Cecchina, is in fact a baroness, so all ends happily. It is said that Piccinni wrote some 130 operas; with an output of this size it is no surprise that most were turned out according to the easy formula of the time. But one or two, such as *La Cecchina*, show Piccinni's gift for elegance and grace, lyrical melody and comic characterisation. The Piccinni-Gluck 'war' in Paris was fought, not between the composers, but by opposing factions of critics and audiences supporting their respective idols.

PICCOLO – the highest-pitched member of the flute family; it sounds an octave above the concert instrument. Few solo pieces are written for it, but the instrument is particularly useful in orchestral writing when a top line requires underlining at dramatic moments or, because of its agility, when rhythms or runs call for emphasis. It is also useful in wind bands. It is used to charming effect in the Chinese Dance from Tchaikovsky's *Nutcracker* ballet.

PIJPER, WILLEM – the most important Dutch composer in the first half of the twentieth century; his teaching had a marked influence on Dutch composition. Pijper's works show a concern with polytonality (working in more than one key simultaneously) and polyrhythm (working with several metrical units at the same time); but his prime technical device is a 'germ-cell', which serves as the sole material on which a movement or even an entire work is based. One of his best-known works is the

Symphony No. 2 (1922), which clearly displays these compositional techniques and at the same time is full of lyricism and drama.

PISTON, WALTER – American composer who flourished mainly in the first half of the twentieth century. In his early years he played in theatre orchestras and dance bands; he also trained as a draughtsman, which accounts for the excellent lay-out and calligraphy of his original scores; his internationally known book, *Orchestration*, contains diagrams and illustrations most of which he drew himself. On his return to America after study in Paris he was offered a lectureship at Harvard; there he remained until 1960, by which time he held the Chair in Music. His two most famous pupils were Elliott Carter and Leonard Bernstein. Another of his first-class text books is *Harmony*, which has been translated into many languages. Piston's music is unjustly neglected in European concert halls; it is full of expansive melody together with witty or driving rhythm, and always well-fashioned, mainly in a neo-classical style. Two attractive examples are *The Incredible Flutist*, a suite for orchestra created out of his ballet of the same title, and his *Symphony No. 5*. No less than eleven major works were commissioned by the Boston Symphony Orchestra.

PITCH – a term often used but not easy to define in simple language. I'll have a go: pitch is a sound that is coherent and not just a buzz, clonk, clatter or thud; the sound, that is, the note, can be identified on its own by an ear that has 'absolute pitch' ability; very few people possess absolute or perfect pitch, and that includes composers and other musicians; the rest of us have to rely on 'relative pitch', meaning that we are able to identify a note if we know its context. Often an instrumentalist, through training, can develop accurate pitching, chiefly confined to his/her instrument; so a violinist or trombonist will usually pitch a note or tune the instrument with near perfect accuracy. The voice finds greatest difficulty with accurate pitching, since it has no mechanical assistance whatsoever – the singer has inwardly to 'feel' the note being reached for. How do all the members of an orchestra play 'in tune'? Well, no doubt you have seen and heard the first oboe player sound out a note – it is the note A vibrating at 440 frequencies per second – and then all the players tune their respective instruments to that note. Why the oboe? I'm not quite sure, except to say that it can pierce through the instrumental hubbub before the performance proper starts, its initial tuning for the A required is the most reliable, and anyway historically the woodwind section of the orchestra has been built around the oboe. The evolution of pitch has a long and complicated history; the foregoing, however, is, I hope, sufficient for your music-loving purposes.

210

PIZZETTI, ILDEBRANDO – a somewhat conservative Italian composer, whose best works date from the first three or so decades of the twentieth century. Of his substantial opera output, *Fedra* has proved the most interesting. In this genre his aim was to counteract the excess attention given to melody by Puccini; instead he produced a kind of arioso/recitative vocal style which, unfortunately, could become monotonous. His songs and choral pieces are freer and less selfconscious, for example, *Tre Composizione corali* for unaccompanied chorus. Quite attractive is his orchestral suite *La Pisanelle* (She of Pisa).

PIZZICATO – an instruction for instruments that are normally bowed (e.g. violin, viola, cello, double bass) that the string or strings should be plucked. The sound can be very effective, whether produced by a solo instrument or by a string section of the orchestra. The first traceable direction for pizzicato is to be found in Monteverdian opera. Leopold Mozart, Wolfgang's father, comments on its use in his treatise on string playing, and Paganini is the first composer to make the left hand, the fingering hand, pizzicato in combination with the use of the bow. Towards the close of the first movement of his String Quartet No. 2 Bartók writes chordal pizzicato for the cello to great serious effect; the same composer introduced a violent pizzicato known now as the 'Bartók snap'.

PLAINCHANT – in the early monodic music of the Church, Western Europe had five liturgies of chant repertory to Latin texts – Gregorian, Ambrosian, Mozarabic, Old Roman and Gallic. Their roots may be traced back to chant practice in the Jewish synagogue during the apostolic period. No notation record has thus far been traced back to before the ninth century. In due course only the Gregorian chant survived, later to develop from monodic to polyphonic practice. Plainchant refers to the monophonic unison music of all five sets of repertory. Eastern European plainchant came to be dominated by the Greek rite at Constantinople known as Byzantine chant. The primary function of all the liturgies, both East and West, is the continuous rehearsal of the Last Supper in the Eucharist which, in the West, is termed the Mass.

PLAYFORD, JOHN – seventeenth-century English publisher and bookseller. Although he brought out a number of non-musical works, Playford's historical interest lies in his publication of English music of the period; we are indebted to him for preserving important works by Purcell, Locke, the brothers Lawes (William and Henry), Simpson and Dering. The books he issued fall into three categories: the theory of music and tutors for various instruments; collections of songs and instrumental pieces; psalms, hymns and psalm paraphrases. Playford's best-known publication *The English Dancing Master* underwent several editions well into the eighteenth century, probably because of the revival of interest in country dance, and because it was the largest single source of ballad songs. His son, Henry, is remembered for his publication of Purcell's *Orpheus Britannicus*.

PLECTRUM – any item which is used to pluck the strings of an instrument. The Greeks already knew about the plectrum, and in medieval Arabic writings there is reference to the materials used – wood, ivory, quill, bone, even tortoiseshell and eagle's talons. It enhances tremolando effects and gives a timbre closer to plucking with the fingernail rather than with the flesh of the fingertip. Most jazz and pop guitarists invariably use a plectrum made of plastic.

POLKA – one of the most popular ballroom dances of the nineteenth century; it has a lively two-beats-to-the-bar rhythm and is danced in couples. It seems to have originated in that part of Czechoslovakia (as was) known as Bohemia; but before then it may well have stemmed from the Polish *krakowiak* dance-songs. In classical music, polkas have appeared as pieces for solo instrument, orchestra, in chamber music and in opera. Smetana used the polka in his opera *The Bartered Bride*, in his String Quartet No. 1 (*From my Life*) and in his symphonic poem *Vltava* (The Moldau). Later examples are in Walton's *Façade*, Shostakovich's ballet *The Golden Age*, and there is Stravinsky's cheeky *Circus Polka*.

POLLINI, MAURIZIO – outstanding and highly versatile twentieth-century Italian piano virtuoso. As evidenced in his concert and broadcast performances and in his many recordings, Pollini's command of a composer's style is remarkable, be it Bach's preludes and fugues or Boulez's *Second Sonata*. He gets to the very centre of the music's intention; even with a work such as Nono's *Como una ola de fuerza y luz* for soprano, piano and orchestra, which employs electro-acoustics, Pollini shows that he certainly knows his 'avant from his elbow'. He is unreservedly my favourite pianist. His recording of Schoenberg's complete solo piano music will make you think of that polemical composer afresh and you will be highly attracted to his interpretations of Beethoven, Chopin, Brahms and Liszt.

POLONAISE – a dance from Poland which now carries a French nomenclature, because its development in classical music has occurred outside its country of origin. In Poland it is still danced at festivities, particularly weddings. Its character is dignified and its pulse is three-beats-to-the-bar;

212

its use as a courtly dance created international interest in it. Bach wrote a polonaise in his keyboard *French Suite* No. 6 and orchestral *Suite* No. 2. Later Beethoven (*Polonaise* in C major, Op. 89) and Weber (*Polacca brillante*) were among the composers who wrote examples for the piano; but the genre is inseparable from Chopin's sixteen polonaises, of which the *Polonaise* in A flat, Op. 53 is the *crème de la crème*. Other composers who turned out polonaises include Schumann (*Papillons*, Op. 2 No. 11), Liszt (*Fest-Polonaise*) and even Wagner (*Polonaise* in D major Op. 2). Tchaikovsky wrote a polonaise for his ballet *Sleeping Beauty*, Musorgsky used its rhythm in the prologue to his opera *Boris Godunov* and Glinka turned out a *Polonaise* in E for orchestra.

PONCHIELLI, AMILCARE – an Italian opera composer, a contemporary of Verdi. His operas received fair circulation, mainly in Italy. An eclectic style and a lack of individual spine have not given his stage works long life. The exception is *La Gioconda*, which still appears to some extent in the modern repertoire; it contains three outstanding arias and the 'Dance of the Hours' ballet, often played on its own in the concert hall and which has earned additional popularity as a cartoon sequence in Disney's *Fantasia*. La Gioconda is a Venetian ballad singer who is in love with a nobleman but at the same time is sought after by a villain; the nobleman in turn loves a Venetian senator's wife; when the senator discovers his wife's infidelity, she is saved by the humble ballad singer because she rescued the singer's mother from a mob. The ballad singer then kills herself. Ponchielli was for a time professor of counterpoint at the Milan Conservatory; his best-known pupils were Puccini and Mascagni.

PONTE, LORENZO DA – See *Da Ponte, Lorenzo*.

POPULAR MUSIC – we all enjoy some branch or other of popular music, so what does this term refer to? It refers to any kind of music that is easy to listen to, usually having clear, simple melody, and which attracts a majority of people in any particular musical culture. It is obvious that popular music existed long before the twentieth century; for example, if we go back to the sixteenth, the lighter madrigals, with the use of part-books, were much in circulation; in the seventeenth century Purcell and his contemporaries turned out tavern songs, often in the form of canons and not infrequently spiced with naughty words and sentiments; then there was in England the rich selection of ballad songs in the eighteenth century and in Europe a plethora of divertimentos and serenades; the nineteenth century pupped arias, choruses and ballet numbers from opera as well as song and dance music – waltzes, polkas and the like. By this time industrialisation had created large communities of people who needed and received a steady flow of music that made for easy listening, to be memorised then whistled or sung; and music-making at home, mainly around the piano, flourished among the middle classes. Operetta and the music hall led to the twentieth-century musical, in which the influence and achievement of the American genre became paramount, along with the writing of single songs, centred in New York.

Commercialism in general and through recording in particular has turned popular music into a multi-million pound/dollar industry over the past six or seven decades. Postwar popular music has been dominated by the tastes of adolescents, and has a rapid turnover. The dichotomy of sound between popular and classical music today is enormous compared with, say, Mozart's time; this widening had already begun in the latter half of the nineteenth century, and can be explained by a complex set of social, cultural and musical factors. But we classical music lovers should not pooh-pooh popular music; in fact, a great deal of the sort of works we listen to may be described as popular according to my opening definition, from Bach onwards; hence the success of recordings entitled 'popular classics'. Another thing that needs to be remembered is that popular music at its best is musically often ingenious, inventive and remarkably well-formed. It is a pity that twentieth-century classical composers have not made more use of popular music material, as was the normal habit in the past. Do I hear you whistling *Yellow Submarine* or humming *White Christmas* or belting out *Land of Hope and Glory*?

POULENC, FRANCIS – twentieth-century French composer and pianist, perhaps the finest writer of the type of French song known as *mélodie* since Fauré. His seemingly simplistic style of composition belies a great subtlety of thought and highly refined compositional technique. Poulenc was taught the piano by his mother, and at fourteen experienced a deep excitement on hearing Stravinsky's *The Rite of Spring*. He established his reputation as an important composer after the presentation in Paris of *Les biches* (The Darlings) in 1924, aged twenty-five; this was a ballet commissioned by Dyagilev. His attractive piano piece *Trois mouvements perpétuels* had already been in circulation for several years, while another piano piece, *Rapsodie nègre*, dedicated to Satie, was his first published item, composed at the age of nineteen. Poulenc's association with the singer Pierre Bernac proved a kick-off point for the output of his songs, and his sacred choral music must be reckoned close or even equal to that of Messiaen in this field of French twentieth-century composition. His serious side reached full expression in his opera

214

Dialogues des Carmélites, about the sufferings of a group of nuns in the French Revolution. He was a member of Les Six; of this group his life-long friend was Auric. Poulenc's music is spicy, often droll, fluent, full of lively rhythm and suffused with catchy motifs. Three samples for you: *Quatre petites prières de Saint François d'Assise* for male chorus, Concerto for organ, strings and percussion, Trio for oboe, bassoon and piano.

POUSSEUR, HENRI – contemporary Belgian composer, theorist and teacher. An early influence on his music was Webern and later, in his association with them, he was influenced by Boulez, Berio and Stockhausen; so, as you would deduce, Pousseur is an avant-garde com-poser. Two contrasting works are his electronic ballet *Electre*, and *Répons* (Response – in the liturgical sense) for flute, harp, two pianos, percus-sion, violin and cello; unfortunately neither is yet recorded. Pousseur founded an electronic music studio in Brussels and is a lecturer at Liège University; his essays include discussion on the harmony of Stravinsky's *Agon* and *The Rite of Spring*, the semantics of music and music's current role in society.

PRAETORIUS, MICHAEL – a late sixteenth- and early seventeenth-century German composer. He was active in Wolfenbüttel, Regensburg, Kassel, Dresden and Magdeburg, and he visited Prague, Leipzig, Nuremberg and Bayreuth; this moving around illustrates that within the German musical world of the time he was greatly appreciated. Praetorius was at the core of Lutheran musical development; he is known to have associated with Schütz. Considering his short lifespan, his prolific output is remarkable. In the latter part of his career – he was largely self-taught – he became aware of contemporary Italian music, appreciating especially the masses and motets of Palestrina. Praetorius was also a distinguished organist. In addition to his compositions he is known historically for his theoretical work *Syntagma musicum*, which deals with the principles and liturgical constituents of religious music; gives a full account of Johann Walter's collaboration with Luther; provides detailed information on the instruments of his day; and, finally, discusses contemporary musical form. The following motets are worthy examples of his style: *Wachet auf, ruft uns die Stimme*, the seven-part *Resonet in laudibus* and the four-part *Maria Magdalena*. There are several other musical Praetoriuses of the time, but Michael is the most important.

PRAGUE – one of the most musical cities of Europe. In 1918 it was the capital of the Czechoslovakian Republic, newly formed; before that the capital of Bohemia, within the Austrian Empire; now it is simply the capital of the Czech nation, split off from its Slovak cousins by mutual agreement. Prague has the first Central European university; modelled on Paris, it was established in 1348 when the city became an imperial capital. It is renowned for its beautiful Baroque architecture, built under the Habsburgs. Its first musical distinction emerges with the excellent opera productions of the seventeenth and eighteenth centuries brought in from Italy. High-quality performances of concert music followed, including works by Mozart, Weber, Beethoven and Spohr; Mozart's opera *Don Giovanni* had its première there. Prague, with its setting on the Vltava river and its growing musical reputation in terms of audience appreciation, became a must for travelling virtuosos. Gradually native composers of quality began to make an impression – first Dušek and Tomašek, followed by Smetana and Dvořák, then Janáček, Martinů and Hába. Until the Second World War and domination by the Soviet Union, Prague was an important centre for the performance of modern music. That Schoenberg, Shostakovich, Milhaud, Hindemith, Ravel, Weill, all had important performances of their works in Prague shows the praiseworthy open-mindedness of its musical directors and its audiences. Presently its long-standing reputation is being revived.

PRELUDE – an instrumental piece intended to precede a further piece or group of pieces. It has no specific form; the prelude evolved from the brief introductions rendered by Renaissance and early Baroque lutenists, keyboard players and organists before 'getting down to it', as it were. These introductions were improvisatory, and usually preceded a suite of dances and, later, instrumental suites. The very apotheosis of the attached prelude comes in Bach's oeuvre, with his preludes for the fugues in his harpsichord and organ works, in due course imitated by Mendelssohn, Liszt, Brahms and Franck. The independent, short piece described as a prelude was firmly established by the piano set of Chopin; here the music deals with a motif or mood. In his footsteps there followed similar pieces by composers such as Skryabin, Szymanowski, Debussy, Rakhmaninov, Messiaen, and not forgetting Gershwin.

PRÉLUDE À L'APRÈS-MIDI D'UN FAUNE – see *Après-Midi d'un Faune, Prélude à l'*.

PRESTON, SIMON – leading twentieth-century English organist; under the influence of George Malcolm he became a first-class harpsichordist to boot. Currently he is organist and lecturer at Christ Church, Oxford. Preston has given many organ recitals both in England and abroad, as well as making recordings; in addition to the normal repertoire his distinctive interpretations may be heard in performances of works by Liszt and Messiaen, while his recording of the Handel organ concertos under Menuhin is much admired. Preston is also no mean conductor of choral music. In 1981 he became first organist of Westminster Abbey.

PREVIN, ANDRÉ – twentieth-century American composer, pianist, broadcaster and conductor; a versatile musician, born in Germany. Because of the Nazi régime his family was forced to leave, and settled in Los Angeles in 1939. Previn became a very fine professional jazz pianist, as well as an orchestrator for MGM film studios; in due course he became MGM's musical director, as well as producing a continuous flow of film music of great distinction, for example *Bad Day at Black Rock* starring Spencer Tracy. His film music won him four Oscars – an impressive achievement. Previn then turned to a conducting career; from 1969 to 1979 he was music director of the London Symphony Orchestra, bringing to its performances a new distinction and many engagements; with them he recorded the symphonies of Vaughan Williams and Walton. He has a particular feel for twentieth-century English music. His compositions reflect both his classical and popular sides, and include scores for the musicals *Coco* and *The Good Companions* as well as *Bowing and Scraping* for jazz ensemble and a Concerto for piano and orchestra.

PRICE, LEONTYNE – a black American soprano of international stature. She started to sing seriously while training as a teacher; performances in operas by Virgil Thomson and Barber, the roles of Bess in Gershwin's *Porgy and Bess* in the theatre and Tosca in the opera of that name on television brought her firmly into the limelight. There followed a steady stream of roles in the traditional operatic repertoire, of which the most acclaimed has been the title role in Verdi's *Aïda*. Price has made numerous recordings, both of complete operas and of compilations.

PRINTING – the printing of music has been a boon to composer, performer and listener, since it has proved a primary means of distributing a great variety of music worldwide. Even to this day it requires skill on the technical side and adroit marketing, despite the advent of recording and broadcasting. From the sixteenth century onwards there has been steady development in materials and engraving procedures. For a long time the good engraver was worth his weight in gold to a publishing house. Because of new techniques of reproduction the music engraver has almost died out, to be replaced by various types of reprographic machines. And now we have arrived at the printing of music by computer; almost with each year that passes, computer music programmes are becoming more versatile and sophisticated. In fact, if he so wishes, the composer, because of the computer, can become the complete narcissist. For it is possible for him to compose, perform, listen to and reproduce his music, taking not one step out of his studio.

PROGRAMME MUSIC – it was Liszt who invented the term 'programme music', as he invented the term 'symphonic poem'. What he meant was a piece of music to which the composer added a description, to guide the listener as to the piece's poetic intentions, to ensure that the listener's reaction was not independent but rather followed the composer's literal conception of the piece from its beginning to its end. In time Liszt's definition took on a narrower meaning and was applied to pieces which had a clear narrative purpose, almost telling a story in sound. A very apt example of such a piece is Richard Strauss's orchestral *Don Juan*. A quasi-programmatic idea lies behind Beethoven's Symphony No. 6 (the *Pastoral*), in which each of the five movements is given a specific title and leads the listener's thought along in a mixture of the narrative and the emotional. For a work to be given a title does not mean that it must be programmatic; Debussy's three-movement *La Mer*, however impressive, does no more than evoke atmosphere and the mood of the sea; this aspect of musical expression is far more common, and may be traced back as far as the sixteenth century to Janequin's chanson *La guerre* or Byrd's *Battel*, a fifteen-piece keyboard suite. Imitation, such as Daquin's harpsichord piece *Le coucou*, is not programme music, neither is any music involving words – song, story (Prokofiev's *Peter and the Wolf*) or opera (Wagner's *Ring* cycle), although in the last-named example the mutation and transmutation of the plethora of *Leitmotifs* is certainly meant to guide the listener in the narrative and emotional progress of, say, the character of Siegfried. In sum, programme music is less important than it at first seems, in the panoply of music.

PROKOFIEV, SERGEY – one of this century's greatest and most attractive composers. All his life he wrote stage music of prime quality, but at the same time his contribution to the genres of piano sonata, concerto and symphony reveals a world of the utmost invention and musical imagination. As with his compatriot, Shostakovich, he was not by nature cut out to pursue a radical path in musical language, such as is to be noted in the works of Debussy, Schoenberg and even Stravinsky, another compatriot. Rather, Prokofiev was content to treat as his roots the heritage of eighteenth-century classicism, but to this he brought his own distinctive musical character, full of original melodic line, harmonic twist, wild rhythm and colourful orchestration. His piano virtuosity enabled him to add significantly to that instrument's repertoire.

He was born in the Ukraine of cultivated and well-off parents; composition burst out of him from the early age of five and never ceased to flow obsessively right up until his death – ironically, Prokofiev died on the same day as Stalin, of whom he had fallen foul. He left for the USA in 1918, shortly after the Russian Revolution, and did not return to resettle permanently until 1936. As will be appreciated, in the Soviet Union his output was a mixture of music written according to his own creative desires and music written to fulfil the politicised aesthetics of the Soviet authorities. Prokofiev's return was due to a desire to be in his native cultural milieu and with his old Russian friends, not at all for political reasons. In fact, he showed a marked lack of political consciousness, even a political naïveté; he seemed only to be able to tune in, as it were, to the music bubbling out of him.

He suffered a ghastly experience when his Spanish-born wife, Lina, was arrested and, under the madness of the Stalinist régime, committed to a labour camp on charges of espionage. Happily, she managed to get to England with their second son, Oleg, after Prokofiev's death. Now a Prokofiev Foundation has been created, based in London at Goldsmiths College (which is to house an archive of Prokofiev's works) and the Blackheath Concert Halls. Recordings of Prokofiev's music are numerous; here are three for a start: the Violin Concerto No. 1 Op. 55; Orchestral Suites Nos. 1–3 from the ballet *Romeo and Juliet*; Symphony No. 1 in D Op. 25 (the *Classical*).

PSALM – the word refers to a sacred song or poem. In our musical history it concerns the Psalter or the Book of Psalms of the Bible, with its 150 poems; these are divided into several categories – poems of exile, of pilgrimage, of those ascribed to David. Psalm settings go back to before Gregorian chant, but starting from monodic (single-line) delivery they gradually diverge, on the one hand involving the church congregation – this later develops into hymn writing – and on the other being taken up by professional composers in their motets and anthems. Examples of psalm-setting from Monteverdi onwards are his *Vespers of 1610*, Handel's *Chandos Anthems*, Bach's cantatas, whose texts include excerpts from the psalms, Mendelssohn's *Psalm 95*, Schumann's *Psalm 40*, Liszt's *Psalm 19*, Brahms's *Psalm 51* Op. 29, Kodály's *Psalmus hungaricus*, Stravinsky's *Symphony of Psalms*, Penderecki's *Psalmy Dawida*.

PSYCHOLOGY OF MUSIC – this aspect of musical investigation examines the different processes our brain uses to make sense of the sounds our ears take in. It is a complicated study, essentially scientific, and still in its early stages of development. While the psychology of music may

219

appear to be a cold-hearted business when we think of our passionate reaction to a Bach cantata, Beethoven string quartet or Verdi opera, it is deeply interested in understanding that arousal of passion, in following our cognitive processes, how we make sense of music. Ask yourself why one piece of music soothes you, another elates you and yet another brings tears to your eyes. Your answer is likely to be very personal, perhaps illogical and incoherent as well; your explanation will be one-sided and insufficient. In the end we are inclined to remark, 'music is something magical'. The areas of investigation for the psychology of music include: pitch, loudness, timbre and texture, rhythm and tempo, melody and harmony, tonal memory, attention span, performance skills, musical creativity, technical and aesthetic change. As a music lover one is inclined to dismiss all this as unnecessary, but one must surely grant the psychologist the right to investigate the phenomenon of music, since it is such a fundamental element in individual and collective social behaviour. What a tiresome matter it all is. Excuse me while I put on a CD of Schubert songs, or should I rather hear some Debussy preludes or ...

PUCCINI, GIACOMO – over the last hundred years the most popular opera composer. He wrote only twelve operas and little else; of these, five are perennial hits – *Manon Lescaut*, *La Bohème*, *Tosca*, *Madama Butterfly*, and *Turandot*. Puccini began his musical career as a choirboy, then an organist. He began to compose in his late teens; in Pisa he heard a performance of Verdi's *Aïda* which set flowing his still untapped operatic genius. After three years at the Milan Conservatory, where one of his teachers was Ponchielli, composer of *La Gioconda*, he met Giulio Ricordi, who became a lifelong friend and Puccini's exclusive publisher. His third opera, *Manon Lescaut*, was a resounding success, and brought him international recognition; even George Bernard Shaw, wearing his grumpy music critic's hat, after the opera's London production acknowledged its quality. Some regard Puccini's next opera, *La Bohème*, as his masterpiece, though initially it did not achieve the same immediate success as *Manon Lescaut*.

From 1909, after *Tosca* and *Madama Butterfly*, Puccini did not compose another opera for six years, because of a family scandal: his wife, Elvira, with whom Puccini had had quite a long affair before they were married, accused one of their maids of having an intimate relationship with her husband; the maid was driven to suicide; an autopsy established her innocence and a following court case found against Elvira. The whole affair caused a sensation in Italy, and badly affected the creativity of the hypersensitive Puccini. He composed his last opera, *Turandot*, in his mid-sixties, a work over which he struggled more than on anything he had written before. He did not live to complete it or to see its first performance, given unfinished under Toscanini at La Scala.

Puccini could not draw on the range of character that is to be found in the operas of Mozart, Verdi or Wagner, but within his narrower field – seven of his works are named after their heroines – he expressed pathos, despair, erotic passion and tenderness with an unmatched certainty of dramatic and musical skill. With a succession of lyrical, vocal lines supported by perfectly balanced orchestral accompaniment he could build up tension to an outburst which completely swamped the singers and the audience. Each opera succeeds in swiftly pulling the audience into its world. To underline his still evergreen appeal there are, for example, currently twenty-one complete recordings of *La Bohème*, fifteen of *Madama Butterfly*, seventeen of *Tosca*, not to speak of dozens of excerpts from almost all his operas.

PULCINELLA – Dyaghilev commissioned this ballet with song from Stravinsky in 1920. Léonide Massine was the choreographer and Picasso did the décor and costumes; its first performance in Paris was a great success. The music draws on material from the works of Pergolesi, the eighteenth-century Neapolitan comic opera composer, and is a delightful example of Stravinsky's neo-classical mode.

PUNCH AND JUDY – to date perhaps Birtwistle's finest opera, and certainly the first English opera to make a mark since Britten's *Peter Grimes*. It is in one act, split into several tableaux, and received its first performance at Aldeburgh in 1968 (it is hard to believe that it is already twenty-six years old). *Punch and Judy* is built from non-evolving formal units; it is highly ritualised (a process to which Birtwistle is much attracted), and the characters are static figures representing abstract ideas. Violence and cruelty are paramount features. Nevertheless the power and drama of the music, both vocal and instrumental, are completely absorbing.

PURCELL, HENRY – seventeenth-century English composer who sang both bass and countertenor as well as being a first-rate organist. Some consider that, following the Tudor period, the two greatest composers were Monteverdi and Purcell. The latter's claim to this position may be acknowledged in the range and quality of his compositions and, following from this, the consistent attention they have received until the present day. He died aged but thirty-six, and his surviving works go back only to 1680, when he was twenty-one; during this fifteen-year period he produced one opera (*Dido and Aeneas*), five semi-operas, a mass of incidental music for plays, anthems, services and other sacred pieces, odes and welcome songs, solo songs, and music for string ensembles as well as pieces for harpsichord. He also wrote nearly eighty catches, one as attractive as the next and some a bit lewd, which, with his technical fluency, he must have dashed off after breakfast, or a pint or two, for his own and friends' amusement. All his works reveal the special and attractive quality of the English melodic genius.

Purcell's music was widely known – by the populace at large through his involvement with the theatre, by the church through his writing of sacred music, and by the court through his odes and welcome songs. He had a remarkable ability to paint aurally an effect or description, such as the Frost Scene in the semi-opera *King Arthur*. The string fantasias and sonatas for violas or violins exhibit easily flowing contrapuntal ingenuity, while his anthems, for example *Like as the hart* or *Haste Thee, O God*, can be deeply moving. Purcell's handling of chromatic harmony is unique in the whole of late seventeenth-century music and anticipates the sophistication of the later Baroque period. His setting of the English language is, perhaps, unmatched; this is what Britten, among other aspects, learnt from him. His imaginative use of ground-bass technique, in which so often the melodic phrasing runs across the ground-bass unit, acts as an evergreen model for composers. Enter Purcell's world with the following: Chaconne in G minor for strings, *March and Canzona* in C minor for brass, *Ode for St Cecilia's Day* (Hail, Bright Cecilia) and the anthem *I was glad*.

QUADRILLE – a dance performed by sets of four, six or eight couples, having a fairly intricate routine of steps; very popular in nineteenth-century ballrooms. Its origins lie in both Italy and Spain, via a dance form used in French eighteenth-century ballet and opera. As a popular dance it arrived in London from Paris in 1815. Its structure is made up usually of five sections, and its lively rhythm is in two-beats-to-the-bar. Composers of dance music in the nineteenth century, including the Johann Strausses, senior and junior, wrote piles of quadrilles; classical music composers were inclined to make fun of it, especially the French, such as Chabrier with his *Souvenirs de Munich* (on themes from Wagner's *Tristan und Isolde*) and Fauré with his *Souvenirs de Bayreuth* (on themes from Wagner's *Ring*). Sacrilege, making fun of Wagner. While working in the Powick Asylum as a conductor, Elgar wrote some quadrilles, using bits of this material in his *Wand of Youth* suite.

QUANTZ, JOHANN – quite a talented eighteenth-century German composer; he was a very fine flautist and flute-maker. Quantz also wrote a fair amount on musical subjects, the most important of which is his treatise on the flute; it consists of three parts: performance on the instrument, ranging from simple to complicated matters such as ornamentation and style; commentary on how accompanying instruments should carry out their tasks; and finally an acute comparison of the characteristics of French, German and Italian playing styles. Quantz was the son of a blacksmith but rose to become a favoured personal musician to King Frederick the Great of Prussia. He only turned his attention to the flute when he found he could not make much of a living as an oboist. His compositions, it will by now have been gathered, are mainly for flute – with continuo, sonatas and concertos. If you are moved to hear some Quantz, there is the Concerto in D or the Trio Sonata, also in D, for flute, bassoon and continuo.

QUARTAL HARMONY – a harmonic system based on the interval of the fourth as opposed to the normal, traditional system built on the interval of the third. Quartal harmony appears in early two-part organum (in the eleventh century and earlier); in the twentieth century, harmonic thinking in fourths is to be found in the music of Debussy and Hindemith. Nowadays composers, as a matter of course, freely interchange between quartal and tertiary harmonic and melodic material.

QUARTER-TONE – as you might expect, a quarter-tone is an interval that is half a semitone. It is approximately one twenty-fourth of an octave and cannot be obtained on an instrument whose pitches are fixed, such as a piano or xylophone; but where the player has to 'find' his notes – good examples are the violin or the trombone – quarter-tones can be played – although it is not easy and requires some diligent practice. The Czech composer Hába has made a special feature in his music of the use of this tiny interval; other composers who have used quarter-tones are Ives, Boulez and Bartók.

Quartet

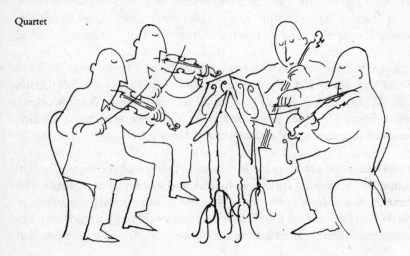

QUARTET – a piece, obviously, that is written for four parts, vocal or instrumental. In the Renaissance many madrigals and chansons were four-part and the same applies to nineteenth-century partsongs. Orchestral accompaniment to vocal quartets appears in oratorio and opera. By far the most significant four-part writing is for the string quartet; then there are piano quartets – normally for piano, violin, viola and cello – and wind quartets. Hindemith and Messiaen have written for the combination of clarinet, piano, violin and cello.

QUEEN OF SPADES, THE – the penultimate opera of Tchaikovsky, in which he combines a certain reworking of eighteenth-century musical clichés, the supernatural and characteristics of melodrama. He wrote it in six weeks during a stay in Florence. The plot: a presentable young man, a passionate gambler, falls in love with a presentable young girl, the granddaughter of a countess who in her youth was herself a gambler; her success was based on her knowledge of a combination of three cards; one night the young man hides in the old woman's bedroom, hoping to force her to tell him the three-card combination; when she sees him the shock kills her; her ghost then reveals the three cards to him; he plays a game against the young girl's fiancé; winning twice, he stakes everything he possesses on the third card and loses; he sees the countess's ghost smiling at him in triumph; now desperate, he ends his life. In her time the old lady had earned the nickname 'Queen of Spades'.

QUILTER, ROGER – English composer who flourished in the first half of the twentieth century; he made a significant contribution to the development of English song. He wrote more than 130 examples, many of which entered the repertoire of important recitalists, e.g. *Three Songs of William Blake*, Op. 20, *Love's Philosophy*, Op. 3 No. 1, *Seven Elizabethan Lyrics*. Quilter also wrote several successful light orchestral pieces such as *A Children's Overture*; these Sir Henry Wood frequently included in his Promenade Concert programmes. Quilter was a founder-member of the Musicians' Benevolent Fund.

QUODLIBET – a foxy bit of composing in which well-known melodies appear in combination; these can be written in sequence, which is not at all as clever. Such pieces are produced lightheartedly or to show off a modicum of contrapuntal technique; texts would often be a part of the operation. *Incatenatura*, as a matter of interest, refers to poetry made up entirely of lines quoted from other works. Musical quodlibets may be traced back to the late fifteenth century. Bach and Mozart both had some fun writing quodlibets; the former with his *Hochzeitsquodlibet* and the final one of the *Goldberg Variations* where he combines the theme with two popular German songs – *Cabbage and Beetroot* and *It is so long since I visited you*; Mozart with his *Gallimathias musicum*.

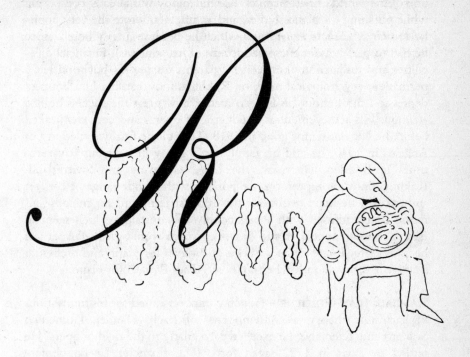

RAINIER, PRIAULX – South African composer who settled in London. After initial study at the South African College of Music, now part of the music department of the University of Cape Town, she won a scholarship to continue her studies at the Royal Academy of Music; later she spent a period in Paris studying with Nadia Boulanger. Rainier played and taught the violin before becoming a professor of composition at the RAM in 1943. Her works are finely fashioned and independent of the various modish trends in composition; this is evident in her *Quanta* for oboe and string trio and in her String Quartet.

RAKE'S PROGRESS, THE – a three-act opera with epilogue by Stravinsky; the libretto is by Auden and Kallman; stylistically the work is the epitome of Stravinsky's neo-classical writing. First performed in Venice in 1951, it is based on Hogarth's series of engravings and draws out their sardonic wit in highly individual vocal and instrumental composition.

RAKHMANINOV, SERGEY – Russian composer, pianist and conductor who settled in the USA. He is the last of the late Russian Romantics such as Rimsky-Korsakov and Tchaikovsky; in his time he proved to be one of the world's finest pianists. Rakhmaninov was already composing while pursuing his piano studies, and at nineteen wrote the very popular *Prelude in C sharp minor* (with which he became utterly bored, since he had to play it as an encore at dozens of his concerts). Financial difficulties and disharmony between his parents during his boyhood left a permanent psychological mark on Rakhmaninov, causing him bouts of depression throughout his life, no matter how great the success he had attained. His achievement as conductor of operas and concerts peaked before he left Russia for good in 1918. Though he finally settled in Los Angeles in 1940, he and his family led a gypsy life, staying at various times in Sweden, Denmark, the USA, Germany and Switzerland. Rakhmaninov's compositions are popular with a wide range of concert audiences. The main reason for this is his striking gift for melody; his music is also infused with a melancholy and nostalgia which seem to have a constant appeal. A trio of works which would give a fair idea of his music are: *Rhapsody on a Theme of Paganini* for piano and orchestra; *The Isle of the Dead* for orchestra; *Twenty-Four Preludes* for piano.

RAMEAU, JEAN-PHILIPPE – French composer noted for his innovations in harmonic theory, a contemporary of Bach, Handel, Domenico Scarlatti and Telemann; he excelled particularly in the field of opera. He settled in Paris in 1723, aged forty. The financier La Pouplinière became his lifelong patron, and this, combined with his theatre work, meant that he was never short of a penny or two. Especially in the last two decades of his life, Rameau believed his composition to be of secondary importance in relation to his research work on musical theory; he would rather have been remembered for the latter. His opera output, however, has proved, at least historically, to be equally significant; he turned out a versatile parade of the fashionable operatic and theatre forms – *opéra-ballet, comédie-ballet, tragédie-lyrique, comédie-lyrique, pastorale*. Rameau succeeded in advancing opera beyond Lully and Gluck, though remaining in their Italian-influenced French tradition. Particularly in the *tragédie-lyrique* (known also as *tragédie en musique*), Rameau shows more of a concern for the emotional and descriptive aspects of the text rather than for the architecture of the drama; suitable examples are *Castor et Pollux* and *Hippolyte et Aricie*. On the other hand, *Platée* is a fine example of his comic opera writing (the *comédie-ballet*); the subject is an ugly nymph who thinks everyone is in love with her; his music imaginatively portrays and expresses her ungainliness, the cruel fun made of her; there is additionally a display of animal noises – birds, frogs, cuckoos and a donkey. To his stage works should be added his collections of harpsichord pieces, for instance, Volume I Nos. 1–10, which contain dance, character and experimental material.

RAPE OF LUCRETIA, THE – Britten's opera in two acts with libretto by the poet Ronald Duncan. The work, in fact, is the first of Britten's chamber operas, the purpose of which was to seek to bring the operatic experience out of the confines of the traditional opera house to a much wider audience. *The Rape of Lucretia* contains five characters supported by an ensemble of twelve instruments; its music is of great eloquence, and retells from a Christian standpoint the testing of the Roman Lucretia's fidelity and her eventual rape. The Male and Female Chorus draw the Christian moral.

RATTLE, SIMON – perhaps the most talented and versatile English conductor currently active. After his appointment as assistant conductor of the Bournemouth Symphony Orchestra he made his South Bank début with the Philharmonia Orchestra, aged twenty. Rattle was the youngest conductor ever to appear at the BBC Proms and at Glyndebourne. Currently he is the music director of the City of Birmingham Symphony Orchestra, as well as being a visiting conductor of important orchestras in Europe and the USA. His numerous recordings and broadcasts underline his authoritative grasp of the traditional orchestral repertoire and his unswerving support for the works of living composers.

RAVEL, MAURICE – turn-of-the-century composer. Although his father's background was largely Swiss and his mother's Basque, the family spent most of their lives in Paris. At the Paris Conservatoire he studied counterpoint and orchestration with Gédalge and composition with Fauré. Interestingly, Ravel made three unsuccessful attempts to win the Prix de Rome; his musical style and language were too off-beat for the judges, which is not to say his submissions were especially avant-garde for the time. By the age of twenty-eight, however, his writing had achieved technical and poetic mastery, as is evident in his orchestral song-cycle *Shéhérazade* and his String Quartet. In his personal behaviour Ravel, like Baudelaire, enjoyed dandyism as a mode of behaviour. Dyagilev commissioned his most ambitious stage work, the ballet *Daphnis et Chloé*, which emphasises his genius for orchestration; yet much of his orchestral material originated either in piano score or as piano pieces in their own right. Ravel and Stravinsky were mutual admirers and dedicated works to each other. During World War I he became a driver in the motor transport corps, having been rejected as a foot soldier because he was seriously underweight. His deepest human affection was for his mother, and her death in 1916 proved a traumatic experience. For the remainder of his life no human relationship matched this particular bond, and for a time the loss slowed Ravel's creative process. In 1928 he made a four-month tour of the USA, and in the same year an honorary doctorate was conferred on him by Oxford University. Vaughan Williams was one of his few private pupils. From a long list of Ravel's music that could be recommended the following must suffice: the opera *L'heure espagnole*, the Piano Concerto in G, and the piano set *Miroirs*.

RAWSTHORNE, ALAN – twentieth-century English composer of the generation of Walton and Tippett; before becoming hooked on composition he tried first dentistry, then architecture. In his creative development, which really did not mature until after World War II, he was much influenced by Hindemith's approach to tonality and structure. There is a certain steely, austere quality to his style, but warmth, humour and melodiousness frequently manifest themselves. Fine examples of his music are the orchestral overture *Street Corner*, the Concerto for piano, strings and percussion and the Quartet for oboe and strings. Rawsthorne was a close friend of Walton and Lambert and at one time occupied the same set of rooms that Chopin rented on his visits to London, in St James's. Among the twenty-two films for which Rawsthorne wrote the music is *The Flying Dutchman*, starring Ava Gardner (the film is based on the original legend, not on Wagner's opera).

RECITATIVE – this term describes a mode of singing, usually applicable to opera; more often than not it is meant for a single voice, and the music follows closely the rhythm and accentuation of ordinary speech and is not cast within a particular form or tempo. The term may also refer to a section of music. Recitative may be said to have been launched with the birth of opera around the beginning of the seventeenth century. Well into the nineteenth century in sung dramatic works its purpose was to promote the action or narrative of the plot, in contrast to the aria, which would dwell on emotion and enhance characterisation. An in-between device is arioso, which often serves to move recitative into aria.

RECORDER – this blowing instrument was already well-established in northern Italy in the sixteenth century; by the eighteenth it was in effective use in solo, chamber and orchestral music. Bach, Handel and their contemporaries wrote for the instrument but from the latter part of the eighteenth century until well into our own day it was almost completely neglected. After World War II it reappeared in strength in the classroom, in the performance of early music and even as a concert solo instrument, for which a number of composers have written pieces of some ambition. The recorder is a woodwind instrument with seven finger-holes and a thumb-hole; it is the chief member of those flutes with a whistle mouthpiece known as fipple flutes. The modern recorder follows the three-sectional design of the eighteenth-century Baroque model. The instrument is made of wood, but for school use is mass-produced from plastic material. Currently there are four sizes in use – treble, the main one, above it the descant, below it tenor and bass, much like the four-part vocal lay-out of SATB; in each case the compass is normally two octaves and a note. The younger Dolmetsch brought the twentieth-century recorder to virtuoso level. English composers who have written for it include Britten, Berkeley, Arnold and Rubbra.

REFRAIN – in music this term refers to a section that is repeated at regular intervals within a larger form; usually it appears in songs, alternating with the verses. Sometimes the verse is expected to be sung as a solo while the refrain is taken up by the chorus. The refrain principle has been around for ages and is found in both classical and folk music as well as in poetry alone.

REGER, MAX – a German composer who flourished at the close of the nineteenth century and the beginning of the twentieth. As a boy he, with his father, a schoolmaster, rebuilt a scrapped organ, which they took home for domestic use. Reger's distinguished keyboard technique enabled him early on to enter the concert circuit as pianist, organist and accompanist. He enjoyed a drink or two, which would always increase his natural affability. Considering his short productive life (he died aged forty-three), his output was large and varied; the only area in which he did not compose was for the stage, although he much enjoyed the theatre. Reger's style is a combination of Bachian counterpoint with Wagnerian chromatic harmony; at the same time he was a great admirer of all the German Romantic composers, from Mendelssohn and Schumann onward. He proved to be the most important composer for the organ since Bach, up to his own day. Much of his music is now considered somewhat dry; of particular interest, however, are the orchestral *Variations and Fugue on a Theme of Beethoven*, Op. 86, the Sonata for violin and piano No. 7 in C minor, Op. 139, and the organ piece *Introduction and Passacaglia* in D minor. His widow was very generous for many years with his estate, giving assistance to both composers and performers.

REICH, STEVE – twentieth-century American composer who first studied philosophy at Cornell University, when he was much influenced by the work of Wittgenstein, and then went on to study composition at the Juilliard School and later at Mills College under Milhaud and Berio. In 1970 he spent an intense summer in Ghana studying African drumming. While his music has its own personal stamp, it belongs to the genre that became an antidote to the over-intellectualisation of music as represented by Boulez, Stockhausen, Berio and Xenakis, and is known as minimalism or systems music; here the pitch content, texture and form is far simpler, but there is much subtlety in the treatment of rhythm and short motifs. Often performances of his music are presented only by ensembles of which he is a member. Worth hearing are *Music for a Large Ensemble*, *Clapping Music* for two performers or *Six Marimbas*.

REICHA, ANTOINE – a Czech composer who settled in Paris and who straddled the late Classical and early Romantic periods. He was adopted by an uncle, a virtuoso cellist and, less significantly, a conductor and composer. Like Quantz, his first instrument was the flute, and like Rameau he was much concerned with musical theory; he had a predilection for mathematics and philosophy. Having already achieved a name for his compositions he nevertheless took further lessons from Albrechtsberger and Salieri; he became a good friend of Haydn and Beethoven. An important piece of writing on music is his *Traité de mélodie*, which examines melody outside its harmonic context, melodic phraseology, the differences between rhythm and metre, and discusses sonata form in relation to thematic development rather than to key relationships. His *Cours de composition musicale*, written during his appointment as professor of composition at the Paris Conservatoire, is one of the first classroom harmony textbooks; *Traité de haute composition musicale* of 1826 is his most important theoretical work, and discusses aspects of counterpoint and harmony well above, as he put it, 'school music'. Despite writing operas, choral and solo voice pieces, orchestral and piano works, his best music lies in his chamber compositions, of which the most popular today are his wind quintets. Try any one of the six, Op. 100. Incidentally, Berlioz and Liszt studied with Reicha.

REQUIEM – the Mass for the Dead; its essential structure was established by the fourteenth century and its full lay-out consists of an introit, Kyrie, gradual and tract, sequence, offertory, Sanctus and Benedictus, Agnus Dei and finally communion. It is celebrated in memory of the faithful departed on All Souls' Day, 2 November, but it may also be sung on the day of the burial and on succeeding anniversaries. Musical settings have continued to the present day, for example Britten's *War Requiem* and John Tavener's *Celtic Requiem*; other composers who wrote Requiem Masses include Mozart, Berlioz, Cherubini, Dvořák, Brahms, Verdi, Bruckner, Fauré. These are not always full settings and may contain texts outside the liturgy.

RESPIGHI, OTTORINO – Italian composer who bestraddled the nineteenth and twentieth centuries. He visited Russia, where he had lessons from Rimsky-Korsakov; the result was Respighi's masterly treatment of the orchestra. Two obvious and popular examples are the symphonic poems *Fontane di Roma* (The Fountains of Rome) and *Pini di Roma* (The Pines of Rome), which were written in 1916 and 1924 and are still going strong today. These works underline Respighi's particular talent for being able to express visual impressions through music. As a conductor he promoted his own works as well as those of his Italian contemporaries, in Europe and in the USA. Later he took a growing interest in Renaissance and medieval Italian music, one result being his arrangement and realisation of lute material entitled *Antiche arie e danze per liuto* (Ancient Airs and Dances). Respighi's list of compositions is not large, but a great proportion of his music has been recorded. His wife, Elsa, was herself a composer and also a singer, and her husband's first biographer.

REVERBERATION TIME – term to describe how long it takes for an uttered sound to die out in the area in which it is enclosed. If the surroundings – walls, ceiling, floor – are made of absorbent material the sound will die out quickly; it will have a short reverberation time and is termed 'dry' sound. On the other hand if the surroundings are highly reflective – hard walls, tiles or glass – the reverberation time may be as long as four or five seconds, and the sound is termed 'lively'. To create a balanced reverberation time in a concert hall is a most complex operation; usually the result is open to discussion, as with the Royal Festival Hall on London's South Bank and its sister, the Queen Elizabeth Hall – some listeners prefer the one to the other in terms of acoustical performance. In a recording studio a dry sound is aimed for so that the music or speech is directed as completely as possible to the microphone; the sound is then 'treated' by the recording engineer.

RHAPSODY – a title used in the nineteenth century; it was first adopted by the Czech composer Tomašek in his *Six Rhapsodies* for piano, dated 1803. In ancient Greece the professional reciter or rhapsodist would declaim or chant selected passages in epic poems. Today the rhapsody does not have any particular form, nor is it confined to any particular medium, though it is mostly found in piano or orchestral works; its character is usually heroic and even wild. Some examples: Liszt, nineteen *Hungarian Rhapsodies* for piano; Dvořák, three *Slavonic Rhapsodies* for orchestra; Bartók, *Rhapsodies* Nos. 1 and 2 for violin and orchestra; Brahms, *Rhapsodie* Op. 53 for contralto, men's chorus and orchestra; Vaughan Williams, *A Norfolk Rhapsody* for orchestra.

RHENISH SYMPHONY – the popular name for Schumann's Symphony No. 3 in E flat, Op. 97, which to some degree gives his impression of the atmosphere of the Rhine near Düsseldorf. Actually this symphony is chronologically his fourth, the one now numbered 'Four' having been written some ten or eleven years earlier. But don't let this confuse you; simply enjoy both symphonies for themselves and fiddlesticks as to when they were written.

RHYTHM – a tricky subject; basically it is the pattern of movement in time. In European music it refers not only to motor movement but also to the pattern of melodic flow and harmonic flow, and even to the pattern of structure in a piece. Rhythm can only be accepted by the ear if its shape is clear. This means that some reiteration is necessary, otherwise the element of indeterminacy enters, thus confusing the ear; this applies to melodic, harmonic and structural considerations as well as to the motor element. The physical feel of motor rhythm requires metre, stress and pulse to be clearly enunciated, after which elaboration and alteration can make sense. Often, as listeners of classical music, we underestimate the fundamentally important role generally played by rhythm in causing us to understand and appreciate a particular piece. This applies to any period in our musical history. A Palestrina Kyrie is better appreciated if its polyphonic rhythm is grasped; Bach possesses a superior imagination to Vivaldi in the use of harmonic rhythm; Bartók's subtlety in the use of motor rhythm is unmatched; once the structural rhythm of Penderecki's *Threnody* is understood it becomes a meaningful, exciting piece. The understanding of any type of rhythm does not require conscious comprehension; rather, it has to be felt. This means the ear has to 'tune in' to these differing rhythmic genres. More often than not you are most probably doing this without realising it.

RICERCAR (*ricercare*) – an instrumental composition popular in the latter half of the sixteenth and much of the seventeenth century. Two types existed side by side: the homophonic ricercar was essentially a rhapsodic piece, acting as an introduction or prelude to a dance. The polyphonic ricercar, more sophisticated and more compositionally demanding, requires interplay between the parts, exploiting motifs and themes; part-writing is a *sine qua non*. The latter type of ricercar heralds the fugue. Attractive examples of twentieth-century ricercar writing, used deliberately, are the two in Stravinsky's *Cantata*.

RIGAUDON – a folk-dance originating in southern France, becoming, in the seventeenth and eighteenth centuries, a popular court dance; it was normally executed by individual couples, but a simplified form could be danced by several couples at once. The rigaudon was inserted into many ballets and operas of the time – Rameau was particularly fond of it and, like others, also wrote purely instrumental versions. It is similar to the bourrée, jolly in spirit, in two-beats-to-the-bar and starting with an upbeat. Sometimes I think it worth reviving the rich variety of Baroque dances; they seem so much more interesting than the present-day gyrations to rock music seen in our dance-halls.

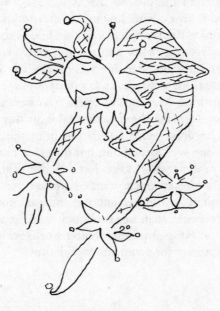

Rigoletto

RIGOLETTO – a three-act opera by Verdi, first performed in 1851 and still doing well in our opera houses; one of his best and most popular, full of much-loved tunes. Rigoletto is a court jester who sets out to murder his boss the duke, for having seduced his daughter, but things go badly wrong and instead it is the daughter who is killed. The opera is the first of what is called Verdi's 'romantic trilogy', the others being *Il Trovatore* and *La Traviata*.

RILEY, TERRY – a twentieth-century American composer, one of the pioneers of the musical style known as minimalism. He took his MA in composition at the University of California at Berkeley and then moved to New York. He has an abiding interest in Indian classical music, with special reference to its scales and rhythms. Minimalism is a reaction to immediate postwar concerns regarding pitch, harmony and motivic development, but retains an interest in texture; attention is especially paid to rhythm and shifting pulses, which give this type of music a certain static, almost ritualistic quality. You should try to hear some Riley; you might enjoy it immensely: say, *In C* for unspecified instruments – any number can theoretically join in – and *Salome Dances for Peace*, for string quartet.

RIMSKY-KORSAKOV, NIKOLAI – the most important Russian composer in the second half of the nineteenth century, after Tchaikovsky, and a member of the 'mighty handful' or the Five (the others being Musorgsky, Balakirev, who greatly influenced R-K, Borodin and Cui). Of this band he was closest to Musorgsky; in their early days they shared a room together, with the proviso that Musorgsky would compose in the mornings and Rimsky-Korsakov in the afternoons. Until the age of nearly thirty Rimsky-Korsakov led a double life, as naval officer in the Russian fleet – one voyage took him as far as Brazil and included a call at Gravesend – and as composer. He was particularly imaginative as an orchestrator – listen, for example, to his symphonic suite *Sheherazade* – and did much work on Musorgsky's opera *Khovanshchina*, and other of his friend's works, to make them performable in this respect. Like his contemporaries, he drew much inspiration from peasant folksong and dance. His operas are well turned out, but they lack characterisation and dramatic power in their vocal realisation – *Sadko*, *The Golden Cockerel*. Interestingly, he wrote an opera entitled *Mozart and Salieri*. His outstanding command of instruments and the orchestra not only influenced his Russian successors, such as Prokofiev and Stravinsky, but also Debussy, Ravel and Respighi. Entertaining works are *Capriccio espagnol*, Op. 34 and the Quintet for piano and woodwind.

RING DES NIBELUNGEN, DER (The Ring of the Nibelung) – Wagner's mega-work, consisting of four full-length operas – *Das Rheingold*, *Die Walküre*, *Siegfried*, *Götterdämmerung* (The Rhinegold, The Valkyrie, Siegfried and The Twilight of the Gods): a good sixteen hours of music, never mind the intervals. The Ring, as it is colloquially referred to, was first performed complete as a cycle at Bayreuth – Wagner's and all Wagnerians' temple – in 1876. The work most closely conforms to his theories on drama and music. The theme is his personal version of the Teutonic epic, *Nibelungenlied*; it develops as a parable of humanity and its search for power while the narrative tells of the theft of the Rhinegold and the misfortune it brings to all those who possess it. Characters include gods, giants, dwarfs (these were pre-P.C. days), nine war-maidens and a flying horse, and the stupidest hero in opera (Siegfried). If you get hooked you enter a cavernous world of legend in which generations of opera-goers have revelled – but it sure ain't everyone's cup of tea.

RIPIENO – a Baroque term that mainly applies to concerto-writing of the period; when the orchestra is playing in full flood, so to speak (or *tutti* – meaning 'all'), in a movement, this is the *ripieno* passage or section; when the solo instrument or group of solo instruments has/have a go, these moments are referred to as *concertino*. Good examples are to be found in Handel's larger vocal works and the *concertino/ripieno* principle is shown at its best in the six *Brandenburg Concertos* of Bach.

RITORNELLO – a form of refrain widely used in the Baroque period. The word is the diminutive of the Italian *ritorno* meaning 'return'. In an aria or concerto movement a type of prelude would introduce the main substance of the piece; this prelude would return at certain moments, either exactly as it was or modified or developed, thus acting as a refrain and known as the ritornello. In eighteenth-century operas, cantatas and other works, the ritornello would often anticipate the aria material and later take on a quite elaborate character. This approach was transferred to the Baroque concerto, as may be heard in examples by Albinoni and Vivaldi and in the ambitious works of Bach such as his *Mass in B minor* and the *St Matthew Passion*. Mozart's late piano concertos show a particularly sophisticated treatment of the ritornello principle which has been carried on into later concerto writing.

RODNEY BENNETT, RICHARD – See *Bennett, Richard Rodney*.

RODRIGO, JOAQUÍN – middle-of-the-road, twentieth-century Spanish composer who is widely known for his very popular *Concierto de*

Aranjuez (Guitar Concerto). His compositional style is essentially neo-classical with a Spanish flavour and has not changed much over the years. It is a pity that the fame of the guitar concerto has overshadowed his other music – the *Concierto de estio* for piano and orchestra or the *Concierto pastoral* for flute and orchestra. Rodrigo became blind at the age of three. He has travelled widely to attend performances of his works. During the Spanish Civil War he lived mostly in Paris; he married the Turkish pianist Victoria Kamhi.

RONDEAU – three fixed forms dominated French poetry and song in the fourteenth and fifteenth centuries – the *ballade*, the *virelai* and the *rondeau*. The most common form of the *rondeau* has eight lines in the pattern ABaAabAB – here the capital letters indicate a refrain. Machaut in the fourteenth and Dufay in the fifteenth century are known for their polyphonic *rondeau* settings and were but two of the many composers of the period that produced them. The first known polyphonic treatment of the *rondeau* is from the thirteenth-century trouvère Adam de la Halle.

RONDO – term referring to a piece or a movement with a variable number of sections in which a theme or a passage recurs several times. This part of the music is known as the refrain or rondo, and alternates with sections which may be termed couplets or episodes. Usually the refrains are in the opening key, whereas the episodes appear in contrasting keys; transition passages and codas are 'worked in' to the rondo. Of particular interest to us is the rondo form which matured in the Classical period; it provided the main alternative to sonata and sonata-related forms and ended up as the standard final movement of concertos, sonatas and symphonies. In contrast to the first movements of such works, which were serious in intent and mood, the final rondo movement normally allowed the composer to let his hair down, as it were, and to write in a lighter vein – which is not to say that the rondo movement was free of all manner of ingenuity in terms of theme treatment, harmonic surprise or clever instrumentation and orchestration. Independent rondos, on occasion with slow introductions, were written in the Classical period (Mozart and Beethoven), and in the nineteenth century Chopin, Mendelssohn and Liszt, amongst others, wrote rondos for piano with the accent on the display of virtuosity.

ROSBAUD, HANS – an Austrian conductor who throughout his career championed the music of twentieth-century composers. Rosbaud was closely associated with Schoenberg, Webern, Berg, Bartók, Stravinsky and Hindemith (with whom he studied for three years), undoubtedly the leading composers of their generation. His interpretation of their works was authoritative; first performances include Schoenberg's *Four Songs* with orchestra, Op. 22, Bartók's Piano Concerto No. 2 with the composer as soloist, and the first radio, stage and recording performances of Schoenberg's opera *Moses und Aron*. Rosbaud travelled widely on concert engagements and broadcast and recorded prolifically. He could speak nine languages fluently, three of which he taught himself while flying from one concert appearance to the next.

ROSENBERG, HILDING – twentieth-century Swedish composer and conductor, of the generation of Stravinsky, Bartók and Vaughan Williams; he lived to the ripe old age of ninety-three. Rosenberg exerted a major influence on younger Swedish composers through his composition and teaching, and took a positive interest in Swedish folk music. Influences ranging from Sibelius to Hindemith and Schoenberg may be traced in his works. Rosenberg's output is wide-ranging and includes incidental music for over forty plays; but he is best heard in his chamber music, for example the String Quartet No. 8 and, in contrast, the *Suite in D* for violin and piano.

ROSENKAVALIER, DER (The Knight of the Rose) – Richard Strauss's three-act opera, first performed in Dresden in 1911; a graceful, comic opera, in which the music, full of melody and successfully expressing intimate relationships in the setting of Maria Theresa's Vienna, rides on the cleverly constructed libretto of Hofmannsthal. The plot: a charming and elegant princess, the Marschallin, is faced with the perennial problem of the older woman who must lose her youthful lover; generously, she enjoys the satisfaction of finally seeing him marry a nice, attractive girl, who had been threatened with marriage to the princess's boorish cousin.

ROSSINI, GIOACHINO – we are talking here of one of the most important composers in the history of opera; and while we are about it, here is my list of prime opera composers to date, the equivalent of a premier league football eleven: Monteverdi, Gluck, Mozart, Rossini, Verdi, Wagner, Puccini, Strauss, Janáček, Britten, Birtwistle (reserves: Handel and Donizetti); second eleven: Lully, Bellini, Beethoven, Meyerbeer, Musorgsky, Tchaikovsky, Debussy, Berg, Prokofiev, Stravinsky, Ligeti (reserves: Purcell, Rameau, Gershwin). Remember, these twenty-seven names come from dozens of composers who wrote operas as a matter of course in the eighteenth and nineteenth centuries, and a large number in the twentieth century. In the first half of the nineteenth century no composer, of opera or otherwise, had the popularity and repute, wealth

241

and influence of Rossini. Yet, for the last forty years of his life he did not again compose an opera; his output in this genre was written between the ages of eighteen and thirty-seven. After this he wrote haphazardly, mainly light piano pieces, songs and choral works; to date there has been insufficient research into the music of this post-opera period. Rossini first made his reputation from the composition of Italian *farse* (one-act farces), which already displayed his musical sense of humour and wit. Of his thirty-nine operas the most long-lived and successful is *Il barbiere di Siviglia* (The Barber of Seville), the epitome of *opera buffa* style. *La Cenerentola* (Cinderella) is not far behind. But his *opera seria* works, such as *Tancredi*, are also significant. It has been suggested that the reasons for Rossini's stopping the composition of opera are threefold: sheer creative exhaustion, important advances heralding the Romantic age which affected attitudes to opera-writing, and the fact that Rossini had become exceedingly well-off. At least a good portion of his wealth had come from his share in the company run by the Neapolitan theatre impresario Barbaia, who had installed profitable gaming tables in the foyer of the Teatro S. Carlo (and whose mistress became Rossini's first wife). Some of the contributions Rossini made to the development of opera include the extension of singing technique, the role of music in defining and shaping the drama, an invigorating vocal melodic style, the use of opera subjects deliberately no longer associated with Greek classical mythology, a rhythmic vitality influenced by Mozart, and a highly individual treatment of the overture. Rossini said of Mozart, 'He was the admiration of my youth, the desperation of my mature years and the consolation of my old age.' The two operas Rossini wrote in his Paris years were *Le Comte Ory* and *Guillaume Tell*. He and Meyerbeer became good friends; on the latter's death in 1864 Rossini was moved to write *Chant funèbre* as a tribute. Of his non-operatic works, the best-known are his *Stabat Mater* and *Petite messe solennelle*, which he later orchestrated ('in order to prevent someone else doing it', he said), and which was originally scored for twelve voices, two pianos and harmonium.

ROSTROPOVICH, MSTISLAV – Russian cellist, conductor and pianist. In the mid-fifties Rostropovich made his début in London and New York, providing ample proof of his virtuosic technique and acute sense of intonation – a demanding and difficult requirement for all cellists. He is an excellent interpreter of contemporary cello music. Composers who have written works for him include Glier, Khachaturian (Cello Concerto), Prokofiev (*Sinfonia concertante* and the unfinished *Concertino* Op. 132 which he and Kabalevsky completed after the composer's death in 1953) and Britten. With the last-named he developed a friendship that produced the Sonata Op. 65 for cello and piano, the Symphony for cello and orchestra and the three Suites, Opp. 72, 80 and 87, for unaccompanied cello. Shostakovich wrote his Cello Concerto No. 1 for him. With the London Philharmonic Orchestra he recorded all the Tchaikovsky symphonies and made the first recording of Shostakovich's opera *Lady Macbeth of Mtsensk*. With his wife, Galina Vishnevskaya, a distinguished soprano, he has given many song recitals. British accolades include the Royal Philharmonic Society's Gold Medal and an honorary doctorate from Cambridge University.

ROUND – usually a perpetual canon for three or more voices; it is essentially an English term – on the Continent the word 'canon' is used colloquially. In medieval Latin the word used was *rota* (wheel). The text could be either sacred or secular; in the sixteenth, seventeenth and eighteenth centuries the English used 'round' for a serious piece and 'catch' for a light one. Composers who have knocked out rounds for fun include Purcell, Haydn, Mozart, Beethoven and Schoenberg. In school music the round is particularly useful in teaching pupils to sing independent parts. 'Round' may also describe a simple type of collective peasant dance; one known to us is *Sellenger's Round* through Byrd's set of keyboard variations on it.

ROUSSEAU, JEAN-JACQUES – eighteenth-century Swiss philosopher, music theoretician and composer, of French Protestant descent. Through his writings and his work for the theatre, especially *Le devin du village* (The Village Soothsayer), Rousseau paved the way for the genre known as *opéra-comique*, though he was a poor composer. A radical claim of his was that opera was not possible in the French language. The only true music for him was song, delivered in a sort of declamation, which, with painting and poetry, should be a primeval expression of nature; he believed that song had to do with the emotions, whereas music, with increasing civilisation, had degenerated into a language that appealed only to the intellect – the sole exception being Italian music. Declamatory song, he thought, should be confined to national culture and could not display an international outlook. This is in contrast to Haydn's attitude that all the world understood his musical language. Yet Rousseau's tenets led indirectly to the Wagnerian theory of music drama.

ROUSSEL, ALBERT – French composer active at the turn of the century and beyond. Like Rimsky-Korsakov, he first embarked on a naval career and saw service at home and overseas; but at twenty, with his urge to write music ever increasing, he resigned his commission and in due course studied with d'Indy at the Schola Cantorum in Paris. There he was appointed professor of counterpoint, a post he held for twelve years until 1914; among his pupils were Satie and Varèse. One of Roussel's first major works, written in 1908, is his Symphony No. 1, sub-titled *Poème de la forêt* (Poem of the Forest); another three symphonies were to follow. Aspects of Asian music influenced his writing after an extended tour in 1909 of India and south-east Asia, evidenced, for example, in his orchestral suite *Evocations* (not yet recorded) for soloists, chorus and orchestra. Two further apt examples of Roussel's eclectic style are to be found in his *Divertissement* for wind quintet and piano and his *Sinfonietta* for strings. His music incorporates the French symphonic tradition of Franck and d'Indy and a graphic penchant going back to the French eighteenth-century harpsichord composers.

RUBATO – the technique of playing rubato appears in the eighteenth century, when it was used in slow movements as an expressive nuance. The solo part or melody minutely lengthens or shortens the note values while the accompaniment holds the pulse steady. It is referred to and used by C. P. E. Bach, Quantz and Mozart. In the nineteenth century the composer *par excellence* who specified rubato is Chopin. The common understanding of rubato nowadays is a change in rhythmic figuration, speeding up (accelerando) or slowing down (ritardando), in which all the parts of a piece are united in such an alteration. Excellent examples of this effect may be found in the six string quartets of Bartók.

RUBBRA, EDMUND – an important twentieth-century English composer who is currently somewhat neglected. He made a valuable contribution to the English symphony, of which he wrote eleven; some of his most felicitous work is to be found in his chamber and instrumental music. Rubbra came from a poor working-class family and left school at fourteen to become a railway clerk; at nineteen he won a scholarship to Reading University and another to study at the Royal College of Music under Holst. He was appointed lecturer in music at Oxford University and taught composition at the Guildhall School of Music and Drama. His language and style are by no means revolutionary, but his music has an individual stamp, displaying a rare lyrical gift and ingenious treatment of motifs and themes in building up large-scale structures; his sense of polyphony is clearly apparent in his music. Rubbra became heavily involved with the philosophical aspects of religion, not only Christianity but also Buddhism and Taoism. An idea of his style may be gained from his Symphony No. 7 in C and his Sonata for violin and piano, No. 2.

RUBINSTEIN, ARTUR – renowned twentieth-century piano virtuoso; he impressed Joachim with his keyboard gifts at the age of three. He was born in Poland but later became a naturalised American. His musical education was supervised by Joachim and Bruch; later he had some piano instruction from Paderewski. Despite a very large repertoire it seems that, because of a natural pianism, unique sight-reading ability and a prodigious memory, he appears to have practised very little. After extensive touring, in 1932 he took time off from the concert circuit, to contemplate and rethink his playing; the result was a rejuvenated and even higher standard of performance. Rubinstein is today considered the twentieth century's most gifted interpreter of the piano works of Chopin. He championed the music of composers such as Szymanowski, Debussy, Ravel, Shostakovich, Prokofiev, Poulenc and Stravinsky, while at the same time rendering with the greatest insight the works of Bach, Mozart, Beethoven and Brahms. His numerous recordings include all the piano works of Chopin and the five piano concertos of Beethoven. He was vigorous in his concert-giving well into his eighties, when it was not uncommon for him to perform in one evening three Beethoven concertos or the two by Brahms.

SACHS, HANS – sixteenth-century German *Meistersinger* made immortal by Goethe's tract, *Erklärung eines alten Holzschnittes, vorstellend Hans Sachsens poetische Sendung* (An account of an old shoemaker, Hans Sachs, and his poetic message) and, from this, Wagner's opera, *Die Meistersinger von Nürnberg*. While learning his craft he travelled around Germany, 'to see the world', so to speak, and then settled in Nuremberg to become a wealthy master-shoemaker; at the same time he joined 'ye ancient guild', a sort of hangover from German Minnesinger days of yore which actively promoted the creation and performance of poetry and music. Hans was pretty energetic himself in this respect, perhaps eating lots of spinach and potatoes, for the archives reveal that he wrote more than 6000 master-songs, satirical and didactic poems, prose dialogues, comedies and tragedies; he was responsible for introducing the master-song into the service of the Reformation and, being an angelical citizen of flourishing Nuremberg, was inspired to bring religious and secular enlightenment to his fellow-men, both humble and rich, through his artistic creations.

SACRE DU PRINTEMPS, LE (The Rite of Spring) – Stravinsky's full-length ballet of 1913, which he also arranged for piano four hands. Its first performance in Paris at the Théâtre des Champs-Elysées caused a scandalous uproar, yet, in 1981, for example, there was not one day in the year when 'The Rite' wasn't being performed on the concert platform or the stage in some or other part of the world (popular fifth symphonies or not, cry your eyes out Beethoven and Tchaikovsky). This music, at its first appearance, was a blast of fresh air with its rhythmic vitality, new thrusts in melody and harmony and highly original treatment of the instruments of the symphony orchestra. The setting is ancient pagan Russia; Part I is entitled The Adoration of the Earth, while Part II is The Sacrifice – of a chosen virgin, natch.

SADIE, STANLEY – one of the most important writers on music in the twentieth century; as musicologist, writer and critic he has a highly respected international reputation. A Cambridge man, for a time he taught at Trinity College of Music, after which he became editor of the *Musical Times* monthly journal, the general editor of the *Master Musicians* series and music critic on *The Times*. Sadie was appointed editor of the sixth edition of *The New Grove Dictionary of Music and Musicians*, the most renowned general music reference source in the world, published in 1980, and having nearly 2500 contributors, many of them universally recognised authorities. Sadie has prepared critical editions of J. C. Bach, Boyce, Boccherini, Handel and written illustrated studies on Handel, Mozart and Bach. His reviews in *The Times* and the *Gramophone* have been informed, catholic in outlook, sympathetic to the subject and always very readable.

SADLER'S WELLS – a leading pleasure garden of London for nearly two hundred years, approximately from the end of the seventeenth century to the end of the nineteenth. In it an edifice called the Music House, opened in 1765, provided entertainment; later this was converted into the Sadler's Wells Theatre, which was reconstructed in 1931 with the aim of also being able to offer opera and ballet performances. The Vic-Wells companies turned into the Sadler's Wells Opera and Ballet and in 1935 settled exclusively in the theatre. The opera company moved in 1968 to the Coliseum, which was more central and had better facilities; in 1974 its name was changed to the English National Opera. The ballet company became the Royal Ballet in 1956, having moved to Covent Garden. Sadler's Wells Theatre remains one of the most important performing arts centres in London.

ST MATTHEW PASSION – down the ages quite a few St Matthew Passions have been set, but by far the most important is Bach's, one of the outstanding religious choral works in our musical history; it is written for soloists, two choruses and orchestra. It was first performed in 1724, and Bach revised it twelve years later. The work shows that he was aware of earlier settings; in the tradition, Bach retains the biblical text for the Evangelist, Jesus, Pilate and the *turba* or crowd choruses, while the more contemplative sections are set to verses written by Picander. A special feature is the frequent appearance of very moving four-part chorales, some repeated with altered harmonisation. Two other Passions by Bach are known, the *St John*, not as inspired as the *St Matthew*, and the *St Mark* of which the text alone survives – the only full copy was destroyed during World War II.

SAINT-SAËNS, CAMILLE – nineteenth-century French composer, a first-rate organist and pianist, who wrote on music with authority and wit. As a child prodigy, he gave a concert which included concertos by Beethoven and Mozart, and as an encore he offered to play any Beethoven sonata from memory. Incredible, would you not say? He helped to popularise Bach, Schumann and Wagner among his country-men, and edited the complete works of Rameau. He visited England frequently, when he would play for Queen Victoria, who allowed him to examine Handel manuscripts in the library at Buckingham Palace.

As Ravel was displeased with the popularity of *Bolero*, so was Saint-Saëns with *Le carnaval des animaux* (Carnival of the Animals), which he dashed off as a private joke in a few days whilst on holiday. He did not teach for long but he did have two famous pupils, Messager and Fauré, the latter becoming a lifelong friend. Unfortunately Saint-Saëns never hit it off with Debussy, and spent ill-considered time in attacking the man and his music. Saint-Saëns's output is not altogether special in lan-guage and style, but it is always clearly and inventively produced, with warm, melodious lines; he had to suffer the remark from his detractors that his was 'bad music well-written'. Nevertheless I guess that you'll enjoy the *Danse macabre* in G minor, *Introduction and Rondo capriccioso* in A minor for violin and orchestra and the music from his opera *Samson et Dalila* (Samson and Delilah).

SALIERI, ANTONIO – Italian-born composer who dominated Viennese musical life for a number of decades at the close of the eighteenth and the early nineteenth centuries. Salieri is mainly known to us on the basis of utterly unfounded nonsense that he poisoned Mozart; an attrac-tive bit of melodrama, contradicting the fact that he assisted Mozart on several occasions, and there is no evidence that there was the slightest degree of animosity between them. At twenty-four Salieri was appointed composer and conductor of Italian opera at the Viennese court of Joseph II, one of the most important musical positions in

Europe. He wrote more than forty operas; you might like to compare his *Falstaff* (1799) with Verdi's (1893). His orchestral and instrumental music is of lesser importance, though not unattractive, for instance, the Concerto in C for flute, oboe and orchestra. He was essentially an Italianate musician, his strengths concentrated on the expression of *cantabile* melody centred round the voice. Salieri's influence and the regard in which he was held were widespread in Europe; this was due in no little measure to his administrative talents. He kept the archival material at the Viennese court in logical order, looked after the welfare of musicians and encouraged the efforts of the younger composers.

SALÓN MÉXICO, EL – one of Copland's most attractive orchestral pieces, completed in 1936 and inspired by a dance hall in Mexico City which he visited in 1932. The music contains material based on Mexican folksong and is rich in tunefulness, rhythmic punch and breezy orchestration. Nice to relax with while sipping your *tequila*.

SALZBURG – an Austrian city, nowadays specially noted for its annual festival founded in 1920. Its history goes back more than a thousand years. Until the early nineteenth century it was the seat of prince-archbishops; in the early medieval period it was the centre of liturgical enterprise for the southern German-speaking lands, and was favourably disposed towards music and the other arts. During the sixteenth century its reputation for building organs of high quality grew, and in the seventeenth it welcomed the earliest appearance of Baroque opera north of the Alps. The interest for us in the next century is that it was the town of residence for the Mozart family and Michael Haydn, brother of Joseph, who entered the archbishop's service as a composer of church music. As the town became part of greater Austria it suffered a loss in funds, with the result that its musicians had to seek their bread at Vienna and elsewhere. A great Mozart Centenary Festival was held in 1856 at which one of Mozart's sons, Carl, presented valuable Mozartiana to the town's Mozart Archives centre. Although the birth of the International Society for Contemporary Music took place at Salzburg in 1922, the town is not known for its support of twentieth-century composers; it has, however, held two ISCM festivals, in 1923 and 1951. Those of you who have visited Salzburg and its environs will know how attractive it is, with its proximity to the complex of lakes known as the Salzkammergut – very romantic.

SAMMARTINI, GIOVANNI – eighteenth-century Italian composer who was born, lived and died in Milan. His output consists mainly of *concerto grosso*-type orchestral pieces, later to develop into the symphony, in which he was a forerunner of Haydn, and numerous chamber music items including trio-sonatas, string quartets and quintets. His extant church music shows him to be a confident master of the genre. More research is still required to ascertain his true worth, and this, in due course, should produce more recordings; but from what is presently issued it is of interest to listen to the Flute Concerto in G and his Symphony in D major. He influenced J. C. Bach and Boccherini and vigorously supported the young Mozart, who visited Milan with his father in 1770.

SARABANDE – of the Baroque suite, the sarabande was a standard movement together with the allemande, courante and gigue; its character was stately, but with a slight sexual innuendo. It originated in the sixteenth century in both Latin America and Spain, then migrated to Italy in the seventeenth century in the guitar repertoire. In the process of becoming 'classicised' it took on two tempos: the French and Germans preferred a slower, the English and Italians a faster one; both emphasised the second beat of its three-beat pulse. Seventeenth-century English composers who wrote sarabandes include Locke, William Lawes and Purcell, and in the eighteenth century Boyce joined the French Rameau and Couperin in writing them. In the late nineteenth and early twentieth centuries sarabande writers included Saint-Saëns, Satie, Roussel, Tailleferre and Busoni. It seems that in its sixteenth-century Spanish origin the sarabande was a fast, noisy, dance-song affair accompanied by guitar, castanets and other percussion instruments, expressing lewdness to such an extent that it had to be banned for a time. To see and hear a reconstruction might well prove interesting – for musicological purposes, of course.

SARASATE, PABLO – one of the finest violin virtuosos of all time. His intonation has been described as faultless, as was his brilliant technique; he was Paganini's successor on the worldwide concert circuit. Joachim, the master-violinist of Germany, whose playing style was quite different, acknowledged the Spaniard's artistry. Among an impressive collection of composers who wrote pieces especially for him were Bruch, Saint-Saëns, Lalo, Joachim, Wieniawski and Dvořák. His best-known pieces from a limited list of compositions are his *Zigeunerweisen* (Gypsy Melodies), Op. 20, for violin and orchestra and his four books of *Danzas españolas* (Spanish Dances), Opp. 21–23, 28, for violin and piano. Sarasate bequeathed his two Stradivari violins to the Paris and Madrid Conservatoires.

SARGENT, MALCOLM – one of Britain's most popular twentieth-century conductors, both at home and abroad. His father, a coal merchant in Lincolnshire, was an enthusiastic amateur organist and choirmaster. Henry Wood brought Sargent to the attention of the public by inviting him to conduct the Queen's Hall Orchestra, first at Leicester, then in London at a Promenade concert. An unending string of successes followed: chief conductor of the Robert Mayer children's concerts, of the Hallé Orchestra and the Liverpool Orchestra; conductor of the BBC Symphony Orchestra; chief conductor at the Promenade Concerts for nearly twenty-one years from 1948. Sargent's greatest gift was in directing large choral forces, who became utterly devoted to him – the Royal Choral Society, the Huddersfield Choral Society. At the Leeds Festival of 1931 he gave the world première of Walton's *Belshazzar's Feast*; in the theatre he conducted first performances of operas by Vaughan Williams and Holst, and Walton's *Troilus and Cressida* at Covent Garden in 1954. And he was not averse to conducting Gilbert and Sullivan operas and making music with provincial and amateur forces, and with children. He was a firm supporter of contemporary music up to Britten and Shostakovich. Sargent was good-looking, urbane, an entertaining public speaker, approachable; he was knighted in 1947. Quite a hero in the musical world of his time.

SATIE, ERIK – French composer, contemporary of Debussy with whom he had a close friendship for a quarter of a century, though they did not always see eye to eye over matters musical. There is a certain parallel between Webern, the Austrian, and Satie, the Frenchman; both were miniaturist composers at their best; both opened radical paths in compositional thinking. The marked difference between the two, however, is that Webern was rooted in an intellectual, scholarly tradition coming from two centuries of Austro-German domination of classical music, whereas Satie came from a culture of refined instinct, independent thought, artistic epicureanism and a strong, regular association with painting and literature. Webern had to overcome a series of do's-and-don't's, Satie enjoyed the freedom to be anarchic. Satie's importance in twentieth-century music may be seen in his influence over composers such as Debussy, Ravel, Poulenc, and later composers such as Cage, helping to break down musical shibboleths. His pieces are shockingly simple in conception and structure, in melodic line and harmonic construction. One need only listen to the *Trois Gymnopédies* (perhaps translated as Three Naked Dances), either in the original piano version or the orchestration (not his), and a string of other piano pieces such as *Trois Préludes flasques* (Three Powder-Flask Preludes), *Trois Sarabandes*, or *Six Gnossiennes* (Six Mystical Concepts). There is also the orchestral piece *Five Grimaces for A Midsummer Night's Dream* and his ballet music *Parade*, a collaboration with Cocteau to a commission by Dyagilev, with décor and costume by Picasso and choreography by Massine. Only in his last ten years or so did Satie find wider recognition outside a small but consistent circle of admirers, including Les Six; much was done to promote him by Cocteau; otherwise he led an exceedingly impecunious and mostly lonely life. Understandably, he hit the bottle, finally sinking into a deep melancholy and dying from cirrhosis of the liver. It is a sadness, for despite a parade of behavioural drolleries, clowning and bizarre situations, Satie seems to have been at heart a shy, retiring and refined person. Musically, he inaugurated that off-beat element characteristic of an important slice of much twentieth-century classical music.

SAXOPHONE – most other instruments have evolved gradually, but the saxophone is among the few that was more or less invented – certainly the only one in this category that not only survived but rose to great popularity. Its inventor, Adolphe Sax (1814–94), after whom it is obviously named, came from a Belgian family of wind-instrument makers. There is little doubt that he was a remarkably fecund instrument maker and developer, and the saxophone is his gift to posterity. Today it is an essential part of the dance-hall band, has produced outstanding virtuosos in jazz (Parker, Mulligan, Rollins, to name but a few) and has its place in classical music. For instance, it makes a sound-colour contribution to military and concert wind band music, to the orchestra – Ravel's *Bolero*, Khachaturian's *Sabre Dance*, Vaughan Williams's Symphony No. 6, Prokofiev's *Lieutenant Kije* – and there are flourishing saxophone quartets, of which the London Saxophone Quartet is the most esteemed in Britain. The most popular member of the saxophone family is the alto, the others, in order, being tenor, baritone and soprano. Pieces for alto saxophone and orchestra include Glazunov's Concerto in E flat major, Ibert's *Concertino da camera* and Debussy's *Rhapsody*. One of the reasons for the instrument's popularity is that it is comparatively easy to play. (My doctor, who knows as much about music as I know about medicine, has taken it up in his fifties to help ease his stressful life.) The saxophone combines a single-reed mouthpiece with a wide-bore conical tube of metal and overblows at the octave; at the open end it expands into a small flare; most of the holes are controlled by keys. The soprano model is straight, but the other three have a U-bend in order to make the length of tube more manageable. In the hands of a poor player (my doctor, for instance) the sound is depressing, but with a gifted performer it can be exceedingly expressive in fast or slow music.

SCALE – nothing more than a sequence of notes going up or down. A scale may consist of any number of notes, usually from five to twelve. All music has its scale, and is drawn from this clutch of notes some of which may be temporarily raised (sharpened) or lowered (flattened) in pitch. A piece written in, say, D major, means that all musical thought in terms of pitch, harmony and melody is centred around the scale of D, of which the first note is D; the same goes for a piece written in G minor; the difference is that the intervals between the notes in sequence are differently spaced. Both these eight-note scales are described as diatonic because each consists of five tones (major seconds) and two semitones (minor seconds). Classical music uses other eight-note scales, especially in the 16th century and earlier, such as the Dorian or Phrygian, which have different harmonic implications. The chromatic scale of twelve notes is built entirely of semitones; the whole-tone scale of seven notes is built entirely of tones. Young performers (vocal or instrumental) 'practise scales' in order to become fluent in dealing with, say, the major scale starting at different pitches, and to develop technical facility. Another name for scale is 'mode'.

SCARLATTI, ALESSANDRO – the surname seems to be of Sicilian origin; it belongs to a family of musicians of which Alessandro and the sixth of his ten children, Domenico, are the most famous. Alessandro's achievement lies in the production of operas and cantatas, and the founding of the Neapolitan school of eighteenth-century opera. He was born in Palermo in the generation before Bach, Handel and Telemann; portraits show him as a handsome young man. He was sent to Rome for musical training, and gained his first operatic success at the age of nineteen. This won him the patronage of the exiled queen Christina of Sweden, who had a court in Rome, and two cardinals. In 1684 Alessandro moved to Naples, and for the following two decades half the operas performed there were written by him. His industry is truly remarkable; by the age of forty-five he had written eighty-eight stage works, although this did not guarantee financial security. As newer approaches to opera emerged, Alessandro turned more to cantata, oratorio and instrumental writing. His opera plots do not receive much exposure today because the characters are stylised, with no inner life, and the orchestra is usually limited to strings and continuo, sometimes calling for additional trumpets and/or horns. It is clear that one factor in his large output was his ability to write speedily in an established convention. You can get on Alessandro's wavelength with recorded excerpts from his operas *Il Pompeo* and *Il Pirro e Demetrio*, and the aria *Con voce festiva* for soprano, trumpet and strings.

SCARLATTI, DOMENICO – evidence seems to show that this Italian composer of masterly keyboard music received no instruction other than from his father in boyhood and adolescence; it is likely that his later move to Portugal and Spain stemmed from a wish to escape the domineering interference of his doting parent in his own musical development. Domenico's own gifts did not run to the composition of vocal music, either secular or sacred, though he did turn out several operas, oratorios and cantatas. He spent four years in Venice and a further ten in Rome, when, for a time, he too received the patronage of an exiled queen – this time Maria Casimira of Poland. In 1719, at the age of thirty-four, he went to Lisbon where he worked for nine years, overseeing the musical education of King John V's younger brother, Don Antonio, and his daughter, the Infanta Maria Barbara, an extremely gifted keyboard player. With her he developed a lifelong musical relationship, and when she married into the Spanish royal family in 1728 he moved with her, content to remain in the employ of the Spanish court until his death nearly three decades later. It is during this long period in the Iberian Peninsula that Domenico created his musical treasure: a collection of more than five hundred one-movement keyboard pieces, all simply called 'sonata'. There is still musicological disagreement over the order in which they were written, but what is indisputable is their endless variety of character and keyboard technique. All are in binary form, yet there is an incredible range of invention in figuration, harmony, melodic line, the influence of guitar, dance and brass fanfares, and the expression of non-musical subjects. Domenico's influence on the extension of keyboard writing is of major importance. Poor old Alessandro; for all his massive list of operas and other vocal compositions, his music today pales into insignificance by comparison with the excitement of his son's sonatas. There are numerous recordings to be had, by both pianists (Horowitz, Lipatti, Michelangeli) and harpsichordists (Rowland, Tilney, Leonhardt).

SCHENKER, HEINRICH – musical theorist; born in Poland, he settled in Vienna. His foremost achievement is a system of analysis which essentially applies to the corpus of music lying between Bach and Brahms; but his pioneering work also gave rise, especially after World War II, to the young discipline of musical theory and analysis. Simply put, Schenker illustrated that the masterworks of this period were indeed masterworks in contrast to lesser pieces, standing up to the scrutiny of his three-layered analytical method. First there was the so-called *foreground* – a composition's most prominent note-to-note progress; second, the *middle-ground* – this reveals the structurally important harmonies and melodic elements occurring within and between musical phrases; and finally the *background* – here we have the bare bones of the piece, namely, the fundamental harmonies shown in their linear relationship, in which an entire series of phrases may be basically dominated by one chord. In analytical practice, both by Schenker and his later followers, the examination of a piece is much more detailed and complicated. Though Schenker believed that all music – including Wagner – outside his chosen 150-year period was inferior, he nevertheless laid the foundation for a more logical approach to musical analysis, as may be seen in the writings of Forte and Whittall, amongst others. His work underlined that most classical music consists of layers of various elements which, if understood, either consciously or instinctively, can do nothing but increase one's listening pleasure.

SCHERCHEN, HERMANN – German conductor who was an extremely sympathetic promoter of twentieth-century music. He worked with Schoenberg in preparing *Pierrot Lunaire* for performance; he founded the avant-garde musical journal *Melos* and the Scherchen Quartet, which had a brief but illustrious life. He was involved in the foundation of the International Society for Contemporary Music, and appeared frequently at its later festivals as principal conductor. In 1933 he settled in Switzerland where, after the war, he established an electro-acoustic research studio. His first performances include *Three Fragments* from Berg's opera *Wozzeck* (1924), Dallapiccola's opera *Il Prigioniero* (1950), and the original version of Henze's opera *König Hirsch* (1956). His Darmstadt performance in 1951 of *Dance round the Golden Calf* was the first music to be heard from Schoenberg's opera *Moses und Aron*; he conducted the complete work at the Berlin Städtische Oper in 1959.

His daughter by the Chinese composer Hsiao Shu-sien, Tona Scherchen-Hsiao, studied composition with Henze at Salzburg; her pieces, in common with those of the Japanese composer Takemitsu, are influenced by contemporary French music.

SCHERZO – in Italian *scherzo* mean a joke or jest; its appendage to a musical piece has rather given it the meaning of 'playful', in Italian, *scherzoso*. Beethoven first introduced it as a replacement for the minuet in the third movement of a four-movement symphony; but he enjoyed making exceptions to the rule, and often placed the scherzo in a different spot. In his Symphony No. 9, to take one example, the scherzo is the second movement and contains strong elements of fugal and sonata-form writing – a marvellous bit of imaginative composing. The pulse is commonly in fast triple time; yet even with Haydn, and certainly in the nineteenth and twentieth centuries, a scherzo might be delivered in two or four beats-to-the-bar. One already finds the term as a description in the lighter madrigals of the early seventeenth century. From Schubert onwards, nearly all nineteenth-century composers wrote scherzo movements; a weighty contribution was Chopin's four Scherzos for piano. One-movement scherzos began to appear orchestrally, not necessarily so-called but certainly *scherzando* in spirit – Strauss's *Till Eulenspiegel*, Dukas's *L'apprenti sorcier*, Saint-Saëns's *Danse macabre*. In the latter it takes on a devilish guise, developed in some of the scherzo movements in the symphonies of Prokofiev, Shostakovich and Vaughan Williams (his Symphony No. 6). Because it has a dance-like character, some composers replaced the scherzo with another dance rhythm – Tchaikovsky with the waltz, Mahler with the *Ländler*, Dvořák with the *furiant*. In one form or another the scherzo is today still alive and kicking.

SCHIKANEDER, EMMANUEL – an eighteenth-century impresario, active in Vienna mainly; a man of many talents – dramatist, composer, singer, actor, theatre director – assisted greatly in his enterprises by his elder brother, Urban. Schikaneder is of particular interest to us because of his dealings with Mozart – he met the family when his touring company landed up in Salzburg in 1780. By the time he commissioned Mozart to set his own text of *Die Zauberflöte* (The Magic Flute) in 1790–91, Schikaneder's interests had moved on to opera and *Singspiel*. He was responsible for the establishment of the new Theater an der Wien in 1801, which has functioned in an almost unbroken line until today. As so often happens with this type of man of the theatre, his fortunes rose and fell; regrettably he died somewhat demented and in penury. Schikaneder is recognised as one of the most talented theatre personalities of his age.

SCHNABEL, ARTUR – one of the most sensitive and intelligent piano virtuosos of the twentieth century. He was born in Austria, became naturalised in the USA and died in Switzerland. Like most instrumental virtuosos, going back to Mozart and earlier, his concert life began before the age of ten. Schnabel lived in Berlin until 1933, when he moved to the USA; while in Berlin he married the contralto Therese Behr and together they presented recitals of *Lieder* by Schubert, Schumann and Brahms. He also took part in early performances of Schoenberg's *Pierrot Lunaire* – very avant-garde for those days. Schnabel made a deep study of Beethoven's piano music and produced an authoritative edition of the master's sonatas. His Beethoven performances, many of which are on record, are now legendary; also worth listening to is his interpretation of Mozart and Schubert. A nice read is his autobiography *My Life and Music*.

SCHOENBERG, ARNOLD – one of the musical giants of the earlier twentieth century. Even if you do not like this Austrian composer's music he is important enough for you to have to know something about him. Realise that, directly and indirectly, his compositions, writings and teachings opened the flood-gates for the radical change that has taken place in most contemporary composition. And so, read on. From after Debussy until about the 1950s the composers who made the greatest impact on the course of classical music are Schoenberg, Bartók and Stravinsky; but unlike the other two, Schoenberg, despite his many disciples and recognition from the professionals, has hardly entered the concert repertoire. Schoenberg, who was steeped in traditional compositional thought, was a master of writing music in a key signature; indisputable proof lies in his *Verklärte Nacht* (Transfigured Night) for strings, his textbooks, especially *Harmonielehre* (Theory of Harmony), and his writing of *Überbrettl* (cabaret) music in Berlin. If he so wished, he could have been an outstanding composer of Hollywood film music. However, to continue to write music in this way seemed to him a sterile procedure, and he came to believe that a new way of dealing with pitch/note/chord organisation had to be found; thus evolved his 'composing with twelve notes' (all the notes in a chromatic scale).

Schoenberg did not sit down at his desk one Saturday night, saying, 'Now, let's see ...' and after several hours shout 'Eureka!'; his twelve-note 'method' had a gestation period of nearly two decades. His seeking for order out of chaos resulted in the establishment of a 'note-row' – the laying out of the twelve notes of the chromatic scale in a sequence which a composer himself ordains and from which a rich variety of technical processes ensues. The rub for us listeners is that twelve-note music does not usually produce the melodic lines to which our ears are drawn, and a barrier is therefore set up between ourselves and Schoenberg's compositions. We need to concentrate our listening on the other elements of music such as rhythm, instrumentation, texture, orchestral interplay, dynamics, overall musical shapes; this is not easy, and a piece based on a 'note-row' requires several listenings before a gut enjoyment can be experienced.

Schoenberg remains somewhat of a tragic figure. As composer and theorist he gave much and received little; he was unwilling or unable to compromise, what with his sharp intellect, his powerful personality, his creative turbulence and his high principles. With the advent of Nazism, like many others he emigrated from Germany to the USA in 1933. A way into feeling for his music is through his piano works – *Six Little Piano Pieces*, Op. 19, *Five Piano Pieces*, Op. 23, *Piano Suite*, Op. 25, *Piano Pieces*, Opp. 33a and b, as well as his *Violin Concerto* and the *Five Orchestral Pieces*, Op. 16.

SCHOLES, PERCY – renowned for his excellent popular music dictionary, the *Oxford Companion to Music*, the first edition of which came out in 1938; it is still going strong. Scholes made a lifelong commitment to bring musical knowledge to the man in the street; he gave numerous lectures on music appreciation, spent some years as a teacher and was associated with the founding of the *Music Teacher* journal. He wrote attractively, sympathetically and with insight on all manner of musical subjects and had spells as music critic for the *Evening Standard* and *The Times*. Scholes was an early supporter of radio and recording in the 1920s, giving talks for the BBC and acting as the editor of its *Radio Times*. In the 1940s he became a member of Oxford University's Faculty of Music; he received the OBE in 1957.

SCHUBERT, FRANZ – a compositional phenomenon of the nineteenth century as regards quality and quantity of output; he produced hundreds of works – symphonies, operas and other theatre music, instrumental pieces, sacred and secular works for voice and more than six hundred songs. This would have been impressive enough had he lived to 'three-score-years-and-ten', but he died at the age of thirty-one. That's no misprint. He easily matches, if not outstrips, Mozart's composing rate. Schubert is one of the great songwriters of all time. Take, say, his seventeenth and eighteenth years: not counting other works, he wrote 245 songs including the remarkable *Gretchen am Spinnrade* (Gretchen at the Spinning-Wheel) and *Der Erlkönig* (The Elf-King). A knowledge of his musical achievement in general is essential to an overall understanding of nineteenth-century music. Why? Because of two important features:

his use of melody as a developmental device in symphonic writing, and his innovations in harmony and key relationships.

Schubert, by all accounts, showed a genial and generous nature, and had a happy family background. One has to remind oneself that psychologically he knew only youth and early manhood; all mature adult thinking was confined to his musical writing. He relished the company of his many friends, with whom he would converse, play music and lark about in the café-bars of Vienna; in a way, he largely wrote his music for them. He never kept high society – in fact, when he became better-known and started to receive 'establishment' invitations, he would frequently not roll up, preferring to mix with his mates. At the age of twenty-five, tragically, he became infected with syphilis, for which at that time there was no cure; the disease not only eroded him physically but also caused him periodic mental suffering. His hero was Beethoven, and the silly thing is that he and Beethoven both lived in Vienna but never met, until Schubert visited him on his deathbed. They are buried close to each other.

Although he was not a success at composing opera, he had an excellent sense of musical drama, expressed supremely in his songs and instrumental writing. In his final years he wrote two outstanding song-cycles, *Die schöne Müllerin* (The Miller's Beautiful Wife) and *Winterreise* (Winter Journey); in the same period there is his song-set *Schwanengesang* (Swan Song – a title given to a group of late songs by their publisher) and the wonderful String Quintet in C. Of his symphonies the two finest are No. 8 (The Unfinished – only the first two movements were completed) and No. 9 (The Great). In 1967 the New Schubert Collected Works was launched; the editors are still at it – there's a pile of music to get through ...

SCHUMANN, CLARA (*née* Wieck) – though best known as the wife of Robert, she was a distinguished musician in her own right, a child prodigy pianist and a fine composer. In those days a professional female musician was a rare thing, a fact which did not hinder her successful concert career. Clara's character reveals intelligence and strength, integrity and sensitivity. By the age of eighteen she came into conflict with her domineering father, a situation made worse by her desire to marry Robert Schumann; in the end court action had to be resorted to and the pair wed in 1840, aged thirty and twenty-one respectively. It may well be imagined how matrimony and the birth of eight children in thirteen years interfered with Clara's professional life.

In 1853 Brahms appeared on the scene, a year before Robert had to be committed to an asylum. The friendship that developed was deep and long-lasting; while there is little recorded evidence that Brahms and

Clara were lovers, the nature of the relationship, some authorities consider, makes this almost certain, at least for a period. Brahms was fourteen years her junior. For the remainder of her life, she gave concerts and taught; she also composed steadily – songs, piano pieces, chamber music; her musical insight allowed her to make intelligent and helpful critical appraisals of the music of both Schumann and Brahms. She prepared a complete edition of Schumann's works and published a collection of his letters under the title *Jugendbriefe* (Letters of Youth).

SCHUMANN, ROBERT – the arch-romantic of the nineteenth century; perhaps the only other composer to stand comparison in this respect is the Frenchman Berlioz. The fantasy, day-dreaming and wayward nature of Schumann fitted hand-in-glove with the ideal and aesthetic of German Romanticism. No matter how he tried to follow the rigorous technical requirements built on a long tradition of classical composition, Schumann was a law unto himself. What saved him from landing up as a mere musical hack was an inborn creativity, which expressed itself uniquely through small-scale works – songs and piano pieces – often strung together like a necklace of beads: for example, the eight songs that make up *Frauenliebe und -leben* (A Woman's Love and Life) or the twenty-one piano pieces that comprise *Carnaval*. Until he began to suffer numbness in his right hand his playing was of the standard of a concert pianist. The piano was so much his instrument that most of his compositions were born at the keyboard; there is an improvisatory element that seems to stem from excursions on it, manifest not only in the Piano Quartet in E flat, Op. 47, and the Piano Quintet, also in E flat, Op. 44, but in his symphonic writing as well. He was a poor orchestrator and a weak conductor, but his grasp of the piano is only matched by Chopin's and Liszt's; he advanced the instrument's technique by the way he used the pedal, introduced cross-rhythms and syncopations, delivered bold and swift harmonic changes and spattered these scores with a rich variety of runs and arpeggio figurations. In the accompaniments to his songs, the piano frequently becomes as important to the interpretation of a text as the vocal line. More often than not the inspiration for a work stems either from a literary source or from highly personal, enigmatic or esoteric thought processes.

Schumann was wayward all his life; he stopped womanising once he married Clara, but not before he, like Schubert, had contracted syphilis. The final two years of his life were spent in an asylum. Though his chronic syphilis must have contributed to this terrible final phase, it may be that there was also a genetic cause, and there is no doubt that Schumann was aware of this. For many years he expressed a fear of going mad; he suffered frequent bouts of depression and several times attempted suicide. Like Wagner, Schumann was also a literary man; he edited and contributed to the journal *Neue Zeitschrift für Musik* (New Journal for Music) on and off for over twelve years, showing much sympathy for fellow composers and other musicians of the day.

SCHÜTZ, HEINRICH – undeniably Germany's finest seventeenth-century composer, whose works are exclusively confined to the genre of sacred choral music, with or without instrumental accompaniment, with texts drawn mainly from the Bible. His pieces put Germany on the international compositional map and represent the best in Lutheran church music. Schütz spent most of his life in the service of courts in Dresden and its nearby towns; his main benefactors were Johann Georg I, Elector of Saxony, and his son, Johann Georg II. He left more than five hundred compositions; a new authoritative edition of his extant works was launched in 1971. By the beginning of the eighteenth century his music fell into neglect, until about 1840 when research scholars began to make a study of his language and style; luckily his life was well-documented during his own time. To his credit he was consistently caring over his musicians, both singers and instrumentalists; for lengthy periods when neither he nor the musicians received any salary, he would fork out from his own resources to assist those in greatest need. This hardship was due in part to the negligence of his benefactors, and in part to the Thirty Years War (1618–48), which gravely disrupted life in much of the territory of north Germany. Most of the texts he set were in German, the rhythm and accent of which clearly affected his musical style, and they played a major part in establishing the Lutheran ideal of using the vernacular in liturgical practice. Good evidence of this is provided by the following examples: *Königs und Propheten Davids 119. Psalmus* (119th Psalm of King and Prophet David) for double choir and continuo, *Symphoniae Sacrae* for various combinations, and the six-part motet *Hodie Christus natus est*.

SCHWARZKOPF, ELISABETH – as Dietrich Fischer-Dieskau is the great postwar baritone interpreter of the German *Lied*, so is Schwarzkopf the soprano equivalent; in fact, the pair have given recitals together. Her name is equally renowned in the world of opera. She made her début at Covent Garden in 1947 as a member of the Vienna Staatsoper. Though she has sung many of the important roles in nineteenth-century Italian opera she has concentrated on Mozart and Strauss. At Venice in 1951 she created the part of Anne Trulove in the first performance of Stravinsky's *The Rake's Progress*, and she has sung in many oratorios including Tippett's *A Child of our Time*. Schwarzkopf's voice, as can be heard in the many recordings she made under the guidance of her husband, Walter Legge – one-time artistic director of EMI records – is silky, yet with a wide range of register and dynamic; it is most effectively versatile in adjusting to mood and character. Her interpretations of *Lieder* are sensitively detailed. Here are two recorded items for you to check her out: *Schwarzkopf Sings Opera Arias* and *Elisabeth Schwarzkopf Lieder Recital*. She has been created a Dame.

SCHWEITZER, ALBERT – a multi-talented humanist whose relevance to music was his involvement in Bach studies; he was born in Alsace and died in the Gabon, West Africa, aged ninety. Schweitzer's *J. S. Bach: Complete Organ Works* is his monument to Bach scholarship, edited in collaboration with Widor and with Nies-Berger; the introductions to each of these volumes are especially enlightening. He was an authority on organ construction and claimed that the best organs were built by the French in the period 1850–80 (which shows a somewhat Romantic period bias). He himself was an organist of fully professional standard; during his periods of leave he gave recitals in Europe and the USA. At Lambaréné in the Gabon he established a leprosy hospital, where he lived and worked for some forty years. In preparation for this lifelong commitment he took a medical degree, while lecturing in theology at Strasbourg University and practising as a Lutheran minister. To be sure, a man of unusual quality.

SCORE – no more nor less than the visual presentation of music on paper. It usually describes a manuscript or printed book showing the lay-out of all the parts of an orchestra; here the term 'full score' has been commonly used. The term 'score' may also be applied to piano music or a song. The normal order of an orchestral score, starting from the top, is woodwind, brass, percussion, strings. In each section its instruments are laid out from high to low sound; thus, for example, in the woodwind section the order is flutes, oboes, clarinets, bassoons. You can appreciate that the function of a score is to record the music that has been made, and for the conductor to direct the parts from the whole or for the performer of, say, a piano piece to comprehend all that has to be played. A conductor or musicologist has to be a first-class score reader in order to grasp fully the details contained in a score. Often the composer's original will have been written in haste, or untidily, or have abbreviations and short-cuts; here the musicologist's function is often to act as editor, to prepare the score for publication. As you would imagine, the use of some form of score or other has been in existence for hundreds of years in classical music. While a large number of twentieth-century scores, by the nature of their musical language and style, do not lend themselves to this sort of thing, some score readers who possess a special talent and keyboard facility can play an approximation on the piano of a Beethoven symphony or a symphonic poem by Strauss from the full score.

SCULTHORPE, PETER – twentieth-century Australian composer, perhaps the most original the Antipodes has yet produced. Sculthorpe's music has great boldness, without being esoteric to the ordinary listener. Like the Japanese composer Takemitsu, he is able to express an aural picture or feeling reflecting his environment, yet technically and directionally the writing is very much part of twentieth-century classical development. Because he is nearer to the Far East than to Europe, it is understandable that Sculthorpe has taken an interest in the music of that geographical area. Full of attractive features are his compositions such as *Koto Music I* for piano, *Songs of Sea and Sky* for clarinet and piano, and *Irkanda IV* for solo violin, strings and percussion.

SEARLE, HUMPHREY – twentieth-century English composer of unusual literary cultivation – he wrote his own opera librettos. Searle's refinement and clarity of musical thought are to be heard in his *Poem* Op. 18 for twenty-two strings and the *Zodiac Variations* Op. 53 for small orchestra. His *Piano Concerto* Op. 5 reveals a romantic streak which he never quite lost, and his setting of Lear's *The Owl and the Pussy Cat* for speaker, flute, cello and guitar shows much musical wit and charm. In 1937–8 Searle studied privately in Vienna with Webern, who greatly influenced his compositional thought, though not his style. Searle was one of the earliest English composers to use the twelve-note method. He belonged to the generation, following Elgar, then Vaughan Williams and Bax, that included Walton, Britten, Lambert, Rawsthorne and Lutyens, all of whom helped to place English composition firmly back on the twentieth-century musical map. Searle was an international authority on the music of Liszt and edited and translated *Hector Berlioz: a Selection from his Letters*.

SEASONS, THE – a popular oratorio by Haydn, completed in 1801, for soloists, chorus and orchestra; the text is a German translation based on an English poem by James Thomson. The sequence of the four parts of *The Seasons* is spring, summer, autumn and winter, unlike Brahms's Piano Concerto No. 2 in B flat major, in which the supposed seasonal sequence is summer, autumn, winter, spring. The work also contrasts greatly with the Baroque *Four Seasons* of Vivaldi.

SEA SYMPHONY, A – this is the title of Vaughan Williams's Symphony No. 1 for soprano and baritone soloists, chorus and orchestra; the texts are based on Walt Whitman's *Leaves of Grass*. Though *A Sea Symphony* was completed in 1909, it was subjected to revision, as the composer was wont to do with nearly all his other nine symphonies. In this instance the final revision was made fourteen years later, in 1923. The work began life as a group of songs of the sea and blossomed into a full choral symphony. In feeling it moves between contemplation and vigorous optimism.

SEGOVIA, ANDRÉS – Spanish guitarist who took the instrument out of its folk and popular traditional setting and placed it firmly in the concert hall, where he was able to engage the delight of an audience over an entire evening. He blazed the trail for an illustrious stream of artists, including Julian Bream, John Williams (who received coaching from him) and Timothy Walker among the English-speaking players. His musicality and the excitement of Segovia's technique inspired composers to produce works for him – Villa-Lobos, Rodrigo, Falla, for example. Listen to *The Art of Segovia* and *Danza – Dances of Spain and Latin America* to get a good idea of his playing. His special sound is due to the way in which he alters his plucking technique between fingertip and nail, backed by great virtuosity. He gave masterclasses in Spain and the USA and made many guitar transcriptions from music by the leading eighteenth- and nineteenth-century composers.

SEIBER, MÁTYÁS – twentieth-century Hungarian composer who settled in England in the 1930s; he was a pupil of Kodály, whom he accompanied on several field trips collecting Hungarian folk music. He was an early European authority on jazz and at the Frankfurt Hoch Conservatory was appointed professor of jazz in 1928, a daring academic appointment for that time. Besides his always finely fashioned compositions he became an important figure in British contemporary musical life through his thorough and critical knowledge of European musical and aesthetic trends and his open-minded observations on British composition; he frequently represented Britain at international meetings and conferences and wrote articles for English and foreign journals. Seiber became the leading composition teacher in Britain; those that passed through his hands include Banks, Fricker, Gilbert, Glasser, Joubert, Lidholm, Milner and Wood. Believing that the composer should first and foremost be a craftsman, willing to tackle any writing task coming his way, he set an example by composing, in addition to his important works, music for radio plays, film advertisement jingles, music for cartoons; he even wrote a tutor for accordion. The cantata *Ulysses* for tenor, chorus and orchestra (the soloist at its first performance was Peter Pears) and the chamber work *Three Fragments* display Seiber's instrumental and orchestral mastery, a sharp dramatic sense and a range of feeling from driving power to the utmost delicacy. Of a rich variety of works his String Quartet No. 3 (*Quartetto Lirico*) is one of the finest postwar examples in this genre, and received a special award at the 1953 ISCM Festival in Haifa. Worth hearing on CD are his *Concertino* for clarinet and string orchestra and the *Four Hungarian Folksongs*. In 1960, on a lecture tour of South African universities, he was tragically killed in a motor car accident on a visit to the wild animal reservation, the Kruger National Park.

SERENADE – a term to describe a piece meant for evening relaxation, consisting of one or more movements involving several players. The serenade originates in southern Europe – Italy and Spain – and would be performed by strolling players on wind and string instruments. As you might expect, it would consist of music that is light-hearted or gentle or sentimental, for wooing a young lady was a part of its function. It grew from the close of the seventeenth century until the time of Mozart who, more than any other composer, established its classical music credentials; by now the serenade, akin to the *divertimento*, could consist of any number of movements with attention to form and instrumentation, and exploitation of orchestral niceties. Two choice examples by Mozart are his *Serenade* K375 and *Eine kleine Nachtmusik* K525 (A Little Bit of Night Music). A serenade was often inserted in an opera – Rossini's *Barber of Seville* and Mozart's *Don Giovanni* contain examples. Serenades or serenade-type pieces have been composed ever since, no matter the language or style – Dvořák, Elgar (*Serenade* in E minor Op. 20 for string orchestra), Tchaikovsky (*Serenade* in C Op. 48 for string orchestra), Sibelius (*Two Serenades* Op. 69 for violin and orchestra), Stravinsky (*Serenade* in A for piano).

SERIALISM – see *Twelve-Note Composition.*

SERVA PADRONA, LA (The Maid as Mistress) – this two-act comic opera by Pergolesi, in which a pretty and astute servant girl foxily manoeuvres her master into wedlock, was originally conceived as an intermezzo to be performed between the three acts of his opera seria *Il prigioniero superbo* (The Haughty Prisoner), first produced in Naples in 1733. Dyagilev, the colourful Russian impresario, drew Stravinsky's attention to some of Pergolesi's music, and from it Stravinsky composed the ballet *Pulcinella* using soprano, tenor and bass soloists with a chamber-sized orchestra. Later he made a *Pulcinella Suite* for chamber orchestra out of the music as well as a *Suite italienne* – one version for violin and piano, another for cello and piano.

SESSIONS, ROGER – one of the most important twentieth-century American composers after Ives. Like many of the composers of his generation he was European-orientated and made regular visits, some quite extended, to France and other countries; yet in his works may often be found lyrical sweeps of melody which have an American character. Through his teaching and writing he had a major influence on two generations of American composers, and with Copland promoted concerts of home-grown music, particularly in New York. He studied with Bloch for a time; he held professorships at Princeton, Harvard, the University of California at Berkeley and at the Juilliard School of Music. Besides Bloch he was also influenced by the music of Stravinsky and Schoenberg, which is not to deny the independence of his musical persona. The orchestral suite *The Black Maskers* and Symphony No. 5 will show you what Sessions's music is about.

SHARP, CECIL – the first important collector and scholar of English folksong. After reading mathematics at Cambridge he went to Australia. Shortly after his return he saw the Headington Morris side dancing at Oxford, and later heard a gardener singing folksongs while mowing the lawn; these two events aroused his interest in folk music and caused him to examine the importance of music as a social and cultural function in society. From 1904 he became a collector and analyst of folksong and dance and an energetic propagandist whose aim was to 'restore their songs and dances to the English people'. For many years he had a devoted amanuensis in Maud Karpeles. Sharp collected nearly five thousand items. His importance in the renaissance of twentieth-century English classical music lies in the fact that composers such as Vaughan Williams, Holst and Butterworth became interested in his work, accompanying him on several field trips, and drawing on the material he had gathered.

SHNITKE, ALFRED – an important post-Shostakovich/Prokofiev Russian composer. His musical studies were pursued in Moscow; at the same time he gained some experience in electro-acoustic composition. His growing reputation in the West has earned him performances and commissions to the extent that Shnitke has spent increasing time outside Russia. He is quite unselfconscious in inserting, in a functional role, quotations of material as varied as Beethoven, Baroque music and modern dance-hall elements. His works are diverse: the Symphony No. 2 (sub-titled 'St Florian'), *Canon in memory of Stravinsky* for string quartet and *Hymn* for cello, harp and timpani. Shnitke has also written a number of important articles, such as *Notes on the orchestral polyphony of Shostakovich's Fourth Symphony* and *The characteristics of Prokofiev's orchestral writing*. Though he has a strong following in England, thus far no recordings are yet available. So your chance to see whether or not you like his music must wait, unless you catch a concert or broadcast which includes a work of his.

SHOSTAKOVICH, DMITRY – he and Prokofiev are the two greatest Russian composers after Stravinsky. His music is less immediately melodious than Prokofiev's, but much more discursive; hence his impressive output of symphonies and string quartets (fifteen of each). His music also includes an attractive set of *Twenty-Four Preludes and Fugues* for piano and an excellent opera, *Lady Macbeth of Mtsensk*, banned by Stalin in 1936 and revived in Russia only in 1962, nine years after the dictator's death. The relationship between Shostakovich and Soviet authority is complex and not easily explained. On the one hand he retained the original ideal of the Soviet state, a desire to promote at all times the interests of 'the people'; on the other he could not stomach the aesthetic of the Communist Party line interfering with his creative musical thought. He was immensely loyal to his country, yet one wonders what kind of music he might have written had he lived and worked outside the Soviet Union. One thing can surely be relied on, namely, that it would have been just as great. There is, in his core works – the symphonies and string quartets – a consistent brooding grief, a melancholy, great outbursts of protesting violence; is this merely a reaction to official dictatorial authority or an expression of a major part of his temperament? There are, however, many examples in his music of high spirits, wit, comedy, a satirical sense of humour, largely absent in the works of 'Western' composers – Hindemith, Schoenberg, Webern, Messiaen, Boulez, for instance. Shostakovich held back the scores of a number of works because of the likely disapproval of the Soviet establishment; one example is his song-set *From Jewish Folk Poetry* Op. 79 for soprano, alto, bass and piano, which he completed in 1948 but did not release until 1955 and which he orchestrated in 1964.

In health Shostakovich was always frail and nervy; his strength lay in his spirit and creative propulsion. He wrote with tremendous rapidity. His composition teacher was Glazunov and in his early years he was much influenced by the music of Stravinsky, Prokofiev, Krenek and Hindemith; he took a serious interest in Mahler and greatly appreciated Berg's opera *Wozzeck*. Shostakovich was also a pianist of concert platform standard, often performing his own works. As a youth, in order to help support his widowed mother and siblings, he had earned roubles playing the piano in a cinema. Listening musts, for starters, since much of Shostakovich's work is recorded, are his Symphony No. 5 in D minor Op. 47 and his String Quartet No. 8 in C minor Op. 110, which contains the motto notes D–E flat–C–B, derived from the initial of his first name and the first letters of his surname, D–S–C–H. After Sibelius he is the twentieth century's most important symphonist.

SIBELIUS, JEAN – Finnish composer, with Grieg the greatest to come out of Scandinavia. As Grieg was involved with Norwegian culture, so was Sibelius with the legend and history of Finland. His continuous sources of inspiration were myth and nature, hardly ever the flux of human relationships. The listener can pick up this bias from his symphonic poems such as *En Saga* and *The Swan of Tuonela* – one becomes transported to another world, magical, isolated, crystalline. As Debussy's *La Mer* evokes images of the sea, Sibelius's last important work, *Tapiola*, conjures up the forests of northern Europe. His seven symphonies create their own world and underline the composer's independent sound cosmos; a good example is the Symphony No. 5 in E flat Op. 82, which shows Sibelius's manner of building up a momentum of excitement from rhythm patterns, gradation of dynamics, sweeping melody and transformation of thematic material.

It should be remembered that until 1917 Finland was part of the Russian Empire, so it is not surprising that Sibelius was strongly nationalist. To some extent this turned him musically inward, so that he had little interest in pursuing the paths blazed by Schoenberg, Stravinsky or Les Six. An overt expression of his nationalism is the orchestral piece

Finlandia, which sometimes comes dangerously near to the bombastic. Sibelius virtually stopped composing from 1925. On his ninetieth birthday he was internationally celebrated; Toscanini sent him tapes of his recordings of Sibelius's music and Churchill sent him a box of cigars! His greatest popularity was gained in England and the USA, and he is an early example of a composer achieving wide recognition through gramophone recording.

SICILIANA – a slow, dance-like, instrumental or vocal piece in triplets, having two or four beats-to-the-bar and starting with an upbeat; it is gentle in character, sometimes bordering on the melancholic. It is most frequently found in Baroque music and is often associated with pastoral scenes. Nineteenth- and twentieth-century composers are not averse to writing the odd siciliana, but it is best displayed in the vocal music of Bach (e.g. the aria 'Stirb in mir, Welt' – Die in me, world – from his cantata *Gott soll allein mein Herze haben* – God alone will have my heart) and Handel (the aria 'Your charms to ruin led the way' from the oratorio *Samson*). Telemann, Domenico Scarlatti and Couperin wrote siciliana movements in several of their keyboard works. Fauré includes a siciliana in his incidental music for Maeterlinck's play *Pelléas et Mélisande*.

SIGNATURE – in music, a sign placed at the beginning of a piece. The *clef* sign comes first and shows the pitch area of the music (high or low). There are two other types of signature, the one which tells you what 'key' the piece is in: its key signature; the other, what 'metre' is to be used: its time signature. (See also *Key* and *Time signature*.) Much music of this century does away with key signatures but retains time signatures. From the seventeenth to the early twentieth century all music was written in a certain key – a tonal centre or tonic or key note – from which the remaining notes of a scale were assigned their harmonic functions. The key signature indicates which notes in the scale have to be raised or lowered; the raised note is made 'sharp' and the lowered note is made 'flat'. A piece in the key of C sharp has seven sharps, for example; a piece in the key of A flat has four flats; the sharp or flat signs indicating which notes are to be so treated are placed on the stave (five parallel lines) at the point where the relevant note occurs. A piece with no sharps or flats is in the key of either C major or A minor. This is all quite a mouthful, but don't worry too much about it. A time signature, on the other hand, is a doddle – it simply tells you how many beats there are to the bar.

270

SINFONIA – simply the Italian for 'symphony'; musicologically, however, the term is used as far back as the late sixteenth century to describe a work for instrumental ensemble, the music for which can take a variety of forms. In the seventeenth century the term was frequently interchangeable with 'sonata'. Before sinfonias were established as three- or four-movement orchestral pieces, becoming precursors of the eighteenth-century symphony, they could appear as canzonas, overtures or as a set of dances. Nowadays 'sinfonia' is sometimes used as part of the title of a small orchestra.

SINFONIETTA – this term has no origin in Italian and seems first to have been used by Rimsky-Korsakov in its French form 'symphoniette'; now the term simply describes an orchestral piece of several movements, less ambitious and lighter than a symphony. As with 'sinfonia' it is also used as a title for a performing ensemble of small-orchestra dimensions, such as the crack London Sinfonietta of international renown. A good number of twentieth-century composers have enjoyed writing sinfoniettas – Prokofiev, Janáček, Britten, Poulenc, Hindemith, Berkeley and Milhaud.

SINGSPIEL – a German term for a play with singing. The *Singspiel* was a particularly popular form of theatre in German-speaking countries for fifty or more years from the middle of the eighteenth century. It was largely influenced by the English ballad opera, with its use of the vernacular, as opposed to the high tone of opera texts, and the liberal delivery of songs with modest orchestral accompaniment and even some dancing. The greatest example is Mozart's *Die Zauberflöte* (The Magic Flute). Many American musicals, especially pre-war, may be described simply as a more sophisticated form of the old *Singspiel*.

SIX, LES – a name given to a group of composers flourishing in Paris as young, musical upstarts in the 1920s. They themselves went under the name of *Les nouveaux jeunes* (The new youth); the *Les Six* title was coined in an article by the journalist Henri Collet and stuck, not necessarily pleasing all its members – Milhaud, Poulenc, Auric, Honegger, Durey and the one woman in the group, Tailleferre. All were students at the Paris Conservatoire and first appeared together in a song recital programme in 1917. Their father figure was Satie, who encouraged not only an anti-Wagnerian attitude but a dismissal of the music of Debussy, Stravinsky, Schoenberg and Strauss; the replacing aesthetic was the writing of short pieces, matter-of-fact, sardonic, the use of popular music idioms, and epigrammatic sound-shots. Another of their champions was Cocteau. In due course they split up as their careers developed in different directions. The one member who retained a streak of the original aims and attitudes in his compositions was Poulenc.

SKALKOTTAS, NIKOLAOS – twentieth-century Greek composer who studied with Schoenberg, Jarnach and Weill during a sojourn in Germany from 1921 to 1933. On his return to Greece he received hardly any encouragement in an environment which was still musically parochial, and led an isolated and depressed existence, beset by ill-health and financial worries, working as a back-desk orchestral violinist for the rest of his life. Skalkottas's music is generally stern, unrelenting and concentrated; it is not easy to perform. Although he employs Schoenberg's twelve-note method of composition in many of his works, his approach is quite independent. Regrettably, Skalkottas had minimal interest in the rich variety of Greek folk music lying at his door. There is a sterile period of some three or four years after his return from Berlin, followed by an outburst of creativity which lasted until his death; of the seventy works he left behind forty-eight were written in this second period. His output merits further investigation and performance. The only works thus far recorded are the *Concertino* for trumpet and piano and his Symphony, sub-titled 'The Return of Odysseus'.

SKRYABIN, ALEXANDER – an off-beat, nineteenth-century Russian composer of marked originality and with a highly inventive harmonic gift; he was also a fine pianist, a talent inherited from his mother. Unfortunately she died of consumption during his boyhood; his father spent long periods abroad in the employ of the Russian consular service, with the result that Skryabin was cared for by a collection of female relatives who, damagingly, pampered him. The St Petersburg patron and publisher Belyayev took over the domination of Skryabin from his womenfolk, treating him kindly and generously until he himself died in 1908; he published the composer's works and sent him on concert tours abroad. Skryabin's philosophising leanings ultimately centred on theosophy, at which time his egocentricity became extreme and he believed himself to be a rare genius. He began to develop a theory of association between notes and colours, which he most embracingly expressed in his *Prométhée* for large orchestra. One of his literary efforts was a poem entitled 'Poema extaza', which ultimately inspired his one-movement orchestral work *Le poème de l'extase* (Poem of Ecstasy). His piano output is of particular interest; both here and in his other works he uses harmony instead of themes as developmental material. The bulk of his music is for piano – an example or two: Sonata No. 9 in F major Op. 68 (subtitled 'Black Mass'), *Vers la flamme* Op. 72 (Towards the

Flame) and *Two Pieces for Left Hand* Op. 9, written during a period when he had injured his right hand.

SMALLEY, ROGER – one of the leading figures of the postwar British avant garde, who for the time being has settled in Perth at the University of Western Australia. He studied with Fricker, White, and Goehr; he was appointed composer-in-residence at King's College, Cambridge, in 1967. With Souster he formed an electro-acoustic music group called Intermodulation which gave a series of impressive performances of improvised and notated music pieces, including his *Beat Music*, which was commissioned for the 1971 Proms. The London Sinfonietta under Atherton has featured first performances of Smalley's works, not least the admirable *Pulses for 5 × 4 players* for brass, percussion and ring modulators. His articles on contemporary music are rich in scope, for example, *Debussy and Messiaen, The Sketchbook of The Rite of Spring, Some recent works of Peter Maxwell Davies*. The main influence on Smalley has been Stockhausen, to which, in his early development, he was almost slavishly devoted. As yet, unfortunately, none of his music has hit the CD shelves.

SMETANA, BEDŘICH (Czech for 'Friedrich') – he is to Czech music what Glinka was to Russian or Grieg to Norwegian music. It's nice to know that Smetana was passionately fond of dancing; his output is brimful of national dance forms and rhythms. It is interesting to note that most middle-class Czechs, then subjects of the Habsburg empire, spoke German; Smetana had to teach himself Czech – his first letter in Czech was written at the age of thirty-two, and his diaries are in German until he was thirty-seven. He took part in the abortive Prague revolution of 1848.

Smetana is the first Czech composer to present the sights and sounds of his country through musical works of distinction, paving the way for Dvořák, Suk, Janáček and Martinů. Throughout his life, however, he failed to gain the full recognition he deserved from fellow musicians, critics and audience. In his early period he wrote almost entirely for the piano, including more than twenty polkas, the popular Czech dance, ingeniously treated, for example, *Quatre Souvenirs de Bohème en forme de polka*; also there is a fine parade of other dance rhythms in his *Fourteen Czech Dances*. Of his eight operas the most popular is *The Bartered Bride*, full of lively tunes and rhythms, light-heartedly and imaginatively orchestrated. One of his best chamber works is the String Quartet in E minor, while his most distinguished orchestral music lies in the series of six symphonic poems called *Má vlast* (My Fatherland), the most frequently performed being No. 2, *Vltava* (or Moldau, the name of the great Czech river). Like Schubert and Wolf, Smetana contracted syphilis which brought about deteriorating health, including steadily increasing deafness which, as you may imagine, must be sheer torture for a musician. He died in a Prague lunatic asylum.

SMYTH, ETHEL – the first important English woman composer, a contemporary of Elgar. Since her day the UK has witnessed an ever-increasing number of women composers to the extent, not yet explained, that it has more pro rata than any other country. Smyth studied in Leipzig and had the opportunity of meeting Brahms, Dvořák, Grieg, Tchaikovsky and Joachim. The Mass in D, her first important work, was performed at the Albert Hall in 1893. In the 1900s she strongly identified herself with the women's suffragette movement and in musical support wrote *The March of the Women* for soprano, chorus and orchestra. The most successful of a series of operas was *The Wreckers*, the overture of which is on CD. Its plot is somewhat bizarre: the folk of a Cornish village seek to rob ships wrecked on the coast; the wife of the headman and her lover decide to light warning fires to deter vessels from approaching the unfriendly coastline, but are discovered and incarcerated in a cave where they will drown with the rising tide. Smyth was also a fine writer; the best of a series of very readable autobiographies is *Impressions that Remained*. She wrote the librettos for all her operas including *Der Wald* (The Wood), a one-acter performed with success not only at Covent Garden but also in Berlin and New York. Smyth was created a Dame in 1922.

SOCIOLOGY OF MUSIC – this is a comparatively young discipline in which attempts are made to understand the relationship between society and music. The sociology of music differs from musicology as such, in that musicology essentially seeks to examine the musical product, although much observation of the society in which it is produced must perforce be involved; on the other hand the sociology of music tries to determine, for instance, why a society during a particular historical period will produce a certain kind of music, and how musical, social and cultural structures are related to each other. Since it is not concerned primarily with the aesthetics of music, folk and popular music are of equal interest. Sociology of music is also different from ethnomusicology, which concentrates on the study of national or ethnic features of musical style or production. But, in essence, musicology, ethnomusicology and sociology of music cannot help but overlap.

Two approaches currently hold sway: the one stems from the music theorist Adorno, and suggests that the most advanced or progressive musical circle in a culture is its seminal point for commentary, being, in sum, a constructive criticism of the state of that culture. The other approach is Marxist-orientated; here the viewpoint is that the economic or material condition of a society brings about changes in musical style and aesthetics. In a nutshell, this is what the sociology of music is all about. As for the two aforementioned approaches, take your pick; or you may work out your own viewpoint on the subject.

SOLER, ANTONIO – an important eighteenth-century Spanish composer. He studied with Domenico Scarlatti and, like his master, Soler's significant achievement lies in the numerous sonatas he wrote for keyboard – nearly one hundred and fifty. Various selections from these are on CD and worth listening to. Of unusual interest, in addition, are his six quintets for organ and string quartet, an uncommon instrumental combination for the time. Unlike Scarlatti's sonatas, which are in one movement or paired, Soler's sonatas are mainly in three or four movements. He also produced an important theoretical work, *Llave de la modulación* (1762) (An explanation of modulation procedures), which discusses in great detail the movement from one tonal centre to another through the twenty-four possibilities within the chromatic scale. Soler took holy orders and spent his life attached to the monastery at El Escorial; this did not deter him from using Spanish dance rhythms – *jota*, *bolero*, *polo* – and other secular influences in his keyboard music. He was also an authority on organ construction, as well as a respected mathematician.

SOLTI, GEORG – British conductor of Hungarian birth. In Budapest he studied with Bartók, Kodály and Dohnányi; he left Hungary owing to restrictions imposed on Jews and spent the war years in Switzerland. His début in England was with the London Philharmonic Orchestra in 1949. Since then he has achieved world fame through regular concert tours, and has made many recordings including the first issue ever of the complete cycle of Wagner's *Ring* operas in 1966. Solti was Covent Garden's music director for ten years from 1961; there he conducted the British première of Schoenberg's *Moses und Aron*. He was knighted in 1972. His interpretations are both subtle and full of verve, and cover a large repertoire of traditional and contemporary works for concert hall and opera house.

SONATA – this term describes a piece, usually of more than one movement, most often in three or four movements, for a solo instrument or instrumental duet, sometimes for a chamber ensemble. A sonata's first movement is, as a rule, ternary in structure; the sections, in sequence, are called exposition, development and recapitulation. (See *Sonata form*, below.) The second and final movements are respectively slow and fast; an additional movement, especially in nineteenth-century works, is sometimes inserted between the second and final movements. Sonata is the weightiest of all instrumental composing ambitions. Its roots go back to medieval times, and until the Classical period the term was one among several used to describe an instrumental piece without vocal attachment. The Baroque sonata, in character, functioned rather as an entertainment. The sonata became more clearly defined and more ambitious from the Classical period, when the examples by Haydn, Mozart, Beethoven and Schubert reflect a discursiveness in musical thought, also to be found in the string quartet and the symphony. The Romantic era saw the sonata spreading more widely geographically, embraced by the French and the Russians, for example, and also extending the personal expression and foibles of the composer, here modelled, no doubt, on some of the sonatas of Beethoven and Schubert – one thinks of compositions in this genre by Brahms, Liszt, Franck or Fauré. In the twentieth century composers have continued to write sonatas but with a less rigid adherence to traditional paths; the common element is that a work so titled is serious in intention. Some very moving examples have come from Debussy, Stravinsky, Berg, Prokofiev, Shostakovich, Bartók, Carter and Boulez.

SONATA DA CAMERA – Italian for 'chamber sonata'; the term describes a seventeenth- or early eighteenth-century instrumental piece for one or more melody instruments (violin, flute, oboe) and keyboard continuo. Corelli was one of the most successful composers of the *sonata da camera*, the movements of which would consist of an 'opener' – a prelude – followed by several dance or dance-derived pieces such as allemande, sarabande, gavotte or gigue.

SONATA DA CHIESA – Italian for 'church sonata'; this type of composition flourished at much the same time as the *sonata da camera*, but its intention was more serious. Movements were more sombre in mood, there was significant use of fugal technique, an absence of dance references and, often, use of the Corelli format of four movements in alternating tempos, slow-fast-slow-fast. At church performances the parts were sometimes doubled, so that the works were performed by what amounted to a small orchestra.

SONATA FORM – this is an unfortunate – because confusing – term to describe the structure of a movement, usually the first, of a three- or four-movement sonata. I suppose the term evolved because the first movement of a sonata is usually its 'heaviest', most serious or ambitious.

Hence, sonata form is also referred to as 'first-movement form'; but it should be underlined that the other movements may use sonata form or variations or modifications of it. What is marvellous about sonata form is that it has richly served composers from Haydn right up to Boulez. The secret of its strength and usability is the purely musical drama contained in its tripartite structure; this allows for creative expression whatever the language and style of the composer. Its first section (exposition) presents the material to be varied, and offers surprises; the same applies to the second section (development), in which the composer really goes to town, showing his ingenuity and range of invention; while the third and final section (recapitulation) reminds us of the musical ideas originally presented, but again allowing for variation and for a convincing dramatic climax – which does not necessarily mean ending the movement as loudly as possible! Sonata form is so widely and interestingly used that, not surprisingly, much has been written about the way various composers have dealt with it, and, believe me, some of these composers can come up with some pretty complicated treatments.

SONATINA – as you have no doubt jumped to it, this term refers to a small-scale, more lighthearted version of the sonata. Sonatinas normally consist of one to three movements of comparatively short duration; 'sonatina' is the Italian diminutive of 'sonata'. Mozart and his contemporaries knocked out sonatinas for piano or piano and violin with obvious pleasure, but the genre took a nose-dive in the nineteenth century, composers being too serious about themselves to bother with it. In the twentieth century, however, the sonatina has been revived to good effect. There are examples by Bartók, Ravel and Prokofiev for piano, by Françaix for trumpet and piano and by Boulez for flute and piano.

SONG – the late John Blacking, social anthropologist and ethnomusicologist, held that *homo sapiens* sang before he could speak. When one considers the glory of song throughout the ages, and if one believes that the human voice is the most beautiful of all musical instruments, Blacking's theory is very tenable. A song may be defined as a form of musical expression uttered by a solo voice presenting a text, with or without instrumental accompaniment. While there is a rich repertoire of song in the folk, popular, religious and theatre genres, we are here paying attention only to classical song from the eighteenth to the twentieth centuries and perforce ignoring that of the Baroque period and earlier: we are talking of the so-called 'art song'.

The emergence of the art song runs parallel with the rise of the middle-class stratum in European society. At the close of the eighteenth century the middle classes became important consumers of music. At the same time the hardier piano not only succeeded the more delicate harpsichord, but its price to the public became increasingly affordable. Composer and publisher cottoned on to the fact that here was a steadily growing market to exploit. As a consequence the nineteenth century produced, in purely musical terms, the golden age of song with piano accompaniment. You'll agree with me when you consider the song output of Schubert, Schumann, Brahms, Wolf, Mahler and Strauss in Germany; in France, Berlioz, Duparc, Fauré, Debussy; in Russia, Musorgsky; in Norway, Grieg; in Bohemia, Dvořák. English and American song arrived later, in the first half of the twentieth century – Vaughan Williams, Britten, Tippett; Ives, Copland, Barber. Now the tradition of song with piano accompaniment seems to be slipping away; instead the inclination is to produce songs with accompaniment by a chamber ensemble or orchestra. There are of course notable exceptions to be found in the music of Webern, Messiaen, Poulenc and others. But one way or another song writing is still going strong.

SONG-CYCLE – this term refers to a group of songs which have a central theme or tell a story; the texts are usually by one poet and the accompaniment is usually with piano. The best-known examples are Schubert's *Die schöne Müllerin* and *Winterreise* (both texts by Müller). In complete contrast is Britten's *Serenade*, in which the accompaniment to the tenor voice is for horn and strings and in which the texts of the songs are by different poets. A few of the many examples of song-cycles are Beethoven's *An die ferne Geliebte*, Schumann's *Dichterliebe*, Brahms's *Liebeslieder*, Mahler's *Kindertotenlieder*, Schoenberg's *Pierrot Lunaire*, Fauré's *Les chansons de Bilitis*, Vaughan Williams's *On Wenlock Edge*, Copland's *Twelve Poems of Emily Dickinson*, Berio's *Circles*, Crumb's *Ancient Voices of Children*, Maxwell Davies's *Eight Songs for a Mad King*.

SORCERER'S APPRENTICE, THE (*L'Apprenti sorcier*) – a very effective symphonic poem by the French composer Dukas, based on Goethe's ballad *Der Zauberlehrling*. It was first performed in 1897 and well received by both critics and audience. Its imaginative orchestration as well as its taut structure influenced Debussy and Stravinsky. The work's wit and high spirits always make it a welcome concert item.

SOUSTER, TIM – a postwar English avant-garde composer who died prematurely at the age of fifty-one. He took his music degree at Oxford and then attended Stockhausen's courses at Darmstadt. He was composer-in-residence at King's College, Cambridge, after a spell as a BBC music producer, during which he worked with Berio, Henze and Feldman. With Roger Smalley in 1969 he formed the live electronic music ensemble Intermodulation, which had an active life of some seven years. He had a natural facility for electro-acoustics, as well as a liking for and an informed interest in non-Western musics and in rock. He also turned out some very effective film and television scores. Souster strove assiduously for composers' rights and was regularly involved in the work of the Association of Professional Composers. Attractive examples of his music are *Pelvic Loops* for two-track tape and *Afghan Amplitudes* for keyboards, synthesisers and percussion.

SPOHR, LOUIS – nineteenth-century German composer who boasted a musical reputation equal to Beethoven's; yet, as time has decreed, he is today of more importance to the musicologist than to the performer or concert audience. Spohr was a first-rate violinist, and a noted conductor who used a baton, a rare thing for those days. He was essentially an orchestral and instrumental composer, though his opera output introduced several innovations: the use of blank verse, running on from episode to episode as opposed to set numbers, and the anticipation of the Wagnerian *Leitmotif* principle. He extended the importance of the clarinet with his four concertos for it (No. 4 in E minor is worth a listen) and increased the exposure of the harp (*Fantasia* in G minor and Sonata in E flat for violin and harp are apt examples). Particularly appealing are two of his larger chamber works – the Octet in E major and the Nonet in F major. He was friendly with Weber and Beethoven and appreciated and was supportive of Wagner's early operas. His memoirs, never completed but which cover his life up until about 1830, give a valuable account of musical affairs of the period.

SPRECHGESANG – literally the German for 'speech-song'; in musical terms this refers to the use of 'speech-voice' in a composition. In practice the sound lies between speaking and singing and is most effective in the German language, from which it originated. Though *Sprechgesang* had been tentatively used before Schoenberg (for example, by Humperdinck in his opera *Königskinder*), it was he who firmly established the device, which is to be found in his *Gurrelieder*, *Die glückliche Hand* (The Lucky Hand) – a concert platform music drama – and in his opera *Moses und Aron*. To English and French ears *Sprechgesang*, which, according to Schoenberg, should resemble neither speech nor singing, can sound comic or even ridiculous. It is best employed to obtain fantasy or distortion effects. Of his two main disciples, Webern and Berg, the former had no use for it, while the latter put *Sprechgesang* to convincing dramatic effect in his operas *Wozzeck* and *Lulu*.

STABAT MATER – the full title of this poem, often attributed to the thirteenth-century Franciscan monk Jacopone de Todi, is *Stabat mater dolorosa* (The sorrowing mother stood); it refers to the Virgin Mary standing at the foot of the cross. It was adopted as a sequence and as a hymn in the Roman Catholic liturgy in 1727. Numerous settings have been composed right up to the present day. Palestrina and Lassus made eight-part *a cappella* settings; Alessandro Scarlatti and Pergolesi wrote versions for soprano, alto, two violins and continuo. In the nineteenth century, chorus and orchestra *Stabat maters* came from the pens of Dvořák, Liszt and Rossini. In the twentieth century a variety of treatments have been given by Szymanowski, Berkeley, Poulenc; an impressive avant-garde version is by the Polish composer Penderecki.

STACCATO – Italian for 'detached'. It is a term used to indicate a note or notes to be played very short, not to be sustained; the opposite term is *legato* (smooth). A note to be sounded staccato has a dot above it; there are degrees of staccato determined by additional signs such as a horizontal dash above the dot, or by the use of a slur across a group of staccato notes. Staccato may create a variety of effects – dramatic, comic, energetic – and its use by different instruments can often determine the character of the music: on the bassoon clowning, on the flute sprightly, on the violin delicately charming.

STAMITZ – the name of a family of musicians who originated in Bohemia and settled in Germany. The best known are Carl and his father Johann; between them they covered the entire eighteenth century. The more important musically is Carl, who wrote piles of symphonies, sinfonia concertantes, concertos and instrumental chamber music. He was also a fine violinist and violist, earning much of his income from concert-giving. At The Hague, the court of William V, Prince of Orange, he gave no fewer than twenty-eight concerts, one of which featured the twelve-year-old Beethoven playing the piano – and receiving a higher fee than his older fellow-musician! Rather infra dig. for Carl ... He was never able to find a sinecure, although the King of Prussia irregularly patronised him. The publishers Hummel and later Breitkopf brought out quite a few of his works, but income from these sources was never sufficient to provide a living, and he fell increasingly into debt. At his death all his possessions had to be auctioned, and the painful thing is that no one wanted his music manuscripts, which, wastefully, simply disappeared. His compositional style belongs to what is known as the Mannheim School, so called because a group of fine composers and performers, including Carl and his father, worked at the court in Mannheim; in the mid-eighteenth century the town boasted the leading orchestra in Europe. Quite relaxing to listen to are Carl's concertos – say, the Concerto for Flute in G major and the Concerto for Horn in E major; and it is worth comparing Carl's *Sinfonia Concertante* in D major for violin, viola and orchestra with Mozart's same line-up in his *Sinfonia Concertante* in E flat major.

STANFORD, CHARLES VILLIERS – British composer and teacher, an immediate predecessor of Elgar. He grew up in Dublin, and at Cambridge read Classics as well as being impressively active as organist and conductor. He then went to Leipzig specifically for musical study; during his German sojourn he met Brahms, Meyerbeer and Offenbach, and was present at the opening of the Bayreuth Festival Theatre. Stanford was elected professor of music at Cambridge at the age of thirty-five and had a long innings as professor of composition at the Royal College of Music – Vaughan Williams, Holst, Lambert, Bliss, Howells are a few from the impressive list of pupils who passed through his hands. He was a prolific composer, an undoubted trail-blazer for the twentieth-century English renaissance. Compared to his predecessors he made important contributions to cathedral music (Service in G Op. 81 for chorus and organ), choral music (*Songs of the Sea* Op. 91 for baritone, male chorus and orchestra) and song-writing (*A Sheaf of Songs from Leinster* for voice and piano).

STEINITZ, PAUL – British conductor, teacher and organist who founded the London Bach Society in 1947; with it in the course of his lifetime he performed every known Bach cantata, a unique achievement. During his tenure as organist and choirmaster at St Bartholomew-the-Great, London, from 1952 he gave complete performances of the *St Matthew Passion* in German, and with the appropriate Baroque forces; this was the first such interpretation in modern times and in marked contrast to the traditional English Victorian rendering. While funds permitted, Steinitz made a point of including in his Bach programmes a commissioned work by a British composer. His widow Margaret continues to administer the London Bach Society and the Steinitz Bach Players. Steinitz was a greatly respected teacher in his double posts at Goldsmiths College and the Royal Academy of Music, and published several books on harmony and counterpoint based directly on the works of the great composers.

STERN, ISAAC – twentieth-century American violin virtuoso of Russian birth. In his teens he played concertos under the batons of Monteux and Klemperer. During the war he played for troops all over the world, and later gave concert tours in numerous countries,

281

including the Soviet Union in 1956. He has regularly sought to assist young musicians in advancing their professional careers. Stern owns two Guarneris, which contribute to the warm, expressive tone of his playing; at the same time he is a flawless technician.

STOCKHAUSEN, KARLHEINZ – twentieth-century German composer, indisputably one of the two leaders, with the American John Cage, of the postwar avant garde. Cage's music is more user-friendly and contains wit and humour, which help to bridge the gap between revolutionary musical ideas and the comparatively innocent listener; Stockhausen's music, on the other hand, is relentlessly serious and inward-looking, despite his protestations that he composes music for the world. The many performances of his works are the result of his being cosseted by respectful contemporary music promoters in charge of radio stations, arts councils and various other arts-promoting organisations, supported by specialist music critics and writers as well as, not unnaturally, adventurous young music students; enthusiasm has not come from the large corpus of concert audiences. Just as Schoenberg was fated to exert a major influence on music of the first half of the century but failed to achieve popularity for his own compositions, does the same perhaps apply to Stockhausen in the second half of our century? What cannot be disputed, and needs to be recognised, is that Stockhausen has a brilliant intelligence and intellect which are poured into a sonic world of acoustics and electronically-sourced apparatus and devices. Added to this is his knowledge of non-European musics and other art forms, phonetics, mathematics and several branches of philosophy. All this combines to express through music his constantly developing theory about the creation and performance of the most magical of all the arts. Stockhausen may be said to be an engineer of sound, and certainly this century's most authoritative and original composer of electronic music, either studio-based or live. Largely due to his own difficult early background – he was orphaned during the war and had to keep himself by undertaking a parade of hack jobs – he has become a lucid and influential composition teacher whose pupils have been drawn to him from all over the world; he is also a clear and effective exponent of his artistic beliefs as lecturer and writer. You might introduce yourself to examples of his music with *Michaels Reise um die Erde* (Michael's journey around the earth, from his opera *Donnerstag* – Thursday) for trumpet and orchestra, *Mantra* for two pianos, percussion and ring modulators, and *Klavierstück XII* (Piano Piece 12).

STOKOWSKI, LEOPOLD – London-born American conductor of Irish-Polish parentage; a good mixture, it seems, for he had a long and distinguished career and lived to ninety-five. It is forgotten that he studied at the Royal College of Music with Parry and Stanford, and at Oxford; he made his début in the first decade of this century. Stokowski's career is truly remarkable. He catapulted to new heights the standard of orchestral playing in the USA; through research into acoustics and electronics he advanced the fidelity of orchestral recording; and through his reworking of scores from Beethoven to Puccini, greatly irritating music scholars, he popularised a host of important works. He was a showman, cultivating gestures pleasing to the audience, and was one of the first conductors this century to abandon the use of the baton. By 1971 he had given some 7000 concerts and, to his great credit, conducted the premières of over 2000 works by contemporary composers, including Rakhmaninov and Varèse – quite disparate composers in language and style. He also involved himself in the conducting of film scores, the best known being Disney's unique *Fantasia*. He was still appearing publicly at the age of ninety-three and made his last recording shortly before his death. Stokowski had three wives, consecutively of course.

STRAUSS, JOHANN – here I refer to Johann Strauss II or Jnr, the most famous of Viennese waltz composers. He flourished for most of the nineteenth century, producing an endless stream of dance hits, mainly waltzes of course, but also polkas, galops, mazurkas, as well as arrangements and paraphrases of symphonic and operatic works. His father, Johann Strauss I or Snr, together with his fellow composer Lanner, had inherited a hundred-year-old Viennese dance tradition which

283

culminated in the orchestral dances of Haydn, Mozart, Beethoven and Schubert; both blazed the trail for son Johann. Like his father, he was both orchestral leader and violinist; he might be compared to Duke Ellington playing the piano and at the same time leading his jazz band from the front. By the age of nineteen he was running his own orchestra of about twenty-eight players; at twenty-five he was appointed 'Imperial-Royal Director of Music for Balls' by the Emperor Franz Joseph I. When Vienna fell under the influence of Offenbach's *opéras bouffes*, Strauss wrote several examples in the genre himself; the two best, still frequently given, are *Die Fledermaus* (The Bat) and *Der Zigeunerbaron* (The Gypsy Baron). Their recommendation is not so much plot or structure as their lively, charming, elegant vocal and instrumental melodic material. Even old Brahms in his crotchety years loved Strauss's music and had him round to coffee several times. The format Strauss employed for the 'number' normally consisted of a slow introduction, five waltzes – each flowing naturally into the next – and a coda. Let me rattle off a few Strauss waltzes, which you're bound to know anyway: *Tales from the Vienna Woods*, *Voices of Spring*, *On the Beautiful Blue Danube*, *Accelerations*, *Roses from the South* and *Wine, Women and Song*. Get ready to take your partner and start to gyrate. And don't forget the polkas, galops and mazurkas to follow.

STRAUSS, RICHARD – German composer, contemporary of Mahler and Debussy (no relation to Johann); in his heyday he was dubbed the successor to Brahms and Wagner. His works may be divided into three broad areas: symphonic poems, operas and songs. The symphonic poems make use of large orchestral forces, not unusual for the time (consider Mahler, for comparison), and are equivalent to major symphonic movements in scale; they are usually programmatic or semi-programmatic in character. Each has a fresh structure; for example, *Don Juan* (one of his best and most popular) is in sonata form with added self-contained episodes; *Till Eulenspiegel* is in rondo form; *Don Quixote* (perhaps compositionally his finest orchestral work) is made up of variations; *Eine Alpensinfonie* (An Alpine Symphony) consists of twenty-two sections and employs a force of 150 players. He was without doubt an excellent orchestrator.

In his mid-thirties Strauss turned with great success to opera-writing, causing a sensation with his one-act *Salome* (based on Oscar Wilde's play), which was followed shortly after by another one-acter, *Elektra*. In all he wrote about fifteen operas; the one most frequently performed in the international repertoire is the light-hearted but clever and tuneful *Der Rosenkavalier* (The Knight of the Rose). *Salome*, with its titillating sexuality and brutality, appeared in fifty opera houses in the space of two years. Strauss's operas are major contributions to the genre. Of interest is the knowledge that his favourite two operas were Mozart's *Così fan tutte* and Wagner's *Tristan und Isolde*.

Throughout his life Strauss wrote songs, and must be considered as an important contributor to the German *Lied* tradition. The song with orchestra was a type which particularly attracted him – his *Vier letzte Lieder* (Four Last Songs), first performed a year before his death, is a fine example. Shortly before this song-set, he produced a work for twenty-three strings, a sort of symphonic adagio, *Metamorphosen*. Strauss earned the reputation of being a first-rate conductor, and in the concert hall he frequently promoted the works of fellow composers – Mahler, Sibelius, Elgar. He has been accused of collaborating with the Nazi régime; rather, as has happened with other composers, he was politically naïve as well as psychologically centred on his music. This may be considered by some as no excuse; however, in defence, he had a Jewish daughter-in-law whom he forcefully protected. He was an obsessive card player, his favourite game being skat.

STRAVINSKY, IGOR – twentieth-century Russian composer; he, Bartók and Schoenberg form a troika of the greatest composers in the first half of this century, following Debussy, Mahler and Strauss. His sound is unique, created by varying mixtures of rhythmic invention, bold instrumentation and orchestration, and the inimitable use of parody technique. The melodic surface of his music, whether motivic or consisting of extended phrases, is also instantly memorable. In the first period of his composition, which evolved slowly in comparison with other great composers, he was influenced mainly by folk music and the works of the Russian composers of the previous generation – Borodin, Balakirev, Tchaikovsky and his mentor Rimsky-Korsakov. His international reputation was launched by his music for the ballet *L'oiseau de feu* (The Firebird), commissioned by the impresario Dyagilev and performed by his Ballets Russes Company in Paris in 1910. Two further ballets quickly followed, *Petrushka* (1911) and *Le sacre du printemps* (The Rite of Spring, 1913); the latter, which caused an uproar at its first performance for a number of reasons (new sounds, inaccurate dancing, confused audience), is today one of the most popular works in the orchestral repertoire. A major part of Stravinsky's oeuvre is theatrical: in addition to ballets, there is his opera-oratorio *Oedipus Rex* (Jean Cocteau wrote the original libretto), the full-length opera *The Rake's Progress* (libretto by Auden and Kallman) and the remarkable *Les Noces* (The Wedding) for vocal soloists, chorus, four pianos and percussion ensemble, which is almost symphonic in its conception and proportions. Then there is his entertaining, small-scale *Histoire du soldat* (The Soldier's Tale) for three actors, female dancer and seven instruments, to be read, played and danced, which he wrote during his stay in Switzerland from 1914 to 1920.

Stravinsky next lived in France and then in the USA until his death. He was buried, according to the wishes of his second wife, Vera (with whom he was in love long before his first wife, Katrina, died), in Venice on the island of San Michele, not far from the grave of Dyagilev. His orchestral and instrumental music is mainly couched in what has been termed 'neo-classical' style; this really means that, like many other composers of his period, he sought to revitalise musical language and style by leap-frogging back over the nineteenth century to scour the eighteenth century for models on which to base the process of composition with a new clarity and conciseness, opposed to the over-emotional thrust of the nineteenth-century masters such as Wagner or Tchaikovsky. But my generalisation hardly gives you an idea of Stravinsky's achievement. Rather than go into detail I recommend that you listen to the *Symphony in Three Movements*, the Octet for wind instruments, or the Sonata (1924) for piano.

From 1953 onwards Stravinsky turned to the pitch organisation device of twelve-note technique, a step that greatly surprised many of his followers; but as usual he handled this element in his own way, thereby extending and widening the scope of this pitch discipline. His lifelong tendency to draw ideas from music written in the last four or five hundred years or from other genres such as folk music or jazz shows on the face of it a magpie-like syndrome. Always, however, the result is extremely original; Stravinsky's own voice is paramount. He anticipates the main characteristic of twentieth-century composition, namely, its freedom to draw on any and every musical source for ideas and indeed for inspiration.

STRETTO – the Italian for 'intimate', 'close', 'tight'; the term refers to a passage in a piece of two or more parts in which the motif or theme piles up its entries on top of one another. Strettos are already found in seventeenth-century instrumental pieces such as the ricercar or fantasia, but they are used to greatest effect in fugues from the eighteenth century onwards. Here the stretto passage normally appears towards the end of the piece, acting as an exciting climax. Each part announces the theme (fugal subject) and before it is completed, the next part enters with the theme, and then the next, and so on; some of the parts may even have another go with the subject, so that a four-part piece, for example, may have a stretto consisting of six entries of the theme. For a simple conception of the stretto effect think of a jolly round, such as *Three Blind Mice*, and the pleasure one receives on hearing each voice come in with the opening phrase.

STRING QUARTET – this is the term for a particular kind of composition, consisting of two or more movements, written for an ensemble of two violins, viola and cello; the term also refers to the ensemble itself. Acoustically, the string quartet offers an infinite variety of rich sounds; as a medium through which musical ideas may be expressed, it has extracted from composers some of their finest creative efforts, from Haydn to Penderecki. The string quartet is the chamber ensemble *par excellence* of Western classical music; because of its nature and function it demands from the listener more concentrated attention than for other genres, including the symphony. Of course, before Haydn, four-part writing for strings was not unusual; these earlier compositions included a continuo part as a rule and, more often than not, the most interesting material was given to the top part, the leading violin. Haydn is regarded as the originator of our present notion of the string quartet; he evolved to this stage only after he had composed some twenty-eight examples with a variety of aims and intentions deriving from the Baroque style and its transition to the Classical period.

True string quartet writing from Haydn onwards demands that each of the four instruments plays an equal, or nearly equal, part in the unfolding of the music. While there are lots of exceptions, the usual composition consists of three or four movements. There is a handsome list of composers after Haydn who wrote important string quartets – Boccherini, Mozart, Beethoven, Schubert, Mendelssohn, Brahms,

Dvořák, Borodin, Tchaikovsky, Franck, Debussy, Ravel. In the twentieth century the two great exponents are Bartók, who opened up a whole new vista of string quartet writing and whose six examples may be confidently compared with the late quartets of Beethoven, and Shostakovich, who, though less revolutionary or exploratory than Bartók, nevertheless produced an impressive sound world in this medium. Other important string quartets have been written by Milhaud, Schoenberg, Webern, Berg, Nielsen, Prokofiev, Janáček, Ives and Carter; even Berio and Boulez have had a go. In England distinguished examples have come from Britten and Tippett in particular, and also from Walton, Rubbra, Seiber, Berkeley, Maconchy, Rainier, Lutyens and Gerhard. So you see, you have a sparkling treasure of string quartet music available and I doubt if you can call yourself a true-blue classical music lover if you are not familiar with at least four or five examples. Just take your pick.

SUITE – the term derives from the French word meaning 'continuation', 'sequel', 'sequence'; thus, musically, a suite consists of a string or chain of pieces. The word entered musical terminology at the close of the sixteenth century and was used as a title for sets of dance pieces; synonyms, used well into the eighteenth century, were 'partita' and 'ordre'. By this time the pieces were not necessarily dance-orientated; in the latter part of the century such titles as 'divertimento', 'serenade' or 'cassation' could be said to be suites. In the nineteenth century the suite took a bit of a nose-dive, but emerged again, quite forcefully, in the twentieth. The suite is suitable for orchestra as well as for a solo instrument. The pieces that make it up may emerge from a variety of ideas: Schoenberg's Suite Op. 25 for piano is essentially dance-orientated; Holst's *The Planets* for orchestra expresses the poetic image of them; Couperin's *ordres* for harpsichord are collections of graphic accounts of life around him; Berg's string quartet, *Lyric Suite*, is simply a musical utterance of six expressions – cheerful, amorous, mysterious, passionate, excited, desolated. Essentially, a suite is a collection of pieces derived from and united by an idea outside the music. This also applies to suites which are drawn from, say, ballet (Tchaikovsky's *Nutcracker* Suite) or opera (Prokofiev's *Love for Three Oranges*).

SUK, JOSEF – Czech composer and contemporary of Janáček; he became Dvořák's favourite pupil at the Prague Conservatoire and later married the latter's daughter Otilie. He was also a distinguished violinist; he was second violin in the Czech Quartet, which, on its international tours over a period of forty years, gave more than 4000 concerts. Oddly enough, despite his string quartet playing, he wrote very little for the medium; his strengths lay in works for orchestra, piano pieces and songs. The loss within the space of fourteen months of both his wife and Dvořák left a lifelong indelible sadness in him, but also led to the creation of his most important work, the symphony *Asrael*. Of his piano music, of particular interest are the ten pieces which comprise *Things lived and dreamt*; his *Serenade* in E flat major, composed when he was not yet twenty, remains one of his best-known works. Suk has proved to be an important contributor to the post-Dvořák development of Czech music.

SULLIVAN, ARTHUR – England's most important nineteenth-century composer. Although throughout his life Sullivan remained ambitious to write worthy works of classical proportions such as operas, symphonies and concertos, his creative talent pulled him in the direction of light music; here he produced outstanding examples of very English songs and comic operas, pitched at the centre of Victorian culture. If you are curious to hear the 'serious' side of his work, then two good examples are the *Overture di ballo* and the Symphony in E. He also wrote a mass of 'drawing-room' vocal solos, duets and trios, of which the best-known is *The Lost Chord* and the most ambitious the song-cycle *The Window*, to words by Tennyson.

Sullivan's fame, however, rests on the fourteen comic operas he created with the writer W. S. Gilbert between 1871, starting with *Thespis*, and 1896, ending with *The Grand Duke*. Most of these were presented by the canny impresario Richard D'Oyly Carte at the Savoy Theatre in the Strand, and are sometimes referred to as 'the Savoy operas'. From *Trial by Jury* (1875) until *The Gondoliers* (1889), each production was a sure-fire success. The material well-being which ensued allowed Sullivan to indulge in racing, gambling and socialising with enviable freedom. In contrast Gilbert's character was stoic and ascetic; the result was that these two personalities, perfectly matched in their artistic partnership, had a relationship in which warmth was lacking but professional duty unshakeable. Apart from *The Mikado*, their stage works, because of their peculiarly English emphasis on satire, wit, turn of verbal phrase or melodic line, have never gained a foothold in Europe; in English-speaking countries, however, to this day, the creations of Gilbert and Sullivan have been exceedingly popular, respected and admired; and there's little doubt that they have influenced the development of the American musical.

Sullivan was knighted at the age of forty-one. As often happens, towards the end of his life his invention declined, but his is a happy and fulfilling record of achievement and recognition, something which too few composers have been blessed with.

SWEELINCK, JAN – Dutch composer of the late sixteenth and early seventeenth centuries. As well as composing a great deal of choral music – motets, psalms, canticles, madrigals and chansons – and pieces for keyboard, he was a virtuoso organist and noted teacher. Pupils came to him from all over northern Europe, often subsidised by their city councils; it may be said that the North German organ school which culminated in Bach was launched by his students. For some as yet unexplained reason he took his mother's maiden surname, for his father, with whom he had an amicable relationship, was called Swybbertszoon; maybe the reason was no more nor less than that 'Sweelinck' is easier to remember than 'Swybbertszoon', even in Dutch. For over forty years Sweelinck was required to provide organ music at the Oude Kerk in Amsterdam twice a day, and it is at these recitals that he gained a reputation as an outstanding improviser. The English composer and harpsichordist John Bull was a good friend; it is largely through him that English keyboard music had a marked influence on the early development of European keyboard writing. Worth listening to are Sweelinck's third volume of the settings of the *Psalms of David*, the five-part motet *Hodie Christus natus est*, and two examples of his keyboard writing, *Est-ce Mars* and a pavan, *Malle Sijman*.

SYLPHIDES, LES – an early twentieth-century one-act romantic ballet, still popular in the current repertoire, first produced in Paris in 1909. The musical material is drawn from the works of Chopin, orchestrated by Glazunov, and the original choreography is by Michel Fokine, who was an important component of Dyagilev's Ballets Russes company.

SYMPHONIE FANTASTIQUE – see *Fantastic Symphony*.

SYMPHONIC POEM – a one-movement orchestral piece in which the wellspring of the material comes from a poem or programmatic idea illustrated in the music. The symphonic poem flourished in the latter part of the nineteenth century and the early twentieth. Its predecessors are programmatically inclined symphonies such as Beethoven's *Pastoral* and Berlioz's *Symphonie fantastique*, and certain overtures which give either a concentrated summation of a play, like Mendelssohn's *A Midsummer Night's Dream*, or a general impression or mood, like the same composer's *Calm Sea and Prosperous Voyage*. It is Liszt, one of the most colourful and multi-talented of nineteenth-century composers, who truly launched the symphonic poem; in fact, the term derives from his own description of such a work, 'symphonische Dichtung'. To some extent it emerged from his predilection for one-movement orchestral pieces, though he composed symphonies as well; he also typifies the nineteenth-century composer's energetic interest in poetry, literature, the fine arts, nationalism, philosophical expression. Wagner's *A Faust Overture* hints that if he had not been so involved with opera he may well have proved an outstanding composer of symphonic poems. Liszt's contributions, such as *Hamlet, Orpheus, Prometheus*, are presaged in his sets for piano – for instance the three entitled *Années de Pèlerinage* (Years of Pilgrimage).

The post-Lisztian German symphonic poem composer *par excellence* was Strauss, who lifted the form to new heights of subtle organisation, orchestration and variety of subject matter – *Till Eulenspiegel, Don Quixote, Also sprach Zarathustra*. He was sufficiently concerned to split the symphonic poem from its symphonic connections by insisting that his examples be called *Tondichtungen* (tone poems). Czech, Russian and French composers took up the writing of the genre. Smetana, expressing his nationalism with his set of six which he called *Má vlast* (My Fatherland), was followed by Dvořák (*In Nature's Realm*) and Janáček (*Taras Bulba*, after Gogol's poem). In Russia they were produced by Tchaikovsky (the fantasy overture *Romeo and Juliet* and the fantasy *Francesca da Rimini*), Skryabin (*Poem of Ecstasy*) and Rakhmaninov (*The Isle of the Dead*). In France, Debussy's *Prélude à l'après-midi d'un faune* and Dukas's *L'Apprenti sorcier* are examples of two different approaches; in Debussy's, the music seeks to be descriptive of a character, in the case of Dukas it is directly narrative. An enjoyable French creation is Koechlin's *Les banda-log*, based on Kipling's *The Jungle Book*. We should bear in mind Schoenberg's two examples, *Pelleas und Melisande* and *Verklärte Nacht*, the latter being a rare example of the non-orchestral symphonic poem, here written for a string sextet. Sibelius composed over twelve symphonic poems covering most of his creative life, from *En Saga* (1892) to *Tapiola* (1926). In England two fine instances are Elgar's excellent portrait of *Falstaff* and Bax's *Tintagel*.

In the progress of the twentieth century the inclination to become more abstract, the dying out of feeling for nineteenth-century Romanticism and the thrust to forge other kinds of association with words has caused the demise of the symphonic poem. From the foregoing, however, it may be seen that the genre is brimful of a variety of exciting music and you have a plethora of riches to choose from. In large measure the aesthetic of the latter half of the nineteenth century may be understood from a study of the symphonic poem.

SYMPHONY – from the mid-eighteenth century until the early part of the twentieth, the symphony is by far the most prominent expression of Western orchestral writing. I am not here concerned with the earlier use of the terms 'symphony' or 'sinfonia', interchangeable with 'overture', or with explaining what these terms meant and their function; suffice to say that it is the early eighteenth-century opera overture, with its three fast-slow-fast movements (best exemplified in the examples by Alessandro Scarlatti), which acts as the immediate precursor of the symphony proper. The symphony may be defined as a technically ambitious work for orchestra, usually consisting of three or four movements; it is the orchestral counterpart of the sonata and the string quartet. The literature of the symphony reveals that through the medium of music, which we may describe as the dramatic organisation of sound, the feelings and emotions of the human condition are constantly rehearsed. A truly high-class symphony is one of the most difficult tasks for a composer to succeed at. Great symphonies have been written by composers from Haydn and Mozart to Mahler and Sibelius. And to this day, despite revolutionary changes in compositional thought which the twentieth century has imaginatively evolved, the symphony is still alive. To cite but a few cases, I have in mind the moulding of this genre by the hands of Shostakovich, Prokofiev, Vaughan Williams, Walton, Britten, Nielsen; even avant-garde composers such as Maxwell Davies and Penderecki have seen fit to write symphonies.

To my mind, the apotheosis of symphonic thought was achieved by Beethoven. He it was who charted the territory of the symphony; other important symphonists, for all their most admirable creations, have simply filled in what he mapped out. The normal lay-out of the symphony is four movements: usually the first is the most ambitious and uses the versatile *sonata form*; the second, often the most emotionally intense, is in a slow tempo and may employ a variation or an abridged version of sonata form; the third movement is, as a rule, a dance-like piece which, in mood, can be melancholy as well as light-hearted; the final movement is frequently in *rondo form* (the opening section reappearing in various guises as the music progresses), and in expression may range from no more than an *envoi* to the very climax of the entire work. There are numerous variants to the foregoing. If you wish to delve deeper, then refer to Volume 18 of the sixth edition of the *New Grove Dictionary of Music and Musicians*, which devotes no less than fifty-one columns to a discussion of the genre; it does not make for difficult reading. Meanwhile I offer you a selection of symphonies from twelve different composers: Haydn (No. 94, *Surprise*), Mozart (No. 41, *Jupiter*), Beethoven (No. 6, *Pastoral*), Schubert (No. 8, *Unfinished*), Brahms (No. 4), Tchaikovsky (No. 4), Mahler (No. 4), Sibelius (No. 2), Ives (No. 3), Shostakovich (No. 5), Walton (No. 1), Lutoslawski (No. 3). This little lot should keep your ears occupied.

SYMPHONY OF PSALMS – this is a most attractive work by Stravinsky, composed in 1930 and revised in 1948. It is written for chorus and orchestra minus violins and violas; perhaps the reason for this was Stravinsky's desire to produce a detached, impersonal, ritualistic form of liturgical expression. The words are taken from the Psalms in the Latin Vulgate version. The work, in three movements, uses the term 'symphony' in its pre-Classical meaning, as a preparation to what follows, perhaps here suggesting the act of worship; or perhaps Stravinsky had in mind the derivation of 'symphony' from the two Greek words 'together' (*syn*) and 'sounding' (*phōnē*).

SYNTHESISER – an instrument that produces sounds electronically. Theoretically it can produce any kind of sound from a dog's bark to a set of strings playing a melodic line; all this is made possible by electronically controlled means. Early machines for synthesising sounds were already being experimented with nearly seventy years ago. Today the synthesiser is an exceedingly sophisticated instrument, and its reproduction of, say, a trombone, is near-perfect, although violin sounds are still very inaccurate. As the programming of synthesisers improved so its versatility widened and it achieved greater fidelity; its ideal is to have complete control over frequency, waveform, intensity and envelope, which together go to make up a musical sound. The synthesiser consists of a number of modular components that can be connected in a large variety of ways. The final signal selected is sent electronically to the loudspeaker and is turned into sound; control is exercised by knobs and/or keyboards.

Synthesisers became commercially viable only in about 1964, when the American Robert Moog succeeded in making voltage control viable. At first its use was confined to the electro-acoustic studio, to be used in conjunction with tape recorders; later, however, it became possible to produce small, flexible, inexpensive machines suitable for use in live performance. Computer technology has led to automated control of many synthesiser functions and to direct digital synthesis of sound; one beneficial consequence has been the opportunity to re-record many performances by important artists and orchestras of yesteryear on to CDs. You can take it from me that, one way or another, electricity in music has come to stay. As with other musical inventions of the past, the synthesiser awaits the advent of a composer who is going to create with it important music that we will like.

SZIGETI, JOSEPH – one of the great violin virtuosos of the first half of the twentieth century, born in Hungary. He promoted works by a handsome number of contemporary composers including Bartók, Stravinsky, Martin, Bloch, Prokofiev, Berg, Milhaud, Ravel and Busoni, thus showing the adaptability of his high musicianship to various musical languages and styles. Szigeti's artistry developed gradually, reaching maturity only in his early thirties, which is unusual for a recognised violin virtuoso. He played, in the first part of his career, sonatas with Busoni and Myra Hess, and in 1940 gave the première of Bartók's *Contrasts*, a trio dedicated to him, with Bartók at the piano and the jazz clarinettist Benny Goodman (who commissioned the work). Szigeti was much admired for his interpretations of the violin music of Beethoven and Brahms and for his performances of Bach's compositions for solo violin.

SZYMANOWSKI, KAROL – an important Polish composer of the first half of the twentieth century. Warsaw, where he began formal musical studies, was, in the early 1900s, conservative and backward-looking, and he sought guidance and stimulation further afield, visiting Leipzig, Berlin, Vienna, Italy and North Africa, where he was aroused by his discovery of aspects of ancient Arabic and Christian cultures. In London he met Stravinsky, with whom he maintained a warm relationship, as evidenced in their correspondence. His individual voice as a composer emerged after World War I and his creative period in this vein was comparatively short, since he died a couple of years before World War II. His patriotic fervour was such that, though he could have settled in the USA, he preferred to remain in Poland. While he was much influenced by Polish folk music, especially that of the Tatra mountain people and of the Kurpie plainsmen, his music, like Bartók's, transmuted these influences to produce the individual Szymanowski sound. A treatise he wrote around 1930, *The educational role of musical culture in society*, provides an insight into his attitude to a complex of matters involving sociological, aesthetic and musical observations.

Deservedly, Szymanowski's music is currently undergoing a revival, and if you are interested to find out whether you agree, then listen to *Litany to the Virgin Mary* Op. 59 for soprano, female chorus and orchestra, or the *Stabat Mater* Op. 53 for soloists, chorus and orchestra; then there is the Concerto No. 2 Op. 61 for violin and orchestra and the Symphony No. 4 Op. 60 (*Symphonie Concertante*) for piano and orchestra; from a substantial collection of pieces for piano one might consider *Masques* Op. 34, the set of *Twenty Mazurkas* Op. 50 (of which Artur Rubinstein has recorded the first four) and *Four Etudes*

Op. 4. In sum, Szymanowski, in the history of Polish composition, succeeded Chopin and paved the way for Lutoslawski, Penderecki and Gorecki. Much worthwhile 'ski/cki' music here.

TABLATURE – to write our music today we use what is called 'staff notation'; this means that we place notes on a five-line horizontal lay-out, known as a stave, moving from left to right; each note describes both its pitch and its duration. Tablature is a notational system which uses letters, numbers or other signs, and in contrast to conventional notation, there is usually one sign for pitch and another for duration. Tablature notation may be found in other parts of the world. In Europe it could be found as late as the eighteenth century. In the twentieth century, there are some scores which do not use traditional notation, and their unusual signs may be classified as modern-day tablature. The earliest tablature on record goes back to the fourteenth century. It was used mainly for keyboard music, with different countries – Spain, Germany, Italy, France – having their own systems; the main tablatures for lute music were French or Italian. Give thanks to all those musicologists and performers who have translated tablature music into our present notation, thus enabling us to play and listen to ancient musical treasures.

TAFELMUSIK – the German for 'table music', a term that describes music performed at grand dinners given by both the nobility and the middle class. *Tafelmusik* or *musique de table* was so-called from as far back as the late fifteenth century until the mid-eighteenth; thereafter the term gave way to 'divertimento', 'serenade' or 'cassation'. Obviously, the nature of the music used at these banqueting occasions was light, melodious, high-spirited and sometimes sentimental. The English called this genre 'taffel consort music'. Each of the three sets of *Tafelmusik* that Telemann composed consists of an overture and suite, a quartet, a concerto, a trio sonata, a solo sonata and a sort of epilogue – nicely calculated to see you through a leisurely consumption of a six-course meal and a noggin or two. The three sets are available on CD if you're interested in an unusual *digestif.*

TAILLEFERRE, GERMAINE – a member of Les Six. Her parents were none too happy over her decision to embark on a musical career; however, she entered the Paris Conservatoire in 1904, did very well, and soon chummed up with fellow students Auric, Honegger and Milhaud. Tailleferre's music contains that concision, sparkle and charm that are typically French, as may be evidenced in her *Concertino* for harp and orchestra, *Jeux de plein air* (Outdoor Games) for two pianos and the Sonata No. 2 for violin and piano. She comes from the tradition of Fauré and Ravel, with whom she studied orchestration.

TAKEMITSU, TORU – twentieth-century Japanese composer of much refinement and originality. Other than some initial conventional instruction he is largely self-taught. Takemitsu is an excellent example of a composer outside the mainstream of Western classical music tradition influencing and extending that tradition by his own fresh, independent, creative imagination. Certainly he is an avant-garde composer, but the works he produces are eminently attractive to the ordinary listener, possessing unity, clarity of line and delicate melodic content; this applies whether his work is a tape of recorded water sounds, a piece for two string quartets, a work including traditional Japanese instruments or merely something for piano solo. Takemitsu believes composition to be the process of giving 'a proper meaning to the "streams of sounds" which penetrate the world which surrounds us'. Recommended, with confidence in your enthusiastic reaction, are the Concerto for viola and orchestra (sub-titled *A String around Autumn*), *All in Twilight* (four pieces for guitar) and the two pieces for chamber orchestra, *Rain Coming* and *Tree Line.*

TALLIS, THOMAS – sixteenth-century English composer, a Kentishman and teacher and colleague of Byrd. For most of his life he was a member of the royal household, serving under the Tudor monarchs Henry VIII, Edward VI, Mary I and Elizabeth I. It seems that during this whole period he was greatly respected both personally and for his music. In 1575 he and Byrd were granted a period of monopoly in the publishing and printing of music, which at the time meant a promising lucrative situation; their first venture under this licence was *Cantiones sacrae*, an anthology of Latin motets which included seventeen items by each of them. Tallis also held posts at Waltham Abbey and at Canterbury Cathedral. His very fine music altered in style according to the exigencies of various liturgical reforms. He possessed a remarkable fund of contrapuntal ingenuity, its apotheosis in sheer magnitude being his notorious forty-part (eight five-part choirs) motet *Spem in alium*. His choral writing ranges from intricate polyphonic texture to simple, homophonic settings. Among his best-known works are two settings of the *Lamentations* of Jeremiah, which are unrivalled for their solemn beauty. In addition to his music for Latin and English Services, motets and anthems, Tallis turned out a goodly number of keyboard and consort pieces, of which apt examples are the *Felix namque* variations (to be found in the Fitzwilliam Virginal Book) and the five-part *Fantasia* for consort; *Absterge Domine* and *O Lord, in thee is all my trust* are excellent illustrations of his motet and anthem writing respectively. Tallis must be reckoned as one of the greatest of all sixteenth-century composers. He died at Greenwich and is buried in the chancel of the parish church of St Alphege.

TANNHÄUSER – a three-act opera by Wagner, the full title of which is *Tannhäuser und der Sängerkrieg auf der Wartburg* (Tannhäuser and the Singing Contest at the Wartburg). Wagner to the end of his life was never really satisfied with the opera, despite two revisions after its first performance in 1845. His plot (he wrote the libretto) is a conflation of several legends based on the thirteenth-century *Minnesinger* (German troubadour) Tannhäuser, who participated in the Fifth Crusade and the Cypriot war and spent time at the courts of Vienna and Bavaria. The plot: Tannhäuser has been seduced by the pagan goddess Venus; tiring of this sort of pleasure, he returns to his fellow *Minnesingers* and takes part in the singing contest, the prize for which is the hand of the noble Elisabeth; but the words of his song betray carnal experience and he is ordered to make the pilgrimage to Rome in order to seek absolution; the blighter fails to obtain it, but on his return he is finally saved by the self-sacrifice of the saintly Elisabeth.

TAPE RECORDER – a very worthwhile item of listening equipment to many lovers of music, and essential in the recording and electro-acoustic studios. Tape recording was developed by the Germans for military purposes and then became a valued facility in the recording process, allowing for editing, multi-track recording, higher-quality reproduction and much more economic storage; it heralded time-saving operations in ethnomusicological fieldwork, as well as the advent of the dubious art of *musique concrète*. The essential components of a tape recorder consist of the *deck*, which handles the tape, and the *electronics*, which house the circuitry for processing the signals. The deck contains two hubs on which are mounted the feed reel and the take-up reel. The tape itself moves past several 'heads' that detect magnetic fields on the tape's oxide; in order, the 'erase' head wipes out previously recorded signals, the 'record' head records signals, and the 'playback' detects the signals. The tape is made to move past the capstan and is held against it by a rubber pressure roller; the capstan motor usually operates at two or more speeds. The heads of tape recorders are divided into a number of parallel tracks or channels; the width of tape covered by each channel is called its 'track width'. Professional tape recorders are made with anything from four to twenty-four tracks; thus, for example, each instrument in an ensemble of twenty-four players can be recorded on its own track, so, if necessary, an individual player can be slotted in or out of the music recorded. The tape recorder has controls to operate play, record, stop, rewind, fast-forward. Tape-playing facilities are incorporated in a large variety of commercial audio equipment and tapes allow for as much as forty-five minutes' worth, approximately, of music to be recorded on each side. A, so far unstoppable, illegal activity of recording copyright music, either from radio or LPs, is taking place; but such recording *is* permitted for educational purposes. Tapes of all kinds of music are gradually being superseded by CDs; there is in the wings the possible emergence of CD-type tapes.

TARANTELLA – a concert piece of the nineteenth and twentieth centuries. Composers were attracted to the furious energy of the original dance and produced virtuoso pieces, almost *perpetuum mobile* in style, mainly for the piano: Chopin's Op. 43, Rakhmaninov's Op. 17 and Liszt's *Années de pèlerinage* (Years of Pilgrimage), I, No. 3, *Pastorale*. Weber uses the driving rhythm of the tarantella in his Piano Sonata Op. 70, as do Richard Strauss in his *Aus Italien*, Op. 16, and Mendelssohn in the final movement of his Symphony No. 4 in A, Op. 90 (The 'Italian'). The tarantella is a folk dance of southern Italy; today it is a kind of mimed courtship dance, performed by one couple surrounded by a circle of others and accompanied by singing, tambourines and castanets; the rhythm is a fast two-beats-to-the-bar in triplets. The popular conception that the tarantella was a cure for a mildly toxic spider's bite has now been discredited.

300

TAVENER, JOHN – note the absence of the 'r' after the first 'e' – twentieth-century English composer who has successfully pursued his very own musical path; some think his music long-winded and boring, others say he's the best thing that's happened to English music in years; in any event he has a large and growing following. At the Royal Academy of Music he studied composition with Berkeley and there composed his first cantata, *Cain and Abel*; his second, *The Whale*, was given its first performance at the inaugural concert of the London Sinfonietta in 1968. While aspects of his music have shown influences of Stravinsky and Messiaen his style is very much that of an unselfconscious, independent mind. Tavener's music often has the time-scale of a Mahlerian symphony if not its intellectual rigour; it undulates in long-wave patterns. This, in large measure, may be due to his natural inclination towards religious mysticism, first Catholicism and then the embrace of Russian Orthodox tenets. Religious rite seems to be in the air; it has captured the musical creativity of such disparate composers as Harvey, Pärt and Gorecki, and has attracted a surprisingly large number of listeners. Tavener's *The Protecting Veil* for cello and orchestra has almost met with the success of a pop hit. In a shorter format are his choral pieces such as *Funeral Ikos*, *The Uncreated Eros*, and *Great Canon of St Andrew of Crete*.

TAVERNER, JOHN – this time having the 'r' after the first 'e' – English composer of distinction who flourished in the first half of the sixteenth century; a predecessor first of Tye and then Tallis. Apart from a four-year spell at Christ Church College, Oxford (then known as Cardinal College, founded by Cardinal Wolsey), he spent the whole of his professional life at Boston, Lincolnshire, well-off and involved with the town's civic affairs. Taverner's output is substantial but not extensive; apart from a few secular partsongs and instrumental pieces he devoted his full attention to a series of Masses, magnificats and motets. His music forms the basis on which Tallis and Byrd were able to extend the English polyphonic tradition of the time as well as producing new approaches to liturgical settings. If you wish to gain an idea of high-quality English vocal polyphonic composition in the first decades of the sixteenth century, as well as giving yourself rare listening pleasure, then the following Taverner pieces are for you: the four-part Mass *Western Wynde*, and the two five-part motets *Dum transisset Sabbatum* and *O splendor gloriae*.

TCHAIKOVSKY, PYOTR IL'YICH – indisputably the greatest Russian composer of the nineteenth century. Though he did not belong to Balakirev's circle he was equally nationalist, and came intermittently under the influence of Balakirev's forceful personality. Tchaikovsky, in the last twenty of his fifty-three years, certainly won an international reputation: performances of his works all over the place, many conducted by him, an honorary DMus. from Cambridge University, a triumphant tour of the USA; but this was nothing compared to the continuous popularity his music has enjoyed ever since. In fact, his success is such that the musical establishment, erroneously, has been inclined to look down on his achievements. His Piano Concerto No. 1 in B flat minor, for example, has been recorded by at least fifty pianists, the Violin Concerto in D Op. 35 by some thirty or more violinists; there are dozens of recordings of the orchestral fantasy overture *Romeo and Juliet*, the Symphonies Nos. 4, 5 and 6, the *Serenade* in C for string orchestra, the ballet suites *Swan Lake*, *The Sleeping Beauty*, *The Nutcracker*, and so on and on. Yet, from a purely technical viewpoint, his compositions contain original treatments of harmony, structure and orchestration; his sense of rhythm, while often dance-like, is developmental. Like nearly all his contemporaries in Russia his writing was instinctive rather than intellectually controlled, as may be found in the music of Brahms or Wagner. The nice thing in classical music throughout the ages is that it allows for great music to flow from either of these creative channels. But we all ultimately like a damn' good tune and this is where Tchaikovsky is unmatchable. Irrefutable proof lies in any one of the works mentioned above.

On the personal side, Tchaikovsky was by nature a gloomy, depressed character; this was tragically compounded by his homosexuality, which, in accord with the morals of Russian society of the day, had to be hidden. It gave him untold misery, and compelled him into a cock-eyed marriage which caused him to have a serious mental breakdown; in the end it led him to take his own life. This sexual condition put in train a bizarre fourteen-year relationship with a rich widow, Madame von Meck, pursued exclusively by correspondence; on the two occasions when they were present at the same function, each passed the other without exchanging a single word. Both had a revulsion against any physical contact with the opposite sex; through their letters they discussed their respective intimate thoughts and feelings. Tchaikovsky's brother Modeste proved to be a lifelong friend and helpmate – he gave the subtitle 'Pathétique' to the Symphony No. 6 in B minor Op. 74, the last work Tchaikovsky wrote, and provided the text (from Pushkin's tale) for his best-known opera, *Eugene Onegin*.

TE DEUM – nowadays usually a choral work, with or without accompaniment in praise of God, often in the nature of a thanksgiving; liturgically it appears at the end of Matins on Sundays and feast days. The Te

Deum has also been used as a processional chant, the conclusion for a liturgical drama and even as a hymn of victory on the battlefield. The text's origin is uncertain, and consists of thirty verses. The earliest source of melody goes back to the twelfth century but it is believed that melodic settings stretch back even further, and evidence for this is still being researched. To the present day, composers have continued to set the Te Deum: Lassus, Palestrina, Purcell, Lully, Handel, Haydn, Berlioz, Bruckner, Dvořák, Verdi and Kodály are a few examples. Walton wrote a particularly fine setting for the coronation of Queen Elizabeth II.

TELEMANN, GEORG PHILIPP – a contemporary of Bach and Handel, he outlived them both, dying in his mid-eighties. Prolific as they were, Telemann out-wrote them – he was a veritable music-producing factory, as well as a busy concert organiser, music educator and theorist; he also wrote three autobiographies. He came from an upper-middle-class family; nearly all his ancestors had received a university education and usually entered the church. He himself enjoyed a thorough all-round education, while his musical talent developed alongside – by his early teens he had taught himself to play the violin, flute, zither and keyboard instruments. From the age of twenty or so he committed himself to a fully professional musical career; a succession of posts followed at such places as Leipzig, Hamburg, Eisenach and Frankfurt. It is at Eisenach that he first met Bach, and in 1714 became C. P. E. Bach's godfather. Wherever he worked Telemann succeeded in developing the local musical activities and standards; he attracted and enjoyed having pupils. He was also a long-time friend of Handel, with whom he corresponded in his elderly years. Telemann managed successfully to have one foot in church composition and the other in opera-writing; his dual activity markedly influenced the prospects and pattern of musical life in Germany. At the time he was a better-known man of music by far than Bach and was certainly regarded as the leading German composer. Posterity, however, has ordained that his works, in sum, do not match those of Bach and Handel. Nevertheless his music merits attention, say, *Uns ist ein Kind geboren* (To us a Child is born), a Christmas cantata for SATB soloists, chorus and orchestra; Quartet in B flat for two violins, viola and continuo; Concerto No. 2 in D for three trumpets and orchestra.

TEMPO – this term simply means the speed at which music is played. How is this reckoned? Well, there could simply be an instruction placed approximately above the first bar (unit) of music, such as fast, slow, moderate – usually in music's *lingua franca* which by tradition is Italian;

thus the three tempos mentioned would be *allegro, adagio, moderato*. But if we take 'allegro', there's quite a range of 'fastness', so the composer could add a rate marking such as 120 beats to the minute; the performer can set this with a stopwatch or the second hand on his wristwatch, or use a ticker mechanism called a metronome, which can be set at different speeds. The expressive needs of a piece of music will demand a speeding up or a slowing down at certain moments; these may be written in by the composer or left to the conductor or player – *ritardando* for slowing down, *accelerando* for speeding up, *a tempo* for going back to the original speed. Obviously, the interpretation of a piece that sticks literally to the given tempo would generally produce a lifeless performance. There are exceptions, of course, such as Ravel's *Bolero*, in which very strict tempo is vital to the work's dramatic realisation.

TERTIS, LIONEL – English pioneer of solo viola playing who earned himself an international reputation. He lived to the age of ninety-nine and was still coaching professionals and occasionally playing at the age of eighty-seven. Though a number of solo viola works written especially for him have not stood the test of time, they served the very useful purpose of underlining the beauty, flexibility and rich character of the instrument. Tertis's performance with Sammons of Mozart's *Sinfonia Concertante* K364 remains one of the best interpretations of that work. He also made transcriptions of Mozart's Clarinet Concerto and Elgar's Cello Concerto which somewhat shocked the purists – all things considered, a silly reaction. Later composers who were inspired by his playing include Vaughan Williams and Bliss; as well, he drew from Walton one of the finest viola concertos ever written.

TESSITURA – the term describes the main pitch area in which a piece of music lies; it does not refer to the actual performing range of a particular voice or instrument. Thus, for instance, one Schubert song may have a high and another a low tessitura. Again, the cor anglais has a low tessitura in *Nuages*, the first of Debussy's three *Nocturnes* for orchestra and wordless choir, whereas it has high tessitura passages in Stravinsky's *Rite of Spring*.

TEXTURE – the vertical aspect of music writing – the combination of parts – may cause a work to sound richly thick or translucently clear; we are here then concerned with the work's texture. Take a few simple examples from Bach's *Two-Part Inventions* for keyboard: No. 6 in E major is heavily contrapuntal, both parts are equally giving it a go, the texture here is thick; No. 4 in D minor, by contrast, is dance-like and mostly has only one part at a time in the lead, so here the texture is thin; No. 14 in B major is sort of in-between, a mixture of thick and thin. There are moments when an eighty-piece orchestra can breathe the lightest of textures and an organ can emit the equivalent density of an African forest. Harmonic texture refers to the number of notes and their lay-out in a chord and the rate of chordal sequence. Melodic texture refers to the number of notes in a melodic phrase – the fewer the notes, the thinner the texture. The slow movement in an Albinoni oboe concerto would have a thin texture, usually, in contrast to the slow movement of a Beethoven piano sonata which might have quite a heavy texture with many more notes. To a certain extent the difference between these two examples is due to the nature of the respective instruments – you twiddle much more on the piano!

THOMSON, VIRGIL (note the absence of the 'p') – twentieth-century American composer as well as a highly respected and characterful music critic. In Paris, where he spent many years, he met Cocteau, Satie (whose music and aesthetic exercised a powerful influence on him) and Les Six, and studied with Nadia Boulanger. He also formed a long-lasting friendship with the off-beat poet Gertrude Stein, as well as an artistic association – he set a number of her poems to song, and her writings were the basis for two operas, *Four Saints in Three Acts* and *The Mother of Us All*, both individual and curious pieces of theatre, too unconventional to retain a foothold in the general opera repertoire. He wrote the music for two excellent film documentaries, Lorentz's *The River* and Flaherty's *Louisiana Story*. Despite the European lure, his music is American because of the sources he drew upon – Baptist hymns, spirituals, popular songs, dance music (tangos, waltzes, foxtrots), marches, children's rhymes, unabashed musical quotation, nineteenth-century Americana.

The *New York Herald Tribune* appointed Thomson music critic in 1940, a position he held for fourteen years; many of his notices were ultimately compiled in three anthologies. He wrote numerous piano pieces which he called 'portraits', some eighty-five in all, many entertaining or moving; there is a recorded selection from the 1940 group, *Twenty-Five Portraits*. Also of interest is the orchestral suite made from the film score for the *Louisiana Story*, called *Acadian Songs and Dances*, and the Sonata for violin and piano.

THOROUGHBASS – also known as 'figured bass', 'basso continuo' or simply 'continuo'. Thoroughbass refers to an independent bass line that proceeds throughout the length of the piece; it played an essential role in ensemble music between about 1600 and 1750. With the bass line a

305

harpsichord, or another chord-producing instrument such as an organ or lute, would fill in the harmony and improvise material; with one or more melodic lines above, an attractive, rich texture would ensue. The bass line had figures added underneath it; these figures indicated chords and their positions, either roots or inversions; the keyboard would present a 'realisation' of the harmony in the process of improvising. In its heyday thoroughbass realisation was very much a creative art. In the present revival of early music, talented and authoritative continuo performers have emerged.

THREE CHOIRS FESTIVAL – a fine manifestation of the British choral singing tradition. An annual music festival is held each year, centred on the cathedrals of Gloucester, Hereford and Worcester in turn, and combining choral forces drawn mainly from the three cities. Particularly since the 1950s the Three Choirs Festival has followed the policy of commissioning works from native composers such as Berkeley, Bennett, Maxwell Davies, Joubert, Maw, Dickinson, Williamson; the tradition of featuring organist-conductors such as Willcocks, Meredith Davies and Guest has also been maintained. The Festival seems to have established itself in the second decade of the eighteenth century; a while later the practice of taking up a collection for the dependants of clergy was initiated, and continues right down to our own time. During its first century of life music by Purcell and Boyce was presented, although Handel's music dominated the programmes; in the nineteenth century music by Mendelssohn, Spohr, Verdi and Wagner was prominently featured. At the turn of the century works by Parry and Elgar (who was born near Worcester) were regularly presented; both these composers took an active part in the Festival's proceedings. In the first half of the twentieth century premières of works by Vaughan Williams, Bax, Holst and Bliss were given, though not all of them were necessarily choral.

THROUGH-COMPOSED – this simply means that the verses of a song are given varying musical settings, instead of the music being repeated as in a strophic song.

TIME SIGNATURE – you will have read about clef, key signature and so on under *Key* and *Signature*. Next we come to the time signature, a numerical fraction which indicates the metre of the piece. Thus, 3/4 means three crotchets or quarter notes to the bar, 6/8 means six quavers or eighth notes to the bar; the lower figure gives us the unit of measurement, the upper gives us the number of units in each bar. I doubt if you need to be reminded that usually a waltz is in 3/4, a tarantella in 6/8, a march in 4/4, and don't be foxed by Tchaikovsky using a time signature of 5/4 (in the second movement of his Symphony No. 4).

TIOMKIN, DIMITRI – Russian-born American composer, one of the finest of film music writers. He spent most of his life in Hollywood, where he turned out the scores for more than 140 films; his language and style were essentially late Romantic, tailored to suit a genre – western (*High Noon*), adventure (*The Guns of Navarone*), fantasy (*Lost Horizon*), thriller (Hitchcock's *I Confess*), science fiction (*The Thing*). Shortly after settling in London in 1968 he became music director and executive producer of the Russian-made biographical film *Tchaikovsky*. Tiomkin studied with Glazunov in St Petersburg and with Busoni in Berlin before emigrating to the USA. If you would like to be reminded of his music there are orchestral pieces which he arranged from his film scores: the suites *Lost Horizon* and *The Thing*, and excerpts from *The Fall of the Roman Empire*, *Friendly Persuasion* and *The Big Sky*, amongst others.

TIPPETT, MICHAEL – twentieth-century English composer and contemporary of Britten. Currently he is the most famous of all living British composers and, at the age of eighty-nine, still composing; unbelievable. He was a late starter, gaining modest recognition at thirty and given strong approval by the musical establishment only at forty; from then on his star has continued to rise uninterruptedly. Three pieces chosen to show the range of his technical skill, musical appeal and highly individual sound world are *Concerto for Double String Orchestra*, *Concerto for Orchestra* and the *Concerto for Violin, Viola, Cello and Orchestra*; but for the Tippett fan, of equal attraction are his four symphonies, four string quartets and four piano sonatas, each of which merits many listenings. There is an opinion that his operas, such as *The Midsummer Marriage*, *King Priam* and *The Ice Break* (the librettos for which he wrote himself), though full of splendid sounds, are not that successful as theatre; this may be because their philosophical thrust outweighs the dramatic design. Tippett has always been dead serious over social and political issues; in his lifetime he has worked with and felt for the underprivileged. His pacifist outlook earned him a month's jail at Wormwood Scrubs during the war; at the time he was music director of Morley College and witnessed its destruction in an air raid. His concern over man's inhumanity to man has led him to the belief that each of us has to reconcile the 'light' and the 'shadow' in ourselves. To some extent it is this thinking that lies behind one of his best-known works, the oratorio *A Child of Our Time* for SATB soloists, chorus and orchestra. The essence of Tippett's style is rhythmic polyphony coupled with variable melodic phrasing; while his idiom is very recognisable and individual, influences on his musical language include Stravinsky, Hindemith, English madrigalian writing, folksong and jazz. If there is one aspect lacking in his creative output it is insufficient attention to musical wit and humour. But this may be no more than a true reflection by the artist of the underlying miseries and conflicts of our time.

TOCCATA – a piece usually written for the keyboard and calculated to show off the performer's dexterous fingerwork; generally the listener is much entertained by this type of piece. There is no set form for the toccata – it may be 'through-composed', employ fugue technique or be cast in sonata form. The name derives from *toccare*, Italian for 'to touch'. Many pieces contain toccata-like texture or passages but are otherwise named, such as Bach's *Chromatic Fantasia and Fugue* in D minor, BWV903. In the sixteenth century toccatas were freely composed keyboard pieces which ignored dance, *cantus firmus* or vocal models. The champions of the seventeenth century were the Italian Frescobaldi and the German Froberger, who in turn influenced Alessandro Scarlatti and Bach. The toccata's popularity seems to have died out in Mozart's time and in the nineteenth century; Clementi's Op. 11 and Schumann's Op. 7 in C are worthy exceptions. French organists of the late nineteenth century such as Widor and Vierne entitled the final movements of their organ symphonies 'toccatas'. Moving into the twentieth century, the final movements of Debussy's *Pour le piano* and Ravel's *Le tombeau de Couperin* are toccatas; the Russians have produced toccata pieces, Prokofiev's Op. 11, Khachaturian's of 1932, and there are toccata-like movements in the sonatas and sonatinas of Kabalevsky.

TOCH, ERNST – twentieth-century Austrian composer, pianist and teacher who settled in America in 1936. Toch wrote a number of Hollywood film scores, but his chief creative output was chamber music – he wrote thirteen string quartets. The style of his music is essentially neo-classical. His symphonic poem *Pinocchio* has been favourably compared with Strauss's *Till Eulenspiegel*. His viewpoint on composition was that every composer involuntarily forms a link in an evolutionary chain; the artistic process, like the biological one, is timeless rather than time-bound. Of listening interest is his Symphony No. 5 (with the subtitle *Jephta – Rhapsodic Poem*), the cello piece *Impromptu No. 2* and the four-part unaccompanied choral piece *Geographical Fugue*. The last-named is as well-known to amateur and school choirs as is Ravel's *Bolero* to concert-goers; it was meant as an educational novelty, not sung but chanted in cleverly laid-out lines of rhythm, and can be taught by rote. The words are enjoyable to mouth; for instance, the first line goes:

'Trinidad! and the Big Mis-sis-sip-pi and the town Hon-o-lu-lu and the lake Ti-ti-ca-ca', and the music, for it is music, ends in an exhilarating climax.

TOMÁŠEK, VÁCLAV – Czech composer whose compositions and teaching linked the Classical period with the nineteenth-century nationalist movement. As a teacher, his reputation was such that the nobility were lining up to have their children taught by him. His memoirs provide a rich description of the musical life of the times and show him to have met Haydn, Beethoven, Clementi, Clara Schumann and Paganini; the critic Hanslick was a student of his and he entered into correspondence with Goethe. Tomášek showed contempt for most of the piano virtuosos slushing around salons and concert halls at the time '... with a couple of memorised Chopin studies and a few of the so-called fantasias of Thalberg ... the piano has now become a coffin wherein true musicianship shall sleep until a musical spring wakens it from slumber ...'; not entirely irrelevant to our own day and age. Tomášek pioneered the short character piece in collections which he called eclogues, rhapsodies or dithyrambs; these influenced Schubert, Schumann and their successors. He seems to have written no orchestral music; however, he produced a large number of songs, either settings of German poetry by such as Goethe, Schiller and Heine, or Czech texts influenced by folksong. Would you like to hear some Tomášek on record? You cannot. To date there seems to be no commercial recording of even a single piece of his. Sorry.

TOMKINS, THOMAS – the last in the line of the great Tudor church composers. Very little is known of his life in general, and of his first twenty years in particular. Tomkins was based at Worcester Cathedral, as well as being a member of the Chapel Royal; it is believed he was a pupil of Byrd and by 1601 was well enough considered to have a madrigal included in Morley's publication *The Triumphes of Oriana*. His own publication of 1622, *Songs of 3, 4, 5 & 6 Parts*, reveals his excellence as a writer of secular polyphony, but the high point of his musical creativity is to be found in his liturgical and anthem compositions; he wrote comparatively little for keyboard or consorts. Proof of the high regard for his church music lies in its wide circulation by the 1630s. Tomkins has more anthems and services to his credit than any other important sixteenth- or seventeenth-century composer. Whether his anthems are full (for chorus only) or verse (with soloists), they are imaginative in their treatment of the texts and the 'orchestrating' of the vocal parts, and range from simple to intricate contrapuntal writing. A felicitous selection for your ears would be the verse anthem *My beloved spake*, the full anthem *O God, the proud are risen against me* for eight parts and organ and the five-part lament *When David heard*.

TONALITY – overall this is a complicated subject, if we have to include classical music before 1600, most works written in the twentieth century and non-Western musics. Here, I think we'll restrict the definition of tonality to classical music produced between the seventeenth and the early twentieth century. Tonality deals with the relationships between groups of notes having a central note or 'tonic'; there is a hierarchical connection between each note in a group and its tonic, which is enriched by the chords that can be built up on each note; further enrichment is possible by the chromatic alteration of each of the notes of a chord.

Different considerations govern tonality before 1600 and in non-Western musics. As for the twentieth century, at its beginning the traditional functioning of tonality had become so sophisticated in its development over three hundred years that composers, in a variety of ways, relegated this musical element in importance or found new ways of dealing with pitch relationships.

TONIC SOL-FA – in about 1840, Sarah Glover, a Norwich schoolmistress, devised a way of teaching singing to her children's choir with great success by using the initials of the major scale doh–re–mi–fa–soh–la–te–doh (d, r, m, f, s, l, t, d). The Reverend John Curwen extended and developed Glover's innovation in his zeal to bring the joy of singing to the many who did not have the opportunity to learn musical notation. A similar system had already been devised in France. The progress of the Tonic Sol-fa movement during the nineteenth century can be described as nothing less than sensational and, in schools especially, it brought much musical pleasure to children who would otherwise not have had the opportunity to make music collectively. Throughout the world, even now, there are communities which create and perform music using this non-notational system, which has become thoroughly sophisticated. Essentially the system is most practical when used for non-chromatic music, but nowadays it certainly allows for the frequent use of sharps and flats; it is particularly helpful in ear-training and sight-singing, with its movable tonic device. Tonic Sol-fa's handling of rhythm is also inventive, but it depends on the bar-line and the colon punctuation mark. Subsidiary accents within bars are indicated by shortened bar-lines; the eye is assisted by equal lateral spacing, no matter the number of notes per beat; rests are not used, silence being indicated by an empty space, and slurs are dealt with by lateral lines under the relevant notes. The teaching of the system requires thorough training, for it is essential for the Tonic Sol-fa singer to feel his notes and intervals through his own voice, and initially this is not easy; but to hear an experienced singer using this system is impressive. Despite other current approaches to musical education, there is still a valid place for Curwen's creation.

TORTELIER, PAUL – one of the great cellists in the generation or so after Pablo Casals. Born in Paris, at the Conservatoire there he played Elgar's Cello Concerto at the age of sixteen and by the age of thirty had established an international reputation. His playing is a rich mixture of tonal power and lyrical tenderness, with a rare accuracy of intonation. His three children are themselves professional performers on piano, violin and cello, and frequently appeared with their father in chamber music recitals. Tortelier's master classes were renowned; his series for BBC television (the first given in 1964) was as compelling for viewers as for the participants. Jacqueline Du Pré was a pupil of his. Tortelier believed that performers should undertake a bit of composing, to enhance their interpretative insight.

TOSCA – Puccini's three-act opera, first produced in Rome at the Teatro Constanzi in 1900. It remains one of his evergreens, full of moving and heady arias and apt dramatic twists. The plot in essence: Tosca, a leading opera singer, has a lover, a painter, who helps to hide an escaped political prisoner; the villainous police chief, Scarpia, discovers evidence of this, and has the painter chucked into jail and condemned to death; Tosca offers herself to Scarpia if he will free her lover; he eagerly agrees, but says the execution by firing squad must be seen to take place; he will ensure that the guns fire blanks. Now he steps forward to embrace the singer; as he does so she seizes a knife and stabs him to death; however, Scarpia, the crafty devil, had bluffed her and the painter is shot; in despair, Tosca throws herself over a parapet to her death.

TOSCANINI, ARTURO – one of this century's most colourful and gifted conductors. As a young cellist touring with an Italian opera company in Brazil he suddenly had to deputise for the conductor at a performance of *Aïda*. With informed musicianship, and without a score, he conducted the performance at the age of nineteen; here there is early evidence of his remarkable memory, acute ear and powers of concentration. He conducted the first performances of Leoncavallo's *Pagliacci* and Puccini's *La Bohème*. At the age of thirty-one he became music director at La Scala and in 1908 took over the artistic directorship of the Metropolitan Opera, New York. In the next three decades

Toscanini travelled widely, conducting at all the music centres of Europe and America; the self-discipline and drive he imposed on himself affected his orchestras, over whom he seemed to exercise a magnetic power. In about 1937 he took command of the newly-formed National Broadcasting Corporation's orchestra; it is with them that for the next seventeen years Toscanini made most of his masterly recordings. Though he was not interested in the trappings of fame, he became a great cult figure. He was a superb interpreter of the music of Puccini, Brahms, Berlioz, Debussy, Tchaikovsky and Strauss and particularly of his three favourites – Beethoven, Wagner and Verdi. His achievements mark a high point in the development of the conductor's art. Politically he was unshakeably principled, refusing to conduct in Hitler's Germany or Mussolini's Italy. One of his daughters married the distinguished piano virtuoso Vladimir Horowitz.

TOVEY, DONALD – English music scholar who flourished in the first half of the twentieth century; until 1914 his career was that of pianist and composer. Tovey was then appointed to the Reid Chair of Music at Edinburgh University. By this time he had written a series of programme notes, and it is really in this area that he saw the purpose of his musical scholarship; he considered himself a populariser of classical music rather than a musicologist. Tovey established the Reid concerts, which continue to the present. His programme notes for these concerts ultimately formed the basis for his well-known *Essays in Musical*

Analysis; they reveal a penetrating insight into their subjects, especially the commentaries on the works of German composers, and they led to an elevation of English writing on music.

TRAVIATA, LA (The Fallen Woman) – a three-act opera by Verdi; the first performance, in Venice at the Teatro La Fenice in 1853, was a failure, for several reasons – the audience was not used to seeing an opera in a contemporary setting, the singer who took the role of the hero was hoarse on the evening and the heroine, who was supposed to be dying of consumption, was rather on the stout side. Verdi had complete confidence in his score, though, as was proved by its reception a year later and since: another long-lived Verdi success. The plot's spine: a courtesan, Violetta, falls in love with a handsome, clean-living young man, Alfredo, and renounces her life of pleasure, leaving her 'protector', a wealthy baron; Alfredo's father persuades Violetta to give up his son for his and his family's sake; broken-hearted, she agrees, and returns to her former life; Alfredo, stricken by her about-face, leaves the country to try to forget her; she finds she is dying of consumption and the father, learning of this, writes to his son, revealing to him Violetta's noble sacrifice; Alfredo returns and the lovers are reconciled, but it is too late and she dies in his arms.

TREBLE – this term has two meanings: first, it refers to a high vocal or instrumental part in a piece of music, and in this sense it can be traced back to the fourteenth and fifteenth centuries, when it was first used to refer to the top part in three- and four-part polyphonic compositions. It is peculiar to the English language. The G (or violin) clef has long been called the 'treble' clef in English. The other meaning of the term refers to the unbroken voice of a boy or girl, particularly the former because of the long tradition of using boy trebles in English church choirs. While a solo treble voice is attractive enough, it is at its most appealing in the sound of a group of treble voices singing in unison or in two parts; an excellent example is Britten's *A Ceremony of Carols*, Op. 28, for treble voices and harp.

TRISTAN UND ISOLDE – three-act opera by Wagner, his most lyrical, first performed in Munich in 1865. Wagner derived his plot from Arthurian legend, tightening and adapting it to suit his own ends – there is evidence that it reflects his passion for Mathilde Wesendonk, the wife of a friend. The outline: Tristan, nephew of the King of Cornwall, is sent to collect the king's bride Isolde from Ireland; she, furious, plans to kill him and herself but her maid, silly girl, substitutes a love potion for the poison; the two fall passionately in love, are betrayed and caught *in flagrante* and Tristan is wounded; he flees to his castle, where he awaits her, but dies as she arrives; she too expires, after singing the famous *Liebestod* (love-death).

TROILUS AND CRESSIDA – Walton's three-act opera with libretto by Christopher Hassall, first performed in London at Covent Garden in 1954; the theme is based on Chaucer's, not Shakespeare's, interpretation of the classical story. The score is predominantly lyrical, even harking back to nineteenth-century Italian opera in its outbursts of passion and concern with the lonely individual in a hostile world. Some consider the opera musically and psychologically backward-looking, but there is no denying its theatrical effectiveness.

TROMBONE – a brass instrument classified as a member of the trumpet family. The range of the tenor trombone, the most popular, covers mainly that of the tenor and baritone voices. The bass trombone makes a useful addition to the orchestra when low trombone sounds at a telling dynamic level are required. Its prominent visual feature is its slide action, which is telescopic and allows the player to vary the length of the tube over seven positions; in each position the player can overblow, and with the positions placed a semitone apart from B flat down to E a full chromatic range is available. Accurate intonation, however, is not easy since, like a singer, the player has physically to feel for the right note, and this requires a good ear and much practice. Glissando effects are another characteristic; the comic or light-hearted utterance can be, and usually is, overdone, but a trombone glissando may also sound very dramatic indeed. The mouthpiece is cup-shaped, the tube bore is cylindrical and the bell is flared, emerging from the gradually expanding tube; the instrument is constructed of a nickel alloy. The trombone has an exceedingly wide dynamic range – at times it can purr and then, in a moment, it can blast away. Up to the eighteenth century it was known as the sackbut. Composers love the instrument; yet the repertoire for solo trombone, including concerto-writing, is surprisingly thin. Two items are of interest: Rimsky-Korsakov's Concerto for trombone and military band and Hindemith's Sonata for trombone and piano. Initiatives in playing technique have been largely developed by jazz trombone virtuosos: cantabile lines, glissandos, irregular attacks, mutes, microtones, sounding two or more notes simultaneously (multiphonics). Some of these devices may be heard in Berio's *Sequenza V* for trombone solo.

TROUBADOURS, TROUVÈRES – French lyric poets and poet-musicians who flourished in the twelfth and thirteenth centuries; their German counterparts were called *Minnesingers*. In a way they were the equivalent of Gershwin, Berlin, Kern, Porter and Mercer in our day. Those active in the south of France were called troubadours, those in the north, trouvères, French and Provençal being two distinct languages. The poet-musician was different from his contemporary the *jongleur*, an itinerant minstrel catering for the lower orders of society and with little social status. Troubadours and trouvères were well-educated, sophisticated verse-technicians, well placed in courtly society: indeed, one famous one was Guillaume IX, Duke of Aquitaine and grandfather of Eleanor, in due course Queen of England. For the expert there are important and subtle differences between the southern and the northern poet-musicians, but for us the essence of their art is the creation in word and music of a dizzy world of *fin'amors*, 'refined' or courtly love. Love here is the source of goodness, a great superstructure of imagination and spirituality built on sexual attraction; but there was a wide variety of approaches to this ideal – love and courtesy, the idolising of the lady, resistance to sensual desires, the lady's power, the joy of love and so on. Literary technique was especially refined, using a rich range of forms and masterly play on words. The poetry, however, was not an end in itself; it only came to life in song, for, as one troubadour recorded, 'verse without music is a mill without water'. Research into this world of poet-musicians is far from complete; nevertheless, it is clear that here is one of the richest cultures in the history of European music.

TROVATORE, IL (The Troubadour) – this four-acter was Verdi's most popular opera during his lifetime, despite the fact that it has the sort of confusing plot which gives opera a bad name – for one thing, you're supposed to know what was going on before the opera has hardly begun. The almost unbroken melodiousness of the score, however, more than placates an audience; it is full of spontaneous and stirring music, and with the use of dance rhythms such as the mazurka and waltz Verdi creates passionate and dramatic effects. One must also remember that during the period of writing *Il Trovatore* Verdi churned out fourteen operas in nine years. In sum, the plot deals with the rivalry of two brothers, unaware of their relationship, for a lady's hand, and also with a gypsy who suffers a conflict between the duty to avenge her mother and love for a son not her own. As you might have suspected, there is more than one death; in this instance the heroine takes poison, while the hero is put to death by his brother.

TROYENS, LES (The Trojans) – an opera by Berlioz consisting of a prologue and five acts, divided into two parts. Part II was first performed in

Paris in 1863, but the composer never saw the first part, which had its première in Karlsruhe in 1890; both parts together were first presented in 1921 in Paris. It is the fourth of the five operas Berlioz wrote, remarkable for its dramatic and lyrical power highlighted by his orchestration. It is a costly opera to put on, which may explain why it has not received more performances. Berlioz himself wrote the libretto; part I is headed 'The Capture of Troy', part II, 'The Trojans in Carthage'. The complicated plot may be reduced to its essence, which is that Aeneas escapes from the Greek sacking of Troy with his family to Carthage; there he is welcomed by Queen Dido, who falls in love with him; after a short but blissful period Aeneas leaves Dido to go and found a new empire in Italy, as the gods have decreed; Dido, heart-broken, orders a pyre to be built on the seashore; into the flames she feeds all his love tokens, then ascends the pyre and – you've guessed it – kills herself, with a sword belonging to Aeneas.

TRUMPET – perhaps the most ancient of all instruments; Numbers x:2 in the Bible contains the divine command to Moses, 'Make thee two trumpets of silver; of a whole piece shalt thou make them: that thou mayest use them for the calling of the assembly, and for the journeying of the camps'. Here we already have evidence of fanfare music. A relief showing a trumpeter on the side of an Egyptian temple has been dated to about 1480 BC. In Europe the ancestor of the modern trumpet is first referred to at the beginning of the eleventh century. Its players had a lowly status until kings and princes considered it *à la mode* to have a clutch of ceremonial trumpeters at court. In the latter part of the sixteenth century, the trumpet entered classical music as a brass or consort ensemble instrument; in the Baroque period it played a regular part in the orchestra and earned itself solo status in concerto-writing. From Mozart to the early twentieth century its solo or chamber role declined; as an orchestral instrument, however, it grew to be of vital importance. Nowadays it is back as a solo and chamber instrument, as well as retaining its position in the orchestra: Hindemith (Sonata for trumpet and piano), Françaix (*Le Gay Paris* for trumpet and nine instruments), Shostakovich (Concerto for piano, trumpet and strings), Maxwell Davies (Concerto for trumpet and orchestra) provide but a few examples. The trumpet has always been associated with rite and ritual, so it is no surprise that it plays a major part in fanfares, such as, for instance, Copland's *Fanfare for the Common Man* for brass and percussion.

Two thirds of the length of the trumpet's metal tubing is cylindrical and one third conical, flaring out to the bell. Only in around 1400 did instrument-makers learn to bend its tubing, thus making it more compact while extending its length. As in the trombone, the mouthpiece is cup-shaped, but shallower. When valve mechanisms were introduced to operate its three pistons in the nineteenth century, the instrument's versatility and agility rapidly advanced. Very effective is the trumpet player's ability to reiterate notes at high speed. Again, it is jazz players who have greatly increased its technical possibilities – trilling, extremely high notes, vibrato effects, glissandos, the use of different kinds of mutes; the virtuoso standing of the great jazz trumpeters should not be underestimated – Armstrong, Beiderbecke, Gillespie, Miles Davis, Marsalis. Haydn's *Trumpet Concerto* in E flat is the work that all classical trumpet players have a go at.

TUBA – among brass instruments the tuba is the equivalent of the double bass in the strings. Because of its size and shape you can't help noticing it in an orchestra. It can certainly blast out low notes but is also capable of sweet, even doleful, sounds. It is surprisingly agile, and possesses a wider range of effective utterance than one might expect; it takes a lot of blowing. The first instrument carrying the name of 'tuba' was introduced in Germany in the mid-1830s, so it is a comparative latecomer to the brass section. The tubing has a wide bore and is coiled in an elliptical shape, with the wide bell pointing upright. Its deep cup-shaped mouthpiece gives the instrument a rich, smooth tone. Its bore is conical and it possesses three to six valves, depending on its make. Sizes vary, but the all-purpose one used in orchestras is the bass tuba, whose lowest note is the F two octaves and a fifth below middle C. Berlioz was the first major composer to include tubas in his works. Two very effective pieces are Vaughan Williams's Concerto for tuba and orchestra and

Edward Gregson's for tuba and brass band; then there is America's counterpart of Prokofiev's *Peter and the Wolf*, the entertaining *Tubby the Tuba* by Kleinsinger and Tripp.

TURANDOT – Puccini's last, unfinished opera; he left three sets of sketches for the final two scenes, and from these Franco Alfano, a friend of his and very much a composer in his own right, completed Puccini's last major creative effort. During the gestation of the opera Puccini struggled with it as with no other work; it brought him to curse that all he could compose were operas, and demand why God had not given him the ability to write symphonic works as well. Toscanini conducted its première at La Scala two years after the composer's death, ending the performance where Puccini himself had stopped writing; only on the second night was the completed opera performed. It is of interest to note that, at Puccini's funeral, the young Mussolini gave the oration. The plot deals with a prince in the Peking of legendary times who wins the hand of the ice-cold Princess Turandot by answering her three riddles; had he not solved them he would have been put to death like previous suitors; in turn the prince challenges her to find out his name before the next day; she tortures his father's slave girl, who kills herself rather than reveal the prince's name; in spite of this unpromising behaviour he still wants to marry her and all ends conventionally well.

TURN OF THE SCREW, THE – Britten's opera, consisting of a prologue and two acts, first performed at Venice in 1954; the libretto, by Myfanwy Piper, is derived from a novella by Henry James. The work belongs to Britten's chamber opera set, its forces made up of only six singers and thirteen instruments. The metaphorical 'screw' idea is expressed musically by a circular pattern of key changes. On the surface the opera is a ghost story involving a boy and his sister; underneath, however, there are implications of conflict between evil and innocence, sexual insinuations and psychological upheaval. Musically and dramatically *The Turn of the Screw* is a highly subtle piece of theatre. The plot, briefly: a governess is sent to look after two children in an isolated manor; she comes to realise that they are infected by two evil spirits and has the housekeeper take the girl back to the care of the children's guardian; before she can depart herself with the boy, he confesses his mental conflict between his involvement with the two ghosts and the pull of the everyday world; the strain proves too much for him, and he collapses and dies.

TWELVE-NOTE COMPOSITION – directly or indirectly, most twentieth-century composers have been affected by certain fundamental aspects of composition innovated by Debussy and Schoenberg. Simply stated, both caused an upheaval in the traditional treatment of pitch material; up to their arrival, for more than two hundred years, pitch organisation centred around key relationships, known nowadays as 'functional harmony'. Debussy's sea-change may be described as instinctive and poetic ('sea-change' is very apt for Debussy and his frequent use of water imagery), whereas Schoenberg's approach was more ordered and consciously evolved (but let it be underlined that he was a complete master in the use of functional harmony). Twelve-note (also called twelve-tone) composition is Schoenberg's brainchild; on the one hand it upsets the use of an hierarchical system of pitch based around the main or 'boss' note; on the other, it harnesses the twelve notes of the chromatic scale into an order (described as a series) in which each note has equal pitch weight. Where the listener finds difficulty in appreciating music created in this manner is that melodic material has a new strangeness which is difficult to grasp, so much so that it has caused other attractive attributes of such composition to lie hidden. Schoenberg's shortcoming, if so it may be described, is his desire to squeeze his twelve-note writing mainly into traditional moulds such as sonata form, which demands its own dramatic time-scale based on key relationships; more successful in this respect were his two main disciples, Webern and Berg. In any event, it is worth coming to listening grips with, say, Schoenberg's String Quartet No. 3, *Variations for Orchestra*, or *Piano Piece* Op. 33a. By now, composers have long progressed to other things with regard to composition technique, but whatever their concern it has been largely enabled as a result of Schoenberg's seminal twelve-note concept.

TYE, CHRISTOPHER – sixteenth-century English composer, a contemporary of Tallis; he spent most of his life in and around Cambridge and served at Ely Cathedral. He took holy orders about ten years before his death. It is likely that Tye was both teacher and friend of Henry VIII's son, Edward. In character he seems to have been somewhat wayward, but his music is among the best that was produced in his time. Regrettably, much of it has been lost or is incomplete. His surviving Latin and English church music is not innovative, but it is, nevertheless, full of variety in structure and texture. If he wrote keyboard music there is today no trace of it, but you'll enjoy a selection of his numerous consort works, say, the *In Nomine* in four parts or the five-part *O Lux*, as well as the four-part Mass *Western Wind* and the five-part motet *Miserere mei, Deus*.

UKELELE – a fun, stringed instrument, looking a little like a guitar that's shrunk in the wash. Its four strings are plucked and tuned g, c, e, a, in

the tenor voice range. The ukelele is associated with Hawaii and garlands and swinging hips in grass skirts, and its name is derived from a Hawaiian word meaning 'leaping flea'; but in fact the instrument originated from immigrants who came to settle from the island of Madeira in the late nineteenth century. By the second decade of the twentieth century the ukelele was being exploited commercially by firms in the USA from Los Angeles to Chicago, as a useful little domestic musical item. It became very popular as an ideal accompaniment for the raucous rendering of lively popular songs – with the best will in the world the ukelele cannot be recommended as a serenading instrument. It reached a peak in popularity in the 1940s and early 50s and it's still around today – easily portable, easy to tune and not costly. Something to buy as a present for yourself for Christmas?

ULISSE – Dallapiccola's two-act opera, with prologue and epilogue, first performed in Berlin in 1968. This was his largest and most ambitious work, and he expected it to be performed in a stylised, semi-oratorio manner, for it is a restrained, philosophical meditation on modern man's search for a meaning to existence. The action follows Homer's account of Ulysses's return to Ithaca after the Trojan war.

UNA CORDA – you may be aware that a piano has two pedals; the right one is called the 'loud' pedal and the left the 'soft' or *una corda* pedal. In a modern grand piano the latter pedal shifts the action sideways, so that the hammers strike only two of the three strings from the note C below middle C and upwards, and only one of the two strings of the note below that C going downwards. There is no change in the striking of the single strings of the extreme bass notes. The effect is not only to reduce loudness but to produce a marked change in timbre. By the time of Beethoven the *una corda* pedal was already in active use and he, for one, accordingly marks specific passages in his music for piano.

UNFINISHED SYMPHONY – quite aptly this title is given to Schubert's Symphony No. 8 in B minor because, after he completed the first two movements in 1822, for some reason which the musicologists cannot yet explain, he never finished the succeeding two, although he did sketch a major part of the third, scherzo, movement. The symphony was first performed only in 1865, thirty-seven years after his death.

UPBEAT – the beat or impulse that comes immediately before the downbeat, which begins the following bar, the first and strongest pulse in a unit of rhythm. Another term for upbeat is *anacrusis*, which can refer to an entire musical phrase, even several bars of music, leading to the downbeat material. To achieve a physical understanding of upbeat take a short or long, deep breath and then breathe out quickly and heavily, or even slowly and gently; the intake of breath is the upbeat and the exhaling is the downbeat.

UTRECHT – a Dutch city that was already functioning in the eleventh century; by the fifteenth and sixteenth centuries vocal polyphonic and organ music was well established in its cathedral and surrounding churches. In the seventeenth century Utrecht boasted a handsome corpus of instrumental musicians, including players of the cornett, shawm, crumhorn, trumpet and strings, and there were carillon recitals. In the nineteenth century concerts were given there by Robert and Clara Schumann, Vieuxtemps, Joachim, Brahms and Wieniawski. Organ-building and bell-casting were actively undertaken well into the twentieth century. Today Utrecht has an electronic music studio that has gained an international reputation.

VALEN, FARTEIN – Norwegian composer who flourished in the first half of the present century. In his lifetime his music received very little of the recognition it deserved – even from his own countrymen; asked if he did not regret this neglect, he replied, 'the important thing is that they [his pieces] have been written'. Valen's music is terse and lucid. His atonality is separate from Schoenbergian orthodoxy and must not frighten you away; he is the most important Norwegian composer since Grieg. Here's a selection of his music: three attractive orchestral pieces – *La isla de las calmas* (composed after a sojourn in Majorca), *Ode to Solitude*, *Pastorale*; the song-set *Four Chinese Poems*, Op. 8; *Four Piano Pieces*, Op. 22.

VARÈSE, EDGARD – French composer who settled in the USA. An undoubted twentieth-century musical revolutionary, during the 1920s and 30s he produced a series of innovatory works which exercised a major influence on later composers; the innovations are found in his musical structure, rhythm, use of percussion and atonality. Early studies in Paris were guided by Roussel and d'Indy, and during a visit to Berlin he met and was much influenced by Busoni. He formed close friendships with Satie and the poet Apollinaire and introduced the music of

325

Schoenberg to Debussy. Varèse, finding it difficult to earn his *louis d'or* in France, left for America in 1915; there he promoted contemporary chamber music, including works by Schoenberg, Stravinsky, Berg, Webern and Cowell, and arranged performances of his own works, which, in the 1920s, created quite a hullabaloo. No harm in dropping into the world of Varèse with *Offrandes* (Offerings) for soprano and small orchestra, *Amériques* for orchestra and *Integrales* (Integrals) for eleven wind and four percussion instruments. His well-merited achievement, based on an output of little more than a dozen works, was not recognised until the final decade of his life.

VARIATIONS – an attractive and perennial technique in Western composition, going back to at least the sixteenth century. You will appreciate that in our classical music it is normally the case that a piece cannot jump from one new idea to the next; our ears would not know what in heaven's name to follow. The very act of developing a motif or theme is variation. Technically, variation writing means that a theme is clearly presented, after which it undergoes a succession of decorations, alterations and disguises, with the ear expected never to lose track of the original theme in the foreground, middle-ground or background of the music. Thus many pieces have the title or subtitle of 'Theme and Variations'. Use of variation technique ranges from the obvious to the most sophisticated, and the composer's approach alters from one historical period to another. In the sixteenth century, a *cantus firmus* (a clear melody in even notes) was often used as a midrib around which a series of decorations were written; this technique is best heard in the numerous keyboard variations churned out by the English virginalists such as Byrd, Gibbons and Farnaby (e.g. Byrd's variations on *The Carman's Whistle*). By the mid-eighteenth century other techniques had become common: filigree work over a repeated phrase in the bass; a sequence of changes following a stated melody; treatment of a theme canonically; manipulation of a chorale melody. A fine example which sums up variation technique up to this point is Bach's *Goldberg Variations*. From the second half of the eighteenth century and into the twentieth, variations, either as complete works or in individual movements, can be found in the output of most composers: Haydn (String Quartet, Op. 76 No. 3), Mozart (*Divertimento* K563 for string trio), Beethoven (*Diabelli Variations* Op. 120 for piano), Schubert (*Wanderer Fantasy* D760 for piano), Brahms (Symphony No. 4), Vaughan Williams (Symphony No. 5 in D), Schoenberg (*Variations for Orchestra* Op. 31), Stravinsky (*Septet*), Webern (*Piano Variations* Op. 27), Nono (*Variazioni canoniche* for orchestra). Writing variations excites and challenges the composer's imagination and can provide much pleasure to the listener.

VAUGHAN WILLIAMS, RALPH – one of the most important twentieth-century English composers; he made a vital contribution in putting England back on the map in terms of composition. His language and style are highly individual and are mainly based on his knowledge of native folk dance and song, and of the works of his Tudor ancestors. Vaughan Williams's creative heights are revealed in his symphonies and chamber music; he also wrote very fine songs, choral works and music for the theatre and screen. He was an effective teacher and conductor. An important aspect of his attitude to composition was that he produced music for performance by the semi-professional and amateur; this established a tradition among succeeding English composers which is maintained until the present, and makes English composition amongst the most 'democratic' in the world.

Vaughan Williams read Music and English at Cambridge, followed by spells of study at the Royal College of Music with Stanford, in Berlin with Bruch and in Paris with Ravel. His ethnomusicological activity concentrated on the counties of Norfolk, Essex and Sussex; in addition he edited the Welcome Songs for the Purcell Society and carried out the important task of selecting melodies for the *English Hymnal* (1903).

He refused a knighthood, later accepting the Order of Merit. His first wife, Adeline, died in 1951 and two years later he married Ursula Wood, writer and poet, who provided the texts for a number of his songs. He is buried in Westminster Abbey, near Purcell and Stanford. There is a host of his works to recommend, but three will have to do: Symphony No. 5, *Fantasia on a Theme by Thomas Tallis* for two string orchestras, and *Flos campi*, a suite for viola, chamber choir and small orchestra.

VENICE – renowned throughout the world for its canal system and unique architecture, musically speaking this north Italian city is the birthplace of commercial opera. Its first theatre was opened in 1637 and two years later Monteverdi's *Incoronazione di Poppea* had its première in the city; by 1700 sixteen theatres had been built for the presentation of opera. Leading opera composers associated with Venice include: in the seventeenth century, Monteverdi and Cavalli; in the eighteenth, Vivaldi, Galuppi, Alessandro Scarlatti, Handel and the librettists Goldoni and Gozzi; in the nineteenth, Rossini, Bellini, Donizetti and Verdi; in the twentieth, Stravinsky (*The Rake's Progress*), Britten (*The Turn of the Screw*), Prokofiev (*The Fiery Angel*) and Nono (*Intolleranza*). These last-named had their premières in one of the most elegant of all opera houses, the Teatro La Fenice, as part of the International Festival of Contemporary Music, now discontinued. Rising again like its namesake the phoenix, the theatre was rebuilt after being destroyed by fire in 1837.

Before the advent of opera, Venice was musically important only from about the beginning of the sixteenth century, which is rather late for an Italian city; at this time the music publisher Petrucci established himself, and this in due course led to Venice's position as the dominant music publishing centre in Italy. With the appointment of the Netherlands composer Willaert as *maestro di cappella* of St Mark's in 1527, church music took a significant step forward; his pupil, Zarlino, through his writings, compositions and sound administration, advanced musical activity still further, and the result was the admirable parade of works by Merulo, the Gabrielis (uncle and nephew) and others. A distinctive form of composition emerged, unique to St Mark's, called *cori spezzati*, in which performing groups, both singers and instrumentalists, were placed in the different choir galleries, creating stereo or quadraphonic effects. This very exciting music flourished from about 1575 to 1610.

VERDI, GIUSEPPE – one of the greatest Italian opera composers of all time; only Mozart and Wagner can equal his achievement of having operas permanently in the international repertoire from the moment of their first performance. Verdi had that rare gift of being able to establish character and feeling immediately through melodic line, which was quickly understood and felt by the listener; he also had an instinct for the choice and shaping of a libretto and knew exactly how the orchestra should back and maintain dramatic development. An apt example is *Rigoletto*, which he composed in forty days, and the way Verdi characterises this deformed court jester; when Rigoletto learns of the abduction of his daughter and has come to the palace to search for her, the music at this moment incorporates his surface lightheartedness, his crafty thoughts and his sense of disaster. Remarkable moments such as this recur throughout his operas, including *Falstaff*, his final opera, composed at the age of eighty. In Verdi's time Italy was involved in a long period of struggle for its independence and unification; he strongly identified himself with this movement, Il Risorgimento (The Great Revival), so much so that the Italians used Verdi's name as an acronym for their proposed king, *Vittorio Emanuele, Re D'Italia*. He owned a complete set of the works of each of his two favourite literary heroes Shakespeare and Schiller. Incidentally, in later life, he kept by his bedside pocket scores of string quartets by Haydn, Mozart and Beethoven. Verdi also had a good business brain, thereby ensuring a regular series of lucrative contracts with regard to performances and publications of his music. This allowed him to take a confident and independent approach in all his dealings; he became quite a substantial landowner. It is worth noting three non-operatic works which should grab you – the *Requiem* for SATB soloists, large chorus and orchestra, written after the loss of his great friend, the writer Alessandro Manzoni, and two other choral items, a *Te Deum* and a *Stabat Mater*. He was not, however, religious, having crossed swords with the Church over his union with Giuseppina Strepponi, with whom he lived for more than ten years before they were married. Three years before he died, deeply and universally mourned, he had built in Milan at his own expense a home for aged musicians, saying that this was his last great work. There are a goodly number of other operas from his considerable output that you should know, but if you pay attention to *Aïda*, *Otello*, *Il Trovatore* (The Troubadour) and *La Traviata* (The Fallen Woman) you'll have a very clear picture of why his music is so greatly loved.

VERKLÄRTE NACHT (Transfigured Night) – an early work by Schoenberg, Op. 4, for string sextet, written in 1899 and later arranged for string orchestra. The language and style are very much nineteenth-century late Romantic and the entire work, in one extended movement, is really based on an opening germ-cell motif. It is a remarkable piece with excellent command of string writing, showing that Schoenberg was capable of producing unabashed romantic melody with the best of them. The music is inspired by a poem of Richard Dehmel and depicts a pair of lovers; the maiden confesses she is pregnant by another; there is a massive emotional upheaval, the outcome of which is that the young man accepts the maiden and her condition; love transcends all and the night becomes a heavenly cloud of spiritual ecstasy. Here indeed is a romantic novella in sound for you.

VICTORIA, TOMÁS LUIS DE – Spanish Renaissance composer, one of the greatest of his time; a contemporary of Byrd. I, for one, am a devoted admirer of his music. Listen to his *Officium Hebdomadae Sanctae – Tenebrae Responsories*, the five-part Mass *Surge Propera* or the four-part motet *Ave Maria, gratia plena* and you'll be bound to agree with me. We are reminded that, at least within the Catholic Church, the *lingua franca* was Latin, for it is recorded that in Rome Victoria would talk to his German seminarians in Latin; he was ordained as a priest at the age of twenty-seven. He may have known and studied with Palestrina; certainly his works of this period are clearly influenced by the Italian master. Victoria returned to Spain in the mid-1580s and was appointed chaplain to the Dowager Empress Maria in Madrid, in whose establishment he remained until his death, refusing several tempting and more lucrative offers elsewhere. An example of the way in which early training was given at this time for the budding professional musician may be seen in Victoria's choir in Madrid; the choirboys not only received singing instruction but were also required to learn plainsong, polyphony and counterpoint from their master. It is of further interest to note that while the same techniques and formats were used by church composers of the period, yet the cultural root of the composer was retained – Spanish for Victoria, Italian for Palestrina, English for Byrd.

VIENNA – certainly one of the most famous musical cities in the world, but today, musically speaking, something of a museum, tending to exist on past glories. Now the capital of Austria, it was also the centre of Habsburg rule, established in the latter part of the thirteenth century and greatly expanding into the vast Austro-Hungarian Empire, which was finally dissolved after World War I. Musical distinction really only began in the latter part of the Baroque era, fuelled by a steady stream of Italian musicians and courtly magnificence. Vivaldi died in Vienna. Composers strongly associated with the city in the eighteenth century include Gluck, Dittersdorf, Haydn, Salieri, Piccinni, Paisiello and Mozart, who composed a large number of his piano concertos especially for Viennese performance; in addition to a strong keyboard tradition that had grown up, opera also flourished. Beethoven owed his first successes to his piano-playing in Vienna; in the nineteenth century he was followed by Schubert, Brahms, Bruckner, Wolf, Mahler and Strauss. At the turn of the century Vienna's reputation for being 'with it' began to recede, as witness the struggles faced by the so-called Second Viennese School (Schoenberg, Berg, Webern especially) and others. Nevertheless, the standard of orchestral playing and opera performance has remained consistently high: the Vienna Philharmonic is one of the world's outstanding orchestras. Vienna has produced some fine publishing houses and its university, founded in the fourteenth century, is distinguished; it is also the home of the Bösendorfer piano, a leading make. Viennese operetta is the chief root from which the American musical grew, and the city is the birthplace of the evergreen waltz.

VILLA-LOBOS, HEITOR – exceedingly prolific twentieth-century Brazilian composer, perhaps the most important South America has produced to date. Emerging in what may be termed a second-world country, he naturally leaned towards musical nationalism; from his late teens until the age of twenty-five he made long trips throughout Brazil absorbing the musics to be found in its various territories (no doubt you are aware that Brazil is larger than the USA). Villa-Lobos in the end was self-taught, learning through one or two self-selected models, of which his favourite was Bach, and through his own continuous composition in a great variety of media. He was a competent guitarist and cellist – the cello was his favourite instrument. It is during his seven or so years in Paris, from 1923 to 1930, that his music was first recognised internationally. It has an immediate appeal for both audiences and performers because of its tunefulness, rhythms and clever instrumentation, although the more sophisticated sectors of twentieth-century musical circles may have found it irrelevant to their concerns. An apt sampling may be taken from his series *Bachianas Brasileiras* – No. 7 for orchestra, No. 6 for flute and bassoon, No. 1 for cello ensemble, No. 9 for eight voices, No. 4 for piano. This Bach/Brazil thing was stimulated in Villa-Lobos because he believed that an affinity existed between Bach's compositions and Brazilian folk music; in each instance the parts retain a marked melodic independence. Numerous other pieces of his are recorded.

VIOL – one of the most popular bowed string instruments of the Renaissance and Baroque periods; in the mid-eighteenth century it was finally and fully replaced by the louder and more nimble violin. The viol had frets and was normally played held downwards on the lap; a larger version, the viola da gamba (leg viol), was held between the legs. The instrument first appeared in the fifteenth century and came in a number of different sizes; as the most common grouping stabilised into the viol consort, the sizes used were treble, tenor and bass. Usually the frets, made of gut, number seven and are placed at intervals a semitone apart; the neck is wide, flat and often quite thin; the back of the body is flat and the shoulders are sloped; the usual number of strings is six. The sound is resonant and reedy; the bow is held underhand, not overhand as with the violin. Viols were used as part of the ensembles accompanying stage works and court entertainments. There is a rich anthology of English music for viol consort which includes examples by Taverner, Tye, Tallis, Byrd, Gibbons, Morley, the Lawes brothers, Locke and Purcell. The early music revival in this century has rightly brought to our attention pieces such as Gibbons's *In Nomine a 4*, William Lawes's *Consort Sett a 6* in D minor and Purcell's *Fantasia upon a Ground*.

VIOLA – today the name 'viola' refers to the alto member of the violin family; it was first found in northern Italy, at the same time that the violin family (as opposed to the viol string groups) was establishing itself in the sixteenth century. The viola sound is equivalent to the alto voice with its warmer, darker tones, in contrast to the violin sound allied to the lighter, more brilliant tones of the soprano voice. The viola is less assertive; it is tuned a fifth below the violin – c-g-d'-a', and the c-string produces a marvellously rich, resonant sound. Viola sizes vary, the longest in use being about 43 cm; the fingering and bowing techniques are similar to the violin's. Violas are considered instruments of the middle tessitura of a string group and play a vital part in providing richness of harmony and texture. Their importance is fully emphasised in the string quartets of Haydn, Mozart, Beethoven and their contemporaries.

The violin and viola are treated as equal partners in Mozart's *Sinfonia concertante* K364; here, being both a good violinist and violist, he illustrates how well he understands the viola's character. The same applies in his superb Quintet in G minor for two violins, two violas and cello. The viola's technique was steadily extended throughout the nineteenth century – note the viola solo in Berlioz's *Harold en Italie*, and the demands made on the viola section of the orchestra in works by Brahms, Verdi, Tchaikovsky, Wagner, Strauss, Ravel, Mahler. The Bartók string quartets and Schoenberg's String Trio make the viola player sweat pretty hard. Twentieth-century concertos for the instrument include Hindemith's four and those by Walton and Bartók.

VIOLIN – this is the canary (or nightingale if you like) of all the musical instruments to be found in Western classical music. It is the soprano of the string family of violin, viola and cello. Acousticians regard it as one of the most perfect of our instruments and it has a remarkable versatility; its model is the human voice, which it rivals in emotional range, from the utterly lyrical to the brilliantly dramatic. It has had constant appeal for composers as a solo instrument, accompanied and unaccompanied; it consistently heads the string section, the centre of the European orchestra. It looks a fairly simple instrument but it is acoustically quite complex and is built from over sixty parts, including the neck, pegbox and scroll, with the fingerboard running along the neck and extending over the belly towards the bridge; in contrast to the viol, the fingerboard is unfretted. In essence the body is a hollow box, but its subtleties of construction are numerous and complicated. The violin in the hands of the right player can produce accurate microtones. It is considered that the great age of violin-making was the century between 1650 and 1750, when supreme Italian craftsmen emerged, of whom the most renowned are the Amati and Guarneri families and Stradivari. The last-named is regarded as maker of the Rolls-Royce of violins; a Stradivarius today may be valued at tens of thousands of pounds. It should be underlined that high-class violin-playing depends a good deal on the quality of the bow and bowing technique. Citing repertory for the violin could be an endless task, so I have selected three popular twentieth-century concertos by English composers: Elgar (Concerto in B minor, Op. 61), Walton (Concerto, also in B minor), Britten (Concerto in D minor, Op. 15); then there is Vaughan Williams's highly original *The Lark Ascending*, which he called a Romance for violin and orchestra.

VIRGINAL – a popular keyboard instrument of the sixteenth and early seventeenth centuries; it is a small, harpsichord-type instrument, usually having only one keyboard. Its strings run at right angles to the keys, in contrast to the spinet where the strings run at oblique angles, and the harpsichord where the strings run parallel. Remember that in all these instruments the strings have a mechanism which operates a plucking action, in contrast to the piano's hammer action. No one is quite sure about the origin of the term 'virginal'; derivation from the Latin *virga*, meaning rod, or connection with Elizabeth I ('the virgin queen'), have been rejected, and it is now thought that probably the instrument was associated with female performers or that the tone was associated with a young girl's voice, *vox virginalis*. The Flemish had a leading reputation for virginal-making; the Italian models were louder and less refined. Though one speaks of the English virginalists – Byrd, Bull, Gibbons and Tomkins, amongst others – it should be appreciated that while many of their pieces were suitable for it, they were really meant for larger instruments. The virginal was mainly used as a practice instrument and for making music in the home.

VIVALDI, ANTONIO – Italian composer and contemporary of Bach and Handel. There is little doubt that he was the most original and influential Italian musician of his time; he expanded violin technique and orchestral writing, and introduced orchestral programme music. He inherited his red hair from his father, later earning the nickname 'the red priest' (*il preto rosso*) – he was ordained in 1703. Throughout his life Vivaldi suffered from asthma and a heart condition; perhaps because of his ill-health and the pressure to compose, his execution of his priestly duties was not entirely faultless. His first post in Venice was as *maestro di violino* at the Pio Ospedale della Pietà, an institution for the care of homeless girls. His tasks included the training of those inmates who were considered musically gifted – the Ospedale was expected to provide concerts during the social season for the Venetian nobility and foreign visitors. Later he spent most of his time on various travels, as the flow of concertos and sonatas that he produced had now given him a European-wide reputation, particularly in Germany; additionally, operas, trio sonatas, Masses, oratorios, cantatas poured out of him. It is estimated that he wrote over five hundred concertos – but do bear in mind that these were written within well-known formulae and should not be compared with the grand concept of the concerto from Mozart and Beethoven onwards. Often they would come out in batches of six or twelve, for instance, the twelve concertos under Op. 8, of which the first four are known to us as *The Four Seasons*, and which provide a suitable example of his programme writing. Vivaldi was described as being rather vain, and he had a reputation for toughness over money matters. From about 1723 he had in train two sisters, Anna Giraud, a singer, and

Paolina who was supposed to nurse his ailments; although he denied it, the general belief was that both were his mistresses. On a visit to Vienna, within a month of his arrival, he died and was buried there in a pauper's grave: a great musician, once wealthy, through his profligate life-style ending up in this sad and lonely ignominy. You might like to hear some of the concertos with string accompaniment that he wrote for piccolo, mandolin, flute, oboe, bassoon, sopranino recorder, a pair of trumpets, cello; for most of these there is more than one example. After his death his music was largely neglected; it is only since World War II that interest has been renewed and the musicologists, still hard at it, have produced some real pippins for our listening pleasure. A fair amount of Vivaldi is now available on record.

VOCALISE – a term denoting singing without a text. At first *vocalise* referred only to nineteenth-century exercises produced for voice-training; sometimes these exercises were written with piano accompaniment, and some showed attractive musical merit. In the early twentieth century composers began to turn out the *vocalise* as a serious concert piece, particularly in France; there is, for example, Fauré's *Vocalise-étude* or Ravel's *Vocalise en forme d'habanera*. Vaughan Williams uses *vocalise* for solo voice in his *Pastoral Symphony* and there are his *Three Vocalises* for soprano and clarinet; then there is *vocalise* writing for chorus in Holst's *The Planets* (the Neptune movement) and Debussy's *Sirènes* (the third movement of his three *Nocturnes* for orchestra); a frequently performed example is Rakhmaninov's *Vocalise*, Op. 34.

WAGNER, RICHARD – of the two most striking and influential composers of the nineteenth century Beethoven is one, the other is Wagner. They were both controversial, and adored in their lifetime; both were responsible for major achievements in the evolution of what is known as the 'symphonic principle' – the way in which motifs and themes are developed and varied – Beethoven through instrumental music, Wagner through opera. Counting the 'Ring' cycle's four operas, Wagner's operatic output numbered only thirteen, most of great length. I say 'only' because hitherto, with but a few exceptions, composers churned out operas by the dozen; nothing wrong with this, really, since for them, generally speaking, the purpose of opera, either comic or serious, was to entertain. For Wagner, however, opera was a vehicle that carried the most earnest philosophical and aesthetic concepts, expressed in musical, dramatic and scenic terms in a combination aimed to deliver a virtually traumatic experience for an audience. For many, even to the present, he succeeded in his aim. He preferred to use the term 'music drama' instead of opera; to me, for one, opera is opera by any other name. In any event, opera has never been the same since his day.

Wagner was also a gifted literary fellow; it should be noted that he wrote all his own librettos. Through his numerous essays, articles, commentaries and letters he poured out thoughts on a wide range of subjects, some ill-considered, others of major significance in the world of music. The tone of some of these writings is unquestionably anti-Semitic, though this has to be put into context. For him neither words nor visual images but only music 'penetrated the innermost essence of the world'; on this basis it is understandable if a solo or duet passage in the 'Ring' had a timespan equal to that of a complete Baroque concerto. With his final opera, *Parsifal*, Wagner came to believe that art could become religion and religion, art; although I personally do not concur, this concept is not as crazy as may first appear. Thus the specially designed theatre built at Bayreuth could be – and often is – considered as the construction of a temple.

The quintessence of Wagner's world is best displayed in *Tristan und Isolde* and in the four operas that make up the cycle *Der Ring des Nibelungen*, which he described as a 'Bühnenfestspiel (how the German language loves to join up words) für drei Tage und einen Vorabend' – a three-day festival of stage drama with, as it were, a curtain-raiser (one helluva curtain-raiser is *Das Rheingold*!). *Leitmotifs* (lead or guide themes) appear in a great variety of guises to bind the cycle's musical and dramatic progress. *Tristan und Isolde*, completed between the writing of the second and third Ring operas, is an extraordinary, lush expression of gigantic sexual passion; it has spawned books and dozens of articles.

Wagner's character was an extraordinary mix of the selfish and the generous, the brave and the irresponsible. His mother's first husband was a police actuary, the second a painter, poet and actor; it has not been fully established which of the two sired Richard. In his boyhood a frequent visitor to the Wagner household was Weber, and Wagner states that it was Weber who first aroused in him a passion for music; at fifteen he was already an avid reader of Shakespeare, Goethe and Schiller and in love with the music of Mozart and Beethoven. Until his mid-fifties he was dogged by financial hardship; in no little measure, it must be said, this was due to his own unrealistic attitudes and his extravagance. What is remarkable, though, is the extent of his industriousness during these decades of material struggle. After twenty-two years of marriage Wagner left his first wife in 1858. Ten years later he struck up a relationship with Cosima, Liszt's daughter and wife of the German conductor Hans von Bülow; Wagner and Cosima married in 1870. A present to her on the birth of their son was the *Siegfried Idyll*, adapted from the love duet in Act 3 of that opera. Always a political radical, on several occasions he fell foul of various government authorities. He died in Venice of a heart attack.

WALTON, WILLIAM – one of the finest of twentieth-century English composers, belonging to the generation between Elgar and Britten. To a limited extent he can be compared with Haydn, in that each of his works is perfectly judged and fashioned, though they may not be equally inspired; similarly he can be compared with Mendelssohn, in that he developed an individual language and style very early in his career that did not change much with his creative progress. Nevertheless Walton produced a number of works that are internationally performed again and again, and deservedly so. His Viola Concerto, written for Tertis but first performed by Hindemith, is one of the finest ever written and stands comparison only with Bartók's example; the Violin Concerto, commissioned by Heifetz, brimful of Waltonian lyricism and rhythmic vivacity, is supreme among twentieth-century compositions in this genre. In contemporary English oratorio writing, *Belshazzar's Feast* is a worthy successor to Elgar's *Dream of Gerontius* and only equalled by Britten's choral *War Requiem*. His concert overtures, such as *Portsmouth Point* and *Scapino*, are as lively and breezy and orchestrally athletic as Strauss's symphonic poems; and then there is the very popular *Façade* suite, which originated as a theatre piece with words by Edith Sitwell and which has also been turned into a short, highly amusing ballet. There is little doubt that Walton wrote a number of hits, despite a comparatively short list of works to his name. He seems to have had particular difficulty in maintaining a regular compositional flow; it is known that this was largely due to his being obsessively self-critical, often taking weeks to decide on the final version of a page of score. He found that he was more fluent in his film scores, of which he wrote more than a dozen, the outstanding ones stemming from his co-operation with Laurence Olivier – *Henry V*, *Hamlet* and *Richard III*. Walton had a sardonic wit, an awareness of the absurd; at the time he was working on his opera *Troilus and Cressida*, he was heard to murmur, 'everyone seems to be writing an opera, so I thought I'd better have a go'. In contrast to not a few British composers this century, influenced by the German-Austrian axis, Walton looked towards, and thirsted for, the Gallic and the Mediterranean. He married an Argentinian, Susana Gil, and they settled on the island of Ischia. He was knighted in 1951 and received the Order of Merit in 1967.

WALTZ – the most popular ballroom dance of the nineteenth century; its raving centre was Vienna, where it was also danced in parks and at cafés. It is known that whenever Chopin, Liszt or Wagner, for example, hit Vienna, they would make sure that they took in a visit to some waltz-dancing venue. It was considered a rather sexy dance because, for the first time in public, the dance involved a tight embrace by the couple. Its rhythm in triple time can be very exhilarating and had a major influence on nineteenth- and early twentieth-century composers. The waltz seems to have its origins in a variety of country dances in southern Germany, Austria and Bohemia. Its simple character caused it to overtake the stately minuet in popularity; already by the close of the eighteenth century one commentator could write '... one need only to be able to waltz, and all is well'. Mozart and Beethoven had already written music which was clearly influenced by the waltz, but Schubert is the first major composer to use the term as a title; Weber elevated the waltz to the concert platform with his piano rondo *Invitation to the Dance*. A further projection of the dance came with the rise of composer-cum-dance band leaders such as Lanner, Johann Strauss I and Johann Strauss II, and, later, Waldteufel; Strauss II wrote highly successful waltz operettas such as *A Thousand and One Nights* and *Roses from the South*. By now the waltz had flooded into all Europe and over to the USA. Gounod introduced a full-scale waltz for soloists and chorus in the second-act finale of his *Faust* opera, and waltzes are to be found in the ballet music of Delibes and Tchaikovsky. Brahms (a close friend of Johann Strauss II) in his two sets of *Liebeslieder Walzer* displays all the subtle varieties to be found in waltz rhythm; then there are the attractive waltz collections of Chopin and Liszt for piano. The summation of the waltz world is contained in the two orchestral pieces of Ravel – *Valses nobles et sentimentales* and *La valse*.

WARLOCK, PETER – the pseudonym of Philip Heseltine, one of the most important pre-war English song writers; proof of the richness of his output in this genre lies in examples such as *The Fox*, *Late Summer*, *Autumn Twilight* and the song-cycle *Lillygay*. He was a lifelong friend of Delius, and was greatly influenced by the latter's thoughts on composition as well as by his music; he published a book on him and assisted Sir Thomas Beecham with his Delius Festival in 1929. In commemoration of Delius's sixtieth birthday he wrote a *Serenade* for strings. A later influence on Warlock was the composer Van Dieren. The hundred or more songs he wrote are expertly crafted and show imaginative treatment of the texts; they also swing in mood from the introvert to the extrovert, reflecting accurately Warlock's character. He suffered psychological and material difficulties which led, sadly, to his suicide at the age of thirty-six. A well-written and popular concert-hall work is his *Capriol Suite* for orchestra.

WAR AND PEACE – Prokofiev's opera in thirteen scenes; the libretto, after Tolstoy's great novel, was written by the composer and Mira Mendelson, with whom he lived after the break-up of his marriage. It was audacious, perhaps, to undertake to make an opera out of Tolstoy's masterpiece, yet the result does work as a theatrical event, especially if one is not too familiar with the original. *War and Peace* belongs to his wartime output, and it is likely that the dramatic and tragic circumstances facing Russia during the war were at the root of Prokofiev's inspiration. He revised the work right up until 1952, having finished it in 1944, and it received its first complete performance in Moscow in 1957, after his death. Prokofiev produced a most powerful score. The details of the plot cannot be rattled off in this case, but it deals with the invasion of Russia by the French, a set of personal relationships, the people of Russia and of Moscow in particular, and Napoleon's retreat.

WEBER, CARL MARIA VON – nineteenth-century German composer who was also a talented conductor and writer on music. He shone equally as a virtuoso pianist, but his main significance is as an important founder of the German Romantic movement and as a major influence on the development of German opera. The kick-off point was the success of his opera *Der Freischütz* (The Free-Shooter) in 1821; it has convincing dramatic structure, imaginative orchestration and lots of fine melodic content. Weber's sense of the dramatic spilled over into his instrumental pieces and songs and his unusual treatment of orchestral forces, distinguished for its attention to material for solo instruments or special groupings. Besides operas and songs Weber has left us other stage music, sacred and secular choral pieces, orchestral works including two piano and two clarinet concertos (one of his two favourite instruments, the other being the horn) and a bassoon concerto, as well as chamber music and piano pieces; not bad for a chap who died at forty. Weber was a weakly child, and suffered from a damaged right hip-bone that left him with a permanent limp. While in Vienna in his late teens he learnt folksongs and enjoyed singing and playing his guitar in its taverns. Weber's professional life was gypsy-like, moving around from one post to another – Breslau, Karlsruhe, Stuttgart, Mannheim, Dresden, Prague, Berlin, Vienna; always on the go, but with his musical reputation ever on the increase through his composition, conducting, piano recitals and his writings. As a pianist he was the equal of Hummel, Moscheles and Czerny; he is supposed to have had elongated thumbs that reached to the middle joint of his index finger, which enabled each hand to play with ease four-part chords covering the interval of a tenth. During the last four years of his life his health deteriorated steadily. His last opera, *Oberon*, was a commission from London; he travelled there to supervise the rehearsals and performances, and was overwhelmed with invitations which his generous and kindly nature could not refuse. After one such

341

evening, feeling particularly poorly, he retired to bed and the following morning was found dead. He was first buried in Moorfields Chapel, but eighteen years later Wagner arranged for the coffin to be brought back to Germany. It was conveyed to the cemetery at Dresden accompanied by Wagner's *Funeral Music* on themes from *Euryanthe* and interred to Wagner's *An Webers Grabe* (At Weber's Grave), a piece for male chorus.

WEBERN, ANTON – a disciple of Schoenberg and a member of the so-called Second Viennese School. As a private pupil of Schoenberg he was influenced by the master's philosophy as well as absorbing compositional discipline; at the time he established a lasting friendship with two other gifted pupils, Berg and Wellesz. Though he already displayed marked talent as a composer by 1908, it was only with the *Passacaglia* Op. 1 for orchestra of that year that he established himself as someone to be taken seriously; the style is still influenced by both Brahms and Schoenberg. He soon established his unique musical character, expressed in short, intense pieces with widely spaced intervals, the melodic material frequently split among parts. To hear this sort of music unprepared can prove shocking, and can even make pieces by Schoenberg and Berg sound 'normal'; but for his detractors to regard Webern as writing 'plink-plonk' music means that they are not hearing its beauty of line and sound colour. At the same time, for his supporters to rationalise that Webern is not a miniaturist composer shows an equal bias. It was only to be expected that after the gargantuan operas of Wagner and symphonies of Mahler someone should come along and as a quite natural reaction try to say in three pages what Wagner and Mahler say in thirty. Essentially, Webern removes the rhetoric of music and distils musical thought to its essentials, as in his two-movement Symphony of 1928 which lasts little more than three minutes. Thus he is inclined to turn out works in sets, such as *Six Bagatelles* Op. 9 for string quartet, *Four Pieces* Op. 7 for violin and piano, or *Five Sacred Songs* Op. 15 for soprano, clarinets, violin and cello; but each piece in any of the sets is a little jewel. His use of pitch material is atonal, either free or using twelve-note technique. From all this it may be said that in a way Webern was more radical than Schoenberg, and for many postwar composers he exercised a greater direct influence than his master. Worth bearing in mind is that the rich tradition of German *Lied* writing did not close with Wolf, but continued in the songs of first Mahler and then Webern, whose pieces in this genre reveal tenderness, delicacy and an unquestionable lyricism. Webern's death was bizarre; while he was taking the night air, in the mountains near Salzburg, an American soldier shot him by mistake.

342

WEELKES, THOMAS – a contemporary of Orlando Gibbons and one of the finest English madrigal composers; he was also an excellent composer of sacred music and wrote the greatest number of Anglican services among the major composers of his time. Weelkes's musical corpus may be divided into two periods. The first, until he was about thirty, concentrated on madrigal writing, of which there are some ninety examples. They display contrapuntal invention and a wide range of mood and subject, and are consistently of interest; to mention but three – the six-part *Death hath deprived me*, and the two five-part *Those sweet delightful lillies* and *Hark, all ye lovely saints above*. The second period concentrates on sacred music – services, motets, full and verse anthems. These will captivate you as much as his madrigals; I have in mind the five-part full anthem with organ *Alleluia, I heard a voice*, the verse anthem *Give the king thy judgements* for three solo voices, six-part choir and organ, and the full anthem for six parts *Gloria in excelsis Deo, Sing my soul to God*. In the latter part of his life he started drinking heavily and there is little doubt that he remained an alcoholic; thus was he prevented from attaining the higher positions which his incomparable creativity merited. Unfortunately, in those days there was no Alcoholics Anonymous organisation to help him ...

WEILL, KURT – twentieth-century German composer who became a naturalised American in 1943. In the 1920s Weill was considered only second to Hindemith on the German musical scene; this may be substantiated by a hearing of his Concerto for violin and wind orchestra Op. 12 and his Symphony No. 2. Although his output covers orchestral, chamber and instrumental music, film, theatre and radio scores, operas, operettas, musicals and ballets, his genius lies in the production of songs as a vital part of one or another piece of theatre drama. It was essentially displayed during his brief, three-year collaboration with Brecht – one thinks of *Die Dreigroschenoper* (The Threepenny Opera), *Aufstieg und Fall der Stadt Mahagonny* (Rise and Fall of the City of Mahagonny) and *Die sieben Todsünden* (The Seven Deadly Sins). His unique, melodic gifts make his beautifully constructed songs unforgettable, even songs that popped out on their own such as *September Song* or *Speak Low* – the latter written with Ogden Nash in the space of a half-hour when they retired to a room at a boring Hollywood house party. Weill, in the USA as in Germany, involved himself with theatre works having philosophical undertones and attached to political or social ideals; one consequence was that, whether song or instrumental piece, the music contained a certain melancholy which was of universal appeal. His teachers included Jarnach, Humperdinck and Busoni, whose influences can be detected in the excellent craftsmanship behind seemingly simple music. In Germany Weill catered for an informed middle-class audience, but in the USA he believed that he should satisfy the broad American public; thus in the final ten years of his life he was immersed in composition for Broadway theatre and Hollywood film ventures. Weill's widow, Lotte Lenya, did much to promote the achievements of her husband, but a lot more research is required to reach a truer evaluation of an unusual and unmistakably gifted composer.

WEIR, JUDITH – perhaps the most talented British woman composer – actually Scottish – currently active, and certainly one of the most fecund composers in the current scene. She possesses an individual voice at once lyrical, sardonic, whimsical; her aural imagination brings attractive surprises from one composition to the next. Weir's present leaning is towards music-theatre, the subjects for which are fantasies cloaking a serious comment or notion about human behaviour. Her latest work, the opera *Blond Eckbert*, on the one hand reflects society's current uncertainty over traditional beliefs and on the other ensures an ear- and eye-catching theatrical experience. Works of lesser ambition worth noting are *Airs from Another Planet* for wind quintet and piano and the eight short piano pieces *An mein Klavier*.

WELLESZ, EGON – Austrian composer, musicologist and teacher who settled in England in 1938, escaping the claws of Nazism. Wellesz was an early pupil of Schoenberg and became his first biographer. What caused him to turn to composition was a performance he heard of Weber's *Der Freischütz* conducted by Mahler, after which he would seize every opportunity to attend Mahler's rehearsals. Wellesz had a generous outlook on music, which considered composers and musical subjects beyond the high but inward-looking culture of Vienna at the time; he thus appreciated the value of Gluck and Bartók, Debussy and Ravel, eighteenth-century opera and the aesthetic aims of Les Six. With the Cambridge scholar Dent, in 1922 he pioneered the setting-up of the ISCM (International Society for Contemporary Music), which still functions. He was responsible for bringing to the notice of Continental audiences the music of Vaughan Williams, Bliss and Walton. Wellesz composed across the spectrum of music, including a postwar burst of nine symphonies; thus far, unfortunately, there are no examples of his works on CD. This may be due to his enormous reputation as a scholar, earned through his pioneering work on early opera, his expertise on Byzantine music and hymnography, his important role in the history of the International Musicological Society.

WESLEY – the family name of several important Englishmen associated with church music of the eighteenth and nineteenth centuries. *John Wesley* is the founder of Methodism; he travelled widely as a preacher and believed in the power of music to improve man's nature. Under his influence congregational hymn-singing leapt forward. He did not hesitate to take popular tunes from all sources and have religious words set to them. A nephew of John was *Charles Wesley*, a composer and organist; he studied composition with Boyce and became organist at St Marylebone Church. *Samuel Wesley*, Charles's younger brother, proved to have the greater talent as composer, organist and violin player, but at the age of twenty-one he had an accident and damaged his skull, with the result that for the remainder of his life he suffered head pains and mental disorders. Living a life largely as a freelance musician and having bouts of lethargy, very likely as a result of his injury, he was more often than not near-destitute. But he turned out a significant corpus of church music and orchestral pieces of undeniable value, for instance the motet *In exitu Israel*, psalm 61, *Hear my crying, O God*, the Symphony No. 5 in A major. Samuel Wesley's works merit much more attention than is being currently accorded to them. *Samuel Sebastian Wesley* was the illegitimate son of Samuel, and musically the most talented of the entire brood; his second name was given him because his father's hero was Bach. An excellent organist, in 1850 he became professor of organ at the Royal Academy of Music. Sebastian appeared on five occasions as conductor of the Three Choirs Festival, the first when he was only twenty-four; in 1871 he introduced for the first time to the Festival Bach's *St Matthew Passion*. He seems to have been by nature prickly and controversial, frequently causing difficulties in his relations with clergy and fellow musicians. Like his father he held Bach in esteem, preferred Spohr to Beethoven (!) and was influenced by Mendelssohn. Works such as the organ piece *Choral Song and Fugue*, the hymn *The Church's one foundation* and the six-part anthem with organ *Cast me not away from Thy presence* show him to be the most important composer in the English cathedral tradition between Purcell and Stanford. It has to be said that, in sum, the Wesleys played a not insignificant part in the musical history of the English church.

WHOLE-TONE SCALE – this seven-note scale is associated with the music of Debussy and his fellow impressionist composers, but it already appears in less transparent form among earlier Russian composers, such as Glinka and Dargomïzhsky. The scale is built up of intervals of the major second (whole tones), in contrast to the chromatic scale, exclusively made up of semitones – minor seconds – and the major and minor scales, which are a mixture of whole and semitones. Aurally, the whole-tone scale does not offer a final note and thus gives the ear a sense of 'floating'. Harmonically it spikes the traditional functioning of key and chord relationships; it opens the sluice-gates for radical treatment of pitch material in composition. A nice, gentle example to give you an idea of the whole-tone scale sound is Debussy's piano prelude, *Voiles* (Sails).

WIENIAWSKI, HENRYK – a Polish virtuoso violinist in the generation after Paganini, a friendly rival to Sarasate. Among both fellow musicians and audience his playing became legendary; at one time he was personal violinist to the tsar of Russia. He undertook extensive and demanding concert tours in Europe and the USA with accompanists that included his gifted younger brother pianist, Jozef, and Anton Rubinstein; with Joachim he was a member of the famous Beethoven Quartet Society. Wieniawski's compositions are almost exclusively for the violin (e.g. *Légende*). The most significant are two violin concertos; the second, in D minor Op. 22 (dedicated to Sarasate), is considered by the cognoscenti as one of the most demanding of its genre for technical virtuosity and lyrical profusion. For sheer pyrotechnics his two sets of études, especially the *Études-Caprices* Op. 18, rival Paganini's *Twenty-Four Caprices*. At the same time there is a long list of attractive pieces with piano such as *Scherzo-Tarantelle* in G minor and *Polonaise* No. 1 in G major.

WILBYE, JOHN – a contemporary of Weelkes and Gibbons, considered by some to be the greatest English madrigal writer; he composed almost exclusively in this medium. His *Second Set of Madrigales* (1609) is held to be the finest English madrigal collection; you will be zonked by such items from the set as *Weep, weep, mine eyes, Sweet honey-sucking bees* and *As matchlesse beauty*. The five-part *Draw on, sweet night* I regard as the perfection of the madrigal. It shows Wilbye's ability to vary sonority, his use of alternating major and minor tonality, his way of expressing the essence of a text and his device of achieving dramatic effect by the alternation of chordal with contrapuntal texture. Wilbye seems to have spent most of his life in Suffolk, as resident musician at Brome Hall, the home of Lord and Lady Kytson. Evidence suggests that in the last decade or two of his life he was pretty well-off, holding the lease of a flourishing sheep farm, and was wont to pay more attention to his business affairs than to composition. He never married but had a long liaison with Lady Rivers, the daughter of Lady Kytson. In his will he left his best viol to his friend the Prince of Wales, later Charles II.

WILLCOCKS, DAVID – twentieth-century English organist and conductor with an international reputation. He succeeded Boris Ord as organist and director of King's College Chapel choir, and under his guidance its musical activities flourished more than ever; the Festival of Nine Lessons and Carols at Christmas became an annual national event on radio and television, and many recording engagements were effected. Later a similar parade of successes ensued after Willcocks became conductor of the Bach Choir in London. He was appointed director of the Royal College of Music in 1974 and appeared with its orchestra and choir at several Aldeburgh Festivals. During his war service he was awarded the Military Cross, and was knighted in 1977.

WILLIAMS, GRACE – Welsh composer, prominent in the first half of the twentieth century; she studied composition with Vaughan Williams and Gordon Jacob at the Royal College of Music, and with Egon Wellesz in Vienna prior to his departure for England. Before returning to Wales in 1946 Williams was a highly committed teacher in London; she made a major contribution to BBC educational programmes and was an active member of the Composers' Guild of Great Britain. Her composition concentrates on the voice, with orchestra, ensemble or piano, showing sensitive treatment of the text, natural vocal lyricism and inventive accompaniment. Two examples are *The Dancers* for soprano, female chorus, strings and harp, and *Six Poems of Gerard Manley Hopkins* for contralto and string sextet.

WILLIAMS, JOHN – a distinguished Australian-born guitarist who has toured internationally with great success and frequently given duet recitals with Julian Bream. Live or on record, Williams's playing is characterised by easy facility, refined control of dynamics and penetrative interpretation. He received coaching from Segovia, who admired his playing sufficiently to appoint him frequently as a teaching deputy. He has been visiting professor of guitar at the Royal Northern College of Music since 1973. While Williams is an undoubted master of the traditional guitar repertoire he has taken a radical approach to the function of his instrument, drawing on jazz, folk, pop and non-Western musics for composition and arrangement, as well as using electro-acoustic techniques.

WILLIAMSON, MALCOLM – a composer born in Australia, who settled in London in 1953. He was appointed Master of the Queen's Music in 1975. As a fine organist and pianist he included a keyboard in his early works so that he himself could participate in their first performances. While his language and style are deliberately eclectic, it is evident that the main influence on his composition is Messiaen. Williamson was for a long time unusually prolific, responding to all kinds of commissions, from opera to works specifically for amateurs. The speed of his writing has at times left him short of self-appraisal, but this has been balanced against the absence of a certain selfconsciousness which was not unusual in postwar composers. The range of his subject matter reveals a cultivated mind. His opera *Our Man in Havana* is certainly among the best to come from the pens of postwar British composers. Not enough of Williamson's music is recorded; a rare example is *Now is the Singing Day* for voice and piano trio.

WOLF, HUGO – one of the great nineteenth-century German *Lieder* composers. As a school pupil and student he had a poor academic record and, though inspired by other composers' music, especially Wagner's, his development was a law unto itself. His first worthwhile songs began to emerge in his late teens; at this time he was taken by a well-meaning friend to a Viennese brothel where he contracted syphilis, which brought about his early death. It is remarkable that, despite his frequent outbursts of rudeness and unsocial behaviour, he had the lifelong sympathy of a parade of loyal friends, who not only appreciated his musical gift but also saw the attractive and likeable aspects of his nature. It is well-known that his chronic ill-health contributed in large measure to his stop-go pattern of composition: months might go by in which he could not write a single note, while in contrast, in an eighteen-month period from 1888 to 1889 he poured out 147 songs. His sterile states would cause him almost unbearable mental stress, which he would attempt to ease by attending musical events or participating in performances of his music. Most of his life he lived in penury or as the guest of generous friends. In the last six years madness set in, in which he suffered a series of hallucinations, and his final years were spent in an asylum. For a long time he had been having a deeply felt affair with a married woman, Melanie Köchert, whose response was equally strong; her love did much to alleviate his suffering. Some three years after his death, she died by throwing herself from the fourth storey of her Vienna home.

The unique aspect of Wolf's music lies in the world of song he created. Each song has its own special intensity, each is a vocal tone-poem expressing the quintessence of its text; his harmony adds a new chromatic richness to the German *Lied* and the piano accompaniments are orchestral in nuance and texture. There is much to recommend for listening pleasure, but for a start there are songs to choose from collections recorded under the names of the poets he set – the *Eichendorff Lieder*, the *Möricke Lieder*, the *Goethe Lieder*, and in contrast there is his pleasant *Italian Serenade* for small orchestra and his String Quartet in D minor.

WOOD, CHARLES – Irish composer and teacher active in the late nineteenth and early twentieth centuries. He held the Chair of Music at Cambridge in the final two years of his life and made his mark with the catchy chimes he wrote for the Gonville and Caius College clock. For the opening of the Royal College of Music's new building in 1894 he wrote a setting of Swinburne's *Ode on Music* for chorus and orchestra. In fact, a large part of his early composition consisted of works for voice and/or chorus and orchestra. Later he turned to the production of some very fine church music; apt examples are his *Evening Service* in F major, the anthem *Hail, gladdening light*, and *O thou, the central orb* for chorus.

WOOD, HENRY – the founder of the London season of Promenade Concerts and their leading conductor and director, almost without exception, from their inception at the Queen's Hall in 1895 until his death in 1944, the year he was made a Companion of Honour (he was knighted in 1911). The BBC took over the running of the Proms in 1927, and they were named the Henry Wood Promenade Concerts from 1945. The move from the Queen's Hall to the Royal Albert Hall took place in 1942, after the former was destroyed by enemy bombs. The remarkable career of Wood, who was as genial as he was efficient, did not centre solely around the Proms seasons and their richly diverse programmes, which included a healthy diet of contemporary music. With incomparable industry he undertook conducting engagements up and down the country, seeking to improve the standards of orchestral playing, amateur as well as professional. Wood was consistently occupied with the voice and its workings; in 1928 he even published a manual, *The Gentle Art of Singing*, and in his autobiography of 1938, *My Life of Music*, he makes frequent observations on the subject. It seems he gave singing lessons until the end of his career. No doubt he and I would agree that the voice is the greatest of all instruments. Today the annual season of Henry Wood Promenade Concerts is a central part of British musical life, as well as attracting thousands of overseas music lovers.

WORD-PAINTING – throughout musical history examples occur in which the meaning of words in vocal music is illustrated in sound. As one might expect, this appeals to the composer's imagination and ingenuity and also adds to the attraction of the music for the listener. Early examples are to be found in Renaissance madrigals and in Baroque oratorios. Word-painting can be divided into several categories: emotion – 'longing', 'laugh', 'happy'; time and number – 'slow', 'thrice', 'often'; motion and place – 'jump', 'heaven', 'falling'; then there is the onomatopoeic imitation of bird-calls, drums or flowing water. Word-painting could be stretched to cover a pronoun, such as 'you', when a melisma on this word may well suggest the beauty or the character of the person so addressed. In general the device is treated with greater sophistication in twentieth-century music, the 'word-painting' often occurring in the accompaniment rather than in the voice-part itself.

WOZZECK – one of the greatest of all twentieth-century operas; composed by Berg, who also wrote the libretto, based on a play by the nineteenth-century German writer Büchner. It was first performed at the Berlin Staatsoper in 1925. The underlying motif is that character and circumstance combine to bring about tragedy; at the same time it is a lament for the 'little man'. The orchestration is rich and original, calling at different times for a military band, a restaurant ensemble on stage, and an out-of-tune piano, also on stage; at times, however, there is the chamber-music quality found in a Mahler symphony. Scenes such as the heroine's lullaby to her child, her Bible-reading moment, the terror of the hero (Wozzeck) just before he drowns in searching for the fatal knife, and the child playing in the final scene, unaware of the death of his parents, are uniquely effective. The remarkable, and very successful, compositional technique of the opera lies in its use of established instrumental forms which produce immediately understood dramatic and musical power. A real *tour de force*.

XENAKIS, IANNIS – Greek avant-garde composer and a name awfully handy for music dictionaries, who has settled in France. Xenakis spent five years in the Greek resistance movement, during which time he was badly wounded and lost the sight of one eye; he was captured and condemned to death but escaped to the USA. Having trained as an engineer he obtained a job in France with the great architect Le Corbusier, working on housing projects in Nantes and Marseilles, a French convent, an assembly building in India and a stadium in Iraq. Some preparation for a career in composition, you might say. Yet one's creative oofles, sooner or later, will out, and with Xenakis the composing urge grew steadily, in the course of which he met Honegger, Milhaud and Messiaen; also of marked help was Scherchen, for whom conducting avant-garde music was as natural as a duck taking to water. Xenakis is as much a musical theorist as a composer. For the production of his works he often employs mathematical models such as laws of probability, game theory, group theory and set theory. I simply report all this, for I confess I am not qualified to link this highly cerebral pre-composition activity with the final result in the concert hall. The sound of his music is not at all shocking, were you to hear, for example, *Phlegra* for chamber orchestra, *Akea*, a quintet for piano and strings, or *A R (Homage to Ravel)* for piano. Xenakis belongs to that sector of postwar avant-garde composers who are perhaps best described as acoustic designers – I have in mind Stockhausen, Nono, Kagel, Cage, Pousseur. However much such composers protest their humanism, their creative results are confined, at least thus far, to a hothouse existence. For three decades from about 1950 their influence was strong, but of late it seems to be waning and remains controversial. Their works, however, have succeeded in stirring the musical sediment, and that's always a good thing.

XERXES – also known as *Serse*, a three-act opera by Handel, first produced in London in 1738; the setting is Persia in the fifth century BC. Xerxes' part is written for a male alto castrato; his aria 'Ombra mai fu' is sometimes known as 'Handel's Largo'. Xerxes, King of the Persians, engaged to one lady, falls in love with his brother's betrothed; this sets off the usual chain reactions of jealousy, misunderstanding and despair; comic relief is provided by the incompetence of the first lady's servant; in the end, one may say, 'all's well that ends well'.

XYLOPHONE – the origin of this instrument is not yet fully explained. Trough-resonating xylophones are to be found in Africa and Indonesia; some organologists claim that the instrument migrated from Indonesia to Africa, while others dispute this theory, believing that it is equally indigenous to Africa. The version that consists of a series of bars, usually of resonant wood but nowadays replaced by synthetic materials and arranged in pitch like that of a piano keyboard, is first mentioned in Europe in the writings of sixteenth- and seventeenth-century musical historians. Until the nineteenth century, when it began to creep into the percussion section of the orchestra, the xylophone would be heard only in the hands of itinerant musicians. Today it has become a convincing solo instrument, especially in the hands of a percussion virtuoso such as Evelyn Glennie. It has a compass of about four octaves. The bars are suspended from cords, with each bar lying above its respective tube resonator; the pitch of each bar is determined by its length and thickness. The whole caboodle is placed on a stand. If the mallets are hard-headed a bright sound is created; soft-headed, they will produce a more mellow tone. It is easily possible for a player to hold two mallets in each hand, thus producing four-part chords quite nimbly. Saint-Saëns makes effective use of the xylophone in two instances – the *Danse Macabre* and the 'Fossils' movement in *Le carnaval des animaux*; Mendelssohn, Chopin and Liszt were aware of the instrument. Other instances of its telling use include Mahler's Symphony No. 6, Puccini's *Madame Butterfly* and

Turandot, Elgar's *Wand of Youth*, Debussy's *Ibéria* and Stravinsky's *The Firebird*. The xylophone's importance was further enhanced in postwar compositions, for instance, Tippett's *Concerto for Orchestra*, Messiaen's *Chronochromie* and Boulez's *Le marteau sans maître*. The xylophone has definitely come to stay.

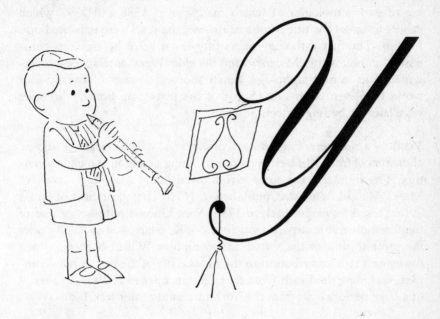

YAMAHA – a Japanese company that manufactures, besides musical instruments, a remarkable range of products including motorcycles and sports articles. The company was founded in 1887 by Torakusu Yamaha, who built Japan's first harmonium. Its musical interests are divided among three firms: one makes pianos, electronic keyboards, brass and woodwind instruments and reproduction equipment for recorded music; one markets all these items; the third does concert promotion in Japan. Its first upright piano came out as far back as 1900 and its first grand piano emerged in 1950, modelled with the advice of a Bechstein consultant; today the Yamaha grand piano is a serious competitor internationally. The company owns the largest brass instrument factory in the world; it also runs a major research and development unit for keyboard, brass and woodwind instruments; further, it has departments for wood processing, metal processing, machine making, electronics and chemicals. A particularly impressive creation is the Yamaha Music School, first established in Tokyo in 1954 and now having branches throughout the world; linked with this operation is the Yamaha Foundation for Music Education, set up in 1966, the main purpose of which is to encourage the making of music by schoolchildren of all ages and by amateurs.

Yonge, Nicholas – early seventeenth-century English singer and music editor. His most important achievement, besides being a regular and respected member of the choir of St Paul's Cathedral, was the editing of two anthologies of Italian madrigals in 1588 and 1597 which came out under the title *Musica transalpina*; the texts were translated into English. The first anthology offers fifty-seven items by eighteen composers, among whom Marenzio and the elder Ferrabosco are best represented; the second anthology, much shorter, consists of twenty-four works by eleven composers. Some of the texts from both anthologies were later set by English composers.

York – a northern English cathedral city in which, evidence shows, choristers of York Minster were already being taught in the eighth century. The minster owns some rare musical items, including a copy of Mace's *Musick's Monument*, published in 1676. The music firm of Banks & Son traces its origin back to 1756. York University possesses one of the foremost music departments in the UK, established in 1963 under the professorship of the writer and composer Wilfrid Mellers, which has made a rich contribution to the musical life of the city. A new complex, including the Lyons Concert Hall, was opened in 1969, as a result of a large personal gift from the Yorkshire industrialist Jack Lyons.

Young, La Monte – a way-out contemporary American composer. He first followed the twelve-note tenets of Schoenberg, but after study with Stockhausen at Darmstadt and familiarisation with the works of Cage his compositions took a more radical turn, paying special attention to theatre and mixed media creations. To some extent this development was also a consequence of his study of the Kirana style of classical Indian vocal music and his marriage to the painter and light-artist Marian Zazeela. Drones, produced vocally, instrumentally or electronically, feature strongly in his pieces, which usually take place in conjunction with light-shows by Zazeela. Thoroughly off-beat are *Composition 1960 No. 2*, which instructs the performer to build a fire, and *Compositions 1961, Nos. 1–29* – here the performer is required to draw a straight line and follow it. Some works continue from performance to performance and in theory can last *ad infinitum*. Since 1964 Young has been working on a single composition which he hopes will be performed throughout his life – its main title is *The Tortoise, his Dreams and Journeys*. There is a CD of his *The Well-Tuned Piano*. So, what do you think?

Ysaÿe, Eugène – a Belgian violinist of international fame and also a bit of a composer; he established the twentieth-century approach to violin-playing and was worshipped by succeeding violinists, including such greats as Kreisler, Thibaud, Szigeti and Enesco. During his stay in Paris he formed close friendships with a rich variety of composers – Franck, d'Indy, Chausson, Fauré, Saint-Saëns, and Debussy, who dedicated his String Quartet to Ysaÿe; other dedications came from Franck (Sonata for violin and piano) and Chausson (*Poème* for violin and orchestra). His conducting career included a four-year spell with the Cincinnati Symphony Orchestra. He performed Elgar's Violin Concerto in Berlin in 1911. Ysaÿe claimed that he learnt most about music from going on tour with the Russian pianist Anton Rubinstein. If you want to know what he was like as a composer, try *Extase* Op. 21 for violin and orchestra and Sonata No. 3 for solo violin.

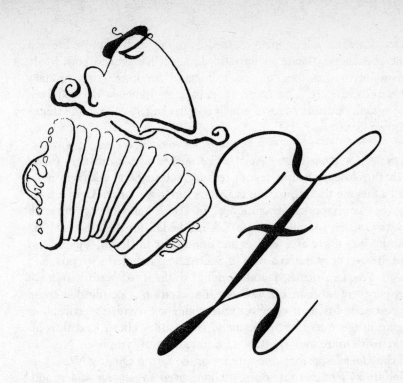

ZARLINO, GIOSEFFO – sixteenth-century Italian theorist. His book *Le institutioni harmoniche* is considered a vital source by historical musicologists in the study of mid-Renaissance compositional concerns and musical aesthetics. Zarlino studied with the Flemish composer Willaert, and it is Willaert's approach to composition that helped to formulate Zarlino's rules on counterpoint. He was also involved with the problems of tuning, the relationship between consonance and dissonance and the function of harmony; he appreciated that vocal and instrumental matters were not necessarily regarded from the same viewpoint. Zarlino aimed to reconcile theoretical speculation on music with its composition; he believed that the composer should not be content with mastering his craft alone, but should seek to understand the reason for doing what he does. His writings may sometimes leave earth and go into orbit; and why not?

ZARZUELA – a theatrical entertainment consisting of song and spoken dialogue. It originated in Spain in the seventeenth century, and because its subject matter was rooted in Spanish national life, with local and topical allusions and much improvisatory speech, it did not migrate to other countries except in limited measure to Spanish-speaking Latin

America. Zarzuela is essentially comedy, dealing with popular life and humble characters; despite its ups-and-downs it has proved both hardy and flexible, so that there is still a demand for it in contemporary Spanish music theatre. The name, it appears, is ultimately derived from the topography outside Madrid which consists largely of bramble thickets, known as *zarza*.

ZEMLINSKY, ALEXANDER – Austrian composer whose career in music began at the close of the nineteenth century. Schoenberg, with whom he formed a lifelong friendship, was taught by him the subtleties and refinements of contrapuntal technique; in fact Schoenberg married Zemlinsky's sister, Mathilde, in 1901. Until he left for the USA in 1933 Zemlinsky was active as a teacher and conductor in Berlin, Vienna and Prague; he was very much a part of Schoenberg's circle in Vienna, and while in Prague organised and conducted the first performance of Schoenberg's monodrama *Erwartung* (Expectation). Zemlinsky could never reconcile his own compositional tendencies with the radicalism emerging in the music of Schoenberg, Berg and Webern, and thus his music remains more user-friendly – for instance, the Symphony No. 2 in B flat, the *Humoresque* for wind quintet or the String Quartet No. 2 Op. 15. Zemlinsky's numerous songs, richly varied in subject and mood, show him to be an important contributor to the German *Lied* tradition.

ZIMMERMANN, BERND ALOIS – twentieth-century German composer who remained impressively independent of the avant-garde vogues of the 1950s and 60s, yet every bit as forward-looking – and his music retained a sense of humour which that of his contemporaries had lost. His one opera, *Die Soldaten* (The Soldiers), is considered the most important German opera since Berg's two of thirty years earlier – *Wozzeck* and *Lulu*. The restrictions imposed by the Nazi régime interrupted his studies at Cologne and Bonn universities; while doing military service in France he came across musical scores by Stravinsky and Milhaud which influenced his early compositions. Zimmermann considered himself a Rhenish mixture of monk and Dionysian; the former is expressed in his pieces for solo instruments, the latter in the Concerto in C for trumpet and orchestra. He turned out a large number of scores for radio and theatre, and enjoyed making arrangements of light music for the radio orchestras of Cologne, Frankfurt and Baden-Baden. If you happen to be an opera buff there is a complete recording of *Die Soldaten*.

ZITHER – this instrument is to be found in Europe, Asia and Africa. Its main feature is that its strings run the length of the body; different body

360

shapes, which act as sounding boards, give the zither sub-names such as cimbalom, autoharp, psaltery and dulcimer. Most zither types are made for the strings, stretched over bridges, to be plucked; but if struck action is included then, believe it or not, the piano could be considered a form of zither. In Europe the most popular instrument of the genre is the box zither, native to Austria and southern Germany. It has four or five metal melody strings passing over a chromatically fretted fingerboard; parallel to these are gut or nylon accompaniment strings, thirty to forty in number. The melody strings are stopped by the left hand; the right-hand thumb, wearing a plectrum, plucks these strings while the remaining fingers of the right hand add accompaniment on the open strings. Probably the most famous zither melody is the 'Harry Lime' theme featured in the Orson Welles film *The Third Man*, played by Anton Karas.

Dates of Composers and Performers

A

Albéniz, Isaac 1860–1909
Albinoni, Tomaso 1671–1751
Arne, Thomas 1710–78
Arnold, Malcolm b.1921
Auric, Georges 1899–1983

B

Bach, Johann Sebastian 1685–1750
Baker, Dame Janet b.1933
Balakirev, Mily Alexeyevich 1836–1910
Balfe, Michael 1808–70
Barber, Samuel 1910–81
Barenboim, Daniel b.1942
Bartók, Béla 1881–1945
Bax, Sir Arnold 1883–1953
Beecham, Sir Thomas 1879–1961
Beethoven, Ludwig van 1770–1827
Bellini, Vincenzo 1801–35
Bennett, Richard Rodney b.1936
Berg, Alban 1885–1935
Berio, Luciano b.1925
Berkeley, Sir Lennox 1903–89
Berlioz, Hector 1803–69
Bernstein, Leonard 1918–90
Birtwistle, Sir Harrison b.1934
Bizet, Georges 1838–75
Bliss, Sir Arthur 1891–1975
Bloch, Ernest 1880–1959
Blow, John 1649–1708
Boccherini, Luigi 1743–1805
Borodin, Alexander 1833–87
Boulez, Pierre b.1925
Boyce, William 1711–79
Brahms, Johannes 1833–97
Bream, Julian b.1933
Brendel, Alfred b.1931
Britten, Benjamin, Lord 1913–76
Bruch, Max 1838–1920
Bruckner, Anton 1824–96
Bull, John c.1562–1628
Busoni, Ferruccio 1866–1924

Butterworth, George 1885–1916
Byrd, William c.1543–1623

C

Cage, John 1912–92
Callas, Maria 1923–77
Campion, Thomas 1567–1620
Carissimi, Giacomo 1605–74
Carter, Elliott b.1908
Chabrier, Alexis-Emmanuel 1841–94
Cherubini, Luigi 1760–1842
Chopin, Frédéric 1810–49
Cimarosa, Domenico 1749–1801
Copland, Aaron 1900–90
Corelli, Arcangelo 1653–1713
Couperin, François 1668–1733
Crumb, George b.1929
Cui, César 1835–1918

D

Dallapiccola, Luigi 1904–75
Da Ponte, Lorenzo 1749–1838
Dargomïzhsky, Alexander 1813–69
Dart, Thurston 1921–71
Davies, Sir Peter Maxwell b.1934
Davis, Sir Colin b.1927
Dean, Winton b.1916
Debussy, Claude 1862–1918
De La Halle, Adam c.1237–87
Delibes, Léo 1836–91
Delius, Frederick 1862–1934
Deller, Alfred 1912–79
Desprez, Josquin see Josquin Desprez
Diaghilev, Sergey see Dyagilev, Sergey
D'Indy, Vincent see Indy, Vincent d'
Dittersdorf, Carl Ditters von 1739–99
Dolmetsch, Arnold 1858–1940
Donizetti, Gaetano 1797–1848
Dowland, John 1563–1626
Dufay, Guillaume c.1400–74
Dukas, Paul 1865–1935
Dunstable, John c.1385–1453

Duparc, Henri 1848–1933
Dvořák, Antonin 1841–1904
Dyagilev, Sergey 1872–1929

E
Eisler, Hanns 1898–1962
Elgar, Sir Edward 1857–1934

F
Falla, Manuel de 1876–1946
Farnaby, Giles 1566–1640
Fauré, Gabriel 1845–1924
Feldman, Morton 1926–87
Ferneyhough, Brian b.1943
Finzi, Gerald 1901–56
Fischer-Dieskau, Dietrich b.1925
Françaix, Jean b.1912
Franck, César 1822–90
Frescobaldi, Girolamo 1583–1643
Fricker, Peter Racine 1920–90
Fux, Johann Joseph 1660–1741

G
Gabrieli, Giovanni 1557–1612
Gay, John 1685–1732
Gerhard, Roberto 1896–1970
Gershwin, George 1898–1937
Gesualdo, Carlo 1560–1613
Gibbons, Orlando 1583–1625
Ginastera, Alberto 1916–83
Glass, Philip b.1937
Glazunov, Alexander 1865–1936
Glinka, Mikhail 1804–57
Gluck, Christoph Willibald 1714–87
Goehr, Alexander b.1932
Gorecki, Henryk b.1933
Gottschalk, Louis Moreau 1829–69
Gounod, Charles 1818–93
Grainger, Percy 1882–1961
Granados, Enrique 1867–1916
Grieg, Edvard 1843–1907
Griffiths, Paul b.1947
Grove, Sir George 1820–1900
Groves, Sir Charles 1915–92

Guido d'Arezzo c.995–c.1033
Gurney, Ivor 1890–1937
Guy, Barry b.1947

H
Hacker, Alan b.1938
Haitink, Bernard b.1929
Halévy, Fromental 1799–1862
Halle, Adam de La see De La Halle,
    Adam
Handel, George Frideric 1685–1759
Hanslick, Eduard 1825–1904
Harris, Roy 1898–1979
Harvey, Jonathan b.1939
Haydn, Joseph 1732–1809
Heifetz, Jascha 1901–87
Henze, Hans Werner b.1926
Hérold, Ferdinand 1791–1833
Hindemith, Paul 1895–1963
Hoddinott, Alun b.1929
Hogwood, Christopher b.1941
Holliger, Heinz b.1939
Holst, Gustav 1874–1934
Honegger, Arthur 1892–1955
Horowitz, Vladimir 1904–89
Howells, Herbert 1892–1983
Humperdinck, Engelbert 1854–1921

I
Ibert, Jacques 1890–1962
Indy, Vincent d' 1851–1931
Ireland, John 1879–1962
Ives, Charles 1874–1954

J
Jacob, Gordon 1895–1984
Janáček, Leoš 1854–1928
Joachim, Joseph 1831–1907
Jolivet, André 1905–74
Joplin, Scott 1868–1917
Josquin Desprez 1440–1521
Joubert, John b.1927

K

Kabalevsky, Dmitry 1904–87
Kagel, Mauricio b.1931
Karajan, Herbert von 1908–89
Keller, Hans 1919–85
Khachaturian, Aram 1903–78
Klemperer, Otto 1885–1873
Kodály, Zoltán 1882–1967
Koechlin, Charles 1867–1950
Koussevitzky, Serge 1874–1951
Kreisler, Fritz 1875–1962
Krenek, Ernst 1900–91

L

La Halle, Adam de *see* De La Halle,
  Adam
Lalo, Edouard 1823–92
Lambert, Constant 1905–51
Landowska, Wanda 1879–1959
Lassus (Lasso), Orlando (Roland) de
  1532–94
Lawes, Henry 1596–1662
Lawes, William 1602–45
Lehár, Franz 1870–1948
Leoncavallo, Ruggiero 1857–1919
Ligeti, György b.1923
Liszt, Franz 1811–86
Locke, Matthew c.1622–77
Lully, Jean-Baptiste 1632–87
Lutoslawski, Witold 1913–94
Lutyens, Elisabeth 1906–83

M

MacDowell, Edward 1861–1908
Machaut, Guillaume de 1300–77
Mackerras, Sir Charles b.1925
Maconchy, Elizabeth b.1907
Maderna, Bruno 1920–73
Mahler, Gustav 1860–1911
Malipiero, Gian Francesco 1882–1973
Marenzio, Luca 1553–99
Martin, Frank 1890–1974
Martini, Padre Giovanni 1706–84
Martinů, Bohuslav 1890–1959

Mascagni, Pietro 1863–1945
Massenet, Jules 1842–1912
Mathias, William 1934–92
Maw, Nicholas b.1935
Maxwell Davies, Peter *see* Davies, Sir
  Peter Maxwell
Mellers, Wilfrid b.1914
Mendelssohn, Felix 1809–47
Menotti, Gian Carlo b.1911
Menuhin, Sir Yehudi b.1916
Messiaen, Olivier 1908–92
Meyerbeer, Giacomo 1791–1864
Milhaud, Darius 1892–1974
Moeran, E. J. 1894–1950
Monteverdi, Claudio 1567–1643
Morley, Thomas 1557–1602
Mozart, Leopold 1719–87
Mozart, Wolfgang Amadeus 1756–91
Musgrave, Thea b.1928
Musorgsky, Modest 1839–81

N

Newman, Ernest 1868–1959
Nicolai, Otto 1810–49
Nielsen, Carl 1865–1931
Nono, Luigi 1924–90
Novello, Vincent 1781–1861

O

Obrecht, Jacob c.1450–1505
Ockeghem, Johannes c.1410–95
Offenbach, Jacques 1819–80
Oistrakh, David 1908–74
Orff, Carl 1895–1982

P

Pachelbel, Johann 1653–1706
Paderewski, Ignacy 1860–1941
Paganini, Niccolò 1782–1840
Paisiello, Giovanni 1740–1816
Palestrina, Giovanni Pierluigi da
  c.1525–94
Panufnik, Sir Andrzej 1914–91
Parry, Sir Hubert 1848–1918

Pärt, Arvo b.1935

Patterson, Paul b.1947

Payne, Anthony b.1936

Pears, Sir Peter 1910–86

Peeters, Flor 1903–86

Penderecki, Krzysztof b.1933

Pepusch, Johann 1667–1752

Pergolesi, Giovanni 1710–36

Perlman, Itzhak b.1945

Pérotin fl.1200s

Petrassi, Goffredo b.1904

Pfitzner, Hans 1869–1949

Piccinni, Niccolò 1728–1800

Pijper, Willem 1894–1947

Piston, Walter 1894–1976

Pizzetti, Ildebrando 1880–1968

Pollini, Maurizio b.1942

Ponchielli, Amilcare 1834–86

Ponte, Lorenzo Da see Da Ponte, Lorenzo

Poulenc, Francis 1899–1963

Pousseur, Henri b.1929

Praetorius, Michael c.1571–1621

Prés, Josquin des see Josquin Desprez

Preston, Simon b.1938

Previn, André b.1929

Price, Leontyne b.1927

Prokofiev, Sergey 1891–1953

Puccini, Giacomo 1858–1924

Purcell, Henry 1659–95

Q

Quantz, Johann 1697–1773

Quilter, Roger 1877–1953

R

Rainier, Priaulx 1903–86

Rakhmaninov, Sergey 1873–1943

Rameau, Jean-Philippe 1683–1764

Rattle, Sir Simon b.1955

Ravel, Maurice 1875–1937

Rawsthorne, Alan 1905–71

Reger, Max 1873–1916

Reich, Steve b.1936

Reicha, Antoine 1770–1836

Respighi, Ottorino 1879–1936

Riley, Terry b.1935

Rimsky-Korsakov, Nikolai 1844–1908

Rodney Bennett, Richard see Bennett, Richard Rodney

Rodrigo, Joaquín b.1901

Rosbaud, Hans 1895–1962

Rosenberg, Hilding 1892–1985

Rossini, Gioachino 1792–1868

Rostropovich, Mstislav b.1927

Rousseau, Jean-Jacques 1712–78

Roussel, Albert 1869–1937

Rubbra, Edmund 1901–86

Rubinstein, Artur 1887–1982

S

Sadie, Stanley b.1930

Saint-Saëns, Camille 1835–1921

Salieri, Antonio 1750–1825

Sammartini, Giovanni c.1700–75

Sarasate, Pablo 1844–1908

Sargent, Sir Malcolm 1895–1967

Satie, Erik 1866–1925

Scarlatti, Alessandro 1660–1725

Scarlatti, Domenico 1685–1757

Schenker, Heinrich 1868–1935

Scherchen, Hermann 1891–1966

Schikaneder, Emanuel 1751–1812

Schnabel, Artur 1882–1951

Schnittke, Alfred see Shnitke, Alfred

Schoenberg, Arnold 1874–1951

Scholes, Percy 1877–1958

Schubert, Franz 1797–1828

Schumann, Clara 1819–96

Schumann, Robert 1810–56

Schütz, Heinrich 1585–1672

Schwarzkopf, Elisabeth b.1915

Schweitzer, Albert 1875–1965

Scriabin, Alexander see Skryabin, Alexander

Sculthorpe, Peter b.1929

Searle, Humphrey 1915–82

Segovia, Andrés 1893–1987

Seiber, Mátyás 1905–60
Sessions, Roger 1896–1985
Sharp, Cecil 1859–1924
Shnitke, Alfred b.1934
Shostakovich, Dmitry 1906–75
Sibelius, Jean 1865–1957
Skalkottas, Nikolaos 1904–49
Skryabin, Alexander 1877–1915
Smalley, Roger b.1943
Smetana, Bedřich 1824–84
Smyth, Dame Ethel 1858–1944
Soler, Antonio 1729–83
Solti, Sir Georg b.1912
Souster, Tim 1943–94
Spohr, Louis 1784–1859
Stamitz, Carl 1745–1801
Stanford, Sir Charles Villiers 1852–1924
Steinitz, Paul 1909–88
Stern, Isaac b.1920
Stockhausen, Karlheinz b.1928
Stokowski, Leopold 1882–1977
Strauss, Johann II 1825–99
Strauss, Richard 1864–1949
Stravinsky, Igor 1882–1971
Suk, Josef 1874–1935
Sullivan, Sir Arthur 1842–1900
Sweelinck, Jan 1562–1621
Szigeti, Joseph 1892–1973
Szymanowski, Karol 1882–1937

T

Tailleferre, Germaine 1892–1983
Takemitsu, Toru b.1930
Tallis, Thomas c.1505–85
Tavener, John b.1944
Taverner, John c.1490–1545
Tchaikovsky, Pyotr Il'yich 1840–93
Telemann, Georg Philipp 1681–1767
Tertis, Lionel 1876–1975
Thomson, Virgil 1896–1989
Tiomkin, Dimitri 1894–1979
Tippett, Sir Michael b.1905
Toch, Ernst 1887–1964

Tomášek, Václav 1774–1850
Tomkins, Thomas 1572–1656
Tortelier, Paul 1914–90
Toscanini, Arturo 1867–1957
Tovey, Sir Donald 1875–1940
Tye, Christopher c.1505–c.1572

V

Valen, Fartein 1887–1952
Varèse, Edgard 1883–1965
Vaughan Williams, Ralph 1872–1958
Verdi, Giuseppe 1813–1901
Victoria, Tomás Luis de c.1548–1611
Villa-Lobos, Heitor 1887–1959
Vivaldi, Antonio 1678–1741

W

Wagner, Richard 1813–83
Walton, Sir William 1902–83
Warlock, Peter 1894–1930
Weber, Carl Maria von 1786–1826
Webern, Anton 1883–1945
Weelkes, Thomas c.1575–1623
Weill, Kurt 1900–50
Weir, Judith b.1954
Wellesz, Egon 1885–1974
Wesley, Samuel 1766–1837
Wesley, Samuel Sebastian 1810–76
Wieniawski, Henryk 1835–80
Wilbye, John 1574–1638
Willcocks, Sir David b.1919
Williams, Grace 1906–77
Williams, John b.1941
Williamson, Malcolm b.1931
Wolf, Hugo 1860–1903
Wood, Charles 1866–1926
Wood, Sir Henry 1869–1944

X

Xenakis, Iannis b.1922

Y

Yonge, Nicholas *c*.1550–1619
Young, La Monte *b*.1935
Ysaÿe, Eugène 1858–1931

Z

Zarlino, Gioseffo 1517–90
Zemlinsky, Alexander 1872–1942
Zimmermann, Bernd Alois 1918–70

List of Recommended Recordings

A

Albéniz, Isaac: *Suite española* No.1, op.47 DECC 433 923-2 DM2
Albinoni, Tomaso: Oboe Concerto in D minor, op.ix no.2 HYPE CDH 88014
Anon: Benedictine Motet from Engelberg RD 77185
Arne, Thomas: Concerto No.5 in G minor HYPE CDA 66509
Arne, Thomas: *Cymon and Iphigenia*, cantata HYPE CDA 66237
Arnold, Malcolm: *Three Sea Shanties* LDR LDRC 1002
Auric, Georges: Trio for oboe, clarinet and bassoon NIMB N15327

B

Bach, Johann Sebastian: *Brandenburg Concerto* No.2 ASV CDQS6041
Bach, Johann Sebastian: *Brandenburg Concerto* No.4 PICK PCD845
Bach, Johann Sebastian: *Chaconne* for violin CDH7 64494-2
Bach, Johann Sebastian: *Chromatic Fantasia and Fugue* in D minor, BWV903
    ARCH 431 659-2AH
Bach, Johann Sebastian: *Fantasia and Fugue* in G minor, BWV542, for organ
    DG 435 381-2GH
Bach, Johann Sebastian: Flute Concerto in E minor RCA GD 86517
Bach, Johann Sebastian: *Forty-Eight Preludes and Fugues* for keyboard
    DG 429 929-2 GD03
Bach, Johann Sebastian: *Goldberg Variations* for keyboard HARM HMC90 1240
Bach, Johann Sebastian: *Italian Concerto* for harpsichord PHIL 426 814-2PH
Bach, Johann Sebastian: *Partita* in D minor for violin EMI CDH7 64494-2
Bach, Johann Sebastian: *St Matthew Passion* ARCH 427 648-2AH3
Bach, Johann Sebastian: Suite No.1 for cello COLL COLL 1379-2
Bach, Johann Sebastian: *Two-Part Inventions* for keyboard DECC 411 974-2DH
Bach, Johann Sebastian: *Von Himmel hoch*, No.9 of the *Orgelbüchlein* DG 431816-2GH
Balakirev, Mily: *Islamey*, oriental fantasy for piano APR CDAPR7021
Balfe, Michael: *The Bohemian Girl*, opera ARGO 433 324-2ZH2
Barber, Samuel: *Adagio* for strings CHAN CHAN 8593
Barber, Samuel: Symphony No.1 RCA RD60732
Bartók, Béla: *Cantata profana* DG 435 863-2GH
Bartók, Béla: *Concerto for Orchestra* DECC 425 039-2DM
Bartók, Béla: *Contrasts* for clarinet, violin and piano CBS CD 42227
Bartók, Béla: *Duke Bluebeard's Castle*, opera DECC 433 082-2DM
Bartók, Béla: *Music for Strings, Percussion and Celesta* DECC 430352-2DH
Bartók, Béla: *Out of Doors* suite for piano DYNA CDS0411-5
Bax, Arnold: *Tintagel*, tone poem LYRI SRCD 231
Beethoven, Ludwig van: *An die ferne Geliebte* for voice and piano ORFE C 140501 A
Beethoven, Ludwig van: *Bagatelles,* op.126 DECC 436 471-2DM
Beethoven, Ludwig van: *Fidelio*, opera EURO GD69030
Beethoven, Ludwig van: Piano Concerto No.5, 'Emperor' PHIL 434 148-2PM
Beethoven, Ludwig van: Sonata op.111 for piano DECC 425 590-2DM 10
Beethoven, Ludwig van: Symphony No.6 in F major, 'Pastoral' PHIL 420 541-2PH
Beethoven, Ludwig van: Symphony No.9 DG 435095-2GCE10

Beggar's Opera, The DECC 430 066-2 DH2

Bellini, Vincenzo: *Norma,* opera EMI CMS7 63000-2

Berg, Alban: *Wozzeck,* opera CBS CD 79251

Berio, Luciano: *Circles* for female voice, harp and percussion
  WERG WER 6021-2

Berio, Luciano: *Sequenza I* for flute WERG WER 6021-2

Berio, Luciano: *Sequenza V* for trombone WERG WER 6021-2

Berkeley, Lennox: *Sinfonia Concertante* for oboe LYRI SRCD226

Berlioz, Hector: *Carnaval romain* PHIL 422 253-2PSL

Berlioz, Hector: *Harold en Italie* (Harold in Italy) PICK PWK 1152

Berlioz, Hector: *Les Troyens* (The Trojans), opera PHIL 416 432-2PH4

Berlioz, Hector: *Symphonie fantastique* (Fantastic Symphony) CHAN CHAN 9052

Bernstein, Leonard: *Chichester Psalms* DG 415 965-2GH

Bernstein, Leonard: *Prelude, Fugue and Riffs* CBS CD 42227

Birtwistle, Harrison: *Punch and Judy,* opera ETCE KTC 2014

Bizet, Georges: *Carmen,* opera PHIL 422 366-2PH3

Bizet, Georges: Symphony in C DECC 417 734-2DM

Bliss, Arthur: *Music for Strings* CHAN CHAN 8886

Bloch, Ernest: *Schelomo* for cello and orchestra BIDD LAB402

Blow, John: *Salvator mundi,* motet PRIO PRCD351

Boccherini, Luigi: Cello Concerto No.9 EMI CMS7 63283-2

Borodin, Alexander: *Polovtsian Dances* from *Prince Igor* DECC 433 625-2DSP

Borodin, Alexander: Symphony No.2 NOVA 150 079-2

Boulez, Pierre: *Pli selon Pli* ERAT 2292-45376-2

Brahms, Johannes: *Academic Festival* overture PICK IMPX 9027

Brahms, Johannes: *Alto Rhapsody* PHIL 426 253-2PH

Brahms, Johannes: Clarinet Quintet EMI CDM7 63116-2

Brahms, Johannes: *Liebeslieder Walzer* (Love-Song Waltzes) for SATB and piano four
  hands PHIL 432 152-2PH

Brahms, Johannes: Symphony No.4 DECC 414 563-2DH

Brahms, Johannes: *Three Intermezzos,* op.117, for piano RCA GD 60523

Brahms, Johannes: Violin Concerto EMI CDM7 64632-2

Britten, Benjamin: *A Ceremony of Carols* for treble voices and harp
  EMI CDM7 64653-2

Britten, Benjamin: *Peter Grimes,* opera DECC 414 577-2DH3

Britten, Benjamin: *Serenade for Tenor and Horn* DECC 417 153-2DH

Britten, Benjamin: *Songs and Proverbs of William Blake* DECC 417 428-2LH3

Britten, Benjamin: *The Rape of Lucretia,* opera DECC 425 666-2LH2

Britten, Benjamin: *The Turn of the Screw,* opera DECC 425 672-2LH2

Britten, Benjamin: Violin Concerto in D minor, op.15 EMI CDM7 64202-2

Britten, Benjamin: *War Requiem* DECC 414 383-2DH2

Bruch, Max: Violin Concerto No.1 EMIL CD27 62519-2

Bruckner, Anton: Symphony No.7 EMI CDM7 69923-2

Busoni, Ferruccio: *Fantasia contrappuntistica* for piano CONT CCD 10006

Butterworth, George: *A Shropshire Lad* NIMB N15068

Byrd, William: *Christe qui lux es,* motet AMON CD-SAR46

Byrd, William: *O magnum misterium,* motet CLLE COLCD 110

Byrd, William: *The Carman's Whistle,* variations L'OI 430 484-2OM3

C

Callas, Maria: *Operatic Arias* EMI CDC7 49005-2

Campion, Thomas: *The cypress curtain of the night is spread*, partsong HARM HMC 90 215

Carissimi, Giacomo: *Jephte*, oratorio MERI CDE 84132

Carter, Elliott: *Night Fantasies* for piano MUSI MACD-604

Chabrier, Alexis-Emmanuel: *España* CFP CD-CFP 9011

Cherubini, Luigi: Symphony in D EURM 350221

Chopin, Frédéric: *Barcarolle*, op.60 RCA GD87725

Chopin, Frédéric: *Berceuse*, op.57 DG 431 623-2 GH

Chopin, Frédéric: *Four Scherzos* for piano PHIL 422 038-2PH6

Chopin, Frédéric, orch. Glazunov: *Les Sylphides*, ballet DECC 433 864-2DA

Chopin, Frédéric: Mazurkas in A minor, op.68 no.4, and in B flat, op.7 no.1 for piano
    EMI CHS7 64697-2

Chopin, Frédéric: *Nocturnes* for piano RCA RD89563

Chopin, Frédéric: *Tarantella*, op.43, for piano SONY CD 46546

Cimarosa, Domenico: *Il matrimonio segreto*, opera RCA GD 60278

Copland, Aaron: *El salón México* SONY CD46559

Copland, Aaron: *Fanfare for the Common Man* for brass and percussion
    RPO CDRPO 7018

Copland, Aaron: *Passacaglia* for piano SILV SONG CD 906

Corelli, Arcangelo: *Twelve Concerti Grossi*, op.6 ARCH 423 626-2AH2

Couperin, François: *Pièces de Clavecin*, Book III, Ordres 13-19 HARM HMA 190 357/8

Crumb, George: *Songs, Drones and Refrains of Death* BRID BCD 9028

Cui, César: *Three Waltzes*, op.31 KING KCL CD 2008

D

Dallapiccola, Luigi: *Due Cori di Michelangelo* PROU PROU CD130

Dargomïzhsky, Alexander: *Russalka*, opera EMI CDH7 61009-2

Davies, Peter Maxwell: *An Orkney Wedding with Sunrise* COLL COLL 3003-2

Davies, Peter Maxwell: *Eight Songs for a Mad King* UNIC DKPCD 9052

Davies, Peter Maxwell: *Lullaby for Lucy*, partsong COLL COLL 3003-2

Debussy, Claude: *Children's Corner* suite SONY CD 48174

Debussy, Claude: *Danse sacrée et danse profane* for harp and strings ASV CDDCA 517

Debussy, Claude: *Images* DG 429 728-2GH

Debussy, Claude: *La Mer* (The Sea) DG 413 589-2GH

Debussy, Claude: *Nocturnes* for orchestra CBS CD44645

Debussy, Claude: *Pelléas et Mélisande*, opera SONY CD47265

Debussy, Claude: *Prélude à l'après-midi d'un faune* (Prelude to a Faun's Afternoon)
    SONY CD 47546

Debussy, Claude: *Préludes*, Book I, for piano DG 413 450-2 GH

Debussy, Claude: *Rhapsody* for alto saxophone and orchestra MARC 8 223374

Debussy, Claude: *Trois Nocturnes* (*Nuages, Fêtes, Sirènes*) DG 435 069-2GGA

Debussy, Claude: *Voiles*, prelude for piano EMI CDH7 6 1004-2

De La Halle, Adam: *Tant con je vivrai*, rondeau DHM RD77155

Delibes, Léo: *Coppélia*, ballet MERC 434 313-2MM3

Delius, Frederick: *On Hearing the First Cuckoo in Spring* PICK BOXD 21

Delius, Frederick: *Summer Night on the River* CHAN CHAN 8330

Dittersdorf, Carl: Oboe Concerto ARCH 427 125-2AGA

Donizetti, Gaetano: *L'Elisir d'Amore* (The Elixir of Love), opera MEMO DR3 104/5

Donizetti, Gaetano: *Lucia di Lammermoor*, opera MEMO HR4287/8

Dowland, John: *Come away, come sweet love*, song L'OI 421 653-2OH

Dowland, John: *Lachrimae or Seven Teares*, for viols and lute HYPE CDA 66637

Dowland, John: *Lamentations* L'OI 436 188-20H2

Dufay, Guillaume: *Ave regina celorum* VIRG VC7 59043-2

Dufay, Guillaume: *Vergene bella*, chanson HYPE CDA 66370

Dukas, Paul: *L'Apprenti Sorcier* (The Sorcerer's Apprentice) PHIL 426 255-2PH

Dunstable, John: *Quam pulchra es*, motet NEWP NC60013

Duparc, Henri: *L'Invitation au voyage*, song EMI CHS7 69741-2(2)

Dvořák, Antonin: Piano Trio No.3 in F minor CHAN CHAN 8320

Dvořák, Antonin: *Stabat Mater* DG 423 919-2GGA2

Dvořák, Antonin: String Quartet No.4 in E minor DG 429 193-2GCM9

E

Eisler, Hanns: *An den kleinen Radioapparat*, song TELD 2292-43676-2

Eisler, Hanns: Septet No.2, *Zirkus* GALL CD-676

Elgar, Edward: Cello Concerto PHIL 416 354-2PH

Elgar, Edward: *Cockaigne* overture ARGO 430 835-2ZH

Elgar, Edward: *Enigma Variations* EMIN CD-EMX9503

Elgar, Edward: *Introduction and Allegro* for strings ARAB Z6563

Elgar, Edward: *The Dream of Gerontius*, oratorio EMI CDS7 47208-8

F

Falla, Manuel de: *Concerto* for harpsichord and instruments DECC 433 908-2DM2

Falla, Manuel de: *El Amor Brujo* (Love the Magician), ballet PHIL 432 829-2PM

Falla, Manuel de: *El Sombrero de Tres Picos* (The Three-Cornered Hat), ballet
    DG 429 181-2GGA

Falla, Manuel de: *Homenaje pour le tombeau de Claude Debussy* for guitar
    RCA 09026 6 1353-4

Falla, Manuel de: *Noches en los Jardines de España* (Nights in the Gardens of Spain), for
    piano and orchestra RCA RD85666

Farnaby, Giles: *Farnaby's Conceit* for keyboard HYPE CDA 66335

Fauré, Gabriel: *Ballade*, op.19 CRD CRD 3426

Fauré, Gabriel: *La bonne Chanson*, song-cycle DENO CO-2252

Fauré, Gabriel: *Pelléas et Mélisande*, suite SUPR 11 0973-2

Fauré, Gabriel: Piano Quintet No.2 EMI CMS7 62548-2

Fauré, Gabriel: *Requiem* EMIN CD-EMX2166

Fauré, Gabriel: *Vocalise-étude* CRD CRD 3477

Feldman, Morton: *Why Patterns* for violin or flute, piano and percussion
    NALB NA039CD

Ferneyhough, Brian: *Superscriptio* for piccolo ETCE KTC 1070

Field, John: Nocturne No.12 for piano CHAN CHAN 8719/20

Finzi, Gerald: *Seven Part-Songs* CHAN CHAN 8936

Françaix, Jean: *Divertimento* for bassoon and strings ORFE C223911A

Françaix, Jean: Piano Concertino ARAB 26541

Franck, César: Sonata in A for violin and piano CRD CRD 3391
Franck, César: *Symphonic Variations* for piano and orchestra DECC 433 628-2DSP
Frescobaldi, Girolamo: *Nine Toccatas* NUOV 6832

G

Gabrieli, Giovanni: *Canzon in echo* for brass EMI CDC7 54265-2
Gerhard, Roberto: *Alegrías* ETCE KTC 1095
Gershwin, George: *An American in Paris* CBS CD 42611
Gershwin, George: *George Gershwin's Song-Book* EMI CDC7 54280-2
Gershwin, George: *Rhapsody in Blue* for piano and orchestra EMI CDM7 64441-2
Gesualdo, Carlo: *Ave dulcissima Maria*, motet ERAT 2292-4519-2
Gibbons, Orlando: *O clap your hands*, anthem PROU PROU CD 125
Ginastera, Alberto: *Tres danzas argentinas* for piano NEWP NPD 85510
Glass, Philip: *Company* for strings VIRG VC7 59610-2
Glass, Philip: *Dances* Nos. 1–5 for chamber ensemble CBS CD45576
Glass, Philip: *Mad Rush* for piano CBS CD 45576
Glazunov, Alexander: Symphony No.7 OLYM OCD 5001
Glinka, Mikhail: *A Life for the Tsar*, opera SONY CD 46487
Glinka, Mikhail: *Spanish Overture* No.1 PHIL 432 826-2PM
Gluck, Christoph Willibald: *Orfeo ed Euridice*, opera ERAT 2292-45864-2
Goehr, Alexander: *Lyric Pieces* UNIC DKPCD9102
Gorecki, Henryk: *Old Polish Music* for brass and strings ARGO 436 835-2ZH
Gorecki, Henryk: Symphony No.3 NONE 7569-79282-2
Gottschalk, Louis: *Bamboula – danza des nègres* EMI CDM7 64667-2
Gounod, Charles: *Faust*, opera EMI CMS7 69983-2
Gounod, Charles: *Petite Symphonie* for wind DECC 430 231-2DH
Grainger, Percy: *Country Gardens* CFP CD CFP 4611
Grainger, Percy: *Handel in the Strand* CHAN CHAN 6542
Granados, Enrique: *Goyescas*, piano suite RCA RD 60408
Granados, Enrique: *Quince Tonadillas al estile antiguo* (Fifteen Songs in the Antique
    Style) DECC 433 917-2DM2
Gregson, Edward: Concerto for tuba and brass band CPRI CAP 21414
Grieg, Edvard: *Holberg Suite* for strings BIS CD 147
Grieg, Edvard: *Peer Gynt Suite* No.1, op.46 EMI CDM7 64751-2
Grieg, Edvard: Piano Concerto DECC 417 728-2DM
Gurney, Ivor: *Down by the Salley Gardens*, song ETCE KTC 1063

H

Halévy, Fromental: *La juive* (The Jewish Girl), opera PHIL 420 190-ZPH3
Handel, George Frideric: *Chandos Anthem* No.1, 'Oh be joyful in the Lord'
    CHAN CHAN 8600
Handel, George Frideric: *Music for the Royal Fireworks* CBS CD 42595
Handel, George Frideric: *Ode for St Cecilia's Day* ASV CDDCA 512
Handel, George Frideric: *Saul*, oratorio TELD 2292-42651-2
Handel, George Frideric: *Serse* (Xerxes), opera DG 435 145-2GX5(1)
Harris, Roy: Symphony No.3 PEAR GEMM CD 9492
Harvey, Jonathan: *Bhakti* for chamber ensemble NMC NMC D001
Haydn, Joseph: Piano Trio No.28 in E DORI DOR 90164

Haydn, Joseph: String Quartet in B flat, op.55 no.3 DG 437 134-2GX2
Haydn, Joseph: String Quartet op.64 no.5 in D major, 'The Lark' DENO CO-1129
Haydn, Joseph: String Quartet op.76 no.2 in D minor ASV CDDCA 622
Haydn, Joseph: Symphony No.94 in G, 'Surprise' PHIL 434 153-2PM
Haydn, Joseph: *The Seasons*, oratorio PREI 93053
Haydn, Joseph: Trumpet Concerto in E flat CBS CD 39310
Henze, Hans Werner: *Ragtime and Habaneras* for brass band TELD 2292-437 13-2
Hérold, Ferdinand: *La fille mal gardée* (The Wayward Daughter), ballet
   DECC 430 849-2DM2
Hérold, Ferdinand: *Zampa*, opera NIMB N15120
Hindemith, Paul: *Die junge Magd* (The Young Maiden), song-cycle WERG 601 17-50
Hindemith, Paul: *Mathis der Mahler*, symphony CHAN CHAN 6549
Hindemith, Paul: Sonata for trombone and piano BIS BIS-CD258
Hoddinott, Alun: *A Contemplation upon Flowers* for soprano and orchestra
   CHAN CHAN 8762
Hoddinott, Alun: *Doubles*, concertante for oboe, harpsichord and strings NIMB N15357
Holst, Gustav: *Hymn of Jesus*, oratorio CHAN CHAN 8901
Holst, Gustav: *St Paul's Suite* for strings KOCH 316 10-2
Holst, Gustav: *The Planets*, suite DENO CO-75076
Honegger, Arthur: *Jeanne d'Arc au bûcher* (Joan of Arc at the Stake), choral drama
   DG 429 412-2GH
Honegger, Arthur: *Pacific 231*, symphonic movement EMI CDM7 63944-2
Honegger, Arthur: *Pastorale d'été* (Summer Pastoral) for chamber orchestra
   MONT MUN 2051
Howells, Herbert: *Chichester Service* ASV CDDCA 851
Howells, Herbert: *Hymnus paradisi*, requiem EMI CDM7 63372-2
Howells, Herbert: *Like as the hart*, anthem ASV CDDCA 851
Humperdinck, Engelbert: *Hänsel und Gretel*, opera CBS CD 79217

I

Ibert, Jacques: *Concertino da camera* for alto saxophone and orchestra KOCH 37094-2
Ibert, Jacques: *Escales*, symphonic poem DENO DC-8001
Ibert, Jacques: *Little White Donkey* for piano SIMA PSC 1067
Indy, Vincent d': *Jour d'été à la montagne*, op.61 ERAT 2292-45821-2
Ireland, John: *Amberley Wild Brooks* and *Remembrance* for piano CHAN CHAN 9140
Ireland, John: *Concertino pastorale* for strings CHAN CHAN 8375
Ireland, John: *Island Spell* for piano KING KCL CD 2017
Ives, Charles: *Central Park in the Dark* CBS CD 42381
Ives, Charles: *The Unanswered Question* NONE 7559-79249-2
Ives, Charles: *Three Places in New England* RCA 09026 61222-2

J

Jacob, Gordon: Concerto for harmonica and orchestra CHAN CHAN 8617
Jacob, Gordon: Suite for bassoon and string orchestra ASU CDDCA 613
Janáček, Leoš: *From the House of the Dead*, opera DECC 430 375-2DH2
Janáček, Leoš: *Glagolitic Mass* SUPR C37-7448
Janáček, Leoš: *Mladi* for flute, oboe, clarinet, bassoon and bass clarinet SUPR 11 1354-2

Janáček, Leoš: *The Makropoulos Affair*, opera DECC 430 372-2DH2
Jolivet, André: Concerto for trumpet and orchestra CBS CD 42096
Jolivet, André: *Petite Suite* for flute, viola and harp ACCO 20229-2
Joplin, Scott: *Maple Leaf Rag* for piano EMI CDM7 64668-2
Joplin, Scott: *Treemonisha*, opera DG 435 709-2 GX2
Josquin Desprez: *Benedicta es, celorum regina*, motet GIME CD GIM001
Josquin Desprez: *Mille regretz*, chanson CENT CRC 2109
Josquin Desprez: *Planxit autem David*, motet FORL UCD 1 6552
Josquin Desprez: *Que vous madame*, chanson EMI CDC7 54659-2
Joubert, John: *Chamber Music for Brass Quintet*, op. 141 MERL HRF 86041
Joubert, John: *Pro Pace Motets* for SATB MSC B34

K

Kabalevsky, Dmitry: *The Comedians*, suite KOCH 37042-2
Kabalevsky, Dmitry: Violin Concerto, op.48 CHAN CHAN 8918
Kagel, Mauricio: *Musi* for strings THOR CTH 2026
Kagel, Mauricio: *Rrrrr: five jazz pieces* MONT 782003
Khachaturian, Aram: Piano Concerto OLYM OCD 236
Khachaturian, Aram: *Spartacus*, ballet suite CHAN CHAN 8927
Kodály, Zoltán: *Dances from Galánta* PHIL 432 005-2MM
Kodály, Zoltán: *Missa Brevis* HUNG HCD 11397
Koechlin, Charles: *Nocturne chromatique* for piano CPO CPO 999 054-2
Koechlin, Charles: Sonata for viola and piano ACCO 20109-2
Krenek, Ernst: *Echoes from Austria*, op.166, for piano CPO CPO 999 099-2
Krenek, Ernst: *Jonny spielt auf* (Johnny Strikes Up), opera DECC 436 631-2DH2
Krenek, Ernst: Symphony, op.34, for wind and percussion THOR CTH 2043

L

Lalo, Edouard: Cello Concerto MERC 432 010-2MM
Lalo, Edouard: *Symphonie espagnole* for violin and orchestra DG 400 032-2GH
Lambert, Constant: *Aubade héroïque* HYPE CDA 66565
Lambert, Constant: *Rio Grande* for piano, chorus, strings, brass and percussion
   EMI CDH7 63911-2
Lassus, Orlando de: *Agibus tibi gratias*, motet ACCE ACC 8855D
Lassus, Orlando de: *Exaltabo te Domine*, motet NIMB N15 150
Lawes, Henry: *Man's life is but vain* and *Sitting by the streams*, songs HYPE CDA66 135
Lawes, William: *Consort Sett a 6* in D minor EMI CDC7 54311-2
Lawes, William: *Pavan of Alfonso* for consort VIRG VC7 59667-2
Lehár, Franz: *Das Land des Lächelns* (The Land of Smiles), operetta EURO 258 373
Lehár, Franz: *Der Graf von Luxemburg* (The Count of Luxemburg), operetta
   TER COTEO 1004
Lehár, Franz: *Die lustige Witwe* (The Merry Widow), operetta DENO DC-8103/4
Leoncavallo, Ruggiero: *Mattinata*, song DG 413 451-2GH
Leoncavallo, Ruggiero: *Pagliacci* (The Clowns), opera RCA GD 60865
Ligeti, György: *Bagatelles* for wind quintet BAYE BR 100052
Ligeti, György: *Hungarian Rock* for harpsichord FINL FACD 367
Liszt, Franz: *Grand galop chromatique* for piano APR CDAPR7021
Liszt, Franz: Piano Concerto No.2 MUSI MACD-625

Liszt, Franz: *Quatre valses oubliées* (Four Forgotten Waltzes) for piano HYP CD A66201
Liszt, Franz: Sonata in B minor for piano NIMB NI 1793
Locke, Matthew: *Consort 'ffor seaverell ffriends'*, suites for violins HARM HMU90 7013
Locke, Matthew: *Musick for His Majesty's Cornetts and Sackbutts* ASV CDQS 6042
Lully, Jean-Baptiste: *Alceste*, opera MONT 782012
Lully, Jean-Baptiste: *Cadmus et Hermione* and *Proserpine*, opera overtures
  HARM HMC90 1267
Lutoslawski, Witold: *Chain 3* DG 431 664-2GH
Lutoslawski, Witold: *Mi-parti* POLS PNCD 043
Lutoslawski, Witold: Symphony No.3 ERAT 4509-91711-2
Lutyens, Elisabeth: *Driving Out the Death* for oboe quartet REDC RR006
Lutyens, Elisabeth: *Verses of Love*, choral pieces CONT CCD 1055

M
MacDowell, Edward: Piano Concerto No.2 in D minor, op.23 RCA GD 60420
MacDowell, Edward: *Woodland Sketches*, op.51, for piano AREM AS55
Machaut, Guillaume de: *Dame, je sui cilz*, motet HYPE CDA 66087
Machaut, Guillaume de: *Dix et sept cinc*, rondeau ADES 13294-2
Machaut, Guillaume de: *Plourés dame*, ballade ADES 13294-2
Maconchy, Elizabeth: String Quartet No.6 UNIC DKPCD 9081
Maderna, Bruno: *Aura* DG 423 246-2GC
Mahler, Gustav: *Das Lied von der Erde* PHIL 432 279-2PSL
Mahler, Gustav: *Des Knaben Wunderhorn*, ten songs with piano CBS CD4 2202
Mahler, Gustav: Symphony No.4 EMI CDM7 69667-2
Malipiero, Gian Francesco: *Grottesco* for small orchestra NUOV 6998
Marenzio, Luca: *Crudele acerba inesorabil' morte*, madrigal DORI DOR 90154
Marenzio, Luca: *Qui di carne si sfama*, madrigal EMI CDC7 47998-2
Martin, Frank: *Petite Symphonie Concertante* for double string orchestra, harp, harpsi-
  chord and piano CASC VEL 2001
Martinů, Bohuslav: *Nonet* for wind quintet, string trio and double bass
  HYPE CDA 66084
Martinů, Bohuslav: Piano Concerto No.3 SUPR 11 0374-2
Mascagni, Pietro: *Cavalleria rusticana* (Rustic Chivalry), opera EMI CDS7 47981-8
Mascagni, Pietro: *Serenata*, canzona DECC 421 052-2DH
Massenet, Jules: *Manon*, opera BUTT BMCD 004
Massenet, Jules: *Thaïs*, opera CHNT LDC278 895/6
Mathias, William: Symphony No.2, op.90, 'Summer Night' NIMB NI 5260
Mathias, William: *Vivat Regina*, op.75, suite for brass band CHAN CHAN 4510
Maw, Nicholas: *Life Studies*, eight movements for fifteen solo strings CONT CCD 1030
Maw, Nicholas: *Odyssey* EMI CDS7 54277-2
Mendelssohn, Felix: *A Midsummer Night's Dream*, incidental music TELD 2292-46323-2
Mendelssohn, Felix: *Andante and Rondo Capriccioso* for piano CBS CD 42401
Mendelssohn, Felix: *Elijah*, oratorio PHIL 432 984-2PH2
Mendelssohn, Felix: String Octet in E Flat, op.20 DENO CO-73185
Mendelssohn, Felix: Symphony No.4, 'Italian' DG 431 038-2GBE
Mendelssohn, Felix: Violin Concerto SONY CD 46542
Menotti, Gian Carlo: *Amahl and the Night Visitors*, opera TER CDTER 1124
Messiaen, Olivier: *Catalogue des Oiseaux* for piano UNIC DKPCD 9062 and 9075

Messiaen, Olivier: *La Nativité du Seigneur* (The Birth of the Lord) for organ
  EMI CZS7 67400-2
Messiaen, Olivier: *Oiseaux exotiques* for piano, wind and percussion and *Des canyons aux étoiles* for piano, horn and orchestra CBS CD 44762
Messiaen, Olivier: *Quatre études de rythme* LINIC DKPCD 9078
Meyerbeer, Giacomo: *L'Africaine*, opera MEMO HR4213/5
Meyerbeer, Giacomo: *Les Huguenots*, opera DECC 430 549-2 DM4
Milhaud, Darius: *La création du monde* (The Creation of the World), ballet
  ERAT 2292-45820-2
Moeran, E. J.: *Fantasy-Quartet* for oboe, violin, viola and cello CHAN CHAN 8392
Moeran, E. J.: *Lonely Waters* CHAN CHAN 8946
Monteverdi, Claudio: *L'Incoronazione di Poppea* NUOV 6737/9
Monteverdi, Claudio: *L'Orfeo*, opera ARCH 419 250-2AH2
Moreschi, Alessandro: *The Last Castrato* OPAL 9823
Morley, Thomas: *Now is the month of Maying* and *My bonny lass she smileth*, madrigals
  CLLE COL CD 105
Mozart, Wolfgang Amadeus: Clarinet Quintet K581 PHIL 420 710-2PSL
Mozart, Wolfgang Amadeus: *Die Zauberflöte* (The Magic Flute), opera
  DECC 433 210-2DH2
Mozart, Wolfgang Amadeus: *Divertimento* K563 for string trio HUNG HRCO 72
Mozart, Wolfgang Amadeus: *Don Giovanni*, opera EMI CDS7 47037-8
Mozart, Wolfgang Amadeus: *Eine kleine Nachtmusik* K525 for strings CIRR CICD 1006
Mozart, Wolfgang Amadeus: *Idomeneo, Re di Creta* (Idomeneo, King of Crete), opera
  ARCH 431 674-2AH3
Mozart, Wolfgang Amadeus: Piano Concertos No.17 in G, K453, and No.27 in B flat,
  K595 EMI CZS7 62825-2
Mozart, Wolfgang Amadeus: Quintet in G minor for violins, violas and cello
  RCA GD 87869
Mozart, Wolfgang Amadeus: *Sinfonia concertante* K364 DG 415 486-4GH
Mozart, Wolfgang Amadeus: Symphony No.41, 'Jupiter' DG 429 668-2GSE3
Musgrave, Thea: *Rorate coeli* for chorus LEON LE 328
Musgrave, Thea: *Song of the Enchanter* ONDI ODE 767-2
Musorgsky, Modest: *Boris Godunov*, opera PHIL 412 281-2PH3
Musorgsky, Modest: *Pictures at an Exhibition*, piano suite PHIL 432 051-2PM
Musorgsky, Modest: *Songs and Dances of Death*, song-cycle CDM LDC 288 031

N

Nicolai, Otto: *Die lustigen Weiber von Windsor* (The Merry Wives of Windsor), opera
  overture CFP CD CFP 4591
Nielsen, Carl: Clarinet Concerto CHAN CHAN 8894
Nielsen, Carl: Wind Quintet RCA RD 86359
Nono, Luigi: *La fabbrica illuminata* WERG WERG 6038-2
Nono, Luigi: *Variazioni canoniche* ASTR E8741

O

Obrecht, Jacob: *Salve crux*, motet, and *Ave regina celorum*, Mass DERV DRVCD 102
Ockeghem, Johannes: *Pro defunctis*, Mass ARCH 415 293-2AH
Ockeghem, Johannes: *Tant fuz gentement*, chanson L'OR 436 194-2OH2

Offenbach, Jacques: *La belle Hélène* (Fair Helen), operetta EMI CDS7 47 157-8
Offenbach, Jacques: *Les Contes d'Hoffmann* (The Tales of Hoffmann), opera
  DECC 417 363-2DH2
Offenbach, Jacques: *Orphée aux Enfers* (Orpheus in the Underworld), operetta
  EMI CDS7 49647-2
Orff, Carl: *Carmina burana*, cantata profana CBS CD76372

P

Pachelbel, Johann: *Canon and Gigue* in D for strings CRD CRDC 4043
Paderewski, Ignacy: *Polish Fantasy* for piano and orchestra OLYM UCD 305
Paganini, Niccolò: *Twenty-Four Caprices* for violin EMI CDC747 171-2
Paisiello, Giovanni: *Il Barbiere di Siviglia* (The Barber of Seville), opera
  HUNG HCD 12525/6
Palestrina, Giovanni Pierluigi da: *Assumpta est Maria*, Mass GIME CDGIM 001
Palestrina, Giovanni Pierluigi da: *Assumpta est Maria*, motet DECC 433 678-2DH
Palestrina, Giovanni Pierluigi da: *Hodie Christus Natus est*, motet
  EMIN CD-EMX 2098
Palestrina, Giovanni Pierluigi da: *Missa Papae Marcelli*, Mass GIME CDGIM 339
Panufnik, Andrzej: *Autumn Music* UNIC UKCD 2016
Parry, Hubert: *I was glad*, anthem EMIL CDZ7 62528-2
Parry, Hubert: *Lady Radnor's Suite* for strings NIMB NI 5210/3
Pärt, Arvo: *Cantus in memory of Benjamin Britten* for string orchestra and bell
  CHAN CHAN 8656
Pärt, Arvo: *De Profundis* for voices, organ and percussion ECM 831 959-2
Patterson, Paul: *Comedy* for wind LDR LDRC 1002
Patterson, Paul: *Mass of the Sea* for solo voices, chorus and orchestra RPO CDRPO 5008
Payne, Anthony: *A 1940s Childhood* for flute and guitar/harp NIMB NI 5247
Peeters, Flor: *Concert Piece*, op.52a PRIU PRCD377
Peeters, Flor: *Variations on an Original Theme*, op.58 MIRA MRCD903
Penderecki, Krzysztof: *St Luke Passion* ARGO 430 328-2ZH
Penderecki, Krzysztof: Symphony No.2 POLS PNCD 019
Pepusch, Johann: *Kammer-Sinfonie* in D minor for strings CHAN CHAN 8319
Pergolesi, Giovanni: *La Serva Padrona* (The Maid as Mistress), intermezzo
  HUNG HCD 12846
Pergolesi, Giovanni: *Stabat Mater* for voices and strings DG 415 103-2GH
Pérotin: *Alleluia, Nativitas* and *Sederunt principes V. Adiuva* ECM 837 751-2
Petrassi, Goffredo: *Nunc* for guitar KOCH 37089-2
Pfitzner, Hans: *Palestrina*, opera DG 427 417-2GC3
Piccinni, Niccolò: *La Cecchina*, opera MEMO DR3 101/3
Pijper, Willem: Symphony No.2 DONE CVCD1
Piston, Walter: Symphony No.5 ALBA AR 011
Piston, Walter: *The Incredible Flutist*, suite RCA RD 60798
Pizzetti, Ildebrando: *La Pisanelle*, suite RCA GD 60315
Ponchielli, Amilcare: *La Gioconda*, opera EMI CDS7 49518-2
Poulenc, Francis: *Aubade* for piano and instruments PEAR GEMM CD 9311
Poulenc, Francis: *Les Biches* (The Darlings), ballet EMI CZS7 62690-2
Poulenc, Francis: *Quatre petites prières de St François d'Assise* for male chorus
  CONI CDCF 151
Poulenc, Francis: Trio for oboe, bassoon and piano PEAR GEMM CD 9311

Praetorius, Michael: *Maria Magdalena*, motet SONY CD 48039

Praetorius, Michael: *Wachet auf, ruft uns die Stimme*, motet GIME CDGIMO 10

Previn, André: *Bowing and Scraping* for jazz ensemble EMI CMS7 64617-2

Prokofiev, Sergey: *Peter and the Wolf* for narrator and small orchestra
EMIN CD-EMX 2165

Prokofiev, Sergey: *Romeo and Juliet*, ballet, suites 1-3 ERAT 2292-45817-2

Prokofiev, Sergey: Sonata for flute and piano ERAT 2292-45839-2

Prokofiev, Sergey: Symphony No.1, 'Classical' SONY CD 48239

Prokofiev, Sergey: Violin Concerto No.1 PEAR GEMM CD 9377

Prokofiev, Sergey: *War and Peace*, opera PHIL 434 097-2PH3

Puccini, Giacomo: *La Bohème*, opera DECC 425 534-2DM2

Puccini, Giacomo: *Madama Butterfly*, opera DECC 425 531-2DM1

Puccini, Giacomo: *Tosca*, opera PHIL 438 359-2PM2

Puccini, Giacomo: *Turandot*, opera DG 423 855-2GH2

Purcell, Henry: *Chaconne* in G minor for strings CRD CRD 3419

Purcell, Henry: *Dido and Aeneas*, opera ERAT 2292-45263-2

Purcell, Henry: *Fantasia upon a Ground* for viols HARM HMC90 1327

Purcell, Henry: *I was glad*, anthem DECC 436 403-2DWO

Purcell, Henry: *March and Canzona* for Queen Mary's Funeral ERAT 2292-45123-2

Purcell, Henry: *Ode for St Cecilia's Day* ERAT 2292-45187-2

Q

Quantz, Johann: Concerto in D for flute RCA RD 60247

Quantz, Johann: Trio Sonata in D for flute, bassoon and continuo THOR CTH 2073

Quilter, Roger: *A Children's Overture* EMI CDM7 64131-2

Quilter, Roger: *Three Songs of William Blake*, op.20 CHAN CHAN 8782

R

Rainier, Priaulx: String Quartet, and *Quanta* for oboe and string trio REDC RR 007

Rakhmaninov, Sergey: Prelude in C sharp minor for piano DECC 414 417-2DH2

Rakhmaninov, Sergey: *Rhapsody on a Theme of Paganini* for piano and orchestra
RCA 09026-6-1265-2(1)

Rakhmaninov, Sergey: *The Isle of the Dead* EMI CMS7 64530-2

Rakhmaninov, Sergey: *Vocalise*, op.34 DECC 425 820-4DH

Rameau, Jean-Philippe: *Castor et Pollux,* opera TELD 2292-42510-2

Rameau, Jean-Philippe: Harpsichord Pieces Volume I Nos.1-10 NAXO 8 550463

Ravel, Maurice: *Daphnis et Chloé*, ballet SONY CD 45842

Ravel, Maurice: *Gaspard de la Nuit* for piano NIMB N15005

Ravel, Maurice: *Introduction et allégro* CALL CAL 9822

Ravel, Maurice: *Le Tombeau de Couperin* CRD CRD 3384

Ravel, Maurice: *L'heure espagnole* (The Spanish Hour), opera DG 423 719-2GH

Ravel, Maurice: *Ma mère l'oye* (Mother Goose), suite COLL COLL 3020-2

Ravel, Maurice: Piano Concerto in G ACCO 20 1052

Ravel, Maurice: *Vocalise en forme d'habanera* PHIL 422 235-2PH

Rawsthorne, Alan: Concerto for piano, strings and percussion CHAN CHAN 9125

Rawsthorne, Alan: *Street Corner* overture EMI CDH7 639 11-2

Reger, Max: *Introduction and Passacaglia* in D minor for organ EURO 610 031

Reger, Max: *Variations and Fugue on a Theme of Beethoven*, op.86 SCHW 311412

Reich, Steve: *Clapping Music* for two performers COLL 1287-2

Reich, Steve: *Music for a Large Ensemble* ECM 827 287-2

Reicha, Antoine: Six Wind Quintets, op.100 no.2 CPO 999 024-2

Respighi, Ottorino: *Ancient Airs and Dances* MERC 434-304-2MM

Respighi, Ottorino: *Le Fontane di Roma* (The Fountains of Rome), symphonic poem
  DG 413 822-2GH

Riley, Terry: *In C* ARGO 430 380-2ZH

Riley, Terry: *Salome Dances for Peace* for string quartet NONE 7559-79217-2

Rimsky-Korsakov, Nikolai: *Capriccio espagnol* OLYM OCD121

Rimsky-Korsakov, Nikolai: Quintet for piano and woodwind CALI CAL 50898

Rimsky-Korsakov, Nikolai: *Schéhérazade* suite CBS CD 44559

Rodrigo, Joaquín: *Concierto de Aranjuez* for guitar and orchestra RCA RD 84900

Rodrigo, Joaquín: *Concierto Pastoral* for flute and orchestra COLL COLL 7005-2

Rosenberg, Hilding: String Quartet No.8 CPRI CAP2 1354

Rosenberg, Hilding: Suite in D for violin and piano CPRI CAP2 1510

Rossini, Gioachino: *Guillaume Tell* (William Tell), opera PHIL 422 391-2PH4

Rossini, Gioachino: *Il Barbiere di Siviglia* (The Barber of Seville), opera
  DG 415 695-2GH2

Rossini, Gioachino: *Petite Messe solennelle* SCHW 31345-2

Rossini, Gioachino: *Stabat Mater* SONY CD 53252

Rossini, Gioachino: *Tancredi*, opera SONY CD 39073

Roussel, Albert: *Divertissement* for wind quintet and piano ADDA 58 1064

Roussel, Albert: Symphony No. 1, 'Poème de la forêt' ERAT 2292-45253-2

Rubbra, Edmund: Sonata No.2 for violin and piano DERV DRV CD 104

Rubbra, Edmund: Symphony No.7 in C LYRI SRCD 235

S

Saint-Saëns, Camille: *Carnaval des Animaux* (Carnival of the Animals) PICK PCD 932

Saint-Saëns, Camille: *Danse macabre* in G minor ASV CDQS 6026

Saint-Saëns, Camille: *Danse macabre*, arranged for piano by Liszt RCA GD87755

Saint-Saëns, Camille: *Introduction and Rondo capriccioso* in A minor for violin and orchestra PHIL 420 887-2PSL

Saint-Saëns, Camille: *Samson et Dalila*, opera EMI CDS7 54470-2

Salieri, Antonio: Concerto in C for flute, oboe and orchestra ERAT 2292-45245-2

Salieri, Antonio: *Falstaff*, opera HUNG HCD 12789/91

Sammartini, Giovanni: Flute Concerto in G SONY CD 47228

Sammartini, Giovanni: Symphony in D major HARM HMA 190 1245

Sarasate, Pablo: *Danzas españolas*, op.21-23, 28, for violin and piano ARAB Z6614

Sarasate, Pablo: *Zigeunerweisen*, op.20, for violin and orchestra EMI CDM7 63533-2

Satie, Erik: *Parade*, ballet HYPE CDA 66365

Satie, Erik: *Six Gnossiennes* for piano VIRG VC7595 15-2

Satie, Erik: *Trois Gymnopédies* for piano CUNI CDCF 512

Scarlatti, Alessandro: *Con voce festiva* for soprano, trumpet and strings
  CHRI CD74599

Scarlatti, Alessandro: *Il Pirro e Demetrio*, opera NIMB N15 102

Scarlatti, Domenico: Sonatas for Harpsichord: A Selection DORI DOR 90103

Schoenberg, Arnold: *Five Orchestral Pieces*, op.16 WERG WER 60 185-50

Schoenberg, Arnold: *Moses und Aron* (Moses and Aaron), opera DECC 414 264-2DH2

Schoenberg, Arnold: *Ode to Napoleon* for reciter and instruments CHAN CHAN 9116

Schoenberg, Arnold: *Pelleas und Melisande*, symphonic poem SUPR 11 0973-2
Schoenberg, Arnold: *Six Little Piano Pieces* op.19 and *Piano Pieces* opp.33a and b
  DG 423 249-2GC
Schoenberg, Arnold: String Quartet No.3 DG 419 994-2 GCM4
Schoenberg, Arnold: *Variations for Orchestra* MUSI MACD-627
Schoenberg, Arnold: *Verklärte Nacht* for strings DG 423 250-2GC
Schubert, Franz: *Die schöne Müllerin* (The Miller's Beautiful Wife), song-cycle
  DECC 436 201-2DM
Schubert, Franz: Impromptu No.4 in A flat major, D899 PHIL 426 128-2PH7
Schubert, Franz: *Schwanengesang* (Swansong), song-cycle CHAN CHAN 8721
Schubert, Franz: String Quintet in C CBS CD 44853
Schubert, Franz: Symphony No.8 in B minor, 'Unfinished' DECC 433 630-4DSP
Schubert, Franz: *Wanderer Fantasia* MUSI MACD-267
Schumann, Robert: *Abegg Variations* for piano DG 435 751-2GDO
Schumann, Robert: *Carnaval* GLOB GLO 5009
Schumann, Robert: *Frauenliebe und -leben* (A Woman's Love and Life), song-cycle
  PHIL 420 784-2PH
Schumann, Robert: Piano Quintet in E flat op.44 DG 435 071-2GGA
Schumann, Robert: Symphony No.3, 'Rhenish' TELD 2292-46446-2
Schütz, Heinrich: *Hodie Christus natus est*, motet CRD CRD 3462
Schütz, Heinrich: *Quo nate Dei*, motet HRI CD 74587
Schütz, Heinrich: *Symphoniae Sacrae* ACCE ACC 9178/90
Schwarzkopf, Elisabeth: *Elisabeth Schwarzkopf Sings Opera Arias* EMI CDM7 63657-2
Schwarzkopf, Elisabeth: *Schwarzkopf Lieder Recital* CHNT LDC 278 999
Sculthorpe, Peter: *Irkanda IV* for violin, strings and percussion SOUT SCCD 1016
Sculthorpe, Peter: *Songs of Sea and Sky* for clarinet and piano TALL TP004
Segovia, Andrés: *Danza – Dances of Spain and Latin America* MNT MM601-2
Segovia, Andrés: *The Art of Segovia* EMI CHS7 6 1047-2
Seiber, Mátyás: *Four Hungarian Folksongs* CNTO CRCD 2366
Seiber, Mátyás: *Notturno* for horn and strings BIS-CD376
Sessions, Roger: Symphony No.5 NEW NW345-2
Shostakovich, Dmitry: Concerto for piano, trumpet and strings CHAN CHAN 8357
Shostakovich, Dmitry: *Lady Macbeth of the Mtsensk District* (*Katerina Izmaylova*), opera
  EMI CDS7 49955-2
Shostakovich, Dmitry: String Quartet No.8 in C minor op.110 NONE 7559-79242-2
Shostakovich, Dmitry: Symphony No.5 in D minor op.47 OLYM OCD 113
Shostakovich, Dmitry: *Twenty-Four Preludes and Fugues* NIMB N1 5026
Sibelius, Jean: Symphony No.2 DG 419 772-2GH
Sibelius, Jean: Symphony No.5 in E flat, op.82 DG 415 107-2GH
Sibelius, Jean: *Tapiola* FINL FACD 023
Sibelius, Jean: *The Swan of Tuonela* COLL COLL 3013-2
Sibelius, Jean: *The Tempest*, incidental music BIS BIS CD448
Skalkottas, Nikolaos: *Concertino* for trumpet and piano CAPR 10 439
Skryabin, Alexander: *Le poème de l'extase* (Poem of Ecstasy) CHAN CHAN 8849
Skryabin, Alexander: *Prométhée* DECC 417 252-2DH
Skryabin, Alexander: Sonata No.9 in F major, op.68, 'Black Mass' for piano
  RCA GD 60526
Skryabin, Alexander: *Two Pieces for Left Hand*, op.9 for piano GAMU GAM CD 520

Smetana, Bedřich: String Quartet in E minor ASV CD DCA 777

Smetana, Bedřich: *The Bartered Bride*, opera SUPR 10 3511-2

Smetana, Bedřich: *Vltava* (Moldau), from *Má vlast* DECC 425 014-2DM

Smyth, Ethel: Overture to *The Wreckers* EMI CDM7 69206-2

Soler, Antonio: A Selection of Keyboard Works ASTR E8778

Spohr, Louis: Octet in E major CRD CRD 3354

Spohr, Louis: Sonata in E flat for violin and harp JECK JD 573-2

Stamitz, Carl: Concerto for Flute in G major ERAT 2292-45835-2

Stamitz, Carl: *Sinfonia Concertante* in D major for violin, viola and orchestra VOX 0011

Stanford, Charles Villiers: Service in G, op.81, for chorus and organ
    CLLE COL CD118

Stanford, Charles Villiers: *Songs of the Sea*, op.91, for baritone, male chorus and orches-
    tra PEAR GEMM CD 9384

Stockhausen, Karlheinz: *Klavierstück XII* for piano SCHW 3100 15

Stockhausen, Karlheinz: *Mantra* for two pianos, percussion and ring modulators
    STOC 16

Strauss, Johann II: *A Thousand and One Nights*, waltz operetta DECC 433 330-2DM12

Strauss, Johann II: *Die Fledermaus* (The Bat), operetta DECC 421 046-2DH2

Strauss, Richard: *Der Rosenkavalier*, opera DECC 425 950-2DM3

Strauss, Richard: *Don Quixote*, tone poem EMI CDH7 63 106-2

Strauss, Richard: *Metamorphosen* for strings DG 410 892-2GH

Strauss, Richard: Oboe Concerto CAPR 10 231

Strauss, Richard: *Salome*, opera DECC 414 414-2DH2

Strauss, Richard: *Till Eulenspiegel*, tone poem PHIL 426 262-2PH

Strauss, Richard: *Vier letzte Lieder* (Four Last Songs) for soprano and orchestra
    EMI CDH7 6 1001-2

Stravinsky, Igor: *Agon*, ballet suite SONY CD 46292

Stravinsky, Igor: *Cantata* SONY CD 46290

Stravinsky, Igor: *Le Sacre du Printemps* (The Rite of Spring), ballet DG 435 769-2GH

Stravinsky, Igor: *Les Noces* (The Wedding), cantata SONY CD 46290(3)

Stravinsky, Igor: *L'Histoire du Soldat* (The Soldier's Tale), music-theatre
    PANG PEA 46 1048-2

Stravinsky, Igor: *Mass* for mixed chorus and double wind quintet SONY CD 46290(3)

Stravinsky, Igor: *Oedipus Rex*, opera-oratorio ORFE CO7 1831A

Stravinsky, Igor: *Petrushka*, ballet music, arranged for piano NIMB NI 1793

Stravinsky, Igor: *Pulcinella*, ballet SONY CD 46292

Stravinsky, Igor: Sonata (1924) for piano SONY CD 46290(5)

Stravinsky, Igor: *Symphony of Psalms* for chorus and orchestra MUSM 67078-2

Stravinsky, Igor: *The Firebird*, ballet EMI CDC7 49178-2

Stravinsky, Igor: *The Rake's Progress*, opera SONY CD 46290(4)

Suk, Josef: *Serenade* in E flat major NOVA 150 022-2

Suk, Josef: *Things Lived and Dreamt* for piano CHAN CHAN 9026/7

Sullivan, Arthur: *Overture di ballo* EMI CMS7 64400-2

Sullivan, Arthur: *The Gondoliers*, operetta DECC 425 177-2LMZ

Sullivan, Arthur: *The Mikado*, operetta TELA CD 80284

Sweelinck, Jan: *Hodie Christus natus est* (Christ Is Born Today), motet
    EMI CDZ7 62852-2

Sweelinck, Jan: *Malle Sijman*, pavan for keyboard GLOB GLO 5030

Szymanowski, Karol: *Stabat Mater*, op.53, for soloists, chorus and orchestra
POLS PNCD 063

Szymanowski, Karol: Symphony No.4, *Symphonie Concertante*, op.60, for piano and orchestra MARC 8 223290

Szymanowski, Karol: *Twenty Mazurkas*, op.50, for piano POLS PNCD 066

T

Tailleferre, Germaine: *Concertino* for harp and orchestra KOCH 37169-2

Tailleferre, Germaine: Sonata No.2 for violin and piano ETCE KTC 1073

Takemitsu, Toru: Concerto, *A String around Autumn*, for viola and orchestra
PHIL 432 176-2PH

Takemitsu, Toru: *Rain Coming* for chamber orchestra VIRG VC7 59020-2

Tallis, Thomas: *Absterge Domine*, motet GIME CDG1M025

Tallis, Thomas: *Lamentations* ARGO 425 199-2ZH

Tallis, Thomas: *O Lord, in thee is all my trust*, anthem GIME CDG1M007

Tavener, John: *Celtic Requiem* EMI CDSAR COR20

Tavener, John: *The Protecting Veil* for cello and orchestra VIRG VC7 59052-2

Tavener, John: *The Uncreated Eros* for chorus and orchestra HYPE CDA 66464

Taverner, John: *Dum transisset Sabbatum*, motet ASV CDGAU 119

Taverner, John: *O splendor gloriae*, motet HYPE CDA 66507

Tchaikovsky, Pyotr Il'yich: *Serenade in C* for strings ERAT 2292-45629-2

Tchaikovsky, Pyotr Il'yich: *The Nutcracker*, ballet TELA CD 80068

Tchaikovsky, Pyotr Il'yich: *The Queen of Spades (Pique-Dame)*, opera SONY CD 45720

Tchaikovsky, Pyotr Il'yich: Violin Concerto in D DG 413 161-2GW2

Telemann, Georg Philipp: Quartet in B flat for violins, viola and continuo, and
Concerto No.2 in D for three trumpets and orchestra L'OR 411 949-2OH

Thomson, Virgil: *Acadian Songs and Dances*, orchestral suite from *Louisiana Story* film
music HYPE CDA 66576

Thomson, Virgil: *Twenty-Five Portraits* for piano KING KCL CD 2005

Tiomkin, Dimitri: *Lost Horizon*, orchestral suite, and *The Big Sky*, film music
RCA GD8 1669

Tiomkin, Dimitri: *The Thing*, orchestral suite RCA GD8 2792

Tippett, Michael: *A Child of Our Time*, oratorio RPO CDRPO 7012

Tippett, Michael: *Concerto for Double String Orchestra* NIMB NI 5097

Tippett, Michael: *The Midsummer Marriage*, opera NIMB NI 5217

Toch, Ernst: *Geographical Fugue* for unaccompanied chorus THOR CTH 2044

Toch, Ernst: *Impromptu* No.2 for cello BIS-CD72

Tomkins, Thomas: *My beloved spake*, verse anthem HYPE CDA 66345

Tomkins, Thomas: *When David heard*, lament GAMU GOUP CD 153

Tye, Christopher: *Miserere mei, Deus*, motet HYPE CDA 66424

Tye, Christopher: *Western Wind*, Mass CRD CRD 3405

V

Valen, Fartein: *La isla de las calmas* and *Four Chinese Poems*, op.8, songs SIMA PSC 3115

Varèse, Edgard: *Offrandes* for soprano and small orchestra, and *Amériques*
SONY CD 45844

Vaughan Williams, Ralph: *A Sea Symphony* VIRG VJ7 59687-2

Vaughan Williams, Ralph: Concerto for tuba and orchestra CHAN CHAN 8740

Vaughan Williams, Ralph: *Fantasia on a Theme of Thomas Tallis* STRA SCD 8011

Vaughan Williams, Ralph: Oboe Concerto DG 419 748-2GH

Vaughan Williams, Ralph: *Romance* for harmonica and strings EMI CDM7 64134-2

Vaughan Williams, Ralph: *Silence and Music*, partsong GAMU CAMCD 529

Vaughan Williams, Ralph: Symphony No. 5 and *Flos campi* for viola, chamber choir and orchestra EMIN CD-EMX2112

Vaughan Williams, Ralph: Symphony No.6 COLL COLL 1202-2

Vaughan Williams, Ralph: *The Lark Ascending*, romance for violin and orchestra STRA SCD 8011

Vaughan Williams, Ralph: *The Wasps*, incidental music EMIN CD EMX 9508

Verdi, Giuseppe: *Falstaff*, opera RCA GD 60326

Verdi, Giuseppe: *Il Trovatore*, opera DECC 417 137-2DH2

Verdi, Giuseppe: *La Traviata*, opera BUTT BMCD 002

Verdi, Giuseppe: *Requiem* for SATB, chorus and orchestra DG 415 976-2GH2

Verdi, Giuseppe: *Rigoletto*, opera BUTT BMCD 001

Victoria, Tomás Luis de: *Ave Maria, gratia plena*, motet HYPE CDA 66129

Victoria, Tomás Luis de: *Surge Propera*, Mass PICK PCD 970

Villa-Lobos, Heitor: *Bachianas Brasileiras*:
  No.1 for cello ensemble HYPE CDA 66257
  No.6 for flute and bassoon KING KCL CD 2027
  No.7 for orchestra EMI CDC7 47433-2

Vivaldi, Antonio: Concerto for bassoon ASV CDDCX 615

Vivaldi, Antonio: Concerto for mandolin HYPE CDA66 160

Vivaldi, Antonio: Concerto for two trumpets NIMB NI 5017

Vivaldi, Antonio: *The Four Seasons* DENO DC-8091

W

Wagner, Richard: *Der Ring des Nibelungen* (The Ring of the Nibelung): four operas:
  Das Rheingold (The Rhine Gold) PHIL 434 420-2PM32(2)
  Die Walküre (The Valkyrie) EMI CDS7 49534-2
  Siegfried DECC 414 110-2DH4
  Götterdämmerung (Twilight of the Gods) DG 415 155-2GH4

Wagner, Richard: *Die Meistersinger von Nürnberg* (The Mastersingers of Nuremberg), opera EMI CHS7 63500-2

Wagner, Richard: *Parsifal*, opera PHIL 416 390-2PH4

Wagner, Richard: *Siegfried Idyll* EMI CDD7 64107-2

Wagner, Richard: *Tannhäuser*, opera PHIL 434 607-2PH3

Wagner, Richard: *Tristan und Isolde*, opera PHIL 438 241-2PH4

Walton, William: *Belshazzar's Feast*, oratorio DECC 425-154-4LM

Walton, William: *Capriccio burlesco* EMI CDM7 63369-2

Walton, William: *Façade* suite ASV CDDCA 679

Walton, William: *Henry V*, film music CHAN CHAN 8892

Walton, William: *Partita* CBS CD 46732

Walton, William: *Portsmouth Point*, overture LYRI SRCD 224

Walton, William: Symphony No.1 RCA GD 87830

Walton, William: *Troilus and Cressida*, opera EMI CDM7 64 199-2

Walton, William: Viola Concerto EMI CDH7 63828-2

Warlock, Peter: *Capriol Suite* NIMB N1 5032
Warlock, Peter: *Lillygay*, song-cycle KOCH 37 118-2
Warlock, Peter: *Serenade* for strings DECC 421 384-2LM
Weber, Carl Maria von: *Aufforderung zum Tanze* (Invitation to the Dance), piano
    rondo MERI CDE 84251
Weber, Carl Maria von: Clarinet Concerto No.2 VIRG VC7 59002-2
Weber, Carl Maria von: *Der Freischütz* (The Free-Shooter), opera PHIL 426 319-2PH2
Weber, Carl Maria von: *Oberon*, opera DG 419 038-2GX2
Webern, Anton: *Five Sacred Songs*, op.15 SCHW 314005
Webern, Anton: *Four Pieces*, op.7 PYRA PYR 13496
Webern, Anton: *Piano Variations*, op.27 DG 419 202-2GH
Webern, Anton: *Six Bagatelles*, op.9 SONY CD 48059
Webern, Anton: Symphony (1928) SONY CD 45845
Weelkes, Thomas: *Death hath deprived me*, madrigal CLLE COLCD 105
Weelkes, Thomas: *Give the king thy judgements*, verse anthem NIMB N15 125
Weelkes, Thomas: *Those sweet delightful Lillies*, madrigal TELD 2292-46004-2
Weill, Kurt: *Die Dreigroschenoper* (The Threepenny Opera), opera PHIL 426 668-2PSL
Weill, Kurt: *Die sieben Todsünden* (The Seven Deadly Sins), opera CBS CD 44529
Weir, Judith: *Airs from Another Planet* for wind quintet and piano LORE LNT 103
Weir, Judith: *An mein Klavier* (To My Piano) for piano NMC NMCD 002
Wesley, Samuel: *Hear my crying, O God*, setting of Psalm 61 EMI CDM7 63100-2
Wesley, Samuel: *In exitu Israel*, motet ASV CDQS 6019
Wesley, Samuel Sebastian: *Cast me not away from Thy presence*, anthem
    HYPE CDA 66446
Wesley, Samuel Sebastian: *Choral Song and Fugue* for organ CRD CRD 3463
Wieniawski, Henryk: *Légende* for violin and orchestra COLL COLL 1045-2
Wieniawski, Henryk: *Scherzo-tarantelle* in G minor for violin and piano and *Polonaise*
    No.1 in G major for violin and piano UNIC UKCD 2048
Wilbye, John: *Second Set of Madrigales* (1609):
    Draw on, sweet night and *Sweet honey-sucking bees* EMI CDC7 49197-2
    Weep, weep, mine eyes CLL COLCD 105
Williams, Grace: *The Dancers* for soprano, female chorus, strings and harp, and *Six
    Poems of Gerard Manley Hopkins* for contralto and string sextet CHAN ABRD 1116
Williamson, Malcolm: *Now is the Singing Day* for voice and piano trio JEW BB002
Wolf, Hugo: *Italian Serenade* for small orchestra ERAT 2292 454 16-2
Wolf, Hugo: Selections from collected songs:
    Eichendorff Lieder CALI CAL 50870
    Goethe Lieder VIRG VC7 59221-2
    Möricke Lieder ORFE C14040 1A
Wood, Charles: *Evening Service* in F major HYPE CDA 66249
Wood, Charles: *Hail, gladdening light*, anthem EMI CDC7 544 18-2

X

Xenakis, Iannis: *A R (Homage to Ravel)* for piano MONT 782005
Xenakis, Iannis: *Phlegra* for chamber orchestra ERAT 2292-45770-2

Y

Young, La Monte: *The Well-Tuned Piano* GVIS R27945-2

Ysaÿe, Eugène: *Extase*, op.21, for violin and orchestra SCHW 311099
Ysaÿe, Eugène: Sonata No.3 for violin NIMB NI 5039

Z

Zemlinsky, Alexander: *Humoresque* for wind quintet SCHW 310100
Zemlinsky, Alexander: String Quartet No.2, op.15 DG 427 421-2GC2
Zimmermann, Bernd Alois: Concerto in C for trumpet and orchestra CAPR 10 482
Zimmermann, Bernd Alois: *Die Soldaten* (The Soldiers), opera TELD 9031-72775-2

These recordings are available from all good retailers or direct from the Classic fM
Music Store: tel. 081 568 4411, Monday to Saturday 8 am to 8 pm. A catalogue comes
free with the order. Post free in the UK. All credit cards, Switch, cheques and postal
orders are accepted.

Index

Note: Pieces of music are included in the entries for composers. Those having their own entries in the A–Z also have separate entries in the index.

Page numbers in boldface indicate main entries devoted to the topics indicated.

The list of dates of composers and performers on pages 363–8 is not included in the index.

birdsong **20-1**, 168

Birmingham **21**

Birmingham, City of, Symphony
Orchestra 21, 198, 231

Birtwistle, Sir Harrison **21**, 52, 91, 111,
148; *Down by the Greenwood Side* **59**;
Punch and Judy 189, 222, 370

Bizet, Georges 7, **21**, 84, 103, 370;
Carmen 21, 33-4, 101, 370

Blacking, John 69, 277

Bliss, Sir Arthur **21-2**, 370

Bloch, Ernest **22**, 370

Blow, John **22**, 370

Boccherini, Luigi 20, **22**, 370

Bohemia **22-3**

Boosey & Hawkes 15

Borodin, Alexander 11, **23**, 47, 370

Boston Symphony Orchestra 52, 138, 210

Boulanger, Nadia 88, 109, 164, 229, 305

Boulez, Pierre **23**, 99, 107, 114, 277, 370

Boult, Sir Adrian 42

Boyce, William 12, **23**, 306

Brahms, Johannes **23-4**, 33, 42, 43, 129,
193, 278, 292, 370; and Clara
Schumann 260-61; fugues 80;
Intermezzos 125, 209; *Liebeslieder* 340,
370; orchestration 192; Piano
Concerto (2) 264; and Strauss 284;
Symphony (4), 36, 200, 326, 370;
Violin Concerto 129, 370

Brandenburg Concertos 42, 80, 239, 369

branle **24**

Brazil 331-2

Bream, Julian **24-5**, 99, 151

Brecht, Bertolt 67, 84, 343

Breitkopf (publisher) 280

Brendel, Alfred **25**

British Electronic Music Society 52

Britten, Benjamin **25**, 32, 35, 36-7, 55, 59,
72, 99, 134, 202, 222, 333, 370; cello
music 242-3; *A Ceremony of Carols* 313,
370; *Peter Grimes* 25, 138, 189, 202, **207**,
370; *The Rape of Lucretia* **231**, 370;
Serenade 56, 278, 370; *Spring Symphony*

20; *The Turn of the Screw* **318**, 370; *War
Requiem* 76, 190, 339, 370

broadcasting **25-6**; *see also* BBC

Bruch, Max **26**, 245, 370

Bruckner, Anton **26**, 370

Bukht, Michael 40

Bull, John **26**, 290

Bülow, Hans von 338

Burgon, Geoffrey 124

Burney, Charles **26-7**, 122

Busoni, Ferruccio **27**, 294, 325, 343, 370

Butterworth, George **27**, 268, 370

Byrd, William **27**, 38, 243, 298-9, 326,
370; *Battel* 218

Byzantine chant 211

C

cabaletta **29**

cabaret **29-30**, 258

cadence **30**

cadenza **30**

Cage, John **30**, 34, 50, 73, 94, 152, 252,
282

call and response **31**

Callas, Maria **31**, 371

Calvin, John 31, 37, 85

Calvinist music **31**

Cambridge **31**, 34, 62, 63, 87, 91, 248,
281, 302; King's College 31, 34, 87,
136, 273, 278, 347

Camden, Archie 159

Campion, Thomas **32**, 371

canon **32**, 243

cantata **32**

canticle **32**

cantilena **32**

Cantiones sacrae 299

cantus firmus **32-3**

canzona **33**

capriccio **33**

Cardew, Cornelius 30

Cardiff Festival of Contemporary Music
113

Carissimi, Giacomo **33**, 371

389

dance **50-51**; *see also* dance forms
Danse Macabre **51**
Dante Symphony **51**
Da Ponte, Lorenzo **51**
Daquin, Louis 218
Dargomïzhsky, Alexander **51**, 371
Darmstadt **51**
Dart, Thurston **51-2**, 114
Davies, Sir Peter Maxwell 11, **52**, 91, 99, 199, 292, 316, 371
Davis, Carl 75
Davis, Sir Colin **52**
Dean, Winton **53**
Debain, Alexandre 106
Debussy, Claude 5, 36, **53**, 61, 63, 78, 88, 138, 209, 252, 254, 319, 345-6, 357, 371; *Golliwog's Cake Walk* **91**, 249; harp music 107; horn music 116; *La Mer* 142, 192, 218, 371; nocturnes 182, 304, 335, 371; *Pelléas et Mélisande* 53, 189, **202**, 371; *Prélude à l'après-midi d'un faune* **5**, 291
De La Halle, Adam **53-4**, 180, 240, 371
Delibes, Léo **54**, 371
Delius, Frederick 16, 20, **54**, 340, 371
Delius Festival 340
Deller, Alfred **55**
Dent, Edward 344
Desprez *see* Josquin
Diabelli variations **55**
Diaghilev *see* Dyagilev
dictionaries **55-6**; *see also Grove's ...*
Dies Irae 51
diminuendo **56**
D'Indy *see* Indy
dirge **56**
discography **56-7**
Disney, Walt 61, 201, 213, 283
dissonance **56-7**
Dittersdorf, Carl Ditters von 56, **57**, 90, 372
divertimento **57**
Dolmetsch, Arnold **57**, 233
Don Giovanni 14, 174, 216, 266, 377

Donizetti, Gaetano 18, **57-8**, 372; *Lucia di Lammermoor* 58, 107, 149, **150-51**, 372
Don Juan 107, 218, 284
Don Quixote 284
double bass **58-9**
Dowland, John 25, 59, 152, 372
Down by the Greenwood Side 59
D'Oyly Carte, Richard 289
Dream of Gerontius, The **59-60**, 69, 190, 372
drum **60**
Dufay, Guillaume 37, **60**, 62, 240, 372
Dukas, Paul 61, 71; *The Sorcerer's Apprentice* 15, 61, 257, **278**, 291, 372
Duke Bluebeard's Castle **61**, 369
dulcimer **61-2**
Duncan, Ronald 231
Dunstable, John **62**, 372
Duparc, Henri **62**, 78, 166, 372
Du Pré, Jacqueline 13
Dvořák, Antonin 42, **63**, 128, 257, 288-9, 291, 372
Dvořák, Otilie 288
Dyagilev, Sergey **63**, 142, 214, 221, 231, 253, 267, 286

E

Early Music Consort 114
Edinburgh **65**, 74
Edison, Thomas **65-6**
editing **66**
education **66-7**
Eimert, Herbert 41
Eisler, Hanns **67**, 372
eisteddfod **67**
electronic music **67-8**, 293, 323
Elgar, Sir Edward 12, 21, 22, 36, **68-9**, 194, 225, 267, 291, 304, 306, 311, 333, 372; *Caractacus* 144; *The Dream of Gerontius* **59-60**, 69, 190, 372; *Enigma Variations* 69, 125, 372; Violin Concerto 167
Ellington, Duke 284
Engelberg, motet from 5

England, eighteenth- to nineteenth-century 22
English Bach Festival 194
English Dancing Master, The 211-12
English Folk Song Society 93
English Opera Group 202
Enigma Variations 69, 125, 372
Enlightenment 17
episode **69**
Esterházy family 110
ethnomusicology **69**, 327
exposition **69-70**

F

Façade 142, 212, 339, 384
Falla, Manuel de 63, **71**, 99, 109, 372
Falstaff 80
fantasia **72**
Fantasia 61, 201, 213, 283
Fantastic Symphony **72**
Farnaby, Giles **72**, 372
Fauré, Gabriel 12, 13, **72-3**, 138, 202, 231, 249, 335, 372; Impromptu 107; siciliana 270; *Souvenirs de Bayreuth* 225
Faust 92-3
Feldman, Morton **73**, 94, 372
Fenby, Eric 54
Ferneyhough, Brian **73-4**, 372
festival **74**
Fidelio **74**, 369
Field, John 182, 372
Fielding, Henry 12
film music **75**, 217, 258, 305, 307, 339
Finland 269
Finlandia 270
Finzi, Gerald **75**, 372
Firebird, The 19
Fischer-Dieskau, Dietrich 14, **76**, 262
Fitzwilliam Virginal Book, The **76**, 203, 299
Flaherty, Robert 305
Fledermaus, Die 169
Florence **76-7**
flute **77-8**
Flying Dutchman, The 146, 168; (film) 232
Fokine, Michel 290

folksong, British 93, 109, 114, 267-8
Françaix, Jean 57, **78**, 88, 277, 316, 372
Franck, César **78-9**, 124, 357, 373
Frankfurt Hoch Conservatory 265
Franz Joseph I, Emperor 284
Frescobaldi, Girolamo **79**, 308, 373
Fricker, Peter Racine **79**
Froberger, Johann 87, 308
fugue **79-80**
Furtwängler, Wilhelm 145
Fux, Johann Joseph **80-81**

G

Gabrieli, Giovanni 31, **83-4**, 204, 328, 373
Gade, Niels 96
galop **84**
Gaspard de la Nuit **84**, 379
Gautier, Théophile 87
gavotte **84**
Gay, John 18, **84**
Gebrauchsmusik **85**
Gédalge, André 231
Geneva **85-6**
genius 21
Gerhard, Roberto **86**, 373
Gershwin, George 4, **86**, 90, 216, 373
Gesualdo, Carlo **86-7**, 373
Gibbons, Christopher 150
Gibbons, Orlando **87**, 332, 373
gigue **87-8**
Gilbert, W. S. 289
Ginastera, Alberto **88**, 373
Gioconda, La 213
Giraud, Anna 334-5
Glass, Philip **88**, 373
Glasser, Stanley 100, 136
Glazunov, Alexander **88-9**, 188, 254, 269, 290, 307, 373
glee **89**
Glennie, Evelyn 204, 352
Glinka, Mikhail 51, **89-90**, 213, 373
glissando **90**
Glover, Sarah 310
Gluck, Christoph Willibald **90**, 107, 189, 209, 373

Holliger, Heinz **114**, 186
Holst, Gustav **114-15**, 244, 268, 374;
    The Planets 288, 335, 374
Holst, Imogen 115
homophony **115**
Honegger, Arthur 75, **115**, 198, 374
horn **115-16**
Hornbostel, Erich von 69
Horowitz, Vladimir 75, **116-17**, 312
Howells, Herbert **117**, 374
Hsiao Shu-sien 257
Huddersfield Choral Society **117**
Hull Philharmonic Society 131
Hummel (publisher) 280
Humoreske **117**
Humperdinck, Engelbert **117-18**, 279, 374
Hungary 24, 61-2, 110, 137-8, 265, 275
hurdy-gurdy **118**
hymn **118-19**, 219

I

Ibert, Jacques **121**, 254, 374
Ibsen, Henrik 97
iconography of music **121-2**
Idelssohn, A. Z. 129
Idomeneo, King of Crete 84, **122**, 377
impromptu **122**
improvisation 41, **123**
incidental music **123-4**
Incoronazione di Poppea, L' **124**, 328, 377
Indy, Vincent d' 78, **124-5**, 244, 374
intermezzo **125**
Intermodulation 273
International Musicological Society 344
International Society for Contemporary
    Music (ISCM) 250, 256, 266, 344
Intimate Revue **29-30**
Introduction et Allégro 69, 107
Iradier, Sebastian 101
Ireland, John **125**, 374
Islamey 11
isorhythm **125-6**
Italian Symphony **126**
Ives, Burl 109
Ives, Charles **126**, 155, 226, 292, 374

J

Jacob, Gordon **127**, 203, 374
Jacopone de Todi 280
Janáček, Leoš 61, **127-8**, 291, 374
Janequin, Clément 37, 218
Jaques-Dalcroze, Emile 85, 161
jazz 31, 41, 85, 217, 265
Jerusalem **128-9**
Jeune France, La 129, 168
Jeux d'enfants 83
jig **86-7**
Joachim, Joseph **129**, 245, 251, 346
Johnson, Dr Samuel 188
Jolivet, André **129-30**, 375
Jones, Inigo 162
Jonson, Ben 162
Joplin, Scott **130**, 375
Joseph II, Emperor 17, 249
Josquin Desprez 33, 37, **130**, 172, 186, 375
Joubert, John **130-31**, 375
journals **205**
Jupiter Symphony **131**, 292

K

Kabalevsky, Dmitry **133**, 242, 308, 375
Kagel, Mauricio **133-4**, 375
Kallman, Chester 112, 229
Kamhi, Victoria 240
Karajan, Herbert von **134**
Karas, Anton 361
Karpeles, Maud 268
Katerina Izmaylova 141
Keller, Hans **134**
Kemp, Ian 159
Kessel, Barney 68
key **134-5**
keyboard **135**
Khachaturian, Aram ix, **136**, 242, 253,
    308, 375
King's College, Cambridge 31, 34, 87,
    136, 273, 278, 347
King's College, London 52
King's Singers **136**, 148
Klangfarbenmelodie **136-7**
Kleine Nachtmusik, Eine **137**, 377

Maderna, Bruno **157**, 376
Madrid, choir 330
madrigal **157**, 160, 197, 343, 346
Maeterlinck, Maurice 202
Magic Flute, The 174, 192, 257, 271, 377
Mahler, Gustav 46, 51, 137, 148, **157-9**, 160, 257, 284, 292, 342, 344, 376
Maitland, Fuller 76
Malcolm, George 216
Malipiero, Gian Francesco **159**, 182, 376
Manchester 90, **159**; Hallé Orchestra 150, 159
Manchester Group 52
mandolin **160**
Manduell, Sir John 159
Mannheim School 280-81
Manning, Jane 201
Manzoni, Alessandro 329
march **160**
Marenzio, Luca 157, **160-61**, 376
Maria Barbara, Infanta 255
Marriage of Figaro, The 14, 174
Martin, Frank 109, **161**, 376
Martini, Padre Giovanni **161**
Martinů, Bohuslav **161-2**, 376
Mary II, Queen, funeral of 33
Mascagni, Pietro 146, **162**, 196, 376
masque **162-3**, 187
Mass **163**, 197, 211; *Requiem* 73, **235**, 329
Massenet, Jules 138, **163**, 376
Massine, Léonide 221, 253
Mathias, William **163-4**, 376
Maw, Nicholas **164**, 376
Maxwell Davies *see* Davies
Mayr, J. S. 58
mazurka **164**
Meck, Mme Nadezhda von 302
Medium, The 167
Meistersinger von Nürnberg, Die 105, **164-5**, 247, 384
melisma **165**
Mellers, Wilfrid **165**, 356
mélodie **165-6**, 214
melody **166**
melos viii, 256

Mendelson, Mira 340
Mendelssohn, Felix 13, 21, 33, 36, 92, 125, 129, **166-7**, 339, 376; *Calm Sea and Prosperous Voyage* 290; *Italian Symphony* **126**; at Leipzig 145-6; *A Midsummer Night's Dream* 55, 124, 166, 290, 376; preludes 216; tarantella 30
Menotti, Gian Carlo 13, **167**, 376
Menuhin, Sir Yehudi **167**, 188, 217
Merry Widow, The 145, 375
Merulo, Claudio 328
Messiaen, Olivier 7, 20-1, 90, **167-8**, 191, 217, 377; *Bird Catalogue* 20-1, 376; organ music 193
Messiah 80, 104, 110
Metastasio, Pietro 90, 147, 179
Meyerbeer, Giacomo 92, 107, **168**, 242, 377
mezzo-soprano **168-9**
MGM 217
Micrologus 98
Midsummer Night's Dream, A 55, 124, 166, 290, 376
Milan 90, 250-51, 329
Milhaud, Darius 75, 129, **169**, 377
minimalism 88, 234, 238
Minnesingers **314-15**
minuet **169-70**
modulation **170**
Moeran, Ernest John **170**, 377
Monteverdi, Claudio 159, **170-71**, 211; *L'Incoronazione di Poppea* 124, 328, 377; *L'Orfeo* 190-91, 377; *Vespers* 219
Montgomery, Wes 68
Moog, Robert 293
Moore, Dudley 30
Moreschi, Alessandro 35, 377
Morley College 114, 307
Morley, Thomas **171**, 309, 377
Morte! 92
Moses und Aron **172**, 241, 256, 275, 279, 380
motet **172**
Mother Goose Suite **172**, 379
Mozart, Carl 250

Mozart, Leopold **172-3**, 174, 211, 251

Mozart, Maria Anna 173, 174, 183

Mozart, Wolfgang Amadeus 7, 14, 17, 21, 78, 83, 110, **173-5**, 183, 190, 192, 228, 242, 249, 250, 251, 257, 277, 326, 377; clarinet music 39, 304, 377; *Don Giovanni* 14, 216, 266, 377; fugues 80; and Haffner 102; *Idomeneo, King of Crete* 84, **122**, 377; *Jupiter Symphony* **131**, 292; *Eine kleine Nachtmusik* **137**, 377; *The Magic Flute* 192, 257, 271, 377; minuet 169; operas 51; piano concertos 42, 377; Piano Sonata (12) 134-5; ritornello 239; serenades 69, 266; *Sinfonia Concertante* 281, 304, 333; in Vienna 330-31

Munrow, David 114

Musgrave, Thea **175**, 377

musicals 188

Musical Times 184, 248

music dealing **175-6**

Music for Strings 22

Musick's Monument 356

musicology **176**

Music Teacher 259

music therapy **176-7**

Musorgsky, Modest 11, **177-8**, 213, 238, 377

Mussolini, Benito 318

Myaskovsky, Nikolay 136

N

Naples 87, **179-80**, 196, 209, 242, 254, 255

Nash, Ogden 343

national anthems **180**

National Broadcasting Corporation 312

Nazism 15, 112, 145, 162, 217, 285, 312, 344, 360

Neue Zeitschrift für Musik 262

neumatic notation **181**

New Grove Dictionary ... 55-6, 248, 292

Newman, Ernest 60, **181**

New York Herald Tribune 305

Nikisch, Arthur 145

Nicolai, Otto **181**, 377

Nielsen, Carl **182**, 377

Noces, Les 286, 382

nocturne **182**

Nono, Luigi 157, **182-3**, 212, 326, 377

Norma 183

notation 98, **183**; graphic **95**; neumatic 181; palaeography **197**; and performance 204-5

note-row 258-9

Novello, Alfred 184

Novello, Vincent **183-4**

Nuremberg 247

O

obbligato **185**

oboe **185-6**

Obrecht, Jacob **186**, 377

ocarina **186**

Ockeghem, Johannes 62, **186-7**, 377

octave **187**

ode **187**

Offenbach, Jacques **187-8**, 284, 378; *Orphée aux enfers* 84, 188, 378; *The Tales of Hoffmann* 188, 378

Ogdon, John 52, 91, 159

Oistrakh, David **188**

Oistrakh, Igor 188

Ondine 112

opera **188-9**

opéra-comique 243

opus **189-90**

oratorio **190**

orchestra **190-91**

orchestration **191-2**

Orchestre de la Suisse Romande 84-5

Ord, Boris 346

Orff, Carl 34, **192**, 378

organ **192-3**, 202, 263

organology **193**

organum **193**

Orkney 52

Orphée aux enfers 84, 188, 378

Orphée et Eurydice 189

Oscars 217

Classic Membership
for Classic fM Listeners

Classic Membership has been designed to offer you, the Classic fM listener, a range of exclusive services and benefits which will reflect not only your interest in classical music and the arts, but also a range of other pleasures – travel, wine, books, cookery, and much more.

Members will receive a personalised membership card and a regular brochure detailing the superb range of high-value special offers★ and services specially arranged by Classic fM on your behalf. In our launch issue two of you will be able to fly with Air UK for the price of one to any of their destinations, purchase discounted tickets to the opera, ballet or classical concerts, take a free consultation lesson with any one of over 200 music teachers★★, receive discounts on classical CDs and cases of wine, and even take in a visit to the Classic fM studios. These are just a few of the offers created to celebrate the launch of Classic Membership which takes place in September 1994.

Classic Membership costs just £15.00 per year. You can join now by sending a cheque/postal order made payable to Classic fM, together with your full name, address and telephone number to: Classic fM, PO Box 829, Slough, Berks, SL1 6BA, to arrive by 30 April 1995. Please quote the reference BK1.

★ Offers subject to availability
★★ Music teachers are registered with the Incorporated Society of Musicians